Umstrittene Katholizität:
Von der zwiespältigen Beziehung
zwischen Vielfalt und Einheit

Catholicity under Pressure:
The Ambiguous Relationship
between Diversity and Unity

Beihefte zur Ökumenischen Rundschau Nr. 105

Umstrittene Katholizität: Von der zwiespältigen Beziehung zwischen Vielfalt und Einheit

Tagungsbericht der 18. Wissenschaftlichen Konsultation der Societas Oecumenica

Catholicity under Pressure: The Ambiguous Relationship between Diversity and Unity

Proceedings of the 18th Academic Consultation of the Societas Oecumenica

Herausgegeben im Auftrag der Societas Oecumenica
von Dagmar Heller und Péter Szentpétery

EVANGELISCHE VERLAGSANSTALT
Leipzig

Bibliographische Information der Deutschen Nationalbibliothek
Die Deutsche Nationalbibliothek verzeichnet diese Publikation in der
Deutschen Nationalbibliographie; detaillierte bibliographische Daten
sind im Internet über http://dnb.dnb.de abrufbar.

© 2016 by Evangelische Verlagsanstalt GmbH · Leipzig
Printed in Germany · H 8014

Das Werk einschließlich aller seiner Teile ist urheberrechtlich geschützt.
Jede Verwertung außerhalb der Grenzen des Urheberrechtsgesetzes ist
ohne Zustimmung des Verlags unzulässig und strafbar. Das gilt insbesondere für
Vervielfältigungen, Übersetzungen, Mikroverfilmungen und die Einspeicherung
und Verarbeitung in elektronischen Systemen.

Das Buch wurde auf alterungsbeständigem Papier gedruckt.

Cover: Kai-Michael Gustmann, Leipzig
Coverbild: © Miklós Szentpétery, Budapest
Satz: Alina Höschele, Möckern-Friedensau
Druck und Binden: Hubert & Co., Göttingen

ISBN 978-3-374-04161-9
www.eva-leipzig.de

Vorwort

Seit ihrer Gründung im Jahre 1978 hat die Societas Oecumenica – auch bekannt unter dem Namen »Europäische Gesellschaft für Ökumenische Forschung« – achtzehn wissenschaftliche Konsultationen an verschiedenen Orten und zu unterschiedlichen Themen durchgeführt. Die jüngste dieser Tagungen, die vom 21.–26. August 2014 in Budapest (Ungarn) stattfand, wird im vorliegenden Band dokumentiert. Das Thema lautete »Umstrittene Katholizität: Von der zwiespältigen Beziehung zwischen Vielfalt und Einheit«.

Das Thema »Katholizität« scheint auf den ersten Blick traditionell und in der einschlägigen Literatur bereits erschöpfend behandelt. Dennoch gewinnt es bei rechter Betrachtung in einer Zeit zunehmender Individualisierung einerseits und wachsender Pluralität andererseits an neuer Aktualität und Brisanz. Während praktisch alle Kirchen in Rückgriff auf die alte Kirche und das frühe Christentum mit dem nizäno-konstantinopolitanischen Glaubensbekenntnis die »Katholizität« als Merkmal der Kirche bekennen (und auch diejenigen Kirchen, die dieses Glaubensbekenntnis nicht verwenden, der Sache nach die Kirche als universal und auf die gesamte Welt bezogen verstehen), ist die konkrete Erfahrung von Christen und Christinnen heute meist eine andere. De facto gibt es an den meisten Orten nicht nur eine, sondern mehrere Kirchen, die je ihr eigenes Profil pflegen und in manchen Regionen dieser Welt nicht viel miteinander zu tun haben. Gleichzeitig ist oft in einer Ortsgemeinde welcher Prägung auch immer weder der Bezug zu Ortskirchen gleicher Tradition in anderen Teile der Welt geschweige denn die

Verbindung mit Christen anderer Tradition besonders stark im Bewusstsein. Die konfessionellen Identitäten sind oft alles andere als stabil, sondern geraten zunehmend durch eine Pluralisierung innerhalb der Konfessionen unter Druck. Viel deutlicher als früher tritt die Erkenntnis ins Bewusstsein, dass der christliche Glaube insgesamt und insbesondere die jeweils eigene konfessionelle Ausprägung in einer pluralen und multireligiösen Welt nur ein Angebot unter vielen anderen darstellt.

Kann also Kirche im Kontext einer spätmodernen Welt den ihr eigenen, theologisch unaufgebbaren Anspruch auf Katholizität in ihrem Leben überhaupt noch verwirklichen und so auch heute noch die »eine, heilige, katholische und apostolische Kirche« sein und bleiben? Oder ist Katholizität als Kennzeichen von Kirche ein theologisches Auslaufmodell? Mit dieser und verschiedenen damit zusammenhängenden Fragen hat sich die 18. Konsultation der Societas Oecumenica in verschiedenen Vorträgen und Workshops beschäftigt.

Die Veröffentlichung der Vorträge im vorliegenden Band folgt dem Konzept der Konsultation.

Der Eröffnungsvortrag der Präsidentin Dagmar Heller (Deutschland/Schweiz) gibt einen einführenden Überblick über die Entwicklung der Bedeutung der Begriffs »Katholizität«, diskutiert seinen Zusammenhang mit den anderen Merkmalen der Kirche, insbesondere der Einheit, sowie die besonderen Herausforderungen in Zeiten der Globalisierung.

Der erste Block von Vorträgen beschäftigt sich allgemein mit den Herausforderungen, denen die Kirchen durch die spätmodernen Prozesse von Individualisierung und Pluralisierung religiöser Überzeugungen ausgesetzt sind. Wie verändert sich dadurch Eigenwahrnehmung und Selbstverständnis der Kirchen nach innen wie nach außen und wie gehen sie mit diesen Herausforderungen um? Dies wird von lutherischer (Risto Saarinen, Finnland), orthodoxer (Georgios Vlantis, Griechenland), römisch-katholischer (Dorothea Sattler, Deutschland) und baptistischer (Henk Bakker, Niederlande) Seite beleuchtet.

In einem zweiten Schritt werden unterschiedliche Konzepte der Verhältnisbestimmung von Vielfalt und Einheit betrachtet, wie sie sich innerhalb des Christentums, aber auch im säkularen Bereich finden. Kirsteen Kim (Großbritannien) stellt die wachsende Vielfalt der weltweiten Christenheit am Beispiel Koreas dar und zeigt, dass der Zusammenhang zwischen

Katholizität und Überschreiten von Grenzen im Wesen des Christentums verankert ist und in die Überlegungen zur Katholizität mit einbezogen werden muss. Wolfgang Lienemann (Schweiz) führt vor, wie in sozialwissenschaftlicher Perspektive Einheit und Verschiedenheit in der Weltgesellschaft allgemein und speziell in Religionsgemeinschaften gesehen werden. Die Frage, ob und inwieweit der theologische Anspruch auf Katholizität angesichts der Eigendynamik einer pluralen polyzentrischen und globalisierten Welt überhaupt noch angemessen vertreten werden kann, wird schließlich von Henk Witte (Niederlande) behandelt.

In der dritten Einheit geht es um den globalen und den lokalen Aspekt von Katholizität. Dabei stellt sich vor allem die Frage, wie der in der Missionstheologie entwickelte Begriff der »Global Christianity« sich zum traditionellen Konzept der Katholizität verhält. Diese Frage behandelt Christine Lienemann-Perrin (Schweiz) aus protestantischer und Dorin Oancea (Rumänien) aus orthodoxer Sicht. Katholizität aus der Perspektive der Kirche(n) an einem konkreten Ort wird anhand des Fallbeispiels des Gastlandes Ungarn von römisch-katholischer (Mihály Kránitz), reformierter (Ferenc Szücs) und lutherischer (Péter Szentpétery) Sicht beleuchtet. Dabei wird insgesamt die Schwierigkeit deutlich, mit der die ungarischen Kirchen nach wie vor konfrontiert sind, dass das Attribut »katholisch« immer noch häufig sofort mit »römisch« in Zusammenhang gesetzt wird. Gleichzeitig werden jedoch Fortschritte im ökumenischen Miteinander verzeichnet.

Im letzten Teil schliesslich wird ein Ausblick in die Zukunft versucht. Friederike Nüssel (Deutschland) tut dies aus evangelischer, Peter De Mey (Belgien) aus katholischer Perspektive.

Auf den Konsultationen der Societas Oecumenica gibt es auch immer Raum für (nicht nur) junge Wissenschaftler/innen Themen und Überlegungen aus ihrem Forschungsbereich, die in Zusammenhang mit dem Konferenzthema stehen, in sogenannten Workshops vorzustellen. Von diesmal zwanzig Workshops (ein bisheriger Rekord!) wurden zehn zur Veröffentlichung eingereicht und hier in alphabetischer Reihenfolge abgedruckt. Sie erweitern die Bezüge des Begriffs Katholizität auf Spezialthemen wie die Frage der Taufe (Augoustinos Bairactaris), des gerechten Friedens (Sarah Gehlin) und der Frauenordination (Margriet Gosker). Zwei stellen das orthodoxe Verständnis von Katholizität näher dar (Mihai Iordache) bzw. beleuchten den orthodoxen theologischen Diskurs anhand zweier bekannter Theologen (Viorel Coman). Die Beziehung zwischen dem biblischen Kanon und der Katholizität der Kirche (Peter-Ben Smit) wird ebenso beleuchtet wie die Bedeutung des Glaubensbekenntnisses für die Einheit der Kirche (Jutta Koslowski). Michael Plathow plädiert für eine »ökumenische Katholizität« und Jelle Creemers untersucht kritisch das jüngste Konvergenzdokument von Glauben und Kirchenverfassung aus freikirchlicher Sicht. Nicht zuletzt bringt James Amanze die afrikanische Diskussion um die Katholizität mit ins Spiel.

Zum Schluss bleibt uns, denjenigen zu danken, die diese Konsultation ermöglicht haben: Aus Deutschland waren es das katholische Hilfswerk Renovabis, das Evangelische Missionswerk (EMW) sowie die Evangelische Kirche in Deutschland (EKD), die finanzielle Unterstützung geboten haben. Aus Ungarn sind zu nennen der Nationale Kulturfonds, der Ökumenische Rat der Kirchen in Ungarn, die Evangelisch-Lutherische Kirche, die Reformierte Kirche als Träger des Ökumenischen Studienzentrums, die den Ablauf der Konferenz in mehrerer Hinsicht unterstützt haben. Einzelpersonen, deren Hilfe für die Logistik unverzichtbar war, können hier nicht alle namentlich aufgeführt werden, stellvertretend wird hier jedoch Marianne Szentpétery genannt sowie die beiden Stewards Mihály Németh und Mária Felegyi, ohne deren tatkräftigen Einsatz die Konferenz nicht so problemlos zustande gekommen wäre.

Für die Fertigstellung des Manuskripts dieser Veröffentlichung danken wir Thomas F. Best und John Robinson für die Korrektur englischer Texte, deren Verfasser eine andere Muttersprache haben. Um das Layout hat sich dankbarerweise Alina Höschele gekümmert. Und schließlich danken wir der Evangelischen Verlagsanstalt in Leipzig für die Aufnahme des Bandes in die Reihe der »Beihefte zur Ökumenischen Rundschau«.

Bossey/Budapest, im August 2015
Dagmar Heller und Péter Szentpétery

Foreword

Since its foundation in 1978 The Societas Oecumenica, which is also known as The European Society for Ecumenical Research has organised eighteen academic consultations in different places and on different issues. The latest of these meetings, which took place in Budapest (Hungary) 21–27 August 2014, is documented in the present volume. The theme was »Catholicity under Pressure: The ambiguous Relationship between Diversity and Unity«.

The theme »catholicity« seems at first sight traditional and treated exhaustively in the relevant literature. But, on closer examination, it gains new timeliness and explosiveness in a time of increasing individualism on the one hand, and growing plurality on the other. While practically all the churches (referring to the early church and early Christianity) confess with the Nicene-Constantinopolitan Creed, the »catholicity« as an attribute of the church (and even those, who do not use this Creed understand nevertheless the church as universal and being related to the whole world), the concrete experience of Christians today is very often a different one. De facto, there are in most places not only one, but several churches, which foster their own profiles and do not have many contacts with each other in some regions of the world. At the same time, even within a church family of the same tradition, there is no awareness of the worldwide relation of the local church, and even less of the connection with Christians of other traditions. The confessional identities are not really stable, but come under more and more pressure through a pluralisation within the churches. In a much clearer way than before, people are aware that in a plural and multi-religious world, the Christian faith in general, and especially the respective confessional form, is just one more offering among many.

Thus, can the church in the context of a late-modern world still realise its specific claim for catholicity, which theologically cannot be given up? Can it therefore still be and remain the »one, holy, catholic and apostolic church« today? Or is catholicity as an attribute of the church a theological concept to be phased out? It is with this and several related questions that the 18th Consultation of Societas Oecumenica dealt in different presentations and workshops.

The order of the papers in this publication follows the concept of the Consultation. The opening lecture of the president, Dagmar Heller, gives a survey on the development of the meaning of the notion »catholicity«, discusses its relationship with the other marks of the church, especially with »unity«, as well as the specific challenges in times of globalisation.

The first part of this volume deals in general with the challenges which the churches are facing through the late-modern processes of individualisation and pluralisation of religious convictions. How is it that they influence self-perception and self-understanding of the churches both inwardly and outwardly? And, how do they deal with these challenges? This is being presented from a Lutheran (Risto Saarinen, Finland), Orthodox (Georgios Vlantis, Greece), Roman Catholic (Dorothea Sattler, Germany) and Baptist (Henk Bakker, Netherlands) perspective.

The second part looks not only at different concepts of the relationship between diversity and unity as they can be found within Christianity, but also in the secular sphere. Kirsteen Kim (United Kingdom) presents the growing diversity in worldwide Christianity with the example of Korea and shows the link between catholicity and the transgression of borders, which is rooted in the nature of Christianity and which needs to be taken into account when reflecting on catholicity. Wolfgang Lienemann (Switzerland) shows how unity and diversity in world society in general, and particularly in religious societies, are understood in a socio-scientific perspective. The question whether and to what depth can the theological claim for catholicity still be held appropriately in view of the self-dynamics of a plural polycentric and globalised world, will be treated by Henk Witte (Netherlands).

The third part deals with the global and local aspect of catholicity. Above all, the question is asked about how the term »global Christianity«, that was developed in mission theology, is related to the traditional concept of catholicity. This question is dealt with by Christine Lienemann-Perrin (Switzerland) from a Protestant viewpoint and by Dorin Oancea (Romania) from an Orthodox one. Catholicity in the perspective of the church(es) in a concrete place is presented with the example of the host country, Hungary, in Roman-Catholic (Mihály Kránitz), Reformed (Ferenc Szűcs) and Lutheran (Péter Szentpétery) views. Here, in general, the difficulty becomes explicit, with which the Hungarian church is still confronted, that the attribute »catholic« is often linked immediately with the adjective »roman«. At the same time, there is progress in the ecumenical togetherness which is to be noted.

Finally, the last part tries to look into the future. Friederike Nüssel (Germany) does this from a Protestant perspective, and Peter De Mey (Belgium) from a Roman Catholic one.

At the consultations of Societas Oecumenica there is always also space for (not only) young researchers to present themes and reflections from their area of research, related to the conference theme, in what we call workshops. Out of – this time – twenty (a record so far!) workshops, ten were submitted for publication and will be printed here in alphabetical order. They enlarge the references of the term »catholicity« to specialised themes such as the question of baptism (Augoustinos Bairactaris), the issue of just peace (Sarah Gehlin) and of the ordination of women (Margriet Gosker). Two of them explain in more detail the Orthodox understanding of catholicity (Mihai Iordache) and shed some light on the Orthodox theological discourse with the example of two well-known theologians (Viorel Coman). The relation between the biblical canon and the catholicity of the church (Peter-Ben Smit) is treated as well as the significance of the Creed for the unity of the church (Jutta Koslowski). Michael Plathow pleads for an »ecumenical catholicity« and Jelle Creemers examines the latest convergence document of the Faith & Order Commission in a critical way from a free-church point of view. Last, but not least, James Amanze brings into play the African discussion on catholicity.

Finally, it remains to thank all those who made the Consultation possible: From Germany it was the Catholic aid agency

Renovabis, the Association of Protestant Churches and Missions in Germany (EMW) as well as the Evangelical Church in Germany (EKD), which offered financial support. From Hungary we need to mention the National Culture Fond, the Ecumenical Council of Churches in Hungary, the Evangelical-Lutheran Church and the Reformed Church as funding bodies of the Ecumenical Study Center, which supported the flow of the conference in many ways. The individuals whose help was indispensable for the logistics cannot all be named here, but who needs to be mentioned are Marianne Szentpétery and the two stewards Mihály Németh and Mária Felegyi, without whom the conference would not have happened in such a smooth way.

For the completion of the manuscript of this publication, we thank Thomas F. Best and John Robinson for the correction of English texts, the authors of which have a different mother tongue. We are grateful to Alina Höschele who took care of the layout. And finally, we thank the Evangelische Verlagsanstalt Leipzig for including this publication in the series of »Beihefte zur Ökumenischen Rundschau«.

Bossey/Budapest, August 2015
Dagmar Heller and Péter Szentpétery

Inhalt/Table of Contents

Vorwort/Foreword .... 5 / 9

OPENING LECTURE/ERÖFFNUNGSVORTRAG

Dagmar Heller
Catholicity under Pressure
The Ambiguous Relationship between Diversity and Unity 19

CHURCHES CHALLENGED BY DIVERSITY

VIELFALT ALS HERAUSFORDERUNG FÜR DIE KIRCHEN

Risto Saarinen
The Changing World as Challenge for the Churches
New Frontiers of Ecumenical Recognition 37

Georgios Vlantis
The Changing World as Challenge to the Churches
An Orthodox Perspective 55

Dorothea Sattler
Ökumenisch eine katholische Kirche werden?
Das Verhältnis zwischen Vielfalt und Einheit aus (einer) römisch-katholischen Sicht 67

Henk Bakker
The Changing Face of Unity, or: Cutting the Right Edges
in the Proper Way 81

CONCEPTS OF DIVERSITY AND/IN UNITY

KONZEPTE VON VIELFALT IN/UND EINHEIT

Kirsteen Kim
Christians without Borders and Churches on the Move
Perspectives on Catholicity from Pneumatology and Mission 93

Wolfgang Lienemann
Einheit und Verschiedenheit von Religionsgemeinschaften
in sozialwissenschaftlichen und theologischen Perspektiven 117

Henk Witte
Is Catholicity Still an Appropriate Concept in a Postmodern World? 155

CATHOLICITY – GLOBAL AND LOCAL

KATHOLIZITÄT – GLOBAL UND VOR ORT

Christine Lienemann-Perrin
»World Christianity« – a New Concept Challenging the
Understanding of »Catholicity« 173

Dorin Oancea
Catholicity as Communion
Three Moments of the Orthodox Experience 193

CASE STUDIES – HUNGARY

FALLSTUDIEN – UNGARN

Mihály Kránitz
Interpreting the Epithet »Catholic«
Living Catholicity: A Case Study in Hungary 209

Ferenc Szűcs
Catholicity and Ecumenism in Hungarian Reformed Perspective
Living Catholicity: A Case Study in Hungary 217

Péter Szentpétery
Catholicity
Case Study: Hungary – from a Lutheran Perspective 225

CATHOLICITY IN THE FUTURE/THE FUTURE OF CATHOLICITY

KATHOLIZITÄT IN DER ZUKUNFT/DIE ZUKUNFT DER KATHOLIZITÄT

Friederike Nüssel
Catholicity – exclusive or inclusive? 239

Peter de Mey
Towards a Healthy Future of Catholicity in the
Roman Catholic Church
Recommendations by Pope Francis 251

WORKSHOPS

James N. Amanze
Misconceptions Regarding the Terms »Catholic« and »Protestant«
and Their Implication in Ecumenical Relations in Africa 275

Augoustinos Bairactaris
Unity in Diversity and the Perspective of Baptism 291

Viorel Coman
Unity and Diversity in the Church
*Vladimir Lossky's Reflection on the Roles of Christ and the Spirit in
the Church, and Its critical Reception in Dumitru Stăniloae's Theology* ...303

Jelle Creemers
The Church and its Characteristics in the document
»The Church« (2013) of the WCC's Commission on Faith and Order
*A Constructive Critique from an Evangelical Free Church
Perspective*... 323

Sarah Gehlin
Catholicity and the Way of Just Peace 335

Margriet Gosker
To be Male is Less Important than It Seems to Be
Catholicity and Gender Focussing on: the Ordination of Women 345

Mihai Iordache
Orthodox Understanding of Catholicity
as the Wholeness of the Church 353

Jutta Koslowski
The Creed as Basis for the Unity of the Church 369

Michael Plathow
Kirchliche Identitäten und ökumenische Katholizität 377

Peter-Ben Smit
From Divisive Diversity to Catholic Fullness?
Canon and Ecclesial Unity Reconsidered 391

Index of Authors/Die Autoren 411

OPENING LECTURE

ERÖFFNUNGSVORTRAG

Catholicity under Pressure
The Ambiguous Relationship between Diversity and Unity: President's Address

Dagmar Heller

»The situation of the world, of its own volition, is pressing Christianity today for reflection on catholicity.« These are the words of the German theologian Wolfgang Beinert from the year 1964. In the original German: »Die Weltsituation drängt heute ganz von selbst das Christentum zu einer Besinnung auf die Katholizität.«[1] He is concerned that there is not enough reflection on catholicity in relation to today's world.

It may be surprising that 40 years later the *Societas Oecumenica* brings up again the issue of »catholicity«. But the world has changed since Beinert's reflection. And although in the meantime many more papers on »catholicity« have been published, the ecumenical situation and the world's situation are challenging the churches even more, and questioning the idea of »catholicity«. Therefore the *Societas Oecumenica* proposed, with good reasons, »Catholicity under Pressure: The Ambiguous Relationship between Diversity and Unity« as the theme of its 18th Academic Consultation.

I will unfold this theme in three steps: First I will give a short historical survey of the meaning and use of the term »catholic«. Then I will show the relationship between »catholicity« and »unity«, before – in a

---

[1] Wolfgang Beinert, *Um das dritte Kirchenattribut: Die Katholizität der Kirche im Verständnis der evangelisch-lutherischen und römisch-katholischen Theologie der Gegenwart*, vol. 1 (Essen: Ludgerus-Verlag Hubert Wingen, 1964), 15.

third part – reflecting on the challenges of today's world for the notion of »catholicity«.

1   What is Catholicity? – An Historical Survey

It is nothing new – of course – that for some, the adjective »catholic« is part of the name of their own church, the one to which they belong. Therefore they are »catholic«. For others this has become a problem, as they feel »we are different« from »the catholics« – even to the point of saying: »we do not want to be ›catholic‹«. But this does not change the fact that both sides – and many others – confess with the Nicene-Constantinopolitan Creed and with the Apostle's Creed: »We believe in one holy *catholic* and apostolic Church« or »I believe the holy *catholic* Church«. This points to a dilemma which some churches have tried to overcome by translating the word »catholic« as »Christian« – »I believe in the Christian Church« – or by using expressions such as »universal« or »general«.

This reveals the ambiguity which the word »catholic« carries today. And when I say »today«, I am thinking especially of situations where we find many »catholic« churches living side by side in the same territory, but separated from each other at the Lord's table. This is already a challenge to the Creed's statement that the church is »one«; but it is also a challenge to the claim of catholicity.

Before going more deeply into this ambiguity, I will seek to understand what the word »catholic« means. The present situation obviously does not help; on the contrary, it complicates the problem. Therefore I propose to look into the original meaning of the word: »kat'holou« means literally »according to the whole«, or »concerning what is whole and intact«. One finds the derivation »katholikos« translated in dictionaries of classical Greek with the word »general«.[2] Beinert points out, in his research about the etymology of this word, that in both secular and profane use in antiquity the adjective »catholicos« is never used for geographical universality.[3] In secular use the term has, according to Beinert, three basic meanings: 1. It is used for the dimension of space and time in the sense of »complete«; 2. As a specific term in rhetorics it means »general«; 3. According to its roots the word also means »perfect«

---

[2]   Cf. Liddell-Scott's *English-Greek Dictionary*.
[3]   Beinert, *Um das dritte Kirchenattribut*, 27. For the Roman Empire and its expansiveness the term is »oikoumenikos«!

or »in fullness«. In summary, Beinert finds that »catholicos« in antiquity until the 3rd century is used in the sense of »all-embracing« (»umfassend«).[4]

This original, *secular* meaning of the term leads us to raise the question: Why has this word been used by the early Christian thinkers for describing the church, as they were formulating the Nicene-Constantinopolitan Creed or the Apostle's Creed?

This question becomes particularly interesting in the search for the understanding of catholicity if we consider that »catholic« is used together with three *other* terms to describe the church: namely the terms »one«, »holy«, and »apostolic«. All three are, to a certain extent, much easier to understand because they are related more clearly and directly to the Bible. They can be drawn almost literally from the Bible, when we ask what Christians are, what they should do, and what the church is. Just to mention two texts, we find there that Jesus wants his followers to be »one«,[5] and that Paul reminds the Ephesians that there is »one body« and »one Spirit«.[6] That the church is »holy« and »apostolic« – meaning »based on the Apostles« – can also be drawn from Paul, when he says to these same Christians in Ephesus: »you are citizens with the saints and also members of the household of God, built upon the foundation of the *apostles* and the prophets, with Christ Jesus himself as the cornerstone. In him the whole structure is joined together and grows into a *holy* temple in the Lord.«[7]

But from where did the Councils of the early church take the idea that the church is »catholic«? There is one biblical text which could be understood as a place where the issue is addressed (although the term »catholic« itself is not used). Or, better: there is one place in the Bible where a description can be found of what the church fathers meant when using the term »catholic« in the Creed. This is Eph 1:22–23: »And he has put all things under his feet and has made him the head over all things for the church, which is his body, the fullness of him who fills all in all.« Paul uses here the Greek term »pleroma« – »fullness«. But why, then, is the church not called »pleromatic«? According to Beinert, one reason could be that »pleroma« was associated too much with the Gnosis, that school of thinking which was seen as a threat to early Christianity. It is probably not by chance that the expression »catholic

---

[4] Ibid., 35.
[5] John 17:21.
[6] Eph 4:4.
[7] Eph 2:19b–21.

church« appears for the first time in a 2nd century anti-Gnostic text of Ignatius of Antioch, namely in his letter to the Smyrneans. It seems, therefore, that the term »catholic« was used rather early to express the Pauline idea of »fullness«, and at the same time to distinguish it from the Gnostic understanding of »pleroma«.[8]

But it needs to be explored more closely, whether what the Creed wants to express here is equivalent to »fullness«. If the origin of the term »catholic« is the letter to the Ephesians, then we need to look more closely at the second of the mentioned verses: »(he) has made him the head over all things for the church, which is his body, the fullness of him, who fills all in all.« (Eph 1:23) In my understanding, »fullness« here is another word for »his body«. »Catholicity« is, then, the fact that the church is the body of Christ in his fullness and perfection. Beinert expressed this by saying that Catholicity means »the fullness of Christian grace, which was given to the church according to God's resolution of salvation, in order to continue Christ's work of salvation until the eschaton.«[9]

If we study further the idea of »pleroma« in Paul's letters and also the early use of the word »catholic« by Ignatius, it must be kept in mind that »catholicity« is based in Jesus Christ – and in such a way that »catholicity« is, in its deepest nature, a quality or an attribute of Christ, and the church is »catholic« insofar as it is rooted in Christ and based in Christ as its head.

But already in the 3rd century the term »catholic« was changed slightly. One of the important texts normally quoted here is the Mystagogical Catechesis 18 of Cyril of Jerusalem from the 4th century, who dedicates an entire paragraph to explaining explicitly the meaning of the third mark of the church. Here catholicity means 1. the worldwide expansion of the church; 2. the universality of the teaching: the church teaches everything that is necessary for salvation; 3. the correct way of venerating God, which is valid for all human beings; 4. the universal power to forgive sins; and 5. the universal work of salvation for all humanity, which is manifest in the fullness of the means of salvation.[10]

---

[8] Beinert, *Um das dritte Kirchenattribut*, 407–409.
[9] Ibid., 462. Original: »Dabei ergab sich, dass dieser Ausdruck die Fülle der christlichen Gnade meint, die nach Gottes Heilsratschluss der Kirche geschenkt wurde, um das Heilswerk Christi bis zum Eschaton fortzuführen.« (English transl. DH).
[10] Cat. 18,23: »It (= the church) is called Catholic then because it extends over all the world, from one end of the earth to the other; and because it teaches universally and completely one and all the doctrines which ought to come to men's

Thus he combines the geographical aspect of catholicity with the aspect of doctrinal and salvific perfection.

A few paragraphs later Cyril speaks of the »catholic church« as the name of the church, and begins using the term in a polemical way to make clear, *which* is the true church.[11] In other words, the term starts to be used in order to differentiate the orthodox, or the true, church from the heretics.[12]

During the following ages the different aspects of the term »catholicity«, as pointed out by Cyril, are emphasized in different ways – and often in a one-sided way. Augustine, for example, focuses on the geographic dimension: in his context, he needs to highlight the universality of the church in order to insist on its authority. But it is also clear to him – and that is an additional aspect – that »catholicity« has an eschatological dimension.[13]

Vincent of Lérins, in the 5th century, combines the idea of continuity with the idea of universality: Catholicity is an identity throughout the ages.[14]

The development during the Middle Ages – which I cannot present here in detail – finally leads to different confessional understandings of »catholicity«. For the Eastern churches, the emphasis is on catholicity as a qualitative notion. For Maximus the Confessor, one of the important reference persons for the Orthodox churches, the catholicity of God is manifested in the image of the catholicity of the church.[15] Or, as a modern Greek Orthodox theologian puts it, »The qualitative catholicity of the church mirrors the fullness of the life of the holy Trinity«.[16] Here it is interesting to note that in the Slavonic branch of Orthodoxy the term »catholicity« was translated into »sobornost«, which puts the

---

knowledge, concerning things both visible and invisible, heavenly and earthly(6); and because it brings into subjection to godliness the whole race of mankind, governors and governed, learned and unlearned; and because it universally treats and heals the whole class of sins, which are committed by soul or body, and possesses in itself every form of virtue which is named, both in deeds and words, and in every kind of spiritual gifts.«

[11] Cat. 18,26; cf. Beinert, *Um das dritte Kirchenattribut*, 70.
[12] Cf. Peter Steinacker, »Katholizität,« in TRE 18 (Berlin/New York: Walter de Gruyter, 1989), 72–80, quotation on p. 73.
[13] Steinacker, »Katholizität,« 74.
[14] Ibid., 75.
[15] Maximus Confessor, Mystagogia 2.
[16] Theodor Nikolaou, »Katholizität, Orth. Verständnis,« in *Ökumenelexikon*, 2nd edition, ed. Hanfried Krüger et al. (Frankfurt a.M.: Otto Lembeck und Josef Knecht), 1987, 628 (English transl. DH).

emphasis on the aspects of community and thus can be described as unanimity (Einmütigkeit) in community.[17]

In the West, »catholicity« is more and more understood during this period in relation to the hierarchy of the church. Probably a certain peak in this development is Pope Innocent III, who understands catholicity to be a »plenitudo potestatis« of the Pope.[18] Especially in the Catholic Reformation (or Counter-Reformation) in the 16th century the term is used in a polemical way; and only in the II Vatican Council is this confessionalistic view reversed. According to the Dogmatic Constitution on the Church, »Lumen Gentium«, art. 13, catholicity is that universality which is a »gift of the Lord himself«, and «[b]y reason of it, the Catholic Church strives constantly and with due effect to bring all humanity and all its possessions back to its source In Christ, with Him as its head and united in His Spirit.« The church is aware of the diversity of the people of God, which leads to the importance of the »common sharing of gifts«, through which each part receives »increase«.

The churches stemming from the Reformation always kept the understanding that they continue the catholicity of the church. Luther sees the catholicity of Rome as being diminished because it is so closely connected with being *Roman*. Catholicity, for Luther, is a spiritual notion which belongs to each church that preaches the Gospel. According to the late German theologian Peter Steinacker, Luther combines the geographical, time-related and theological aspects of catholicity by saying, »daher heist es ein einige heilige Catholica oder christliche Kirche, dass da ist einerlei reine und lautere Lehre des Evangelii und äusserlich Bekenntnis derselben an allen Orten der Welt und zu jeder Zeit, unangesehen, was sonst an Ungleichheit und Unterschieden des äusserliche leiblichen Lebens oder äusserlicher Ordnungen, Sitten und Zeremonien sind.«[19] It is interesting to note that Luther equates here the term »catholic« with »Christian«, thus giving a reason for churches later on to translate the word »catholic« in the Creed into »Christian«. Catholicity, for Luther, is manifested through the same teaching and the same confession in each place and at all times.

---

[17] Gregor Müller, »Sobornost,« in LThK 9 (Freiburg: Herder, 1964), 841f.
[18] Yves Congar, *L'Eglise de saint Augustin à l'époque moderne* (Paris: Cerf, 1996), 254f.
[19] Crucigers Sommerpostille, Epistel am Siebzehnten Sonntag nach Trinitatis, WA 22,299f. (»Therefore it is called one, holy Catholica or Christian Church ...«).

These observations show the close relationship between catholicity and the question of the tension between unity and diversity, to which I will return.

It is especially with the modern ecumenical movement that a new reflection on catholicity was initiated in many churches. The churches discovered that they all claim to be »catholic«. It was especially the fourth Assembly of the World Council of Churches at Uppsala in 1968, which rediscovered the term.[20] Catholicity is described there as »gift of the Spirit ... also a task, a call and an engagement.«[21] According to the introductory words of the Armenian Bishop Karekin Sarkissian to the report of section I at the Uppsala assembly, »catholicity ... is no longer to be considered as a ›mark of the church‹ as the traditional terminology used to describe it ... it is made clear that the Church ›has to become catholic constantly anew‹.«[22] And he points out: »catholicity is not a state of being, a pattern of sheer existence, but rather a way of living ... Catholicity is not to be identified with the outward extension of the Church, the spread, the expansion, the embracing of all men, the presence in all the corners of the earth. Of course this geographical and quantitative dimension is an essential part of the Church's mission. But the question about the catholicity of the Church is how to permeate the world with that spirit and quality of life – fullness of life in fellowship with God – which is the gift of the Father in the Incarnation of his Son, received and made manifest by man in and through the ›Body of Christ‹, the Church enlivened with the Holy Spirit.«

The section report places catholicity within the challenges of the »needs of the world and ... our solidarity with a creation which is ›groaning in travail together‹.«[23] In other words, at Uppsala another dimension of catholicity was highlighted: the fact that catholicity needs to be expressed in the life of the church. The Report of the Assembly also emphasized the close interrelatedness of catholicity with the other marks of the church: oneness, holiness and apostolicity. Catholicity is dynamic through its eschatological dimension, because »Catholicity reaches its completion when what God has already begun in history is

---

[20] Section 1 was dealing with »The Holy Spirit and the Catholicity of the Church«.
[21] Norman Goodall (ed.), *The Uppsala Report 1968* (Geneva: WCC, 1968), 13.
[22] Ibid., 7.
[23] »The Holy Spirit and the Catholicity of the Church. The Report as adopted by the Assembly«, in ibid., 12.

finally disclosed and fulfilled.«[24] Therefore, »the Church is catholic ... in all her elements and in all aspects of her life«.

In one of the most recent documents of the Faith and Order Commission of the World Council of Churches, the new convergence document *The Church: Towards a Common Vision*, catholicity is understood as rooted in the »abundant goodness of God«.[25] It is characterized by the fact that »the Church's mission transcends all barriers and proclaims the Gospel to all peoples«. The document takes up the quotation from Ignatius of Antioch, and sees catholicity expressed in the eucharist. What is important to note is the following sentence: »The essential catholicity of the Church is undermined when cultural and other differences are allowed to develop into division.«[26] A similar formulation can be found already in a previous Faith and Order paper from 2005.[27] Thus it can be said that the ecumenical movement has discovered that *the division among the churches is destroying catholicity*. This is formulated positively in the statement »Called to be the One Church«, a document of the ninth Assembly of the WCC in 2006 in Porto Alegre: »Each church fulfils its catholicity when it is in communion with the other churches.«[28] And the way in which this is lived out and expressed in the life of the churches is called »mutual accountability«.

This again leads to the affirmation that *catholicity* is closely linked with the question of *unity*.

Another Faith and Order text – »A Treasure in Earthen Vessels«[29] – has made this clear by pointing to the fact that the churches »belong to one another in a profound way because of their relationship to God through Jesus Christ.«[30] In other words, each local church perceives itself as embodiment of the one catholic church. Therefore the document discusses catholicity in its relation to contextuality, and states: »Contextual interpretations can contribute to a fuller interpretation of the Gospel and can thereby speak to the Christian community as a

---

[24] Ibid., 13.
[25] *The Church: Towards a Common Vision*, Faith & Order Paper 214 (Geneva: WCC, 2013), par. 22.
[26] Ibid.
[27] Cf. *The Nature and Mission of the Church* (Geneva: WCC, 2005) par. 55.
[28] »Called to be the One Church,« par. 6 in *God, in Your Grace ...: Official Report of the Ninth Assembly of the World Council of Churches*, ed. Luis N. Rivera-Pagan (Geneva: WCC, 2007), 255–261, quotation on p. 257.
[29] *A Treasure in Earthen Vessels*, Faith & Order Paper No. 182 (Geneva: WCC, 1998).
[30] Ibid., par. 43.

whole … Accordingly, catholicity binds all local communities together, thereby allowing them to contribute to one another's understandings and to broaden their horizons.«[31] And further: »catholicity enables communities to free one another from one-sidedness or from over-emphasis on only one aspect of the Gospel. Catholicity enables communities to liberate one another from being blinded or bound by any one context and so to embody across and among diverse contexts the solidarity that is a special mark of Christian *koinonia*.«[32]

In summary we can say that the ecumenical movement has made the different churches aware of several facts: (a) all churches are catholic; (b) catholicity is about togetherness, about the relationship with other churches, and therefore it is damaged by the divisions between churches; (c) catholicity has to be lived out; (d) expressions of catholicity are a common eucharist, mutual accountability and solidarity; and (e) catholicity is dynamic and the churches need to grow into it.

2 Catholicity and Unity

Through this – admittedly short – analysis of the historical development of the understanding and discussion of catholicity, it has become clear that catholicity is closely linked to the question of unity, and thus to the question of the relationship between unity and diversity. Therefore, in order to understand better what catholicity is, I would like to reflect further on these interconnected themes.

First of all: although there is a link between catholicity and unity, both terms are distinct. How, then, are they related and how are they distinct from one another?

In the Creed we clearly have both marks of the church – oneness and catholicity – as distinct categories. Oneness is broken through division – when one community excommunicates the other. In other words: oneness is broken, when there are different churches which deny that they have the same faith. Oneness is thus related to the inner situation of the church; it describes the *relationship* among its members. Catholicity is something different: Catholicity is the conviction that, in Jesus Christ, the fullness of salvation is revealed to the whole of

---

[31] Ibid., par. 47.
[32] Ibid., par. 48.

humanity.[33] Catholicity describes the openness of the church towards the world outside. First of all it is related to the openness of a local community to other communities or churches; but secondly it also describes the mission of the church towards the whole of humanity. Miroslav Volf formulates this by saying: »a local church can be catholic only by way of a connection with an ecclesiological whole transcending it ... this whole is the eschatological indwelling of the triune God in God's whole people«.[34]

John Beckett, following Miroslav Volf, comes therefore to the conclusion that: »catholicity and mission are mutually determinative.«[35] And: »the church's catholic identity becomes a motivation for mission.«[36]

It is sometimes forgotten that it is this outward missionary aspect of the church, even more than the above-mentioned inner aspect, which makes it necessary to reflect on the question of diversity, plurality and unity.

This leads me to say: Catholicity is what holds together diversity and unity, the local aspect and the global view, the contextual and the universal. Yves Congar expressed this in the following sentences: »Catholicity is the feature of the church, due to which the reality of multiplicity within the church is able to be harmonised with the reality of unity. It is the law, which rules the relationship between the multiple and the one.«[37] But he goes further and says: »It [catholicity] can also be looked at from the point of view of the many as well as from the point of view of the one. Considered from the point of view of multiplicity catholicity is based on the material cause of the church, namely the human nature with all its richness, with its enormous diversity and the infinite possibilities of the first Adam to express himself in different

---

[33] Cf. Bernd Oberdorfer, »Katholizität der Kirche,« in RGG, 4th ed., vol. 4, 2001, 902–905, here 902.

[34] Miroslav Volf, *After Our Likeness: The Church as the Image of the Trinity* (Grand Rapids: W.B. Eerdmans, 1998), 272.

[35] John Beckett, »Evangelical Catholicity – A Possible Foundation for Exploring Relational Responsibility in a Global Community?,« ERT 34.2 (2010): 131–135, quotation on p. 133.

[36] Ibid.

[37] Yves Congar, »Catholicité,« in G. Jacquemet, *Catholicisme hier, aujourd'hui, demain, Encyclopédie en sept volumes*, vol 2.12 (Paris 1950), col. 722–725 (quoted by Beinert, *Um das dritte Kirchenattribut*, 471f.): »La catholicité est cette propriété de l'Eglise grâce à laquelle la réalité du multiple, en elle, s'harmonise avec la réalité de l'unité. Elle est la loi qui régit, en elle, le rapport du multiple et de l'un.«

ways … Considered from the point of view of unity catholicity is based on the fullness of Christ's graciousness, who had been installed by God as head of a new humanity and a new universe. … This catholicity of its head is the principle of the ecclesial catholicity.«[38]

In other words, Congar sees diversity and plurality on the human side of the church, while unity is assigned to the divine side. This is a point for discussion: Congar omits the fact that there is already in God a certain plurality, if the Trinity is taken seriously. Therefore, unity and diversity cannot just be attributed to the divine side of the church on the one hand, and the human side on the other. Catholicity is thus more complex, and we can say: catholicity is the task of the church to find the right way of relating both – diversity and unity – to one another in a healthy balance.

It also should not be forgotten – as history has shown – that it is problematic to focus on only one aspect of catholicity. In fact if catholicity is highlighted as keeping the balance between diversity and unity, it is not clear why catholicity is specifically a feature of the *church* – after all each community, each village, each state, has to struggle with this tension. I think only of Switzerland, the country, in which I presently live. There are people of four different languages – and thus also different cultures – living together. And they are kept together through a common history, through a common national day, through common tasks, common enemies, etc. But this is not catholicity, because what holds them together is related to their inner relationship, to something coming from inside. Catholicity, however, is something that comes from *outside*. It is a characteristic of God, one which has a goal, a final aim in the eschaton, that transcends the immediate well-being of human persons. Thus catholicity as *pleroma*, as fullness in which Christ is all in all, is therefore not just a balance between diversity and unity, but embraces diversity and unity in such a way that they are no longer in tension with each other.

---

[38] Ibid.: »Aussi peut-on la considérer soit du côté du multiple, soit du point de vue de l'unité. Considérée du point de vue du multiple, la catholicité se fonde sur la cause matérielle de l'Eglise, à savoir la nature humaine, les potentialités indéfinies du premier Adam, qui s'expriment de différentes manières. … Considérée du point de vue de l'unité, la c. se fonde sur la plénitude de grâce du Christ constitué par Dieu chef d'une humanité nouvelle et même chef d'un univers nouveau … Cette c. de son chef est principe, pour l'Eglise, de sa propre c.« (English translation DH).

3 Today's Challenges for the Catholicity of the Church

At the beginning of my paper I pointed out that the question for the churches today is, *how* to live out their catholicity. In this last part of my paper, I will offer some reflections on this.

I have just reflected on the ambiguity between diversity and unity that is transcended by catholicity. In Christian history we can see that in the early centuries this was lived out by developing several principles, in order to bring diversity and unity together. I remind you only of the ministry of the bishop, of the eucharist, and of the Creed.[39] But today the situation is different. The diversity with which the early church was struggling was a diversity within the Roman Empire – within a certain unity, which was a *political* unity. It also needs to be taken into account that the means of communication were rather poor, compared with today. Thus the difference and diversity with which early Christians were confronted was rather limited, to the diversity within local communities.

As we have seen, Catholicity today is challenged by the fact that the church is both a local and a global phenomenon. Therefore the question today for the churches is how to live their catholicity in the context of globalisation. As the German Roman Catholic theologian Franz Segbers puts it: »Knowing that one lives in a global and globalized world can fulfil a key role in the development of a new understanding of catholicity«.[40]

Globalisation is, on the one hand, the situation of the »world«. It is the situation in which the churches are living and acting; it is the »context« in which the churches today announce the Good News. On the other hand, globalization is also »affecting« the churches, because the implications of globalisation have an effect on the inner life of the churches.

I would like to unpack this a bit more:

---

[39] Cf. Andrew Louth, »Unity and Diversity in the Church of the Fourth Century,« in *Unity and Diversity in the Church*, ed. R.N. Swanson (Oxford: Blackwell, 1996), 1–17.

[40] Cf. Franz Segbers, »Globalization as the Context for a Theological and Ethical Understanding of Catholicity,« in *Globalization and Catholicity: Ecumenical Conversations on God's Abundance and the People's Needs*, eds. Marsha L. Dutton with Emily K. Stuckey, Beiheft zu IKZ 100 (Berlin: Stämpfli, 2010), 147–161, quotation on p. 159

When I speak about »globalisation« I am not talking only about economic globalisation, but also about technological and cultural globalisation; in other words: the fact that one culture tends to become the *only* one for the entire globe, or about the development expressed in the saying that we are living in a »global village«.

Vincent J. Miller, a US theologian, has given a very true analysis of globalisation, one which tells us something about the specific challenges for the catholicity of the church today. He shows, on the one hand, that globalisation is »the imposition of a single culture«[41] and therefore a movement of homogenisation. Since homogenisation leads to the destruction of particular cultures globalisation is, on the other hand, also the origin of counter-movements that try to protect one's own culture. This means that in our globalised world we find an increasing tension between on the one hand a sort of »global culture« characterised and supported through modern technology, fashion brands, etc., and on the other hand movements which highlight the particular, as characterised by the struggle for the right of minorities, indigenous communities, etc.

We can see a parallel in the theological field: While the churches had, and have, the tendency to go with globalisation as can be seen in the history of Christian mission, the missionary movement during the 20th century has become very sensitive to questions of inculturation. And theology in general has become much more aware of the contextuality of every theology.

But there is something more to globalisation: Globalisation, through the modern means of communication such as the internet, social media, etc. produces cultures which »float free of geographical space … The culture within which we relate to one another … is unbound from geographical space – deterritorialized – … The interplay of these two dynamics tends to reduce culture and religion to sources of identity.«[42] Miller points to the problem for the church that there are many subcultures, and people choose their groups. This means that there is a homogenisation in the small group. In other words: everyone chooses the community in which he or she feels good, or where the same kind of people are together (young people, intellectuals, white, black, elderly, homosexuals etc.). »Parishes cease to be places where people with

---

[41] Vincent J. Miller, »Where is the Church? Globalization and Catholicity«, *Theological Studies* 69 (2008): 412–432, quotation on p. 413.
[42] Ibid., 415.

different theological commitments worship together and interact.«[43] And: »Culture ceases to provide common assumptions that form the basis for judgment, deliberation, and conflict.«[44] And finally this leads to the problem that »when society is reduced to a conglomeration of individuals choosing among heterogeneous cultural associations, people lose the ability to conceive of the world as a place of specific moral responsibility.«[45]

This seems to be the serious challenge of globalisation.

Miller tries to give an answer to this: »The challenge is not simply to preserve particularity against erosion ... The mark of catholicity provides both measure and means for engaging these cultural dynamics. An ideal of unity is a harmony of difference that challenges the dominant sectarianism, and a call to the fullness of salvation that cannot settle for purity abstracted from concrete engagement with the world ... By fostering relationships and exchanges not happening elsewhere, the church, as a global community with a global infrastructure of its own, can foster a better form of globalization than the one promoted by the forces of advanced capitalism.«[46]

Vincent Miller is a Roman Catholic, and when he speaks of a »global infrastructure« of the church he is probably thinking of the Roman Catholic Church. But I think that his general idea is also true for all the churches together, as a whole in the ecumenical movement. The reflection on »catholicity« as fullness in God, and therefore as openness to the world, is necessary in each church. It will start naturally from the experience of the local church, and needs to lead to an awareness of its relationship, and interdependence with, the world outside. Beckett emphasizes here the common mission: »This perspective on catholicity ... reinforces that there is a global interdependence between believers as we participate in the missio Dei. This global interdependence is based on a common Spirit-mediated identity and a common Spirit-mediated mission. ... The local church is the normative venue for the believer to enact the relational responsibility that goes hand in hand with this interdependence. However, a broadening of relational responsibility beyond the local church is also necessary.«[47]

---

[43] Ibid., 417.
[44] Ibid., 418.
[45] Ibid., 418.
[46] Ibid., 421.
[47] Beckett, »Evangelical Catholicity,« 134.

It seems to me that the model of *koinonia* as developed by the WCC Commission on Faith and Order[48] – despite all its problems – is a helpful one for this reflection. It helps in understanding »catholicity« as the task of reflecting on community, and on the elements which foster communion. As Segbers says: »For the wholeness and fullness indicated by the term *catholicity* to become visible, exchange and communication are necessary.«[49] The ecumenical movement has, in several instances, highlighted collegiality and conciliarity as important elements in this regard.[50] This needs the cultivation and formation of a spirit of curiosity about the other, and tolerance for the otherness of the other. The above-mentioned Faith and Order document on ecumenical hermeneutics talks about the necessity of mutual confidence and the awareness »of the possibility of an abiding complementarity ... of the values inherent in the ›otherness‹ of one another and even of the right to be different from each other, when such differences are part of the exploration of the divine mystery and the divinely willed unity.«[51] In light of the analysis of the phenomenon of globalisation, it seems to me that another dimension needs to be worked on. And this is the development of responsibility for the other, or to use another word: solidarity.[52] But this cannot be a solidarity just for the sake of solidarity. Solidarity is for the sake of the common message which Christians have: the message of the salvation of humanity, which cannot be separated from the message of peace for the world. Catholicity is lived out when churches live in a spirit of peace and solidarity – on the parish level with one another, and on the global level with other churches looking together towards peace for the whole world.

I would like here also to mention an additional element of catholicity, one to which Edmund Schlink draws attention[53] and which is often forgotten: the aspect of repentance. Schlink says: »The Church is catholic, by repenting for its self-sufficiency and sluggishness, and by

---

[48] Cf. *On the Way to Fuller Koinonia: Official Report of the Fifth World Conference on Faith and Order*, ed. by Thomas F. Best and Günther Gassmann, Faith & Order Paper No. 166 (Geneva: WCC, 1994).
[49] Segbers, »Globalization,« 160.
[50] For example *A Treasure in Earthen Vessels*, par. 35.
[51] Ibid., par. 30.
[52] Cf. Miller, »Where is the Church?,« 425.
[53] Edmund Schlink, *Ökumenische Dogmatik* (Göttingen: Vandenhoeck & Ruprecht, 1983), 588.

subordinating itself anew to the Pantocrator.«[54] Only with this attitude can catholicity – and also the other marks of the church – be lived as gifts of God.

4 Conclusion

In the ecumenical movement it has been discovered that the »catholicity« of the church is the reason *why* the search for unity is necessary. Catholicity and ecumenism are closely related as we seek to find an answer to the ambiguity – noted at the beginning of this presentation – between the churches' claim to catholicity and the fact that they still live in a state of division, especially at the Lord's table. As Lukas Vischer, the former director of the Faith and Order Commission of the World Council of Churches, stated at the fourth World Conference on Faith and Order in 1963 in Montreal:[55] »The ecumenical movement can be described as a movement which contributes to the growth of true catholicity.« This is still true for the common struggle of the churches in today's world of globalisation and growing pluralism, and Beinert's words, with which I began my presentation, are as valid as they were 40 years ago.

---

[54] »Die Kirche ist katholisch, indem sie für ihre Selbstgenügsamkeit und Trägheit Busse tut und sich aufs Neue dem Pantokrator unterstellt.« Ibid., 588 (English transl. DH).

[55] »The Meaning of Catholicity,« Preface in ER 16 (1963): 24f.

CHURCHES CHALLENGED
BY DIVERSITY

**VIELFALT ALS HERAUSFORDERUNG
FÜR DIE KIRCHEN**

The Changing World as Challenge for the Churches
New Frontiers of Ecumenical Recognition

Risto Saarinen

My first visit to Budapest, the venue of our conference, occurred thirty years ago, in the summer of 1984. The Lutheran World Federation (LWF) gathered for its assembly in Hungary, and I represented the Evangelical Lutheran Church of Finland as youth delegate. Hungary was a communist country and Ronald Reagan was the President of the United States.

In that assembly, we decided among other matters that apartheid is an issue of *status confessionis* and suspended the white South African churches from their membership in the LWF.[1] Social-ethical issues dominated the assembly agenda, the key words being peace, justice and equality. While I was enthusiastic about many of these issues, I also wondered why individual ethics was not discussed.

The approach to human rights was somewhat selective in this assembly of 1984. Universal rights of equality were highly appreciated, but rights of individual freedom related to the freedom of expression, individual life choices and freedom of conscience, were often considered as conservative and capitalist matters, issues that Ronald Reagan and Margaret Thatcher had pushed on to the political agenda. They were often referred to as the »third basket« of the European Conference

---

[1] For this, cf. J. H. Schjørring et al. (eds.), *From Federation to Communion: The History of the LWF* (Minneapolis: Fortress Press, 1997), especially 238–239.

of Security and Cooperation. Burning issues like racism were not treated in terms of rights of individual freedom, but as test cases for universal equality.

1 From Universalism to Difference

Today we live in a different world. Issues of peace and justice are still prominent and social ethics continues to be important. The relative importance of individual ethics and freedom rights has, however, increased. Nowadays it dominates the agenda of many churches. In addition to basic equality, societies and religious communities discuss the rights of minorities and the morality of their members' different individual life projects. Human rights are increasingly understood as the structure that enables the flourishing of very different individuals and particular groups.

Political historians and philosophers agree that the end of the Cold War era, around 1990, meant the emergence of a new cultural period which demanded new starting-points for societal reflection. To outline this dramatic cultural change, I will employ some phrases of the Canadian philosopher Charles Taylor.[2] Until 1990 we can adequately speak of the era of universalism, and politics of universalism, that shaped societal discussion at least since the Second World War. A politics of universalism wants to create a homogenous world in which global equality is strongly affirmed, and individual and cultural differences are largely ignored.

This politics of universalism embraces equality and unity. Legal and institutional structures are meant to enable the equal participation of all interested stakeholders. The United Nations, the Socialist International, the British Commonwealth and the European Economic Community can be understood as typical institutions of such universalism. The ecumenical movement, the World Council of Churches and the global Roman Catholic Church as promoted in the documents of the Second Vatican Council all represent the same trend of homogenous universalism in the field of religion.

---

[2] Charles Taylor, »The Politics of Recognition,« in his *Philosophical Arguments* (Cambridge: Harvard University Press, 1995), 225–256. See also Simon Thompson, *The Political Theory of Recognition: A Critical Introduction* (Cambridge: Polity Press, 2006).

After the fall of the iron curtain, however, the premises of such universalism and internationalism changed dramatically. Nationalist ideologies gained new current relevance. Globalization was no longer seen as a merely positive, progressive trend; the dangers of globalization began to be emphasized. Instead of global social issues, the rights of minorities and the conscience of the individual moved to the focus of ethical reflection. Rights of human freedom were moved from the agenda of the political right to the centre of all democratic politics.

While the leaders of the churches may not have been very conscious of this new paradigm, church documents adopted new political trends. Around the year 2000, three large European religious majorities published influential public documents on globalization and social ethics. In Germany, this was done in a common text of the Protestant churches and the Catholic Church. In Finland, the Lutheran bishops' conference drafted a similar document. In Russia, the Orthodox Church published a major document on social ethics, the first of its kind in Eastern Christianity.[3]

Astonishingly, all three documents are critical of globalization, recommending policies that return to locally-normative orders and which fight global neoliberalism. Local and regional policies and institutions are preferred over worldwide forces. In a paradoxical manner, all three documents point to the need to create powers which exercise control over global markets and other forces of globalization. Obviously the churches cannot draft concrete proposals towards such global governance, since they are, *a priori*, critical of universalism and global powers. Rather they recommend a nostalgic return to the roots of their local and regional normative orders, hoping that some anonymous, non-global, force could control global markets and policies.

We may label this new paradigm a »culture of difference«, and call its social agenda a support of differences. The new paradigm focuses on the positive appreciation of differences, and those fundamental human rights that enable different people to voice their different concerns and ideologies so that they are not ignored just because they are a minority. Charles Taylor outlines the various tensions between the claim of

---

[3] For this and the following, see Risto Saarinen, »Die neuesten Soziallehren der Kirchen und ihr europäisches Umfeld,« in *Die europäische Integration und die Kirchen*, ed. H. Duchhardt (Göttingen: Vandenhoeck & Ruprecht, 2010), 89–106. The following are the titles of the documents: *Für eine Zukunft in Solidarität und Gerechtigkeit* (German), *Towards the Common Good* (Finnish), *The Social Doctrine of the Russian Orthodox Church* (Russian).

universal equality and the rights of minorities. He pleads for the preservation of differences and an affirmation of minority rights, even where that would mean the violation of democratic majorities. As a test case, he argues that the French-speaking minority in Quebec, Canada, sometimes needs to have its minority language protected in situations in which the rights of the English-speaking majority are violated. Thus ethnic, linguistic and other cultural identities have, for Taylor, an inherent value; therefore a culture supporting differences is sometimes preferred over a politics of universalism.[4]

The need for such a support of differences has often been approved in recent democratic politics. Theoretical scholars claim that politics in the post-Cold War era can be adequately described as identity politics: that is, as public debates and decision-making concerning the rights and visibility of different identities such as those of sexual, linguistic and ethnic minorities on the one hand, and those of populist, nationalist and fundamentalist groups on the other.

While the earlier, conventional politics of the Cold War era was a struggle for economic distribution between parties and societal classes, the new politics concerns the visibility and flourishing of different identities in the society. Such »identity politics« can be either progressive or regressive, and may lead either towards multiculturalism or to a complete separation between different ethnic identities. Sometimes it can even lead to both simultaneously, as in some Western countries which affirm multiculturalism, but in which the different groups remain segregated from one another in concrete societal practice.[5]

In all these cases the important thing is the particular difference that gives my own group, and myself, its distinctive identity. Identity is not something to be chosen and adopted autonomously; it is primarily something that society needs to recognize: only identities that are recognized through public discussion and political decisions are real identities. They are heteronomous due to this act of recognition. For this reason, identity politics is often characterized, by Hegel's famous phrase, as »a struggle for recognition«. While the old paradigm of

---

[4] Taylor, »The Politics of Recognition.«
[5] See Thompson, *The Political Theory of Recognition*, and Nancy Fraser and Axel Honneth, *Redistribution of Recognition? A Political-Philosophical Exchange* (London: Verso, 2005).

universalism understood equality and toleration as its basic virtues, the cohesive forces of the new era are identities and their recognition.[6]

The overall theme of the present consultation of our *Societas Oecumenica* is *Catholicity under Pressure: The Ambiguous Relationship between Diversity and Unity*. In the following, I build on the historical description outlined above.

During the last 25 years, we have moved from the era of universalism to a new era that emphasizes difference. Diversity is celebrated and ideologies that demand universal validity, or catholicism, remain under pressure. The ecumenical movement is a child of the era of universalism; in order to stay alive, this movement needs to understand that we have moved to a new historical era in which the old paradigm, as such, is no longer valid.

This paradigm change is also a major challenge for the churches in general. The churches need to react to it. As a Lutheran theologian I will give some resources from my Protestant tradition as to how to understand, and react to, this challenge. Basically, however, this is not a confessional issue. It is a theological, philosophical and social issue that concerns all churches and, perhaps, even all religions alike. In addition to recent Protestant theology, I will pay attention to some important Roman Catholic contributions.

Let me summarize the historical paradigms with a description of three symptoms that witness to my claim of paradigm change. The first such symptom is the above-mentioned shift from social ethics to the individualist understanding of human rights, freedom considered as the rights of minorities to promote their own identity. In my own Lutheran tradition, as in many other Protestant and Anglican traditions, recent debates on marriage and homosexuality are prominent examples of this kind. In the Catholic Church, the problem of remarrying after divorce and staying in the church is structurally similar to this issue, as it concerns the legitimate amount of freedom and differing identities within a church.

A second symptom concerns the relationship between Christian and national or local cultural identity. In the era of difference, political leadership is tempted to make religion an ingredient of that national, or even nationalist, identity that promotes a given political program. Church leaders are tempted to follow this program, as it promises

---

[6] Thompson, *The Political Theory of Recognition,* and Axel Honneth, *Kampf um Anerkennung: Zur moralischen Grammatik sozialer Konflikte* (Frankfurt: Suhrkamp, 1992).

influence and good standing for their church. In my view this phenomenon concerns not only openly patriotic countries but it is a real, though unspoken, issue in Lutheran countries such as Finland, Sweden and Norway. These countries have a long tradition of national churches. Moreover, the church parties are, in Scandinavia, often linked to political parties. Given this constellation, the churches seek to defend their local normative orders – which may be progressive or regressive – and they remain critical of global trends.

A third symptom concerns the way in which local churches no longer have international or global visions but remain confined to their closest environment, their own village or small town. Head pastors and bishops are elected as local representatives, who primarily care for their own small region. The faithful see the church in a nostalgic fashion, as a remnant of their own childhood, of everyday life, something that is not concerned with global market or international politics. This nostalgia for the »small circles« of the »good life« may even be labeled as the most pervasive symptom, as it feeds the first and second. A nostalgic person may easily vote nationalist leaders and oppose vehemently all new forms of freedom, in family life and elsewhere.

We need to see that the most ardent followers of a politics of difference, or identity politics, are located at the opposite poles of a society: on the one hand, progressive minority activists and advocates of human rights embrace this politics; on the other hand, a similar critique of globalization also fuels the conservative nostalgia of populist movements.

2 Current Philosophical Theories of Recognition

I now move from this generalizing, paradigmatic historical description towards a more careful academic analysis. I will start with two conclusions which many political philosophers have drawn from the multiculturalism discussions of the last twenty years. When I say that I agree with these two conclusions, I am saying nothing original but am remaining on the common ground of current societal discussion.

First, the choice of a viable paradigm is not a choice between universalism and difference. The most prominent theorists, such as Taylor or the German philosophers Axel Honneth and Rainer Forst, argue that we need both universalism and difference, and that the two notions, taken together can, to some extent, heal each other's weaknesses. Honneth, for instance, considers that human individuals and groups have two basic needs in their societal life. They need respect which is granted to everybody in equal terms by the universal rule of law. They also need individual or collective recognition of their individual features, skills and achievements; this should be granted to each of them separately and according to a proper measure. Thus both individuals and groups need both a politics of universalism, and a support for differences.[7]

Personally I think that ecumenists should adopt a somewhat similar strategy, holding that we need both unity or catholicity, and individual flourishing or striving for perfection. The ecumenical movement discovered costly universalism; but we also need the tools to understand difference. Universality and individual flourishing are not in conflict, rather they may balance one another's weaknesses in ways that, in the field of religion, remain to be unfolded. Because the theory of recognition holds that we need both universalism *and* difference, it may become a friend of the ecumenical movement.

Second, the theorists claim that our era needs a cohesive force which helps to build a harmonious multicultural society. The idea of recognition is often understood as such a force; therefore this idea is currently being studied by many interdisciplinary research groups around the world. Also my own work, and the work of my students in Helsinki, focus on the dynamics of recognition in religion and theology.[8] What is meant by this concept?

A first glimpse can be obtained by saying that recognition assumes more than mere toleration, but less than agreement or consensus. I may *tolerate* Muslims, secularists and fundamentalist Christians in my own society even when I don't want to have anything to do with them. Political theorists claim that such non-committed toleration is not enough: in order to build a successful multicultural society, its stakeholders should relate positively to one another even when they don't agree. When I *recognize* my Muslim neighbours, however, I commit to work together with them to build a good society. In an ideal case, such recognition should be mutual. However, even a one-sided recognition may be better than nothing. This kind of recognition normally entails a

---

[7] Thompson, *The Political Theory of Recognition*; Honneth, *Kampf um Anerkennung*; Rainer Forst, *Toleranz im Konflikt* (Frankfurt: Suhrkamp, 2003).
[8] See my project website: http://blogs.helsinki.fi/reasonandreligious recognition. Among new dissertations, Timothy Lim's »Ecclesial Recognition: An Interdisciplinary Proposal« (Regent University, 2014) deserves mention.

qualification, – a »recognizing as« – of the other as something: as good a neighbour, as Abraham's heir, as a person of good will, etc.[9]

Axel Honneth's theory of recognition, it has been argued, consists of three parts: love, respect and esteem. Persons learn to *love* in their primary parental relationships; on the basis of loving recognition in a family, we can become socialized. As social creatures, persons should learn universal *respect* within the legal structures of society; in addition, we may gain individual *esteem* on the basis of our particular features or achievements. In all three of its variants, recognition is heteronomous: others recognize me.[10] Toleration is often thought of as being a fairly autonomous virtue, whereas recognition occurs in this heteronomous manner. In some sense, recognition is therefore more social. On the other hand, there may not be any strict need to separate toleration and recognition. Rainer Forst, for instance, seems to consider recognition as a full-fledged, and particularly mature, form of toleration.[11]

Following Hegel, many theorists claim that human beings in a society go through »a struggle for recognition«.[12] When we are recognized as children, and later as citizens and as skilled members of the society, we obtain an identity that makes us mature. For this reason, obtaining recognition resembles reconciliation: due to this event, our struggle is appeased. Repressed groups and discriminated individuals should therefore be recognized; this is the way in which they become balanced members of our society. Although different theorists consider the relative importance of personal psychology differently, they are normally optimistic with regard to the good effects of becoming loved, respected and obtaining esteem. Theoretically, however, one can also imagine a society that lacks these virtues so that its members remain permanently unable of creating lasting ties of co-operation and balanced identity. In such a case, the struggle continues and no reconciliation is provided.

---

[9] For the as-qualification, see Risto Saarinen, »Anerkennungstheorien und ökumenische Theologie,« in *Ökumene – überdacht*, ed. T. Bremer and M. Wernsmann (Freiburg: Herder, 2014), and Thomas Bedorf, *Verkennende Anerkennung* (Berlin: Suhrkamp, 2010).
[10] Thompson, *Political Theory of Recognition*; Honneth, *Kampf um Anerkennung*.
[11] Forst, *Toleranz im Konflikt*.
[12] Honneth, *Kampf um Anerkennung*; Ludwig Siep, *Anerkennung als Prinzip der praktischen Philosophie* (Hamburg: Meiner, 2014).

3 Recent Theological Work on Recognition

In what follows, I regard these two conclusions as valid and ask whether religion and theology can receive something from them, or even something contribute to this discussion. Most current theories of recognition do not treat religious matters. Contemporary theologians are, however, paying increased attention to them. This process of reception has, as I see it, three stages, each of which opens up valuable insights to the theological understanding of the contemporary world. In the *first stage*, theologians ask what the current discussion can offer to theological reflection; the first stage thus imports the social discussion to theology. In the *second stage*, one begins to ask whether the resources of Christian theology have any phenomenological correspondence to the issues; the second stage thus opens a comparative perspective. In the *third stage*, one asks whether religion and theology have some resources of their own to offer, for instance, a historical resource or a new insight on recognition that stems from the specific field of religion. My own proposals from a Lutheran or Protestant perspective aim to move to this third stage. Before that, however, I will comment on the current theological discussion taking place on the first and second stage.

In his Catholic fundamental theology, Jürgen Werbick considers that Honneth's ideas of love and recognition can be connected to Christian theology, insofar as they are interpreted as pointing towards a divine subject. God thus fulfills the promise established by the philosophical figure of recognition. Similarly, the Lutheran systematic theologian Jan-Olav Henriksen argues that the issue of recognizing the other is a prominent aspect of Christology. In another recent study, Gregory Walter claims that the promises given and received in an anthropological gift exchange, create a framework for recognizing the other. For Walter, the theological concept of promise can be understood as a bridge, launching the issue of recognition as a theological theme.[13]

These works belong to a larger current in which contemporary phenomenological philosophy (in particular the thought of Emanuel Levinas and Paul Ricoeur) is being discussed in theology. While the concepts of difference and otherness are central to this, the idea of

---

[13] Jürgen Werbick, *Den Glauben verantworten: Eine Fundamentaltheologie* (Freiburg: Herder, 2000); Jan-Olav Henriksen, *Desire, Gift, and Recognition: Christology and Postmodern Philosophy* (Grand Rapids: Eerdmans, 2009); Gregory Walter, *Being Promised: Theology, Gift, and Practice* (Grand Rapids: Eerdmans, 2013).

recognition is discussed only in a rather sporadic way. I consider this current of discussion to be important for today's ecumenical theology, manifesting as it does today's new awareness of differences. But I also think that the resources of Christian theology remain somewhat poorly represented in many of its studies. The first stage of reception is often primarily interested in launching the ideas of French phenomenology into theology.

However, the new extensive study of Veronika Hoffmann, *Skizzen zur Theologie der Gabe*, brings this process of reception to a new level. This work achieves the first extensive phenomenological comparison between the culture of recognition and Christian theology, thus moving the discussion from the first stage of launching ideas to the second stage of fruitful dialogue. Hoffmann's starting point is the theory of recognition as it appears in Marcel Hénaff's study *The Price of Truth*. Hénaff's book became famous after Paul Ricoeur adopted its conclusions in his last book *The Course of Recognition*. As Hénaff's study proceeds beyond the ideas of Taylor and Honneth, its basic ideas need to be briefly mentioned.[14]

For Hénaff the idea of recognition, and the need to overcome otherness, are not issues that emerge only in late modernity. Rather, they are basic elements of anthropology and shape the social dynamics of all or most cultures. For Hénaff, the anthropological idea of gift exchange comes very close to the general idea of mutual recognition. In giving and receiving ceremonial gifts, we grant and obtain recognition with our neighbours. While economic exchange, i.e. buying and selling, avoids creating lasting social ties, the gift exchange is primarily involved in constructing the social sphere by means of granting and obtaining recognition. In and through material gifts, we give and receive recognition. Recognition is thus the hidden spirit of gift exchange; it is the archetypal non-economic modus of interpersonal communication. Through gift exchange, otherness and distinctive identities become established and shaped; at the same time, such differences are not obstacles to communication but can be effectively overcome. For Paul Ricoeur, Hénaff's ideas mean that the event of obtaining recognition is not only a Hegelian struggle, but also a means of peaceful coexistence.[15]

[14] Veronika Hoffmann, *Skizzen zu einer Theologie der Gabe* (Freiburg: Herder, 2013); Marcel Hénaff, *The Price of Truth: Gift, Money, and Philosophy* (Stanford: Stanford University Press, 2010); Paul Ricoeur, *The Course of Recognition* (Cambridge, Mass.: Harvard University Press, 2005).

[15] Henaff, *The Price of Truth*; Ricoeur, *The Course of Recognition*, esp. 233–241.

Hoffmann calls this basic idea of Hénaff »the gift of recognition« and undertakes an extensive phenomenological comparison between it and various traditional themes of dogmatic and ecumenical theology. Here I will give only one example of the many fascinating and well-argued comparisons made in her excellent study. This example concerns the theology of justification, in particular the Lutheran - Roman Catholic *Joint Declaration on the Doctrine of Justification*. As a Catholic theologian Hoffmann, wants to respond to the Protestant criticisms presented by Eberhard Jüngel. (It is noteworthy that Jüngel, too, considers justification to mean basically an act of divine recognition; Jüngel does not, however, participate in the broader theoretical discussion regarding recognition and difference.[16])

Hoffmann argues that the Hénaffian »gift of recognition« manages to avoid the »economic« dimensions of salvation, dimensions criticized by the Protestant Reformation. You cannot buy and sell recognition; it can only be granted and obtained as gift. The justification of sinner, understood in terms of recognition, is thus not obtained through merit or achievement; it remains a strictly non-economic gift. At the same time, however, this non-economic mode of justification is not merely unilateral or monergistic: the gift can only be a gift when both sides are persons, capable of personal acts. Jüngel's typically Protestant problem is that he wants to achieve unilateralism or monergism at any price. When Protestants remain bound to the concepts of merit and achievement, they remain fixed to economic thinking. Instead of non-merit and non-achievement, the Protestant should affirm the possibility of entirely non-economic exchange. This is, according to the Catholic Hoffmann, possible with this idea of the gift of recognition: when Catholics affirm this idea, they are not Pelagians, rather they can affirm the divine initiative without reducing humans to non-personal objects.[17]

Hoffmann argues further that the Pauline act of forensic *logizomai*, imputation or reckoning, is an act of »creative misrecognition«. The lasting difference between the righteous God and sinful human beings cannot be overcome by any consideration of universal justice. Instead, in forensic justification a culture of difference and diversity needs to be assumed. Because God justifies sinners through an act of reckoning, God's recognitive act is an act of misrecognition: God takes the sinner to

---

[16] Hoffmann, *Skizzen zu einer Theologie der Gabe*, 285–346; Eberhard Jüngel, *Das Evangelium von der Rechtfertigung des Gottlosen als Zentrum des christlichen Glaubens* (Tübingen: Mohr Siebeck, 1998).

[17] Hoffmann, *Skizzen zu einer Theologie der Gabe*, 285–320.

be righteous. At the same time this act is creative in the sense that it enables the circulation, the giving and receiving, of gifts within the gift exchange. In the world of otherness and difference, a successful act of recognition needs to be a *mis*recognition of some kind, Hoffmann argues.[18]

In this limited sense, the traditional Protestant doctrine of forensic justification can be compared phenomenologically to the culture of differences that employs the gift of recognition as its tool of social cohesion. Thus Jüngel is right in claiming that justification is an act of divine recognition; he is wrong, however, in remaining constrained to the economic vocabulary of merit and achievement. In order for recognition to occur, we need to move beyond economic vocabularies. Even then, however, a truly *religious* recognition needs to take place, as a sort of *mis*recognition within the sphere of difference that surpasses universal justice.[19]

I cannot here consider Hoffmann's fascinating proposals in detail. I have only taken her as an example of how the discussion about the challenge of difference and diversity can move from the first stage of awareness to the second stage of phenomenological comparison, and thus become fruitful in ecumenical doctrinal dialogue. While scholars like Werbick and Henriksen are to be thanked for creating an initial awareness of recognition, Hoffmann must be thanked for a truly theological discovery of the rich doctrinal resources that can be employed in responding to the challenge of difference and diversity.

4   Recognition as a Classical Theme of Theology

I now come to the *third stage*, of claiming that the theology of recognition is not only a new task to be accomplished in our era marked by difference, but a *classical theological issue* which can be located in the great and long tradition of the Christian church. According to this claim the theology of recognition is of equal value with the philosophical theories of Taylor, Honneth, Ricoeur and Hénaff. Fundamentally this theology is already part of our learning and competence; at the same time, it is something that needs to be detected and put into fruitful use. Until now, Protestant theologians have done little, or almost nothing to

---

[18]   Ibid., 320–326.
[19]   Ibid., 295–306.

accomplish this. In Catholic theology, the situation is somewhat better, as the works of Werbick and Hoffmann have shown.

Obviously I cannot justify this fully in the remaining short section of my paper. I will only give some programmatic fragments. First we need to proceed from a phenomenological comparison to the real intellectual history, the *Begriffsgeschichte*, of religious recognition. We have excellent histories of the idea and concept of toleration,[20] but nothing comparable on recognition. If theologians consider the notion of recognition to be a major virtue in this age of difference and multiculturalism, we need to trace the history of this fundamental concept and idea. This is necessary to understand what religious recognition is, and what it can be: once we know what religious recognition is, we can apply it to the challenges facing our religious communities today.

The concept of recognition, in German: *Anerkennung*, is not something which Hegel created and which social philosophers discovered after the end of the Cold War. Like other notions in its mental neighborhood (for instance, tolerance or agreement), it has an extensive intellectual history that goes back to Aristotle and the Greco-Roman world. This history is particularly rich in Protestant theology; this finding may be surprising, as nobody has investigated it. My historical »fragment« is limited to two major figures of the 20th century, Rudolf Bultmann and Karl Barth. As they employ the concept of recognition in crucial passages of their theology, this small fragment opens up broader perspectives.

In his article on *ginosko* (»to know«) in Kittel's *Theological Dictionary of the New Testament*, Bultmann notes that the biblical notion of »knowing« involves the person who knows. Thus knowing contains an element of *Anerkennen*, of recognizing; it does not remain theoretical but involves will and emotion. This feature stems from Judaism but also permeates New Testament Greek: in the New Testament the knowledge of the divine will is, according to Bultmann, »primarily recognition, an obedient or thankful submission to what is known«. Similarly, the substantive *gnosis* in the Gospels is not theoretical information but »a recognition of God's new plan of salvation«. The verb *epiginosko*, and the substantive *epignosis*, express this recognition in a paradigmatic manner; *epignosis* has »become an almost technical term for the decisive knowledge of God which is implied in conversion to the Christian faith«.[21]

---

[20] Forst, *Toleranz im Konflikt*.
[21] For this and the following, cf. Rudolf Bultmann, »ginosko,« in ThWNT, vol. 1, 688–719.

In addition to human knowledge, the Hebrew and Greek terms are also employed, in a distinctive way, of God's knowledge: God's knowing establishes the significance of what is known. The object of God's knowledge becomes an object of concern and recognition, of *Anerkennung*. In this manner God's knowledge also means election. In many New Testament passages, God's knowledge implies election. Thus both human knowledge and divine knowledge mean an attachment, a recognitive involvement and affirmation of the known object. Christian knowledge is »an obedient and grateful recognition of the deeds and demands of God«.

Bultmann's article on *pisteuo*, »to believe«, in Kittel's dictionary deepens the insights regarding recognitive knowledge. Bultmann believes that the Hebrew concept of faith and trust can also be understood as recognition. Such faith involves a strong mutual relationship, a relationship established by God. The recognition (*Anerkennung*) of Jesus as Lord is intrinsic to Christian faith. In faith, a Christian recognizes Christ as Lord. This faith in the kerygma is »inseparable from faith in the person mediated thereby«. In other words faith as recognition has, as its object, both the doctrinal content and the person mediated through this content.[22] The relationship of recognition, as expressed by the terms *gnosis, epignosis* and *pistis*, is a mutual relationship of involved persons. The doctrinal content, or the kerygma, belongs to this relationship; at the same time, the interpersonal involvement remains a necessary constituent of religious faith and knowledge.

In his *Church Dogmatics* Karl Barth formulates a similar point when he discusses the cognitive content of faith. He teaches that the human act of faith consists of three aspects, namely, recognizing, knowing and confessing (*Anerkennen, Erkennen, Bekennen*).[23] Against Protestant Orthodoxy Barth teaches that the aspect of recognizing must come first. The error of Orthodoxy consists in holding that the Christian first needs to know the object of faith; only then he would perform the acts of recognition and confession. Barth teaches that

> Christian faith is a recognition (Anerkennen) ... Knowing is certainly included in the recognition, but it can only follow it. Recognizing is a taking cognizance which is obedient and compliant, which yields and subordinates itself. This ... is not an incidental and subsequent characteristic of

[22] Rudolf Bultmann, »pisteuo,« in ThWNT, vol. 6, 174–230.
[23] Karl Barth, KD IV/1, 839.

faith, but primary, basic and decisive. It is not preceded by any other kind of knowledge, either knowing or confessing.[24]

Like Bultmann, Barth holds that the primacy of recognition is due to its capability of creating the reference to the person of Jesus Christ and to the fact represented by Jesus: »Recognition as the basic moment in the act of Christian faith has reference to Jesus Christ himself … It has reference to the fact which the community represents in the world, to the person by whom it is constituted and who is its living law.«[25] At this point, Barth explicitly adds that he shares the view of Bultmann.

Here I cannot enter into any larger discussion about the truth-value of the claims of Bultmann and Barth. Let it be added, however, that Barth believes that his view of faith as recognition comes from Luther, and is represented by the Pietism of the 18th century as well as the cultural Protestantism of the 19th century. Both Bultmann and Barth consider that the idea of biblical knowledge and faith as recognitive involvement is not a small detail, but a prominent and pervasive theme of Protestant theology.

The dialectical contrast between knowledge as theoretical information, and knowledge as personal recognitive involvement, reminds us of the paradigms of universalism and diversity. A paradigm of universalism almost inevitably needs to employ a theoretical concept of rational knowledge. The paradigm of diversity can pay more attention to the idea that each person experiences his or her own knowledge, and the known object, differently. A paradigm of diversity may even grant Barth's point that the recognitive appreciation comes first, before any theoretical mastery of official teaching. This may sound »postmodern«, but I am not trying to argue for limitless pluralism. Rather, this paradigm of diversity exemplifies a *fides quaerens intellectum*, faith seeking understanding. The basic trust needs to come first, only then we can proceed to the content. The point of Bultmann and Barth is, therefore, not postmodern but classical.

In his small book *Reification*, Axel Honneth discusses the epistemological grounds of the contemporary philosophy of recognition. For Honneth these grounds are found in childhood psychology, especially in the primary relations between child and parent. A small child does not learn loving trust on the basis of information and evidence. Rather love

---

[24] Ibid., 847–848.
[25] Ibid., 849.

and trust emerge as a primary, objective relationship; only due to the emergence of such a relationship is the child a person who can receive information and perform thinking. Thus knowledge is preceded by constitutive, heteronomous recognition. Honneth claims that the human mind afterwards reverses this order, and performs a problematic act of *Verdinglichung*, of reification. Due to this problematic act, we are accustomed to thinking that we first need to know a given object before we can appreciate and evaluate it. But in human psychology the order differs from this: psychologically we are first constituted by the acts of loving appreciation, and we also form attachments to objects before knowing them.[26]

When Bultmann and Barth teach that recognition comes first in the biblical acts of knowing and believing, these dialectical theologians are surprisingly close to Honneth's theory of recognition. Recognition is a *primary orientation*, one that is grasped in terms of knowledge only afterwards.

5   Ecumenical Visions in the Era of Difference

At this point we can proceed to ecumenical matters. The first lesson is that the era of diversity is, finally, nothing fundamentally new. We experience it as new only because we, as ecumenists, have had a strong belief in the victory of universalism. This was, however, in many ways a false belief since it had no secure epistemological grounds: equality and toleration are great virtues of universalism, but they are not everything. They are virtues of *detachment*, powers enabling us to remain distant from objects, to perform reification. In addition to them, we need virtues of *attachment*, powers that bestow upon us a positive identity and equip us with love and respect.

While detachment may be related to catholicity and universalism, we might say that the virtues of attachment emphasize the mark of holiness. The current era of difference has made these virtues visible in new ways. Theologically this is a positive development, since it links us with the biblical understanding of knowing and believing: we know and believe since we are attached to others and recognized by others. We are deeply heteronomous beings.

---

[26]   Axel Honneth, *Reification: A New Look at an Old Idea* (Oxford: Oxford University Press, 2008).

How are we to evaluate the mark of catholicity on the basis of this insight? We need to rule out two problematic and even false understandings of catholicity. Catholicity is not a seemingly objective theoretical information about religion. Catholicity is in danger of *Verdinglichung*, reification: if it becomes an objective information, it loses its biblical background of faith and recognitive knowledge. However, the opposite alternative is also problematic. If I speak of *my* catholicity, or the catholicity of *our supporters*, I have a colonialist attitude to this virtue. The era of difference asks constantly: whose catholicity, which catholicity? We need to ask this question, and deconstruct the »ownership« of the mark of catholicity. Catholicity needs to be seen between its possessive and theoretical extremes: nobody »owns« catholicity, and we cannot have merely theoretical information about it. It is good that catholicity exists in this way, »under pressure«. Only under pressure can catholicity reveal its true nature. Catholicity needs to be complemented with holiness.

Given that our era of difference has the power of recognition as its cohesive force, how could we employ this power in ecumenical work? Ecumenists have employed the idea of recognition prominently, at least since the 1970s. The extensive reflection on ecumenical recognition in the 1970s, initiated by Heinrich Fries and continued by many others, is in many ways similar to the later insights of Charles Taylor and Axel Honneth.[27] Here ecumenists have really moved ahead of their times. At the same time, the new insights of political philosophy and the new era of difference can show how this concept now works more effectively than in the 1970s. With the help of new philosophical insights, much theological work is currently being done to revive the idea of ecumenical recognition. Basically, however, it is the classical theological insights which make this concept helpful and promising.

Ecumenical recognition is not a universalist solution; it aims to solve targeted, and mostly bilateral, problems of church unity. Ecumenical recognition proceeds through formulating convergences and common doctrinal views. At the same time, however, it cannot be »doctrinal mathematics« or a purely Faith and Order style of work: the interpersonal dimension, and the primacy of personal recognition, must be kept in mind. As Bultmann and Barth point out, personal recognition is theologi-

---

[27] Heinrich Fries, »Was heisst Anerkennung der kirchlichen Ämter?,« *Stimmen der Zeit* 98 (1973): 507–515. This paper is the first one to attempt a theological definition of ecumenical recognition. For an overall history of the older discussion, see Gerard Kelly, *Recognition: Advancing Ecumenical Thinking* (Frankfurt: Lang, 1996).

cally primary; the dimension of theoretical knowledge follows and assumes this primary recognition. Doctrinal recognition of some targeted theme may be the end result of this work, but it starts, in some way, with a primary recognition between persons. Some ecumenists, for instance Walter Kasper,[28] saw this marching order already in the 1970s. Perhaps they were then too much ahead of their times; only now, in the era of difference and in the aftermath of the so-called politics of recognition, are we better able to understand what ecumenical recognition means.

The idea of targeted and limited ecumenical recognition can, in some ways, be understood as being a typically Lutheran idea. Martin Luther understood the essence of faith as consisting in faithfulness and in the so-called apprehensive faith, the personal appropriation which makes the believer a committed stakeholder. At the same time, this appropriation is not of one's own doing but is a gift bestowed and initiated by God.[29] This heteronomous constitution of faith and the whole Christian person links Luther with the 20th century concepts of Bultmann and the current theorists of recognition.

It needs to be added, however, that until now the idea of recognition has for the most part been elaborated by Catholics. One should also note how the concept of recognition has been employed in the documents of the Second Vatican Council. In both *Lumen gentium* and *Nostra aetate*, the concept is used as a criterion of evaluating other religions. *Lumen gentium* states that »God gathers his people among those who recognize him in truth«. Since Muslims »recognize the Creator«, they are related to the people of God. In this manner *Lumen gentium* follows Bultmann's understanding of immediate personal encounter, on the basis of which faith is evaluated. In *Nostra aetate*, the Roman Catholic Church calls people to »recognize those spiritual and moral good things« that are found in other religions.[30] Recognition thus also concerns our interpersonal evaluation. Interestingly, Vatican II thus recommends a targeted and limited recognition with regard to other religions. Perhaps we can say that the council fathers have, in this manner, anticipated the era of multiculturalism and difference and given some advice about how to relate to the issues which it raises.

---

[28] Walter Kasper, »Was bedeutet das: Katholische Anerkennung der Confessio Augustana?,« in *Katholische Anerkennung des Augsburgischen Bekenntnisses?*, eds. H. Meyer et al. (Frankfurt: Lembeck, 1977).

[29] Risto Saarinen, »Glaube,« in *Luther-Lexikon*, ed. V. Leppin and G. Schneider-Ludorff (Regensburg: Bückle & Böhm, 2014), 259–261.

[30] Lumen Gentium 9,16; Nostra aetate 2.

The Changing World as Challenge to the Churches
An Orthodox Perspective

Georgios Vlantis

1 Introduction

> Das ist die Sehnsucht, die durch alle Werke Augustins hindurchklingt: Die Sehnsucht nach ewigem Frieden. Er, der ein Leben lang ruhelos unterwegs war, war doch ruhelos nur um der letzten Ruhe willen, die ihm in diesem Leben fort und fort seine geheime Unruhe blieb. Dass ihm all sein Sinnen und Sehnen in diesem einen zusammenlief, in dem Verlangen nach einem letzten Stille-Sein, zeigt, wie tief er ein Mensch der Antike gewesen ist. Aber dass er diese Ruhe nicht anders fand denn in der Liebe und in dem Frieden (pax!) Jesu Christi, zeigt, wie echt er Christ geworden ist.[1]

In the concluding remarks of his doctoral thesis Joseph Ratzinger is not only summarising central constants in Augustine of Hippo's character and thought; furthermore, he is pointing out the exceptional position of peace and tranquillity in the world of ideals emphasised during antiquity. In various Christian modifications, this – typical for the ancient thought – longing for peace, hesychia, tranquillity, theoria, etc. deeply penetrates the Middle Ages. It also characterises Orthodox spirituality

---

[1] Joseph Ratzinger, *Gesammelte Schriften*, vol. 1: *Volk und Haus Gottes in Augustins Lehre von der Kirche*, ed. Gerhard Ludwig Müller (Freiburg i. Br.: Herder, 2011), 418.

till nowadays.² On the contrary, modernity, according to Hans Blumenberg's analysis, is characterized from its very beginning by a radical reevaluation of the concepts of motion and change. This development is closely connected to the gradual secularisation of the dominant worldview. Motion and change are not any longer mainly associated with the confirmation or disturbance of an eternal order. They do not mark a situation of ontological inauthenticity. They are powers which lead to fullness of life: »Im Anfang war die Tat«³ – and action accompanies life as its most necessary condition. According to the dominant currents of modernity, motion, change, and action do not have a transcendent prime mover as ontological cause, but the human beings themselves. They are regarded as confirmations of the independence and autonomy of the human being.⁴

These thoughts already touch the issue of the complicated relation of the Orthodox world to modernity.⁵ I consider this as a key issue, if we want to understand the Orthodox reaction to the changes and challenges of our world. Therefore, I decided not to offer one more description of crucial problems we are facing today, but to focus on the understanding of change in Orthodox theology and history. A short overview will follow concerning current Orthodox reactions to a changing world. I will conclude with some thoughts on the theological potentials of the Eastern Church concerning modern challenges and will elaborate them in an ecumenical perspective.

---

[2] For an overview of the Orthodox spirituality, see e.g. the classic works of Tomáš Špidlík, *The Spirituality of the Christian East: A Systematic Handbook*, Cistercian Studies Series 79 (Kalamazoo: Cistercian Publications, 1986), and Paul Evdokimov, *Ages of the Spiritual Life* (Crestwood, New York: St. Vladimir's Seminary Press, 2002).

[3] Johann Wolfgang von Goethe, *Faust I*, *Studienzimmer*, v. 1237.

[4] See Hans Blumenberg, *Die kopernikanische Wende* (Frankfurt a.M.: Suhrkamp, 1965) and *The Genesis of the Copernican World*, trans. Robert M. Wallace (Cambridge: MIT Press, 1987); F. Kaulbach and Gerbert Meyer, »Bewegung,« in *Historisches Wörterbuch der Philosophie* 1, ed. Joachim Ritter (Basel: Schwabe, 1971), 864–879; Panajotis Kondylis, *Die neuzeitliche Metaphysikkritik* (Stuttgart: Klett-Cotta, 1990).

[5] See Pantelis Kalaitzidis, *Ορθοδοξία καί Νεωτερικότητα. Προλεγόμενα* (Athens: Indiktos, 2007); Pantelis Kalaitzidis and Nikos Ntontos (eds.), *Ορθοδοξία καί Νεωτερικότητα* (Athens: Indiktos, 2007); Assaad Elias Kattan and Fadi A. Georgi (eds.), *Thinking Modernity: Towards a Reconfiguration of the Relationship between Orthodox Theology and Modern Culture*, Balamand Theological Conferences 1 (Tripoli: St. John of Damascus Institute of Theology 2010); Vasilios N. Makrides, »Orthodox Christianity, Modernity and Postmodernity: Overview, Analysis and Assessment,« *Religion, State and Society* 40 (2012): 248–285.

2 The Ambiguities of Change in Orthodox Theology and History

Either identifying itself as traditional, as »Church of the Fathers«, faithful to the authenticity of the Christian doctrine, or polemised as traditionalistic, archaic, resistant to change, the fact remains that Orthodox theology, mentality and aesthetics are decisively shaped by its past.[6]

Nevertheless, great authorities of the Eastern Church were conscious of the novelty of their theological perspective. They were aware that they developed teachings which had never been articulated in that depth previously: One may think, for example, of Basil of Caesarea and Gregory of Nazianzus who elaborated pneumatology. Both of them saw change not as contradiction to the past but as a legitimate development, a constructive growth in the understanding of biblical truth (both Fathers support their views with numerous biblical citations); they both regarded this process as fruit and gift of the Holy Spirit.[7] One may argue that profane historians are not happy with metaphysically supported notions of historical linearity.[8] However, when the Orthodox Church speaks of an organic growth of doctrine it does not (or should

---

[6] This claim is an empirical observation. On a systematic-theological level, John Zizioulas and other Orthodox theologians emphasise the idea that the Church receives its identity from the future, from the eschaton, not from the past. See John Panteleimon Manoussakis, »The Anarchic Principle of Christian Eschatology in the Eucharistic Tradition of the Eastern Church,« *Harvard Theological Review* 100 (2007): 29–96. Although it is worth discussing on the theological presuppositions and limits of this thought and on its relation to the empirically observable behaviour of the Orthodox, such an undertaking would exceed the framework of this paper.

[7] See Stylianos Papadopoulos, *Πατέρες, αὔξησις τῆς Ἐκκλησίας, ἅγιον Πνεῦμα* (Athens, 1970) and also his *Πατρολογία*, Vol. 1: *Εἰσαγωγή, Β΄καὶ Γ΄ αἰώνας* (Athens, 1977), 17–51.

[8] Taking into account Kant's radical critique to teleology one may say that such schemes seem not to be convincing any more in interdisciplinary scientific discussions. The critique exercised against schemes of historical linearity in the last centuries includes not only theological, but also profane ones, like Hegel's and Marx's. See the classical work of Karl Löwith, *Meaning in History: The Theological Implications of the Philosophy of History* (Chicago: University of Chicago Press, 1949). However, this philosophical critique did (or does) not prevent Orthodox theologians from developing concepts of theology of history with nationalistic teleological implications. See e.g. Victor Roudometof, *Nationalism, Globalization, and Orthodoxy: The Social Origins of Ethnic Conflict in the Balkans* (Westport, CT: Greenwood Press, 2001); Pantelis Kalaitzidis, »The Temptation of Judas: Church and National Identities,« *Greek Orthodox Theological Review* 47 (2002): 357–379.

not) propose a methodology for the study of history: it rather makes a theological confession considering the peaks of its theology as expressions of its continuity with the apostolic origin and as tangible results of the energy of the Spirit in the Church.⁹

Orthodoxy emphasises continuity; but change is also present in its history. The Eastern Church insists on its loyalty to the patristic worldview; but if the above-mentioned Fathers, Basil of Caesarea and Gregory of Nazianzus, could somehow transfer themselves from the fourth to the fourteenth century, they would notice self-evident affinities as well as notable changes in their church: a more profound christological teaching, a conciliarly condemned Origen (their beloved Origen!),¹⁰ a complicated administrative system (and an excommunicated Rome), an almost homogenic ritual and a new paradigm in religious aesthetics. This does not necessarily mean contradiction to the past or betrayal of the Christian faith, but proves that change takes place in the churches, whether they want to accept it and name it as such or ignore it, insisting one-dimensionally on their continuity with the past.

On the other hand, it is true that in the Orthodox context the will for creative theological work gave gradually its place to an over-emphasis on the concern for faithfulness to tradition. Even the word »novelty« (*καινοτομία, νεωτερισμός*) became an accusation implying heretical teaching, inauthenticity of doctrine and break in continuity of faith.¹¹

---

9   See e.g. Stylianos Papadopoulos' works mentioned above; Andrew Louth, »Is Development of Doctrine a Valid Category for Orthodox Theology?,« in *Orthodoxy and Western Culture: A Collection of Essays Honoring Jaroslav Pelikan on His Eightieth Birthday*, eds. Valerie Hotchkiss and Patrick Henry (Crestwood: St. Vladimir's Seminary Press, 2005), 45–63.

10 Gregory of Nazianzus, in cooperation with Basil, even compiled an anthology of Origen's texts called Philocalia. See J. A. Robinson, *The Philocalia of Origen: The Text Revised With a Critical Introduction and Indices* (Cambridge: Cambridge University Press, 1893). Nevertheless, this does not imply a full adoption of his theology by the Cappadocians (see St. Papadopoulos, *Πατρολογία*, Vol. 1, 410).

11 See e.g. Trine Stauning Willert and Lina Molokotos-Liederman (eds.), *Innovation in the Orthodox Christian Tradition? The Question of Change in Greek Orthodox Thought and Practice* (Farnham: Ashgate, 2012), and especially the chapters by Trine Stauning Willert and Lina Molokotos-Liederman »How Can We Speak of Innovation in the Greek Orthodox Tradition? Towards a Typology of Innovation in Religion,« 3–17, and Vasilios N. Makrides »Orthodox Christianity, Change, Innovation: Contradictions in Terms?«, 19–50; as well as Ivana Noble, »History Tied Down by the Normativity of Tradition? Inversion of Perspective in Orthodox Theology: Challenges and Problems,« in *The Shaping of Tradition: Context and Normativity*, ed. Colby Dickinson (Leuven: Peeters, 2013), 283–296.

»I will say nothing of my own«,[12] John of Damascus declares in his *Dialectica*. Some centuries later the Byzantine theologian and philosopher Theodoros Metochites will claim that everything has been said and nothing else can be added; we trace expressions of a *grand ennui* during the last centuries of Byzantium, while it hopelessly struggled for survival.[13]

One may dispute to what extend theological reasons led to this kind of traditionalism; historical and cultural factors should not be ignored, too. The centuries of Muslim and communist oppression and the hard fate of the Orthodox people in general strengthened this concern for preserving tradition untouched and nourished the aversion against anything which may endanger the religious and cultural identity. A faith in danger means also an identity in danger. Under such circumstances the potentials of change cannot unfold themselves easily; innovation may be interpreted as alienation from the very core of the Christian message. But the paradox is that by being focused on preserving everything unchanged, Orthodoxy did actually change compared to its more fruitful and innovative past. Steps undertaken e.g. in the fourth century concerning dogmatic teaching, liturgical expression or administration would be unthinkable for this church nowadays. But who can predict the future?

3   The Orthodox Churches Facing a Changing World Today

Are we allowed to identify Orthodoxy with stagnation, with outmost resistance to change? I think this is too essentialistic to be true. The twentieth century has proven that the Eastern Church and its theology are able to develop creative and inspiring insights when acting in more or less liberal political contexts: the Russian diaspora or the Greek theological generation of the '60s constitute paradigm shifts in the Orthodox thought.[14] Nevertheless, in both cases theologians want to

---

[12] »Ἐρῶ τουγαροῦν ἐμὸν μὲν οὐδέν« (*Dialectica* 2.9) – see Bonifatius Kotter (ed.), *Die Schriften des Johannes von Damaskos*, vol. 1 (Berlin: de Gruyter, 1969), 55.

[13] Hans-Georg Beck, *Theodoros Metochites: Die Krise des byzantinischen Weltbildes im 14. Jahrhundert* (München: Beck, 1952). On the concept of the *grand ennui* in modernity and its implications, see George Steiner's excellent book *In Bluebeard's Castle: Some Notes on the Redefinition of Culture* (London: Faber & Faber, 1971).

[14] See Mary P. Cunningham and Elisabeth Theokritoff (eds.), *The Cambridge Companion to Orthodox Christian Theology* (Cambridge: Cambridge University

establish their new perspective by a hermeneutic approach which regards change mainly as a return to the Fathers, as a coming back to the authenticity of the patristic heredity after centuries of serious alienation. Georges Florovsky spoke of a »babylonian captivity« of the Orthodox theology in categories of the Western thought. The initially Lutheran context of this expression has been easily forgotten; any positive influences of the contact of Western theology with Orthodoxy are hardly seen.[15]

The fall of communism and further global geopolitical changes of the last decades led to a renaissance of religious life in many traditionally Orthodox countries. At the beginning one could experience there the almost absolute dominance of views that attempted to redefine the public role of Orthodoxy in a rather defensive way. Nowadays new voices become audible to criticizing theological nationalism, polemic anti-westernism, aggressive anti-ecumenism and ideological anti-modernism of older theologians. Even taboo issues like the ordination of women or homosexuality are now being discussed in the Orthodox world and certain approaches bringing new impulses are surprising. Younger theologians seek the encounter with the modern world beyond the prejudices of an anti-modern rhetoric and try to benefit from the potentials that modernity and post-modernity offer to Orthodoxy.[16]

One should, of course, be aware of the asymmetries and non-tautochronies in Orthodoxy throughout the globe in their confrontation with a changing world. For instance, the theological profile of the Orthodox Church of Finland differs decisively from the one of the Church of Poland; the ecumenical openness of the Orthodox in Germany is not self-evident for their brothers and sisters living in Bulgaria or Georgia; Greek theologians rejecting modernity do not inspire their modern American Orthodox colleagues.[17] Since Orthodoxy is on its way

---

Press 2008); Pantelis Kalaitzidis, Thanasis Papathanasiou and Theofilos Ambatzidis (eds.), Ἀναταράξεις στὴν μεταπολεμικὴ θεολογία. Ἡ «θεολογία τοῦ '60» (Athens: Indictos, 2009); Karl Christian Felmy, Einführung in die orthodoxe Theologie der Gegenwart, 2nd edition (Münster: LIT, 2011).

[15] See Pantelis Kalaitzidis, »From the ›Return to the Fathers‹ to the Need for a Modern Orthodox Theology,« St. Vladimir's Theological Quarterly 54 (2010): 5–36.

[16] Vasilios N. Makrides, »Orthodox Christianity, Modernity and Postmodernity: Overview, Analysis and Assessment,« Religion, State and Society 40 (2012): 248–285.

[17] E.g. Aristotle Papanikolaou, The Mystical as Political: Democracy and Non-Radical Orthodoxy (Notre Dame: Notre Dame University Press, 2012).

to its Holy and Great Synod, one wishes that this conciliar event makes a serious contribution to overcoming tensions in the polyphonic Orthodox world, which emphasises its unity but cannot – and should not – hide its diversity.[18]

Nevertheless, we should not underestimate the power of Orthodox voices still seeking for a nationalist oriented restoration of an imperial paradigm, suggesting an exceptional, privileged relation between them and the state (*synallelia-symphonia*). In Russia – and this is not the only example – a view is being articulated that almost identifies the message of the church with the values of the nation and interprets the Christian faith in normatively understood terms of culture. From that imaginary identification of church and nation follows implicitly that the non-Orthodox »others« have to be seen as second class citizens concerning their devotion to the state. Various laws against a vaguely defined proselytism show that the very existence of other confessions or faiths is interpreted also as a direct or latent threat to national security.[19]

This kind of theological nationalism in traditionally Orthodox countries is associated with an aggressive anti-westernism which I already mentioned above. according to a theology of history adequate to this view, considerable demands of the liberal society are nothing more than ideological products of the West, which is seen as if it has lost its connection with the authenticity of the biblical message. The history of changes which marks the development of the Western world is understood as history of a fall from an idealised Christian past; therefore one is not willing to differentiate between the theologically acceptable and the legally possible. The demanded free space for the expression of individuality is often regarded as an *ex definitione* illegitimate and sinful variety of individualism.[20]

---

[18] Nevertheless, one should not be over-optimistic concerning the expectations from this event. See the various critical assessments published in the special issue of *Religion und Gesellschaft in Ost & West*, 11–12/2014.

[19] Athanasios Vletsis, »Die letzte Bastion einer byzantinischen ›Symphonie‹? Die Deklaration der Russisch-Orthodoxen Kirche zu Menschenrechten (2008) als Ausdruck einer vormodernen Kirche-Staat Beziehung,« *Ökumenische Rundschau* 59 (2010): 346–362; Pantelis Kalaitzidis, *Orthodoxy and Political Theology*, trans. Gregory Edwards (Geneva: WCC, 2012); Papanikolaou, *The Mystical as Political*; Vasilios N. Makrides, »Orthodoxe Kirchen im öffentlichen Raum: Hintergrund, Probleme, Perspektiven,« *Ökumenische Rundschau* 62 (2013): 350–369.

[20] Angelos Giannakopoulos, »Antiokzidentalismus und ostkirchliche Tradition,« *Zeitschrift für Religionswissenschaft* 10 (2002): 119–129; Pantelis Kalaitzidis, Ελληνικότητα και αντιδυτικισμός στη «Θεολογία του '60» (doctoral dissertation,

This way ascribes to the secular society a solely negative content. It sees no liberating potential in secularization but only a process of demoralisation. Of course similar voices are *mutatis mutandis* observed in other, non-Orthodox churches, too. Some argue for the need of an Orthodox-Catholic alliance against modernity; the aim of it should be not the restoration of sacramental unity, but the establishment of a front for the promotion of what is regarded as traditional Christian values.[21] In many contexts one observes a growing tension between church leadership promoting such views, and more liberal Orthodox theologians who are seeking an alternative way of encounter with the modern world.

4 Towards an Ecumenical Hermeneutics of Change. An Orthodox Contribution

Does the turbulent situation described above imply that Orthodoxy cannot contribute fruitfully to the ecumenical discussion on unity and variety? Sometimes exactly such turbulences carry seeds of change; here I note certain potentials, deficits and tasks:

1. The Orthodox Church is bearing witness to a great theological tradition. In a world of fluid identities it is important to remind of a heredity, which can also be a chance. It is crucial for Christians to offer a sense of continuity, of a community diachronically connected to the biblical message. Stubbornly dwelling in the past is theologically problematic. However, the same can be said for an almost neurotic adjustment to the *Zeitgeist*. Tradition helps Christians discern the spirits and provides them with criteria to exercise their prophetic task. In this respect, Orthodoxy has a lot to offer from its hardly known treasures.
2. The Orthodox emphasis on apophaticism may contribute to an ecumenically fruitful theological re-evaluation of change. The realisation of the limits of reason and language, the respect for the mystery of the unknown, the resignation from any totalitarian herme-

---

Aristoteles University of Thessaloniki 2008); Vasilios N. Makrides, »Orthodox Anti-Westernism Today: A Hindrance to European Integration?,« *International Journal for the Study of the Christian Church* 9 (2009): 209–224.

[21] Daniel P. Payne and Jennifer M. Kent, »An Alliance of the Sacred: Prospects for a Catholic-Orthodox Partnership Against Secularism in Europe,« *Journal of Ecumenical Studies* 46 (2011): 41–66.

neutics gives respectable space for the unfolding of the potential of the »other«. Apophaticism implies that variety does not have necessarily to be subordinated to a pre-existent scheme of unity. It may as well be an opportunity for the enrichment and extension of this scheme. Churches argue against each other on issues which they claim that they know better than their dialogue partners. I think it could be fruitful in the contexts of both ecumenism and evangelisation, if Christians realise and confess together what they do not know. In other words, if they could present themselves as an ecumenical community willing to listen to and reflect on the questions of our world rather than behaving like a group of people who have all the answers already. In this way, they could gain credibility as well as benefit from the openness to inspiring changes.[22]

3. A decisive Orthodox contribution to the discussion on unity and variety depends on the clear response of the Eastern Church on the ecclesiological status of the other churches. One may say that the reluctance of Orthodoxy is related to its above mentioned apophatic tradition, which demonstrates a considerable aversion against scholastic definitions. Nevertheless, *theologia negativa* should not serve as an alibi for an undifferentiated preservation of the ecclesiological model of the ancient heresiology. If one ascribes to the ecumenical partner even only the negativity implied by the term »heresy«, there can be no space for the variety mirrored in them, since their »otherness« is regarded only as alienation and inauthenticity. The Eastern Church should go beyond the bipolar scheme Orthodoxy-heresy, elaborating further towards an ecclesiology which will take generously into account the *in via* situation of churches seeking the restoration of full visible unity. Otherwise, the strong anti-ecumenical tendencies will continue to thrive and be active in the Orthodox world insisting on their argumentation that is based upon a dualistic, undifferentiated use of the old ecclesiological scheme.[23]

---

[22] Georgios Vlantis, »The Apophatic Understanding of the Church and Ecumenical Dialogue,« *The Ecumenical Review* 62 (2010): 296–301.

[23] Stylianos Tsompanidis, »The Church and the Churches in the Ecumenical Movement,« *International Journal for the Study of the Christian Church* 12 (2012): 148–163, and *Ἐκκλησία καὶ Ἐκκλησίες. Ἡ θέση τῶν ἄλλων χριστιανικῶν Ἐκκλησιῶν στὴν ἐκκλησιολογικὴ αὐτοσυνειδησία τῆς Ὀρθόδοξης Ἐκκλησίας στὰ πλαίσια τοῦ οἰκουμενικοῦ διαλόγου* (Athens 2013); Athanasios Vletsis, »Orthodox Ecclesiology in Dialogue with Other Understandings of the Nature of the Church,« in *Orthodox Handbook on Ecumenism. Resources for*

4. Such a dynamic model accentuates the need for a profound eschatological perspective in ecumenism. The Orthodox focus on eschatology and the experience of its foretaste in liturgical life provide impulses for new understandings of catholicity. In Orthodox theology catholicity is indeed no measurable fact, but an eschatological quality, a demand, an appeal and a witness to the world to come. The church is catholic insofar as it is eschatological, insofar as it prepares the world for the anticipated fullness of life. In the spirituality of the Eastern Church positive change is understood in terms of transfiguration, as an experience of grace *in via* towards the eschatological future.[24]
5. But who decides what constitutes an acceptable, positive change and what not? In various cases the »otherness« of the ecumenical partners or certain developments in their churches have been instrumentalised as alibi for ending the dialogue with them. Take for example the reaction of the Russian Orthodox Church to bishop Margot Käßmann's election at the presidency of the EKD.[25] It seems sure that a rapidly changing world will be also a world of considerably changing churches, a world where the »*noi pensiamo in secoli*« will lose a lot of its fascination. Churches claiming that they have definite answers will be surprised to realise that they first have to learn what the questions of this changing world are. Therefore, even if Christians disagree on the solutions suggested, they have to keep on talking to each other; there should be no taboo issues for ecumenism. Of course, a constant focus on difficult themes leads often to frustration; ignoring the sensitivities of the partner proves to be ecumenically unconstructive. The discussion on moral discernment shows exactly how big the challenges are and how difficult it is to keep the desired balance.[26]

Theological Education, eds. Pantelis Kalaitzidis et. al. (Volos: Volos Academy Publications / Geneva: WCC Publications, 2014), 134–152.

[24] See John Zizioulas, *Remembering the Future: An Eschatological Ontology* (London: T&T Clark, 2008).

[25] Reinhard Thöle, »Einleitung in den Brief von Erzbischof Ilarion an Landesbischöfin Dr. Margot Käßmann,« *Materialdienst des Konfessionskundlichen Instituts Bensheim* 61 (2010): 14 (Ilarion's letter is published in German on p. 14–15).

[26] Dagmar Heller and Johanna Rahner, »Moralisch-ethische Urteilsbildung – eine aktuelle Herausforderung für den ökumenischen Dialog,« *Ökumenische Rundschau* 62 (2013): 237–250; Dagmar Heller, »Moralisch-ethische Urteilsbildung in der ökumenischen Diskussion,« *Una Sancta* 69 (2014): 162–170.

5 Epilogue

Ratzinger's text which I quoted at the beginning goes on and concludes as follows:

> Man könnte Augustin kein größeres Unrecht tun als ihn zu lösen aus dem lebendigen Gang seiner Zeit, um ihn zum zeitlosen Denker zu stempeln. Bei ihm ist etwas ganz anderes Ereignis geworden. Das Begreifen der einen Wahrheit Jesu Christi mitten aus der Lebendigkeit der eben gelebten Gegenwart heraus. Und darin freilich steht Augustin für alle Zeiten.[27]

Longing for eternity has to be accompanied by the will to take time in its concreteness seriously and to profit from it. This is the great teaching of the incarnation; the churches have to experience and practice this teaching in apophatic humility, prophetic rigidity and eschatological generosity. And they have to practice it together as changing churches challenged by and also challenging a changing world.

---

[27] Ratzinger, *Gesammelte Schriften*, vol. 1, 418.

Ökumenisch eine katholische Kirche werden?
Das Verhältnis zwischen Vielfalt und Einheit aus (einer) römisch-katholischen Sicht

Dorothea Sattler

1 Hinführung zur Thematik

1.1 Das Haus aus vielen Strichen – ein Bild für die Katholische Kirche?

Die metaphorischen Vorstellungen von der Gemeinschaft der an Jesus Christus Glaubenden sind sehr vielfältig. Eines der Bilder für die Glaubensgemeinschaft, die Kirche, ist das eines Hauses. Diese bereits in biblischer Zeit in der jüdisch-christlichen Tradition vor dem Hintergrund der Frage nach dem Tempel als Ort der Gegenwart Gottes geformte Metapher betont ursprünglich in kritischer Intention die Freiheit Gottes gegenüber jedem menschlichen Anspruch, ihn in seiner Selbstentscheidung für den Ort seiner Gegenwart in seiner eigenen Wahl begrenzen zu wollen. Daher überbringt der Prophet Natan dem künftigen König David eine Botschaft, die Gottes Empörung gegenüber dem Bau eines Tempels in deutliche Worte fasst: »Geh zu meinem Knecht David und sag zu ihm: So spricht der Herr: Du willst mir ein Haus bauen, damit ich darin wohne? Seit dem Tag, an dem ich die Israeliten aus Ägypten heraufgeführt habe, habe ich bis heute nie in einem Haus gewohnt, sondern bin in einer Zeltwohnung umhergezogen« (2 Sam 7,5f). Gott möchte nicht in die Hände der Menschen geraten und gezwungen sein, an einem von ihm nicht selbst gewählten Ort präsent sein zu müssen. Gott lässt sich nicht an einen Ort binden, er sucht vielmehr die lebendige Gemeinschaft mit den auf ihn vertrauenden

Menschen in ihrer konkreten Not. Vor diesem Hintergrund ist es gut verständlich, wenn auch die neutestamentlichen Schriften den personalen Anteil der Glaubenden am Bau der Kirche betonen und mahnen: »Lasst euch als lebendige Steine zu einem geistigen Haus aufbauen, zu einer heiligen Priesterschaft, um durch Jesus Christus geistige Opfer darzubringen, die Gott gefallen« (1 Petrus 2,5). Die von Gott initiierte Hausgemeinschaft der Menschen steht in dem Dienst der Vergegenwärtigung der Lebenspreisgabe – des Lebensopfers – Jesu Christi.[1]

Aus festen Steinen scheint das Haus nicht gebaut zu sein, das auf der Federzeichnung von Hartwig Hamer zu sehen ist.[2]

Das Bild dieses Schweriner evangelischen Künstlers trägt den Titel »Das alte Haus«. Aus leichten Federstrichen besteht es; es ist in den Konturen kaum zu identifizieren; es erscheint noch mehr verworren und verschwommen, je näher es vor Augen gehalten wird. Aus vielen ungezählten Strichen entsteht dieses Haus. Nur wer die Zeichnung aus

---

[1] Vgl. zur Verbindung zwischen Eucharistie und Diakonie als Weisen der Gegenwart Jesu Christi in der einen Katholischen Kirche an anderer Stelle ausführlicher: DOROTHEA SATTLER, Eucharistische Realpräsenz des diakonischen Lebens Jesu Christi. Eine römisch-katholische Perspektive, in: Evangelische Theologie 74 (2014), 447–460.
[2] Original in meinem Privatbesitz.

weiterer Entfernung betrachtet, erkennt deutlich ein Haus mit einem großen und hohen Dach. Ganz von der Nähe aus sind nur Strichlinien ohne Zusammenhang zu sehen. Ist es nicht auch ebenso bei der Kirche, deren Katholizität – Einheit in Zeit und Raum – derzeit nur als ein von Ferne betrachtetes Ideal besteht? Aus der Nähe betrachtet, erscheint die Vielgestalt christlicher Existenzformen verwirrend, konturenlos.

Überall dort, wo lebendige Menschen eine Gemeinschaft bilden, ist die Vielfalt im Miteinander unvermeidbar. Die Lebensgeschichten der Menschen, die an einem Ort zusammenkommen, sind sehr verschieden. Auch in der Ökumene lernen wir heute, den biographischen Zugang zu den theologischen Fragen mit hoher Wertschätzung aufzunehmen. Im Erzählen von der eigenen Lebensgeschichte wird deutlich, wie stark die biographischen Prägungen bei der Bildung unserer Persönlichkeit im gesamten Glaubensleben sind. Niemand ist wie der Andere oder die Andere. Lebendig sind die Striche, die sich zu der einen Kirche zusammenfügen. Jeder Strich ist wichtig und unverzichtbar – möglicherweise vor allem jene Striche, die sich nicht leicht in das Gesamtbild einfügen lassen.

1.2 Vorhaben und Begrenzungen

Meine Aufgabe ist es, die römisch-katholische Sicht der Katholizität der Kirche darzulegen. Ich beginne daher zunächst mit einer assoziativ gehaltenen Skizze der Situation der Römisch-katholischen Kirche heute – mit besonderem Blick dabei auf die Frage der Einheit innerhalb der römisch-katholischen Vielfalt (Abschnitt 2). Ich möchte sodann über den langen und schwierigen Weg orientieren, den die Römisch-katholische Kirche bei ihrer Suche nach einem Ort innerhalb der ökumenischen Bewegung gegangen ist; in diesem Zusammenhang sind insbesondere die Ausführungen des 2. Vatikanischen Konzils über die Katholizität der einen Kirche zu bedenken (Abschnitt 3). Ich möchte abschließend einige Gedanken zu dem aus meiner Sicht zu suchenden Modell der Einheit der Katholischen Kirche formulieren (Abschnitt 4). Bei all dem leitet mich der Gedanke, dass die Römisch-katholische Kirche nicht – ohne die anderen Kirchen – die eine, heilige, katholische und apostolische Kirche ist.

2 Wahrnehmung: Die (römisch-) katholische Einheit und Vielfalt im Pontifikat von Franziskus

Der Römisch-katholischen Kirche gehören weltweit heute ca. eine Milliarde Menschen in hunderten von Nationen unter der Leitung von mehr als dreitausend Bischöfen an. Die Herausforderungen vor Ort sind sehr unterschiedlich. Krisen durchschütteln diese Weltkirche derzeit: die bleibende Gefahr des sexuellen Missbrauchs angesichts der bereits eingestandenen Schuld ebenso wie die finanziellen Intrigen im Weltkontext und auch in regionalen Zusammenhängen. Die Aufgabe ist erkannt, unter Berufung auf die Anliegen des 2. Vatikanischen Konzils Reformen in der Römisch-katholischen Kirche zu bewirken. Papst Franziskus bemüht sich darum, indem er an die drei Grunddimensionen im Sein und Handeln der Römisch-katholischen Kirche erinnert: an die weltweite Diakonie im Blick auf die Flüchtlinge und die Hungernden, an die gemeinsame Freude bei der Verkündigung des christlichen Evangeliums der Versöhnung sowie an die Feier der Liturgie in katholischer Gemeinschaft.

Kurz nach der Wahl von Jorge Mario Bergoglio zum Papst ist ein Foto von seinem Besuch noch als Erzbischof von Buenos Aires in einem Kinderhospiz an einem Gründonnerstag, an dem die römisch-katholische Liturgie die Feier der Fußwaschung optional vorsieht, in den Medien erschienen. Die Fußwaschung ist zu einem Symbol für das Handeln des gegenwärtigen Papstes weltweit geworden. Im ersten Jahr seines Pontifikats war er an Gründonnerstag in einem Gefängnis in Rom und hat auch Frauen die Füße gewaschen und sich damit über eine Vorschrift bei der Gestaltung der Liturgie dieses Tages hinweggesetzt, die angesichts der Berufung nur von zwölf Männern in den Kreis der Apostel die liturgische Feier der Fußwaschung bei Frauen nicht vorsieht. Weitere Bilder sind in den ersten Monaten des Pontifikats hinzugekommen – vor allem seine Anteilnahme am tödlichen Geschick der Flüchtlinge durch einen Blumenkranz im Mittelmeer, das für viele Menschen zum Grab wird.

Mit Papst Franziskus entdeckt die Römisch-katholische Kirche wieder neu alte Seiten an ihrer Katholizität: die Diakonie, die nicht darauf achtet, wer welcher Religion oder Konfession oder welchen Geschlechts ist. Allein der Mensch in Not ist wichtig. Im Sinne des Gerichtsgleichnisses von Mt 25 gilt es zu handeln, da Jesus sagt: »Amen, ich sage euch: Was ihr für einen meiner geringsten Brüder getan habt, das habt ihr mir getan« (Mt 25,40). Im Sinne Jesu wird es sein, auch an die Schwestern in der Not zu erinnern.

In der Römisch-katholischen Kirche fragen viele gegenwärtig, welche Handlungsimpulse sich aus dem Apostolischen Schreiben »Evangelii Gaudium« von Papst Franziskus ergeben.[3] Wir wissen uns streng ermahnt dazu, die Freude an der Verkündigung des einen Evangeliums mit Wort und Tat als die Mitte unseres römisch-katholischen Missionsauftrags zu betrachten. Entsprechende Konkretisierungen sind heute sehr erwünscht. Die Gremien in den Diözesen weltweit machen sich Gedanken über die Frage, wie die neuen Impulse – die Option für die Armen; das Anliegen, aus der Kirchendepression herauszufinden und hineinzugehen in die Freude an der Verkündigung – in die Tat umzusetzen sind.

Bei aller Wertschätzung der Kontextualität auch der römisch-katholischen Verkündigung des Evangeliums bleibt zugleich ein Grundsatz bewahrt: Weltweit gibt es im römisch-katholischen Liturgieraum eine gemeinsame liturgische Leseordnung aus den biblischen Schriften. In jeder römisch-katholischen liturgischen Feier hören alle auf das eine Wort Gottes. Die zur Verkündigung berufenen, ausgebildeten und beauftragten Verkündiger stehen unter dem Wort Gottes, das ihnen vorgegeben ist. In meiner persönlichen Wahrnehmung ist dies die stärkste Quelle der Katholizität: das gemeinsame Hören auf die eine Heilige Schrift an allen Orten zu derselben Zeit.

Die Römisch-katholische Kirche besinnt sich zugleich derzeit auf das Ortskirchenprinzip und damit auf die in einzelnen Themenbereichen bestehende Eigenständigkeit der bischöflich verfassten Kirche weltweit. Gleichwohl gilt: Nicht immer ist alles gut in allen dezentral verantworteten Regionen. Gelegentlich wünscht man sich eine überregionale – auch eine über die Diözesen hinausgehende – Autorität in der Römisch-katholischen Kirche. Das Beispiel der Diözese Limburg lässt einen solchen Ruf angesichts des Umgangs mit den Kirchensteuermitteln sehr dringlich erscheinen. Auch in anderen Themenbereichen – beispielsweise in der Frage des angemessenen pastoralen Handelns in der Begegnung mit geschiedenen und dann wiederverheirateten Menschen[4] oder im Blick auf die Kündigungsgründe im Arbeitsrecht –

---

3   Vgl. PAPST FRANZISKUS, Apostolisches Schreiben »Evangelii Gaudium« über die Verkündigung des Evangeliums in der Welt von heute, Bonn 2013 (Verlautbarungen des Apostolischen Stuhls, Nr. 194).
4   Vgl. das Dokument »Theologisch verantwortbare und pastoral angemessene Wege zur Begleitung wiederverheirateter Geschiedener«. Überlegungen der Deutschen Bischofskonferenz zur Vorbereitung der Bischofssynode (24. Juni 2014), in: Die pastoralen Herausforderungen der Familie im Kontext der

sprechen die Bischöfe in der Römisch-katholischen Kirche in Deutschland nicht immer mit einer Stimme.

Papst Franziskus hat ein sehr hohes Interesse daran, um die Vielfalt der Meinungen innerhalb der Römisch-katholischen Kirche zu wissen. Recht bald nach Beginn seines Pontifikats hat er zur Vorbereitung der Außerordentlichen Bischofssynode im Oktober 2014 in Rom die Bitte an alle Christgläubigen weltweit gerichtet, ihre eigenen Meinungen zum Thema Ehe, Familie und Sexualität zu formulieren. Inzwischen bereitet sich die Römisch-katholische Kirche auf die Ordentliche Weltbischofssynode zu dieser Thematik im Herbst 2015 vor. Im Umfeld dieses Geschehens zeigen viele Veröffentlichungen, wie vielgestaltig Menschen in der Römisch-katholischen Kirche sich in eigenen Stellungnahmen zu diesem Themenkreis äußern.[5] Ratlos und zugleich voller Staunen sind wir in der theologischen Fachwelt angesichts dieser Situation: Wer wird mit welchen Kommunikationsmethoden einen Dialog gestalten können, in dem die erkennbaren Divergenzen in eine konstruktive gemeinsame Handlungsoption überführt werden können? Oder sollte dies nicht das Ziel sein? Möglicherweise sind Enttäuschungen zu erwarten, wenn zunächst alle aufgrund ihrer Lebenserfahrungen nach ihrer Meinung gefragt werden im Blick auf das Zusammenleben von Mann und Frau – ja sogar von Mann und Mann sowie von Frau und Frau – und dann doch am Ende der Beratungen lediglich die Erinnerung an die eine römisch-katholische Lehre erfolgt, wie sie immer schon war und immer bleiben wird? Spannend sind die Zeiten in der Römisch-katholischen Kirche heute. Immerhin ist eines schon erreicht: Die Rede von der Barmherzigkeit Gottes allen Menschen gegenüber ist zum Leitwort des neuen Pontifikats geworden.[6]

Evangelisierung. Texte zur Bischofssynode 2014 und Dokumente der Deutschen Bischofskonferenz, Bonn 2014, 42–76 (Arbeitshilfen, Nr. 273).

[5] Vgl. die Veröffentlichung der Abstimmungsergebnisse bezüglich der Einzelaussagen in der »Relatio Synodi« (Schlussrelatio der Dritten Außerordentlichen Vollversammlung der Bischofssynode), a.a.O., 141–175; vgl. auch die Zusammenfassung der Antworten aus den deutschen (Erz-)Diözesen auf die Fragen im Vorbereitungsdokument für die Dritte Außerordentliche Vollversammlung der Bischofssynode 2014, a.a.O., 7–41.

[6] Vgl. WALTER KARDINAL KASPER, Das Evangelium von der Familie. Die Rede vor dem Konsistorium, Freiburg 2014.

3 Grundlegung: Das 2. Vatikanische Konzil und die Katholizität der Kirche(n)

Mit dem 2. Vatikanischen Konzil hat die Römisch-katholische Kirche ihren Blick gewendet: weg von der kircheninternen Selbstbespiegelung hin auf die Wahrnehmung der Nöte in der Welt. Das Bild von Fritz Weigner mit dem Titel »Urbi et Orbi«[7] bringt dies zum Ausdruck:

Die Darstellung zeigt den Blick, den der Bischof von Rom von seinem Balkon über dem Mittelportal des Petersdoms aus hat, wenn er zu besonderen Anlässen dort steht. Für die Stadt Rom und für die gesamte Schöpfung erbittet der Papst an hohen Festtagen »Urbi et Orbi« den göttlichen Segen. Im Kontext des 2. Vatikanischen Konzils (1962–65) hat die Römisch-katholische Kirche ihre Blickrichtung verändert, mit Papst Johannes XXIII. die Fenster zur Welt geöffnet. Sie schaut nun von Rom aus auf die gesamte Weltgemeinschaft: »Freude und Hoffnung,

---

[7] Vgl. HERMANN-JOSEF SIEBEN, Konzilsdarstellungen – Konzilsvorstellungen. 1000 Jahre Konzilsikonographie aus Handschriften und Druckwerken, Würzburg 1990, 80–84, bes. 82.

Trauer und Angst der Menschen von heute, besonders der Armen und Bedrängten aller Art, sind auch Freude und Hoffnung, Trauer und Angst der Jünger Christi. Und es gibt nichts wahrhaft Menschliches, das nicht in ihren Herzen seinen Widerhall fände« (2. Vatikanisches Konzil, Gaudium et Spes [GS], Nr. 1)[8] – so lautet der Beginn der Pastoralkonstitution des 2. Vatikanischen Konzils, der wegweisend wurde für viele Stellungnahmen zur kirchlichen Situation in der Gegenwart.

In all dem Vielen, was aus Sicht des 2. Vatikanischen Konzils zur Frage der Katholizität der Kirche in Einheit und Vielheit zu sagen wäre, erscheint mit ein Gedanke sehr wichtig: Die Römisch-katholische Kirche weiß um den Unterschied zwischen »katholisch« und »römisch-katholisch«. Das 2. Vatikanische Konzil formulierte diese Einsicht in folgender Weise: »Obgleich ... die katholische Kirche mit dem ganzen Reichtum der von Gott geoffenbarten Wahrheit und der Gnadenmittel beschenkt ist, ist es doch Tatsache, dass ihre Glieder nicht mit der entsprechenden Glut daraus leben, so dass das Antlitz der Kirche den von uns getrennten Brüdern und der ganzen Welt nicht recht aufleuchtet und das Wachstum des Reiches Gottes verzögert wird. Deshalb müssen alle Katholiken zur christlichen Vollkommenheit streben und, ihrer jeweiligen Stellung entsprechend, bemüht sein, dass die Kirche, die die Niedrigkeit und das Todesleiden Christi an ihrem Leibe trägt, von Tag zu Tag geläutert und erneuert werde, bis Christus sie sich dereinst glorreich darstellt, ohne Makel und Runzeln. ... Aber gerade die Spaltungen der Christen sind für die Kirche ein Hindernis, dass sie die ihr eigene Fülle der Katholizität in jenen Söhnen wirksam werden lässt, die ihr zwar durch die Taufe zugehören, aber von ihrer völligen Gemeinschaft getrennt sind: Ja, es wird dadurch auch für die Kirche selber schwieriger, die Fülle der Katholizität unter jedem Aspekt in der Wirklichkeit des Lebens auszuprägen« (2. Vatikanisches Konzil, Unitatis Redintegratio [UR], Nr. 4). Dies bedeutet: Auf der existentiellen Ebene ist die römisch-katholische Kirche bei der jeder Zeit neu aufgetragenen Gestaltung ihrer Einheit, Heiligkeit, Apostolizität und Katholizität auf das Zeugnis der liebenden Lebensgabe der gottesfürchtigen Gerechten aller Zeiten und Räume bleibend angewiesen. Der mit der Pilgerschaft der Kirche verbundene, stets fortdauernde Prozess der immer wieder erforderlichen inneren Erneuerung hat zum Ziel, »die wahre Katholizität und Apostolizität der Kirche immer vollständiger zum Ausdruck

---

[8] Alle Dokumente des 2. Vatikanischen Konzils sind in deutscher Sprache leicht zugänglich in: KARL RAHNER/HERBERT VORGRIMLER, Kleines Konzilskompendium. Sämtliche Texte des Zweiten Vatikanums, Freiburg/Basel/Wien [35]2008.

[zu] bringen« (2. Vatikanisches Konzil, Unitatis Redintegratio [UR], Nr. 4). Katholizität ist kein Ist-Zustand, sondern ein Soll-Zustand – gemessen am Maß des gelebten Evangeliums.

Der römisch-katholische Theologe Hermann J. Pottmeyer hat in den 80er Jahren des 20. Jahrhunderts auf die ökumenische Bedeutung des von Yves Congar und Karl Rahner angestrengten Bemühens, die eine wahre Kirche auch durch die »via empirica« aufzuzeigen, hingewiesen. Seine Schlussüberlegung lautet: »Wenn es richtig ist, dass zur Kirche als Zeichen des Reiches Gottes nicht nur die Zeichenhaftigkeit ihrer Institutionen, sondern auch die des Lebenszeugnisses ihrer Glieder gehört, kann der Erweis der Wahrheit der Kirche durch die Praxis nicht übergangen werden.«[9]

Das 2. Vatikanische Konzil ermutigte zu einer Unterscheidung zwischen der Vollständigkeit der ekklesialen Strukturelemente in der Römisch-katholischen Kirche und der mangelnden, fehlerhaften Gegenwart des verkündigten Jesus Christus in ihrem Erscheinungsbild. Die Kirche ist zugleich Zeichen der Fülle und Zeichen des Mangels. Daher ist die Römisch-katholische Kirche »nur« Sakrament Gottes: Zeichen der Gegenwart des Geistes Gottes im immer auch sündigen Gefüge der Kirche, daher ständig der Reform bedürftig (vgl. 2. Vatikanisches Konzil, Lumen Gentium [LG], Nr. 8). Daher liegt – so ist es zugestanden vom 2. Vatikanischen Konzil – ein »defectus ecclesiae« in der Römisch-katholischen Kirche vor – ein Mangel im Hinblick auf ihre volle Katholizität, solange die Römisch-katholische Kirche nicht lebt, wie sie leben sollte – und zugleich dankbar zu erkennen ist, dass außerhalb ihrer Grenzen Menschen dem Evangelium gemäß leben – auch mit Gefährdungen des eigenen Lebens bis hin zum Martyrium.

Es war ein langer Weg, bis die Römisch-katholische Kirche nach dem 2. Weltkrieg in die ökumenische Bewegung hineingefunden hat, ja ein Teil von ihr wurde. Es gibt einen Gedanken des Dichters Peter Handke, der mir sehr viel bedeutet: »Vor jeder Begegnung: Denk, was der andere für einen Weg hatte«.[10] Es ist in vielfacher Hinsicht lehrreich, sich nochmals sagen zu lassen, wie die Römisch-katholische Kirche – meine Kirche – noch 1928 über die ökumenische Bewegung dachte, als Pius XI. sich in seiner Enzyklika »Mortalium Animos« über jene Menschen sprach, die in den 20er Jahren des 20. Jahrhunderts

---

9   HERMANN J. POTTMEYER, Die Frage nach der wahren Kirche, in: WALTER KERN u.a. (Hrsg.), Handbuch der Fundamentaltheologie, Bd. 3: Traktat Kirche, Freiburg/Basel/Wien 1986, 212–241, hier 240.
10 PETER HANDKE, Phantasien der Wiederholung, Frankfurt 1983, 42.

»Life and Work« und »Faith and Order« gründeten – eben die »Panchristen« – solche, die alles gleich machen wollen. Pius XI. sagt über sie 1928:

> All zu leicht werden manche durch die Vorspiegelung einer scheinbar guten Sache getäuscht, wenn es sich darum handelt, die Einheit aller Christen untereinander zu fördern. Ist es nicht billig, – so sagt man – ja, ist es nicht heilige Pflicht, dass alle, die den Namen Christi anrufen, von den gegenseitigen Verketzerungen ablassen und endlich einmal durch das Band gegenseitiger Liebe verbunden werden? Wie könnte denn jemand den Mut haben zu sagen, er liebe Christus, wenn er sich nicht nach besten Kräften für die Erfüllung des Wunsches Christi einsetzt, der da den Vater bat, dass seine Jünger eins seien. ... Ja, so fügen sie hinzu, möchten doch alle Christen ›eins‹ sein! Um wieviel erfolgreicher würden sie dann an der Bekämpfung der schleichenden Pest der Gottlosigkeit arbeiten können, die jetzt täglich weiter um sich greift und im Begriff ist, das Evangelium vollständig um seine Kraft und Wirkung zu bringen. So und ähnlich reden in stolzer Sprache jene, die man Panchristen nennt. Man glaube nicht, es handele sich bei ihnen nur um vereinzelte kleine Gruppen. Im Gegenteil: sie sind zu ganzen Scharen angewachsen und haben sich zu weit verbreiteten Gesellschaften zusammengeschlossen, an deren Spitze meist Nichtkatholiken der verschiedenen religiösen Bekenntnisse stehen.[11]

Pius XI. weiß um die – nach seiner Ansicht – verführerische, suggestive Kraft des Gebetes um die Einheit. Er beklagt, dass auch viele Katholiken sich haben betören lassen. Der Irrtum, der bei den ökumenischen Bemühungen wirksam werde, besteht nach Pius XI. in der Meinung, die von Jesus im Gebet erflehte Einheit seiner Jünger bestehe noch gar nicht. Der Papst beklagt, dass sich unter denen, »welche die brüderliche Gemeinschaft in Christus Jesus mit lauter Stimme preisen, ... kein einziger [findet], dem es in den Sinn käme, sich der Lehre und der Leitung des Stellvertreters Jesu Christi zu unterwerfen und ihm zu gehorchen.«[12]

Viel ist geschehen zwischen 1928 und heute. Viele römisch-katholische Christinnen und Christen sind heute in der ökumenischen Bewegung engagiert. Wir leben nicht mehr das Modell der Rückkehr-

---

[11] Vgl. PIUS XI., Mortalium Animos (6. Januar 1928), in: ANTON ROHRBASSER (Hrsg.), Die Heilslehre der Kirche, Freiburg 1953, 397–411 (Nr. 669–689), hier Nr. 672.
[12] A.a.O., Nr. 678.

Ökumene. Und zugleich bleibt die Frage: Welches Modell der Einheit der Katholischen Kirche streben wir in der Ökumene gemeinsam an?

4 Einheit in versöhnter Verschiedenheit – ein geeignetes Modell an jedem Ort?

Die Römisch-katholische Kirche weiß heute um die Grenzen ihrer eigenen Katholizität. Dies gilt vor allem auf der Ebene des existentiellen Zeugnisses im christlichen Leben; daher sind Hinweise auf die Ökumene der Märtyrer für Jesus Christus auch in ekklesiologischer Perspektive von sehr hoher Bedeutung.[13] Zugleich fällt es ihr schwer, dem Modell der Einheit in versöhnter Verschiedenheit zuzustimmen.[14] Warum ist dies so?

Erfahrbar – sichtbar – wirksam kann die Kirche nur in einer Gemeinschaft von Menschen werden, die sich im Raum – an den Lebensorten – begegnen. Bliebe die Kirche rein »unsichtbar« – bestünde sie nur in geistlichem Sinn, wäre sie nie leibhaftig erfahrbar, nie konkret, dann wäre sie unwirksam. An ihren Lebensorten suchen Menschen nach Trost, nach Rat und nach einem Halt in den Abgründen der zeitlichen Existenz. In den überschaubaren Lebensräumen, die Menschen in ihrem Alltag erfahren, immerzu mehrere Varianten des Christlichen zu leben und keine Versammlung an einem Ort zu einer Gemeinschaft des Erzählens, des Suchens, des Fragens, kein gemeinsames Gedächtnis der Großtaten Gottes anzustreben, dies kann auch meines Erachtens nicht die zu suchende Gestalt der katholischen Kirche sein.

In der Römisch-katholischen Kirche ist die Bedeutung der Gemeinden für das Glaubensleben einzelner Menschen in jüngerer Zeit wieder stärker in den Blick genommen worden. Angesichts der abnehmenden Zahlen von Menschen, die sich für den priesterlichen Dienst berufen fühlen, stellt sich für die Römisch-katholische Kirche mit Dringlichkeit die Frage, wie weit die Entfernungen bis zu dem Ort werden dürfen, an

---

[13] Vgl. dazu exemplarisch: MARTIN THOEMMES, »Sag niemals drei, sag immer vier«. Das Gedenken an die Lübecker Märtyrer von 1943 bis heute, Hamburg 2012; PETER VOSWINCKEL, Geführte Wege. Die Lübecker Märtyrer in Wort und Bild, Kevelaer ²2010; sowie die Studie TAMARA GRDZELIDZE und GUIDO DOTTI (Hrsg.), Cloud of Witnesses: Opportunities for Ecumenical Commemoration, Genf 2011.

[14] Vgl. als Übersicht über die in der Ökumenischen Bewegung bedachten Modelle der Einheit: JUTTA KOSLOWSKI, Die Einheit der Kirche in der ökumenischen Diskussion. Zielvorstellungen kirchlicher Einheit im evangelisch-katholischen Dialog, Münster 2008.

dem Menschen die Eucharistie feiern können. Die Kirche im Dorf zu lassen – das ist eine Forderung nicht nur älterer Menschen mit geringer Mobilitätsbereitschaft.[15] Offenkundig gibt es bei vielen Menschen noch eine hohe Erwartung an eine christlich-religiöse Präsenz in der Nähe zum Wohnort. Bei Kasualien – Taufe, Eheschließung, Begräbnis – wird dies dann ganz offenkundig. Dabei scheint es für Menschen zunehmend unwichtig zu sein, welcher Konfession die handelnden Personen angehören – die Hauptsache ist: Sie sind erreichbar zur rechten Zeit. Nach meiner Wahrnehmung ist für viele Menschen, die kaum Kirchenbezug haben, vor allem wichtig, ob die im Namen Jesu Christi handelnde Persönlichkeit in einer spezifischen Lebenssituation sensibel handelt, hörbereit ist, sich den Wünschen der Familien öffnet und glaubwürdig erscheint.

Es ist ein Verdienst der Ökumenischen Bewegung, bei ihrer intensiv betriebenen Suche nach dem rechten Verständnis der christlichen Einheit zu erkennen, dass mit ihr nicht Einheitlichkeit im Sinne von Uniformität in den Ausdrucksgestalten des Glaubens gemeint ist. Die Vielfalt birgt einen großen Reichtum: Die Sprachen, die Gesänge und die Bewegungsformen in den Gottesdiensten können unterschiedlich sein. Es gibt mehrere, gleichberechtigte Worte, in denen der eine christliche Glaube zum Ausdruck kommen kann. Legitim ist die Vielfalt der kirchlichen Lebensformen, solange diese als kulturspezifische, auf die Situation bezogene, aktuelle Darstellungen des Wesens der einen Kirchen zu erkennen sind. Dieses Anliegen trägt die Römisch-katholische Kirche mit.

Entscheidend ist bei der Suche nach dem angemessenen Modell der Einheit aus Sicht des 2. Vatikanischen Konzils, dass dabei die Mitte der Bewegung nicht aus dem Blick gerät: das gemeinsame Zeugnis für Jesus Christus. Daher ist für mich das Wagenrad[16] als Sinnbild für die Ökumene wichtig geworden:

---

[15] Vgl. JÜRGEN WERBICK, Warum die Kirche vor Ort bleiben muss, Donauwörth 2002.
[16] Foto aus einem Kalender zu Bräuchen am Niederrhein. Original im Privatbesitz.

Wenn alle Konfessionen sich an der einen sie verbindenden Mitte orientieren, wenn alle diesen Weg zur Mitte als Weg der eigenen Umkehr gestalten, dann kommen die historisch gewordenen Konfessionsfamilien einander näher, weil sie alle nach Christus Jesus suchen. Katholizität bedeutet dann: In das Gesamt jene Früchte einbringen, die in der jeweiligen Sensibilität im Blick auf die veränderten geschichtliche Kontexte gewachsen sind. Konfessionelle Eigenarten sind oft den historisch bedingten Konstellationen geschuldet. Gemeinsam sind wir der Überzeugung, dass die Weisungen der biblischen Schriften nicht in vergleichbarer Weise zeitbedingt sind wie die Zeugnisse aus der Tradition.

Mit einem Bild von einem Haus habe ich begonnen, mit einem Bild von einem Haus möchte ich auch enden. Udo Mathee,[17] ein Künstler aus dem Münsterland, hat diese Holzskulptur gestaltet, die ich mit seiner Zustimmung von Beginn meiner Tätigkeit in Münster an als Leitbild des ökumenischen Handelns in der Metaphorik der »Hausgemeinschaft« gewählt habe: Ein kleines Haus ruht auf dem großen Stein: Der Gottesname erklingt: Ich werde da sein als der, als der ich mich erweisen werde: Ich bin – Ich bin nicht nur da für Menschen in diesem Haus. Ich bin überall jederzeit für alle da. Gott ist wahrhaft katholisch – da auch

---

[17] Vgl. http://www.udomathee.de (Stand: 1. August 2014).

über den Tod hinaus für alle, die in irdischen Häusern keinen Schutz mehr finden.

Die »Katholizität« der Kirche besteht in ihrer an allen Orten des Erdkreises von Gott gewünschten Präsenz zur Erfüllung ihrer universalen Sendung zur Verkündigung des Evangeliums in aller Welt. Der Grund der Sendung der Kirche in alle Welt liegt in Gottes universalem Heilswillen, der schöpfungstheologisch begründet ist: Der Schöpfer von allem, was ist, trägt selbst Sorge dafür, dass alles zu seiner Erfüllung finden kann. Die ersten Kapitel der Bibel lassen Gott als ein Wesen in Erscheinung treten, das alles im Guten begonnen hat und dann bitter erfahren muss, dass Misstrauen, Angst und Neid Menschen in die Sünde treiben. Gott hält trotz seiner inneren Anfechtung, ob er nicht besser das gesamte Menschengeschlecht wieder vernichten solle (Gen 6,5-7), daran fest, seinen Geschöpfen das Leben zu erhalten. Nach christlicher Überzeugung ist Gottes Name im Leben und Sterben Jesu in untrüglicher Weise offenbar geworden. Jesus bleibt in aller erfahrenen Anfeindung den Menschen selbst dann noch liebend verbunden, als er seinen bitteren Tod vor Augen hatte. Gottes Tat der Auferweckung Jesu autorisiert die Verkündigung Jesu: Gott ist wirklich einer, der die Sünderinnen und Sünder liebt. Gottes Erbarmen ist unermesslich. Gottes Güte stellt keine Vorbedingungen. Es besteht Hoffnung für die gesamte Schöpfung: Alle Geschöpfe sollen aus der Finsternis des Todes in das Licht Gottes geführt werden. Gottes Sinnen und Trachten ist wahrhaft katholisch.

The Changing Face of Unity, or: Cutting the Right Edges in the Proper Way

Henk Bakker

The theme of this conference is highly relevant. Catholicity is indeed under pressure, and the relationship between diversity and unity is an ambiguous one. The question of how to deal, as churches, with diversities emerging from growing diversity in a changing world (which for me is chiefly the Dutch world), is an urgent question which makes reflection in ecumenical settings like these of primal importance. My approach to the issue is taken mainly from three sources: (1) my own involvement and engagement with Baptist churches, a minority church in the Netherlands (I speak from a Baptist perspective, which is a congregationalist perspective) and, in particular, with students preparing for the ministry; (2) figures and statistics about church life which have been published by several institutions; (3) and some ecclesiological reflection on the gift of catholicity to the worldwide church. This brings me to the revised title of this short address: »the changing face of unity, or: cutting the right edges.

1 Churches in a Secularized Context

With regards to the situation in Holland, and specifically the Baptist churches in Holland, statistics pertaining to ecclesial involvement do not have a positive outcome. Recently the Dutch Social and Cultural Research Centre published the response of a broad enquiry concerning the Dutch people's overall confidence in the church. Among their conclusions is the observation that personal confidence in the church has never been as low as it is today.¹ For several decades the Netherlands have been number one on the list of secularized countries. In around 2020 secularization should reach its zenith; by then only 2.6 million Dutch citizens (out of ca. 17 million) will be connected to a church, and of these probably only one in five will visit the church on a regular basis. Church attendance is problematic because churches, after all, are not really to be trusted. Churches struggle with the bad image which they have in the public opinion.

Part of this negative image is its divisiveness, its lack of concord and respect when it comes to accepting the form of Christianity practiced by other Christians. The church notoriously seems to talk with two mouths: on the one hand, we firmly believe that the Gospel crosses bridges, unites, reconciles, heals and overcomes breaches between persons and institutions. Yet on the other hand, we just don't care so much about visible unity: building lasting relations with Christians who differ from us is a troublesome, inconvenient and unpredictable undertaking. Many secularized ears not only hear, but also understand this double-sided talk: they conclude that the church is hopelessly divided and beyond the possibility of restoration.

However, the awareness of God – or something (»ietsisme«) like God – is also increasing among the Dutch. People seem to be more susceptible, more open, to the transcendent than they were thirty years ago. And there are more hopeful signs: although church attendance is still diminishing, a growing group of young Christians, between 17 and 30 years old, tends to become more faithful church visitors than their parents and grandparents. They are depicted as »new orthodox« and, in part, even as »neo-fundamentalists«.

2 Church Renewal

What is going on? Old forms of church, and especially old expectations of being church, are being replaced by fresh initiatives for church renewal and church planting. It is a challenging enterprise to visit a church on Sunday morning or at another moment of the day, especially for younger people. This is an interesting development: older members

---

[1] See esp. Joep de Hart, *Geloven binnen en buitenverband: Godsdienstige ontwikkelingen in Nederland* (Den Haag: Sociaal en Cultureel Planbureau, 2014).

of churches tend to skip services or even to withdraw from the church, whereas younger members remain more faithful.

Also among Baptist churches (which as a Dutch denomination are slightly growing) fresh expressions of Christian communal awareness are important. For Baptists in general, ecclesial adaptability has historically always been a means of overcoming times of distress and marginality. Baptists are congregationalists, and find their ecclesial minimum not in the sacraments or institution or ecclesial office, but rather in the community of conviction which covenants together. Baptists like to call themselves a covenanting community, because the presence of Jesus in the community of the Spirit results, by definition, in processes of mutual binding and bonding. A key Bible text in this respect« is Matthew 18:20, »where two or three are gathered in my name«, says Jesus, »there I am in the midst of them.« Jesus brings believers together, and binds them together by commitment, expectation, and service.

Accordingly, the binding and bonding character of a community depends primarily on the presence of Jesus through the Spirit, Jesus who comes and involves himself in the communal life. Therefore, the mark of catholicity is a gift which comes and goes with Christ. »Catholicity« is not an eternal, frozen state but a process of grace, displayed in flux. Consequently catholicity should be described not only in terms of *esse* (being), but also in terms of *fieri* (becoming[2]). Catholicity is the fullness of life mirrored in one, yet nonetheless many-faceted, countenance of the body of Christ, never behaving univocally, but always somewhat ambiguously.[3] The very fibre of unity expressed in the body of Christ is, in itself, diverse and multi-faceted. The church's creative polymorphism may be the heart of its unity. At least, this seems to be occurring at the grassroots level in a couple of Dutch Baptist churches.

---

[2] The *esse* of the *notae ecclesiae* is an abiding predicate only in the presence of Jesus, who is consistently coming to the church, as also the Spirit is.

[3] Cf. Karl Barth, *Kirchliche Dogmatik* IV,1, Studienausgabe vol. 23 (Zürich: Theologischer Verlag Zürich, 1986), 726–765 (745: »die Einheit der Gemeinde, aber auch die Vielfältigkeit ihrer Gliedschaft nicht zu verleugnen«; 753: »legitime ... Vielheit«; 765: »Von ihm her gesehen, wird ja dann bestimmt auch ihre wirkliche Einheit in größerer oder geringerer Ferne sichtbar werden«); cf. the WCC convergence text *The Church: Towards a Common Vision*, Faith and Order Paper No. 214 (Geneva:WCC, 2013), par. 9: »visible unity«, and par. 12: »legitimate diversity«), 783–795. The WCC document, quite consciously or unconsciously, used Barthian categories. See also E.J. Beker and J.M. Hasselaar, *Wegen en kruispunten in de dogmatiek*, vol. 5: *Kerk en toekomst* (Kampen: Kok, 1990), 19, 99–122, 279–290.

3 Catholicity under New Forms of Unity

New forms of unity, concomitant with new forms of diversity, are emergent in our days. I am inclined to consider these new forms of unity as expressions of the imperishable gift of catholicity to the church. Modes of binding and bonding do undergo transformation, due to cultural and societal changes, and so does the formation of shared ecclesial identity. Western culture nowadays may be qualified as a »culture of shining«, or a culture of expressive individualism, or even a culture of expressive materialism.[4] Ours is a culture in which the individual wishes to reflect the world's symbols, especially those of success, beauty and style. Therefore commitments, even in the church, will always be commitments that go along with the expectations of the Western self.

Shared expectations presume a »thick« community, one with many shared values and ideals. Probably we, as churches, should readjust to the present situation and presume more of a »thin« community, a community with many distinct, private expectations about life style, meaningful relations, and the aesthetic imagination. Collective ideals – ideals agreed on by almost everyone at the same time – are simply beyond reach in a country like the Netherlands today.

I do not recommend settling for individualism, and yielding to the dominant »culture of shining«, also in the church. But I do believe that we should not underestimate Christ's lasting gift of *catholicity* to the church. For a long time this gift may have seemed to be absent, even obsolete; yet it is there, in a concealed way, as a mystery hidden within the many complexities of the world. Karl Barth refers extensively to what he describes as an ontological impossibility (»eine ontologische Unmöglichkeit«[5]), namely the fact that the unity of the synagogue and the church – the very root of Christ's body – has been disrupted and, ever since, the identity and self-understanding of the church have been in dispute. However, because the mystery of the church is the mystery of its Lord Jesus Christ, the church works its way to unity in faith and

---

[4] See Hanneke Schaap-Jonker, »Ik geloof in mezelf: Religie, spiritualiteit in een uitblinkcultuur,« *Nederlands Theologisch Tijdschrift* 66.4 (2012): 253–265, and Hessel Zondag, »Terugverlangen naar traditie,« in *Vreemd! Varianten van verscheidenheid en verschil in godsdienst en kerk*, ed. Rein Nauta (Tilburg: Publiekslezingen Departement Religiewetenschappen en Theologie Tilburg; Nijmegen: Valkhof Pers, 2009), 83–107.
[5] Barth, *Kirchliche Dogmatik* IV,1 749, 756.

hope. The gift of catholicity is not at the church's disposal;[6] it is up to Christ to express it, or to conceal it for the time being, under Christ's divine rule. Still – as with Christ himself – it is always there, even if in a concealed way.[7]

There is this story of a sculptor who moulded a fine piece of art. When visitors of the art studio applauded at the results and were amazed by its beauty, they asked him for his technique. The artist simply declared that the image was there all the time. He only had to cut off the right edges in the proper way.

Catholicity is one of the profound marks (*notae ecclesiae*) of the Christian Church which is always there, though we may not always see and be aware of it. And could it be that – due to the fact that it's there, yet hard for us to recognize given our own expectations – the way in which catholicity expresses itself would change more or less dramatically? Sometimes catholicity comes to the fore as we expect it: as the glittering third of the four crown jewels of the church universal (which is one, holy, catholic and apostolic), as a keen and caring predisposition to unity, truly governed by the idea that only united with all the saints shall we »be strengthened to comprehend what is the breadth and length and height and depth of knowing Christ's love«.[8]

However, at another moment catholicity does not express itself in this sovereign way, because it simply changes the face which it presents to us. The *hidden* gift of catholicity may then be displayed through other characteristics of the church. The attributes of the church cannot be sliced up into four or more separate pieces; the pursuit of visible unity, which catholicity represents, can be fulfilled only if all these fundamental gifts work together. Accordingly, the mark of catholicity may occasionally »behave« differently, and may reveal itself in an almost concealed way. The gift of catholicity is the remarkable gift of ecclesial creativity which enables qualities of the church to change in their

---

[6] Barth, *Kirchliche Dogmatik* IV,1 793: »es steht mit der Katholizität und also mit der Wahrheit der Christlichkeit der christlichen Gemeinde objektiv nicht anders als mit deren Einheit und Heiligkeit: die Kirche hat keine Verfügung über sie«.

[7] Unity in salvation history has more of a mystery than of a clarity; see, for example, Ez 37:15-19; John 10:16 and 17:20-23; Rom 11:25-26; Eph 2:15-16; 3:3-6; 4:3-6; Rev 7:4, 9.

[8] Eph 3:18-19.

appearance, and yet to remain the same.⁹ Due to all kinds of circumstances, the appearance of unity may change.

At the time of the early Church, Christians called one-another brothers and sisters. Christian life was like family life. When the Christian community was disrupted, endangered and scattered throughout the region due to persecution or other threats, new avenues were found to for the community to stay in contact. Local authorities frequently endeavored to choke the gift of catholicity out of the community, but most of the time without results. After all, Jesus' words have been instructive: »I was sick, and you visited me; I was in prison, and you came to me«,¹⁰ so that Christians did their utmost to stay connected and to console one another. The Gospel not only established a personal relation to God but also created, almost out of nothing, a vibrant social environment, a new family, a new humanity to care for.¹¹ Radical faithfulness to the commandments of Jesus to love one another, brought forth a radical new awareness of belonging and commitment.¹²

Even a non-Christian writer like Lucian of Samosata (c. 120-190 AD) was amazed by the fact that Christians left nothing undone to rescue or help a certain Christian brother called Peregrinus, who was imprisoned somewhere in Palestine for worshiping a crucified Palestinian man and thereby introducing a new cult into the world. In Lucian's own wording: »Indeed, people came even from the cities in Asia, sent by the Christians at their common expense, to succor and defend and encourage the hero.«¹³ Although Lucian hates to admit it, in the early second century Christians really cared for their own species, wherever and however this might be. This was in their spiritual DNA: an inherent predisposition toward catholicity. Love will always find itself a way.

---

9   Barth, *Kirchliche Dogmatik* IV,1 783-784: »es redet von einer in allen Verschiedenheiten sich überlegen durchsetzenden Identität, Kontinuität, Universalität ... In dem Charakter dieser Selbigkeit existiert sie ...: ich glaube ... die Existenz einer Gemeinde, die ... in allem Wechsel ihrer Gestalt unveränderlich ist«.
10 Matt 25:36.
11 Adolf von Harnack, *Die Mission und Ausbreitung des Christentums in den ersten drei Jahrhunderten*, 4th ed. (Wiesbaden: VMA-Verlag, 1980 [1924]), 174, 189.
12 See John 13:34 and Mark 12:29-31.
13 See Lucian, *De morte Peregrini* 13. Cf. Eusebius, *Historica ecclesiastica* 4,23.

4 Parameters for New Forms of Fellowship

Now back to the Netherlands. If the preconditions are right, vital communities flourishing with creativity may also be bent to the task of shaping new forms of unity. I see at least three vital parameters, culturally embedded and ecclesially relevant in Holland, which may bring to bloom new forms of fellowship in the church.

We have to reckon with the deep conviction of the average Dutch church member that, as such, relationships are more important than truth: after all truth is subjective knowledge, while a relationship is a shared experience.[14] The church is an experiential community of believers who share their life stories with one another. Their relationships *are* their truth. Man's spiritual life is his social life, as James McClendon has written: »the moral life of Christians is a social life«.[15] Obeying Christ implies a moral commitment to caring relations. Therefore, let churches be places of social formation, relationally open for experiential truth.[16]

Understanding new forms of unity implies knowledge of new forms of diversity as well. Diversity is not only to be understood in terms of confessional heresy or liberalism, but more in terms of having no story

---

[14] E.g. one could wonder if a church should necessarily split if the majority of the church allows female elders/ministers to preach. Is the mutual care and love not strong enough to survive the dissent on the issue? Cf. the dynamical coherence of the notions of unity, truth and caring relations in Eph 4:13–16: »until we all attain to the unity of the faith ... But speaking truth in love we may grow ... into him from whom the whole body ... makes itself grow ... in love.« Another example, taken from family life: parents set out rules and norms at home, such as »no smoking here« and they expect their children to respect family ethics. But if a child refuses to do so, and parents have to perpetually raise »red flags« with their child, are they compelled finally to give up their child, and break contact? Do they stop loving their child because their truths are being neglected? I do not say that truth is unimportant, but I defend the Biblical point of view that relation is more important than being persistent in pressing one's truth on someone else. I won't say that truth should never divide a community of believers, but only after effort has been made to build strong relationships.

[15] James Wm. McClendon, *Systematic Theology*, vol. 1: *Ethics* (Nashville: Abingdon Press, 2002), 165.

[16] I use the term »experiential truth« in an ecclesial way. The church comes together to hear the Word of God, and because Christ is in the church, people »experience« the *viva vox Christi* and »know« the truth of the Gospel in their life. The moment they pass on this knowledge, it becomes tradition. So, experiential truth lies firmly embedded in the supporting sidetracks of Scripture and tradition. If experiences are not accompanied and supported by Scripture and tradition, there is a danger of alienation from the faith.

about the miraculous (such as tales of divine intervention), and having no story about the experiential reframing of reality. This is exactly what younger believers in Holland try to find in the church: the experiential confirmation of a God-given restructuring of life. Therefore: let churches be places replete with stories of divine intervention and with the miraculous.

One of my colleagues at VU University examined basic semiotic perspectives on the narrative of conversion in two Dutch churches, an Evangelical Seeker Church (a Baptist Church), and a Pentecostal Church. Her conclusions point in the same direction as indicated above: churches open to creative ways of binding and bonding are committed to sharing a social imaginary world that invites churchgoers to stretch their imaginations.

> Beliefs and belonging are still important, though these concepts must be observed within the context of new modes of binding, constituted through shared narratives, languages and discourses, and aesthetic styles – particularly in the domain of worship music ... This study convincingly puts forward the importance of emotions, affects and bodily experience of (potential) converts, emphasizing the sensuous aspects of religion and the images it cultivates, and acknowledging people's desires ... Deducted from the ethnographic material, I have discussed three distinct semiotic domains at play within each church context; for analytical purposes, these are distinguished as separate fields of signs and meanings: the material domain of worship space, the aesthetic domain of worship music and the discursive domain of language. Bearing in mind the conjunction of these domains of meaning, together they reflect and constitute the social imaginary world – encompassing not only the ways people *think* but also how they *imagine* the world ... – with ontological claims that direct the formation of converts.[17]

Thus in dealing with the growing differences and diversities among church visitors – both believers and non-believers – churches may be able to transcend their current difficulties by emphasizing relationships more than doctrine; divine intervention more than human concerns; and fresh Biblical imagination more than our current, static inertias. In this respect aesthetics has become an important aspect of liturgy. The

---

[17] Miranda Klaver, *This Is My Desire: A Semiotic Perspective on Conversion in an Evangelical Seeker Church and a Pentecostal Church in the Netherlands* (Amsterdam: Amsterdam University Press, 2011), 396–397.

beauty of assembling, glorifying, and proclaiming brings many believers to a new awareness of binding and bonding, and to new perspectives on diversity and unity.

Catholicity is under heavy pressure, and obviously churches deal with these tensions in different ways. My perspective has been to set out some preconditions for enabling the quality of catholicity to find new ways of binding and bonding in the local church. As I said above: the basic capacity is already there in the church. It is possibly disguised or veiled; but it has been there always. We just have to cut off the right edges in the proper way.

CONCEPTS OF DIVERSITY AND/IN UNITY

**KONZEPTE VON VIELFALT
IN/UND EINHEIT**

Christians without Borders and Churches on the Move

Perspectives on Catholicity from Pneumatology and Mission

Kirsteen Kim

1 Introduction

»Christians without borders and churches on the move« is one way of summing up the subject matter of mission studies, which deals with both global and local Christian mission from the multi-disciplinary perspectives of theology, history, and cultural, social, religious and global studies.[1] It is also an apt description of the contents of the Acts of the Apostles. The first Christians experienced the ethnic inclusiveness and geographical universality of their new-found Christian identity and various episodes of travel, scattering, migration and deliberate mission activity led to the growth of church communities, the relocation of others and the establishment of new ones among different peoples across the Roman empire. Not only then but since, »Christians without borders and churches on the move« has continued in the history of Christianity, if it is considered from a global perspective. In fact, it is the stuff of which Christian history is made and one of the things that makes Christianity a world religion.[2] Therefore, any understanding of

---

[1] For examples, see the journal of the International Association for Mission Studies, *Mission Studies*.

[2] Sebastian Kim and Kirsteen Kim, *Christianity as a World Religion* (London: Continuum, 2008); Dana L. Robert, *Christian Mission: How Christianity Became a World Religion* (Chichester: Wiley-Blackwell, 2009).

catholicity must take account of the boundary-crossing nature of Christianity and the mobility of church communities. In this paper I suggest some tools for this task from pneumatology and theology of mission.

I anchor this essay in the recent history of Christianity in one particular context within which »Christians without borders and churches on the move« is a fitting summary of ways of being church. That context is Korea.³ There are striking parallels between the Korean Protestant experience and that of the first Christians in the book of Acts, many of which are drawn by Korean pastors and theologians themselves in their sermons and writings.⁴ Some of these parallels are also suggested by contemporary commentaries on the Acts of the Apostles, especially those sensitive to Pentecostal and post-colonial perspectives.⁵ I use such observations to develop pneumatological and mission theological tools which owe a great deal to Korean theology and to ecumenical discussion.

2   Christians Without Borders: Pneumatological Perspectives

Korea was a unified country with territorial integrity from 676 AD but when they began to study Christianity more than a millennium later, Koreans experienced it as transcending these borders. From 1392 the country was known as Joseon. Confucianism functioned as the state religion and exercised »ritual hegemony«; that is, no other religious practices were permitted.⁶ Foreign missionaries were unable to penetrate the country but Korean scholars heard about the Catholic faith

---

3   Historical details and scholarly references may be found in Sebastian C.H. Kim and Kirsteen Kim, *A History of Korean Christianity* (Cambridge: Cambridge University Press, 2015). Selected sources on Korean Christianity are also included below.
4   See, for example, Kirsteen Kim, *The Holy Spirit in the World: A Global Conversation* (Maryknoll, NY: Orbis Books, 2007), 103–139.
5   Especially, Amos Yong, *The Spirit Poured Out on All Flesh: Pentecostalism and the Possibility of Global Theology* (Grand Rapids, MI: Baker Academic, 2005); Justo L. Gonzales, *Acts: The Gospel of the Spirit* (Maryknoll, NY: Orbis Books, 2001); Beverly Roberts Gaventa, *Acts* (Nashville, TN: Abingdon Press, 2003); James D.G. Dunn, *Christianity in the Making*, vols. 1 & 2 (Grand Rapids, MI: Eerdmans, 2003, 2009); V. George Shillington, *An Introduction to the Study of Luke-Acts* (London: T&T Clark, 2007).
6   Don Baker, »Catholicism in a Confucian World,« in *Culture and the State in Late Chosŏn Korea*, eds. JaHyun Kim Haboush and Martina Deuchler (London: Harvard University Press, 1999), 199–230.

during the annual diplomatic mission to Beijing and studied Catholic literature. Finding it relevant to social issues as well as religiously attractive, they sent one of their number to Beijing for baptism and founded their own Catholic community. When in the late eighteenth century some refused to comply with Confucian ritual, they sparked persecution that lasted for nearly a century. Catholicism survived as an underground movement of small groups and Catholic villages.[7]

In the nineteenth century, a poor economic situation, internal unrest and increasing insecurity caused growing instability. Attempted invasions by Western powers (in the case of France with Catholic support) and threats from Russia and Japan led the authorities to close off Korea to most foreigners, especially missionaries, while it kept its close relationship with China. Dissidents and entrepreneurs alike left in search of freedom and new opportunities. The first Korean Protestants we know of came into one or both categories and were baptised not in Korea but in Manchuria in the late 1870s. With the help of missionaries, they produced gospels in Korean and distributed copies in Korea itself. They also founded small Christian communities there.[8] In these circumstances, those who were open to receive Christianity were in some way dissatisfied with the status quo in Korea. They must have found the Christian gospel extraordinarily attractive since they were prepared to risk the wrath of the state to receive it. Furthermore, they were open-minded enough to receive from people beyond Korean borders. They were aware that Christianity was a universal faith – or at least that it was offered to all.

---

[7] For early Korean Catholic history, see Yu Chai-shin (ed.), *The Founding of Catholic Tradition in Korea* (Mississauga, Ontario: Korea and Related Studies Press, 1996); Jai-keun Choi, *The Origin of the Roman Catholic Church in Korea: An Examination of Popular and Governmental Responses to Catholic Missions in the Late Chosôn Dynasty* (Cheltenham: The Hermit Kingdom Press, 2006); Andrew J. Finch, »A Persecuted Church: Roman Catholicism in Early Nineteenth-Century Korea,« *Journal of Ecclesiastical History* 51, no. 3 (July 2000): 556–580.

[8] For early Protestantism, see Sung-deuk Oak, *The Making of Korean Christianity: Protestant Encounters with Korean Religions, 1876–1915* (Waco, TX: Baylor University Press, 2013).

3   The Universal Spirit: The Reception of Christianity in Korea as a Global Connection

Korean Catholics were connected to the world Church initially through the Jesuits and hierarchy in Beijing and later by the Paris Foreign Mission, links that they struggled to maintain even under persecution. From the 1870s, as Korea reluctantly and under duress opened its doors to Japan and the West, missionaries were permitted to enter the country. Some elite Koreans who were pursuing modernisation argued that Protestant Christianity lay at the heart of the Western societies they admired (chiefly the USA) and that adopting it would be for the good of the country. They invited, and even financed, Western missionaries to come to Korea to share their faith and also their education, medicine and industry with them. When the missionaries arrived, they found believers waiting for baptism. Koreans presenting themselves to missionaries for baptism signalled not only that they wished to worship Christ but also their desire to join themselves to the global Christian movement.

As has been often pointed out, the Korean case presents a striking parallel to the account of the »Macedonian call« in Acts 16.[9] When the apostle Paul crossed into Macedonia, it was because he had heard the call of the Macedonians themselves, and when he arrived he found people already worshipping God in Philippi. Furthermore, the Acts narrative of the initiating, guiding and empowering work of the Holy Spirit suggests that the Macedonians were reaching across borders because that Spirit was already at work in them, prompting their desire for Christ and enabling their response.[10] The Spirit with which the New Testament church was baptised was identified by the Church Fathers as the Spirit of God, the Giver of Life,[11] and as such knows no borders. The same Spirit was at work in the creation and already known in the Hebrew worship of the one God, experienced in the faith of Israel and manifest in the life and ministry of Jesus Christ. Similarly, Korean theologians insist that God was not »carried piggy-back to Korea by the

---

[9]   For example by Juan G. Ruiz De Medina, *The Catholic Church in Korea: Its Origins, 1566–1784* (Rome: Istituto Storico, 1991), 7–9.

[10] David J. Bosch, *Transforming Mission: Paradigm Shifts in Theology of Mission* (Maryknoll, NY: Orbis Books, 1991), 84–122.

[11] Cf. the Nicene Creed.

first missionary«.[12] God's Spirit was already present and active in Korean experience and it was because of this that the first Korean Christians embraced the gospel as both continuous with what they already knew and also a fulfilment of it.[13]

The Korean context is one in which there is awareness of many spirits. In Korean traditional religion there are nature spirits, ancestor spirits and many others.[14] Both the terms *sin* and *ryeong* that were used to translate »spirit« in the first Korean Bibles set the linguistic framework for understanding the Spirit within the many spirits of the complex Korean spirit-world. Therefore it was important that the Spirit of God manifest in Christ was distinguished from the rest as »the *Holy Spirit*« and a strong theology of discernment developed.[15] When the Korean feminist theologian Chung Hyun Kyung chose to present her eco-pneumatology at the general assembly of the World Council of Churches in Canberra, Australia in 1991 in terms of a shamanist exorcism,[16] she was roundly condemned in the Korean churches for her failure to distinguish the Holy Spirit from other spirits and to make explicit the Trinitarian relationship of the Holy Spirit to Christ.[17] Korean theologians appreciated that, although the Holy Spirit is universally at work, not every spirit is on the side of Christ. At the same time as their baptism in/with the Holy Spirit separated them from some other Koreans, it also joined them to the wider Christian community worldwide.

---

[12] Younghak Hyun, »A Theological Look at the Mask Dance in Korea,« in *Minjung Theology: People as the Subjects of History*, ed. Commission on Theological Concerns of the Christian Conference of Asia (London: Zed Press, 1983), 47–54 (quotation on p. 54).

[13] Ryu Tong-shik, *The Mineral Veins of Korean Theology* (in Korean), 2nd edition (Seoul: Dasan Geulbang, 2000); Sung-deuk Oak, »Edinburgh 1910, Fulfillment Theory, and Missionaries in China and Korea,« *Journal of Asian and Asian American Theology* 9 (2009): 29–51.

[14] For listings of the names of the gods, spirits and ghosts of the pantheon of Korean folk religion, see James Huntley Grayson, *Korea – A Religious History*, revised edition (London: Routledge, 2002), 221–225; Hyun-key Kim Hogarth, *Korean Shamanism and Cultural Nationalism* (Seoul: Jimoondang, 1999), 121–249.

[15] Kim, *The Holy Spirit in the World*, 103–139.

[16] Hyun Kyung Chung, »Come, Holy Spirit – Renew the Whole Creation,« in *Signs of the Spirit*, ed. Michael Kinnamon, Official Report of the Seventh Assembly of the World Council of Churches, Canberra, 1991 (Geneva: World Council of Churches, 1991), 37–47.

[17] Kim, *The Holy Spirit in the World*, ix–x.

4   The Korean Pentecost: The Korean Church among the Churches

Protestantism took a distinctively Korean form in a revival movement in the first years of the twentieth century. The first Protestant communities had been connected to transnational denominations by Presbyterian and Methodist missionaries who arrived from 1885 onward. These were mostly from the USA where they had been influenced by the Moody and Sankey Revival of the 1870s that cut across denominational boundaries. As a result they not only emphasised the Evangelical tenets of the Bible, the Cross, conversion and activism but also the perfecting work of the Holy Spirit in the believer. A tendency to pre-millennialism motivated the evangelisation of Korea within the shortest possible time by a unified effort regardless of denomination. To this end, the missionaries adopted the »three-self« mission method[18] which meant they encouraged Korean congregations to be self-supporting, self-propagating and (to a large extent) self-governing. In other words the Korean churches were largely independent of the missionaries and also of one another. In keeping with this method they met for prayer and Bible study in small groups in people's homes, as well as in church and also in larger gatherings known as Bible schools.[19] As in the case of the Catholic Church earlier, the use of small groups made Protestantism resilient to oppression.

In the early years of the twentieth century Holiness spirituality, which focused on the »fullness of the Spirit« or »baptism in the Spirit«, grew among the foreign missionaries in Korea and among Korean Christians. This »revival« movement culminated in 1907 when thousands of Korean Christians exhibited the kind of spiritual outpouring also observed in Wales in 1904 and in India in 1905, and which is associated with the origins of global Pentecostalism.[20] News of the revival was reported around the world and it led to greater mutual respect between Koreans and missionaries now that they recognised one another as filled with the same Spirit.

The revival both demonstrated in the eyes of the international community that Koreans were true believers and at the same time

---

[18]   Known as the »Nevius method« in Korea.
[19]   For recent discussion of early missionary work, see Donald N. Clark, *Living Dangerously in Korea: The Western Experience 1900–1950* (Norwalk, CT: EastBridge, 2003); Oak, *The Making of Korean Christianity*.
[20]   See Allan H. Anderson, *An Introduction to Pentecostalism* (Cambridge: Cambridge University Press, 2004), 136–139.

made both missionaries and Koreans even more confident that there was already a Korean church and that the faith had taken root in Korean soil. The fact that the revival coincided with the establishment in 1907 of the Presbyterian Church of Korea strengthens the case of later Protestant historians who see this as the point at which Christianity became indigenous.[21] Distinguishing features of Korean spirituality were already in evidence by the time of the revival such as early morning prayer meetings, simultaneous prayer, prayer mountains, collective Bible reading and generous giving. As a result of the revival these practices, together with a Bible-based faith and a fervent spirituality, were baptised as authentic Korean Protestantism. Later denominations such as the Holiness churches since the 1920s and the Pentecostal churches from the 1950s both adopted these practices in Korea and also connected their histories to the revival as a sign of their own Korean-ness.[22]

Korean Protestants themselves saw the Korean Revival of 1903–1907 as »the Korean Pentecost« in which the Holy Spirit descended on the people. The description of the Pyongyang revival by the local synod is clearly influenced by the account in Acts 2: »When the Holy Spirit came, one person started crying aloud and confessing his sins and others joined in. In the evening ... there was the presence of a strong wind and then eventually the Holy Spirit descended«.[23] However, Korean theologian Ryu Tong-shik sees the revival as spawning two strands of Holy Spirit movement in Korea: the paternal and the maternal. The former was connected with public responsibility and political activism and emerged as *minjung* theology, a Korean political theology, in the 1970s. The leading *minjung* theologian Suh Nam-dong identified the Holy Spirit as the source of the power of the movements of the masses for their rights in various peasant uprisings in history and in his day in the movements for labour and civil rights under military-backed governments.[24] The maternal movement was characterised by interiority

---

21 For example, Lak-geoon George Paik, *The History of Protestant Missions in Korea, 1832–1910*, 2nd edition (Seoul: Yonsei University Press, 1970 [1929]), 374–375.
22 For example, Young-hoon Lee, *The Holy Spirit Movement in Korea: Its Historical and Theological Development* (Oxford: Regnum, 2009).
23 Quoted in Deok-joo Rhie, *A Study on the Formation of the Indigenous Church in Korea, 1903–1907* [in Korean] (Seoul: Institute for Korean Church History, 2001), 110–111. My translation.
24 Nam-dong Suh, »Historical References for a Theology of the Minjung,« in *Minjung Theology: People as the Subjects of History*, ed. Commission on Theolog-

and individualism which came to the fore in the charismatic revivalism and the growth of Pentecostalism in the same period. Ryu sees these two pneumatologies as running along pre-existing fault-lines in Korean society between Confucian and shamanistic patterns of religiosity which correlate to some extent with class and gender. At a time of polarisation between *minjung* and popular Korean Christianity under military dictatorship, Ryu sought to unify them by both an appeal to a primordial national spirit and a belief in one Holy Spirit active in varied ways in Korean history.²⁵ Ryu's pneumatology treads a fine line between a nationalism that identifies the Korean Spirit with the Holy Spirit and an internationalism of the universal spirit that undermines the particularity of Korean experience. Jong Chun Park, a contemporary Methodist theologian, aims to resolve this tension when he describes how the Holy Spirit is both on the inside and the outside of Korean faith. The Spirit of God both »crawls« with the people through all their troubled history and struggles for life and also breaks into Korean history in »dance« prompted by transnational encounter and resulting in religious revival and social transformation.²⁶

5   The National Spirit: Koreans as the Chosen People of God

Although the 1907 revival may be seen as part of a global Pentecostal movement, the fact that it occurred at a time of national crisis in Korea (Japan had defeated the other major contenders for Korean territory: China (1895) and Russia (1905) and proclaimed a protectorate over the peninsula) suggests that there were nationalist factors at work as well. As the nation was fighting for survival, Korean Christians saw the growth of the church as a form of resistance and hope. In the midst of turmoil, the revival provided a cathartic opportunity for repentance and faith that God was blessing Korea despite appearances to the contrary. When the Presbyterian mission went ahead with its plan, informed by three-self mission policy, to establish the Presbyterian

---

ical Concerns of the Christian Conference of Asia (London: Zed Press, 1983), 155–182, at 167–177.

25   Kirsteen Kim, »Holy Spirit Movements in Korea: Paternal or Maternal? Reflections on the Analysis of Ryu Tong-Shik (Yu Tong-shik),« *Exchange* 35, no. 2 (2006): 147–168.

26   Jong Chun Park, *Crawl with God, Dance in the Spirit! A Creative Formation of Korean Theology of the Spirit* (Nashville, TN: Abingdon Press, 1998).

Church of Korea in 1907 and the first seven Korean pastors were ordained, the Korean Church proudly took its equal place among the churches of other nations. However, when Japan finally annexed Korea in 1910, the nation ceased to exist. The Japanese took over most Korean institutions and the only ones that stood independent of Japanese control were religious.

In spite of their avowed neutrality in politics and refusal to support armed insurrection, the mainline Protestant churches and schools implicitly encouraged nationalism. They were founded on three-self principles which encouraged self-reliance and an alternative modernisation. Moreover, they used the Korean language rather than Japanese and educated Koreans in their own heritage. They networked together nationally and also across the growing Korean diaspora, they acted as a lobbying group on behalf of the people in dealings with the Japanese and they offered leadership skills for Koreans and trained a class of political leaders and intellectuals. Among the religions of Korea – chiefly Confucianism, Buddhism and indigenous religions, the Christian churches especially posed a challenge to the Japanese authorities. Not only did Christians see themselves as protectors of the nation but there is evidence – in the form of church growth – that many other Koreans regarded the churches as part of the nationalist struggle for self-reliance, modernisation and Korean language and culture. Christians taught that God had specially blessed Korea and had chosen her for salvation. In this way the Holy Spirit was construed as reinforcing the national spirit of resistance and self-reliance.[27]

Protestant leaders showed their nationalism in several ways. One way was to lend their strong support to the independence movement of 1 March 1919. This bid for the self-determination promised by US President Woodrow Wilson to other small nations in the aftermath of the First World War was brutally suppressed by the Japanese colonial government but not before news and photographs were flashed around

---

[27] See, for example, Sok-hon Ham, *Queen of Suffering: A Spiritual History of Korea*, trans. E. Sang Yu (London: Friends World Committee for Consultation, 1985); Mahn-yol Yi, »The Birth of the National Spirit of the Christians in the Late Chosŏn Period,« trans. Ch'oe Ŭn-a, in *Korea and Christianity*, ed. Chai-shin Yu (Fremont, CA: Asian Humanities Press, 2004), 39–72; Young-keun Choi, »The Great Revival in Korea, 1903–1907: Between Evangelical Aims and the Pursuit of Salvation in the National Crisis,« *Korean Journal of Christian Studies* 72 (2010): 129–149; Kyoung-bae Min, »National Identity in the History of the Korean Church,« in *Korea and Christianity*, ed. Yu, 121–143.

the world with the help of foreign missionaries.²⁸ The global missionary presence protected the church and it was one reason why Korean churches continued to invite Western missionaries despite the growing autonomy of the churches, complaints about missionary domineering and the difficulties set in the way of foreign mission work by the Japanese.

Another way in which they were nationalist was that Korean Christians resisted being subsumed under Japanese denominations. Japanese theologians applied pressure by arguing that Koreans should join the unified Japanese church in the name of ecumenism and Christian unity. Pneumatologically, they argued that Koreans should experience the freedom of the »New Testament spirit«, which they argued was universal and they criticised Koreans for preferring the limited spirit of the Old Testament faith of Israel. Conveniently for them, the Japanese believed the New Testament spirit was fulfilled in the Japanese church and empire, whereas most Koreans understandably clung to belief in the election of Israel and of Korea.²⁹ Korean Protestants also distinguished the Holy Spirit from the spirits of Shintoism. They condemned as idolatrous the participation in Shinto rituals that was imposed by the Japanese and a minority of conservatives mounted the only significant opposition to it.³⁰ As the Japanese grip tightened, the churches as institutions and church leaders were forced to submit to control of the colonial authorities, who eventually imposed a union on the Korean churches, and the foreign missionaries left as Japan asserted itself against the West. The misuse of ecumenical theology to force unity left a lasting suspicion of ecumenism in the Korean churches for whom the spirit of truth was the only basis of unity. In these difficult circumstances the independency of Korean Christianity and its basis in small groups allowed Christianity to continue as an underground movement

---

[28] For a recent account, see Timothy S. Lee, »A Political Factor in the Rise of Protestantism in Korea: Protestantism and the 1919 March First Movement,« *Church History* 69, no. 1 (2000): 116–142.

[29] Sung-deuk Oak, »Japanese Colonialism and Christianity«, in *Sources of Korean Christianity*, Sung-deuk Oak (Seoul: Institute for Korean Church History, 2004), 323; Gregory Vanderbilt, »Post-War Japanese Christian Historians, Democracy, and the Problem of the ›Emperor-System‹ State«, in *Christianity and the State in Asia: Complicity and Conflict*, eds. Julius Bautista and Francis Khek Gee Lim (London: Routledge, 2009), 59–78, at 63–66.

[30] Allen D. Clark, *A History of the Church in Korea* (Seoul: Christian Literature Society, 1971), 221–226.

until the end of the war in local congregations and small prayer and Bible study groups.

Under Japanese colonisation, which claimed to benefit Korea by carrying out modernisation that it was not capable of achieving by itself, Korean Christian leaders shaped their own vision for national development. This was for a nation founded on Christian values, as they believed the Western nations were, which would be powerful and prosperous, while also democratic and caring. Although the liberated Korea was tragically divided, Christian leaders worked with successive governments in South Korea to actualise these ideals. Pneumatologically speaking, Korean church leaders understood the blessing poured out in the Korean Pentecost as life-giving, including in a material sense. Their pneumatology was informed by indigenous understandings of »spirit« as the life-force or power derived from the Confucian, Daoist and Shamanistic cosmologies prevalent in Korean thought.[31] The leading Protestant pastor in the second half of the twentieth century was Han Kyung-chik whose sermons of that period express the Christian vision for the nation in a pneumatological framework.[32] Han prayed that the church should be »a centre for evangelisation of the Korean people«, »a stronghold of liberal democracy« and »a source of social renewal«[33] and he believed this would be achieved by the power of the Spirit. Han saw the Holy Spirit and religious revival as the non-violent power that would overcome Communism and other spiritual forces[34] and give victory over adversity to both church and nation.[35] This would be through the education and empowering of believers »to live and serve justly«,[36] to create a community of love and sharing[37]

---

[31] Kim, *The Holy Spirit in the World*, 103–139.

[32] In 1992 Han was awarded the Templeton Prize for progress in religion. His collected works are translated and published as Eun-seop Kim (ed.), *Kyung-chik Han Collection*, vols 1–10 (Seoul: Kyung-Chik Han Foundation, 2010). See particularly Yoonbae Choi, »Kyung-Chik Han's Theology of the Holy Spirit,« in *Kyung-Chik Han Collection*, vol. 9: *Theses 1*, ed. Eun-seop Kim (Seoul: Kyung-Chik Han Foundation, 2010), 315–64.

[33] Han, Kyung-chik, *Autobiography of Han Kyung-chik: My Thanksgiving* [in Korean] (Seoul: Duranno, 2010), 377.

[34] One of his favourite texts was »Not by might, nor by power, but by my Spirit, saith the Lord of Hosts« (Zech 4:6).

[35] Kyung-chik Han, *May the Words of My Mouth* (Seoul: Youngnak Church, 2002), 196–212 (sermon from 1966).

[36] Kyung-chik Han, »Another Counsel,« in *Kyung-Chik Han Collection*, vol. 4: *Sermons 1*, ed. Eun-seop Kim (Seoul: Kyung-Chik Han Foundation, 2010), 333–346 (Sermon from 1967), 340.

and to transform the wider society.³⁸ Through more than five decades of struggle and change in South, Han led his church in a holistic ministry of worship, discipline and self-support, together with evangelism, social service, support for modernisation and missionary activity, especially toward North Korea. He regarded the Spirit as the source of the blessing of church growth, democratisation, security and prosperity that South Korea has gained despite the odds.³⁹

Pentecostal mega-church pastor Cho Yonggi (1936–) also preached a pneumatology of development. Cho identified the realm of the Holy Spirit as »the fourth dimension«. This »hovers over« the three-dimensional, material world and the world of evil spirits does not encroach on it, being only »supernatural« and not »spiritual«.⁴⁰ In this world of dreams and visions, Cho taught his disciples to »see by faith« what they want to achieve in accord with »the desire of the Holy Spirit«.⁴¹ Through prayer, fasting and exorcism, Cho taught that the Holy Spirit, who enables believers to overcome the evil spirits and other problems that hold them back, and realise the blessings that God wishes to bestow on them.⁴² In common with some US American prosperity preachers, Cho taught of a »three-fold blessing«, which was based on verse 3 of John 2, which in Cho's interpretation promises »spiritual well-being«, »general well-being« – including material prosperity and »bodily health« to believers. It was strongly criticised by both other Pentecostal and also mainline churches at the time as a gospel for success which manipulated God to obtain wealth.⁴³ However, Cho insisted from his Korean experience that poverty is »a curse from

---

[37] Kyung-chik Han, »Be Filled with the Spirit,« in *Kyung-Chik Han Collection*, vol. 4, 358–371 (Sermon from 1968).

[38] Kyung-chik Han, »The Source of Ability,« in *Kyung-Chik Han Collection*, 311–321 (Sermon from 1970).

[39] Kyung-chik Han, *Just Three More Years to Live* (Seoul: Rev. Kyung-Chik Han Memorial Foundation, 2005), 178, 180.

[40] David Yonggi Cho, *The Fourth Dimension: The Key to Putting Your Faith to Work for a Successful Life* (Secunderabad, India: Ben Publishing, 1999 [1989]), 45–49, 72–73; David Yonggi Cho, *The Fourth Dimension: More Secrets a Successful Faith Life*, vol. 2 (Secunderabad, India: Ben Publishing, 1999 [1983]), 35–37.

[41] Cho, *The Fourth Dimension: The Key*, 51–73; Cho, *The Fourth Dimension: More Secrets*, 50–57.

[42] David Yonggi Cho, *The Holy Spirit, My Senior Partner: Understanding the Holy Spirit and His Gifts* (Milton Keynes, UK: Word Publishing, 1989).

[43] See discussion in Wonsuk Ma, William W. Menzies and Hyeon-sung Bae, *David Yonggi Cho: A Close Look at His Theology and Ministry* (Seoul: Hansei University Press, 2004).

Satan«[44] and that the kingdom of God is one of well-being and good living.[45] Theologians of his »full gospel« tradition have refined Cho's thought into a »holistic approach« in which the power of the Spirit deals with people's suffering and enables them to live a full life.[46] So although Cho placed greater emphasis on visionary and other supernatural means and was more focused on economic success than social change, Cho's confidence in the power of the Holy Spirit to bring about positive and material change was not dissimilar to that of Han Kyung-chik[47] or even some *minjung* theology.

In this section we have seen how Korean Christians have used pneumatological tools to support their existence as »without borders« in the triple sense of openness to transnational influences, participation in world Christianity and sense of identity. In the next section we shall look at the mission theological perspectives that inform the global mobility of Korean Christians in migration and mission.

6   Churches on the Move: Mission Theological Perspectives

The worldwide spread of Christianity in the New Testament is partly due to the sending activity of the church in Antioch and also, presumably, to the sending activity of other churches, with whose apostles or missionaries – like Apollos – Paul occasionally came into contact. Another factor encouraging its spread was the already existing Jewish diaspora. According to Luke, these dispersed Jewish communities extending from Pontus in the north of Asia Minor south to Egypt, from Rome in the west to Elam, east of Arabia, were all represented among the crowd at Pentecost (Acts 2:9–11). Even if the message was not immediately taken back to them at that time, the list in Acts 2 is also

---

[44]   Cho, *The Fourth Dimension: The Key*, 137–138; David Yonggi Cho, *Born to Be Blessed* (Secundarabad, India: Ben Publishing, 1999), 121.
[45]   David Yonggi Cho, *Solving Life's Problems* (Secunderabad, India: Ben Publishing, 1998 [1980]), 27–41.
[46]   Jeong Chong Hee, »The Korean Charismatic Movement as Indigenous Pentecostalism,« in *Asian and Pentecostal: The Charismatic Face of Christianity in Asia*, eds. Allan Anderson and Edmond Tang (Oxford: Regnum Books, 2005), 551–571.
[47]   Cf. Hong Jung Lee, »*Minjung* and Pentecostal Movements in Korea,« in *Pentecostals After a Century: Global Perspectives on a Movement in Transition*, eds. Allan H. Anderson and Walter Hollenweger (Sheffield: Sheffield Academic Press, 1999), 138–160, at 149, 157.

intended as a record of the first Christian churches. This mode of spread through the diaspora is substantiated by the travels of the apostle Paul, who in most cities found a Jewish community with which he made contact first and, despite the usual opposition, from which some of first Christians in each place were drawn. A third factor was the situation of the first Christians within the Roman Empire which, like most empires, dispossessed and displaced individuals and whole communities. Persecutions, like those recorded in Acts 8, 11 and 18, caused Christians to scatter or re-locate. As well as such involuntary movement, the empire also facilitated mobility for some, like Paul himself, his fellow tent-makers Priscilla and Aquila and Lydia, the business woman from Asia Minor.[48]

It is often said that the Acts of the Apostles would be better named »the Acts of the Holy Spirit«.[49] There are repeated Pentecosts in Acts in which the Spirit comes on different communities in the same way as the Spirit had come at first on the Jews in Jerusalem (4:31; Samaritans, 8:14-17; Romans, 10:44-48; 11:17-18; 15:8-9; Ephesians, 19:1-7). The ending of Acts leaves open the possibility of continued manifestations of the Spirit's power in the ongoing life of the church.[50] Not only is the Spirit at work through the church but the Spirit in Acts is seen to be »the principal agent of mission«.[51] Prior to the church, there is a mission of the Spirit in which the church is privileged to participate: »The Church, as the body of Christ, acts by the power of the Holy Spirit to continue his life-giving mission in prophetic and compassionate ministry«.[52] This recognition of the *missio Spiritus* lends both dynamic and fluid dimensions to the church's missionary activity. As stated in the new World Council of Churches statement on mission, »… Christian witness … unceasingly proclaims the salvific power of God through

---

[48] For insight into the colonial and diaspora context of early Christian mission, see inter alia N.T. Wright, *The New Testament and the People of God* (London: SPCK, 1992); Udo Schnelle, *Apostle Paul: His Life and His Theology* (Grand Rapids, MI: Baker Academic, 2005); Alexander J.M. Wedderburn, *A History of the First Christians* (London: T&T Clark, 2004); Dale T. Irvin and Scott W. Sunquist, *History of the World Christian Movement*, vol. 1 (Maryknoll, NY: Orbis Books, 2001); R. Geoffrey Harris, *Mission in the Gospels* (Peterborough: Epworth, 2004).
[49] Cf. Gonzales, *Acts*.
[50] Yong, *The Spirit Poured Out on All Flesh*, 83.
[51] John Paul II, *Redemptoris Missio: On the Permanent Validity of the Church's Missionary Mandate* (Rome: Vatican, 1990), paragraph 21.
[52] World Council of Churches, *The Church: Toward a Common Vision*, Faith and Order paper 214 (Geneva: World Council of Churches, 2013), 5 (section 1.A.1).

Jesus Christ and constantly affirms God's dynamic involvement, through the Holy Spirit, in the whole created world.«[53] In view of the precedence of the *missio Dei*, mission is increasingly understood as an invitation to »find out where the Holy Spirit is at work and join in«.[54]

7   Global Connections: Christians in Exile, Diaspora and Migration

As well as a similar pneumatological orientation, many of the same factors of imperial power, migration and sending observed in Acts can also be seen in the history of the Korean church. Growing instability on the Korean peninsula in the late nineteenth and early twentieth centuries and Korea's absorption into the Japanese empire provoked emigration for economic and political reasons. Koreans worked in Japan's growing factories, laboured on plantations in Hawaii or, if they could, studied in Japan or the USA. As Japan tightened its grip in Korea, thousands left to join the guerrilla fighters resisting occupation and after the 1919 uprising a network of émigrés formed the Korean provisional government in Shanghai. Whole church communities moved en masse to Manchuria and Siberia where they could develop uncultivated land and keep their culture. There they founded their own villages to model a Korean Christian society, enlighten the homeland and resist the Japanese.[55] Later, as the Pacific War gathered pace, hundreds of thousands were conscripted or otherwise forced to move to fight, support the troops or manufacture armaments. Others emigrated in the hope of returning once Korean sovereignty and security was returned. Those migrating to Western countries tended to be Christians, or became so on arrival, and Protestant churches formed the social as well as religious centre of diaspora communities. Often with the help of church workers sent out from Korea, through the church, exiles kept up Korean customs and language, established Korean schools for their youth, were informed of developments at home, put pressure on foreign

---

[53]   World Council of Churches, *Together Towards Life: Mission and Evangelism in Changing Landscapes* (Geneva: World Council of Churches, 2013), 10 (para. 18).
[54]   World Council of Churches, *Together Towards Life*, p. 10 (para. 18), p. 11 (para. 25), 40 (para. 110). Cf. Kirsteen Kim, *Joining in with the Spirit: Connecting World Church and Local Mission* (London: SCM Press, 2012).
[55]   At least until 1931, when Japan created Manchukuo.

governments to support Korean independence, and raised funds for the nationalist effort and those suffering on the peninsula.[56]

Eventually in 1945 Korea was liberated from Japan by the victory of the Allied powers only to be divided into two parts administered by USSR and USA military regimes in the north and south, respectively. The ideological pressures of the emerging Cold War and the mutual antagonism of Communist- and Western-oriented Koreans were major factors contributing to the formation of two separate Koreas: the Democratic Peoples' Republic of Korea in the North and the Republic of Korea in the South. When these went to war in 1950–1953 and were backed by the superpowers, the devastation of the peninsula and loss of life was tremendous.[57] Emigration from South Korea continued and was encouraged from the 1960s as a way of bringing remittances, building foreign relations and relieving political pressure. Large-scale migration to the United States from 1968 resulted in a Korean community there of 2 million that is estimated to be 70 per cent Protestant today. There are also large Korean Christian communities in Canada, Japan, Vietnam, Philippines, Australia, Germany, the UK, Brazil and Argentina. Migrant communities maintain links with the homeland and are also linked to each other forming a global network. Developments on the peninsula are watched with interest and prayed over in all these communities, which may also seek to intervene.[58] The US American diaspora has not only supported and influenced the churches in Korea but the influence is also the other way on the American churches, for example in their use of the cell-group methods, which are held by some to be a key factor in church growth.[59]

---

[56] For the Korean Christian diaspora, see S. Hun Kim and Wonsuk Ma (eds.), *Korean Diaspora and Christian Mission* (Oxford: Regnum Books, 2011).

[57] There are no verifiable figures for the total casualties in the Korean War but recent estimate give 3 million Koreans (roughly 10 per cent of the population) were killed, wounded or missing by 1953. Don Oberdorfer and Robert Carlin, *The Two Koreas: A Contemporary History*, 3rd edition (New York: Basic Books, 2014), 8.

[58] For an insightful study of a particular migrant Christian community, see David K. Yoo, *Contentious Spirits: Religion in Korean American History, 1903–1945* (Stanford, CA: Stanford University Press, 2010).

[59] See, for example, Donald A. McGavran and C. Peter Wagner, *Understanding Church Growth*, 3rd edition (Grand Rapids, MI: Eerdmans, 1990).

8   A Light to the World: The Return and Gathering of the Nations

Although they crossed national borders to bring the gospel to Korea, when it came to establishing churches, the Protestant missionaries had been very bound by the notions of territory that prevailed in Europe. Moreover, their denominations were in competition with each other so they divided up the Korean peninsula between them under the system known as »comity«; that is, Christians within one region were expected to belong to the same denomination. The massive internal displacement of Koreans during the colonial period and even more so during the Korean War largely broke down that system. From 1945 until the 1960s, South Korea was a country of refugees as returned exiles and those displaced by colonial policy were joined by others fleeing from the communists in the north. The majority of Protestants had been northerners and Pyongyang was such a Christian enclave that it had been known as »the Jerusalem of the East«. Many of these refugees now formed new congregations in the south. Because they tended to be better educated and more fervent and conservative in their faith, the existing structures of the denominations were placed under strain as the northern refugees remade the southern churches in their image.[60] Meanwhile in North Korea all religious activity was suppressed and the functional substitute of Juche-Kimilsungism was imposed.[61] It is possible that the cell formation allowed Christianity to survive underground for some time despite its suppression by the communist regime but this is not possible to verify.

To the denominational divisions brought by the missionaries, from the 1950s in South Korea were added new Presbyterian denominations born of the struggles under occupation and partition (Koshin and Kijang) and the Cold War (Tonghap and Hapdong), and other splinter groups. In addition to the Catholic, Presbyterian, Methodist, Holiness,

---

[60]   For details of the influence of the northerner migrants on the churches in the south, see In-cheol Kang, »Protestant Church and Wolnamin: An Explanation of Protestant Conservatism in South Korea,« *Korea Journal* (Winter 2004): 157–190. Kang argues that the comity system did play a part in the denominational divisions.

[61]   For religion in North Korea and Juche-Kimilsungism, see for example, Charles K. Armstrong, *The North Korean Revolution, 1945–1950* (Ithaca, NY: Cornell University Press, 2004); Bruce Cumings, *North Korea: Another Country* (New York: New Press, 2004); Shin, Eun-hee, »The Sociopolitical Organism: The Religious Dimensions of Juche Philosophy,« in *Religions of Korea in Practice*, ed. Robert E. Buswell, Jr. (Princeton, NJ: Princeton University Press, 2007), 517–33.

Baptist and Anglican churches and the Salvation Army that were there before the Pacific War, returning Koreans converted elsewhere established Pentecostal, Nazarene, Adventist, and Church of Christ congregations. The massive aid effort mounted by the UN and by Western churches brought more denominations into the country, including Lutherans and Quakers. In addition the chaotic spiritual atmosphere of the 1940s and 50s led to many new Korean-founded movements.

Christians were disproportionately represented in the political leadership in the south, and in particular in the person of former exile Syngman Rhee, first president of South Korea and a Methodist, who held power until 1960. Rhee believed that freedom and equality would be assured if the nation was founded on Christianity. Christian leaders shared his vision of a Christian nation as opposed to the Communist one promoted in the north. Foundational to this vision was religious freedom, including not only freedom of belief and practice but also the freedom to propagate one's faith. In the democratic context of South Korea and as a challenge to the regime in the North, church leaders set themselves targets to increase Christian numbers by mass evangelisation in addition to local church growth efforts. These bore fruit in the much-vaunted membership figures which roughly doubled every decade up to the early 1990s. Mass events which were held every 3–4 years during this period, which drew millions of people, were ecumenical in the sense that they were supported by almost all the Protestant denominations.[62] However, the imposed union of the late colonial period had created a great suspicion of ecumenism among many Korean Christians and the inclusion of Communist-approved churches in the World Council of Churches turned most against it. Furthermore, the religious and denominational plurality of South Korea, combined with capitalist models of enterprise and a belief in the positive value of market forces, encouraged competition for growth between local churches that militated against structural or visible church unity. What is more, rapid urbanisation created the conditions for the emergence of the megachurches for which South Korea is famous.[63]

The churches tended to see the growth of Christianity, which was unique in modern Asia, as a measure of the »success« of the gospel in

---

[62] For post-war Protestant evangelisation of the South, see Timothy S. Lee, *Born Again: Evangelicalism in Korea* (Honolulu: University of Hawaii Press, 2010).

[63] See for example, Soo-han Gil, *Social Sources of Church Growth: Korean Churches in the Homeland and Overseas* (Lanham, MD: University Press of America, 1994).

Korea, evidence of Korea's election and vindication of Korean ways of practising the faith. From the 1970s, Christians from other parts of the world came to see the phenomenon and study it, and Korean Christians began to think of their calling as centripetal; that is as being a light to Asia and the world, a city set on a hill to which the nations gather. In the early 1980s, theologian Han Chul-ha, for example, insisted that Korea would evangelise the world, not according to the Western colonial model of »triumphalistic missionary sending«, but by an ethical mission of demonstrating a righteous national life like »Jerusalem of old«.[64] The climax of this view of mission as bearing witness to what God had done in Korea was in 1988 when the Olympic Games were held in Seoul. South Koreans were able to showcase their country's economic »miracle« and also its religious and other achievements to the other nations of the world, including China, the USSR and other Communist countries – with the exception of North Korea, of course, and a few of its allies. The event was a triumph for the South Korea and set it on the world stage. The churches took full advantage of the opportunities for evangelism and were also very active in hosting the visiting teams.

9   Sent to All Nations: Korean World Mission

However, by the end of the 1980s, the energy behind the »explosive« growth of Korean Protestant churches was being channelled into a centrifugal mission from Korea to the world helped by growing financial resources and a surplus of clergy. The impulse to world mission from Korea went back to the origins of the Protestant churches in gratitude for what they had received and a desire to »repay the debt of the gospel« that had been brought to them. Not content with sending missionaries to the diaspora, Korean Protestants understood that taking the gospel to another people was the sign of a mature church and in 1913, soon after its establishment, the Presbyterian Church of Korea had commissioned three men for church planting in Shandong province in China.[65] Such cross-cultural mission was considered more

---

[64]   Chul-ha Han, »Involvement of the Korean Church in the Evangelization of Asia,« in *Korean Church Growth Explosion*, eds. Bong-Rin Ro and Marlin L. Nelson (Seoul: Word of Life Press, 1983), 51–68.

[65]   Young-woong Choi, »The Mission of the Presbyterian Church of Korea in Shandong, North China, 1913–1957,« in *Transcontinental Links in the History of*

prestigious than pastoral work among diaspora communities.⁶⁶ Missionary sending continued on a small scale but when the churches collaborated to organise the »World Evangelization Crusade« in 1980, they declared their intention to start a »Korea-modelled and Korea-led [world] missionary movement« and launched a programme to send 100,000 missionaries and volunteers overseas in the next decade.⁶⁷ The global missionary movement mushroomed as South Korea's foreign relations became multi-lateral, governmental restrictions on overseas travel and foreign exchange were relaxed and globalisation brought greater freedom of movement. Furthermore Western-based mission agencies actively recruited Koreans because they saw their potential for evangelising the rest of Asia, especially areas closed to Westerners.

The Korean world missionary movement cannot be separated from national aspirations for global recognition and national and business interests. Nor can it be easily distinguished from the diaspora communities which, like the Jewish diaspora in the New Testament, provided bases and logistical support for mission or were themselves missionary toward their respective contexts. The growing number of Protestant missionaries saw themselves as ambassadors for South Korea and exported not only a Korean gospel but also Korean culture and products wherever they were sent. By making global networks, South Koreans were also protecting themselves from the threat from North Korea and even understood themselves to be bringing about a global peace that would eventually solve the problem on the peninsula. By 2010 there were estimated to be 20,000 Koreans serving abroad in evangelism, church-planting and service of various sorts, including medical work and IT development and support.⁶⁸ These included a growing

Non-Western Christianity, ed. Klaus Koschorke (Wiesbaden: Harrassowitz, 2002), 117–30.

⁶⁶ Cf. Donald N. Clark, »History and Religion in Modern Korea: The Case of Protestant Christianity,« in *Religion and Society in Contemporary Korea*, eds. Lewis R. Lancaster and Richard K. Payne (Berkeley, CA: University of California Institute of East Asian Studies, 1997), 169–214, at 185.

⁶⁷ Joon-gon Kim, »Korea's Total Evangelization Movement,« in *Korean Church Growth Explosion*, eds. Bong-rin Ro and Marlin L. Nelson (Seoul: Word of Life Press, 1983), 17–50, at 35. For Korean missionary thinking in the 1980s and 1990s, see also the other articles in this volume and in Bong-rin Ro and Marlin L. Nelson (eds.), *Korean Church Growth Explosion*, 2nd edition (Seoul: Word of Life Press, 1995).

⁶⁸ For further details, see Steve Sang-cheol Moon, »The Protestant Missionary Movement in Korea: Current Growth and Development,« *International Bulletin of Missionary Research* 32, no. 2 (2008): 59–64; »Missions from Korea 2012:

number of Catholics who formed a national society of apostolic life in 1975 and had become increasingly oriented toward global mission by the twenty-first century for similar motives of »gratitude« and »requital«.[69]

Although Western missionaries encouraged the Korean churches to be self-propagating, it is clear that this did not extend to the expectation of a world mission from Korea. In fact in the post-colonial period earlier expansionist theologies were giving way to a new paradigm of *missio Dei*, that is, mission should be primarily understood not as sending from one territory to another but as a participation in the sending activity of God the Father – the sending of Christ and the Holy Spirit into the world.[70] Both the *missio Dei* and its corollary that each local church is missionary were originally formulated at the meeting of the International Missionary Council in Willingen, Germany, in 1952 in a post-War and post-colonial world in which sending of Western missionaries was becoming difficult and contentious. Western churches were forced to withdraw from what had been their main mission fields of India and China and some churches in the Third World, wishing to assert their independence from their former colonial masters, called for a moratorium on mission.[71]

Whereas the theology of *missio Dei* was intended for a world in which churches stayed put, today's theology of mission must take into account that churches are »on the move« as well as new intentional and expansionist mission movements. Korean churches have never had a settled history. Even in the Catholic Church, which has the longest history in the peninsula, it was not possible to establish a parish system until the 1960s. The churches have existed within a context of repeated threat and radical change and this has contributed to their global mobility and their dynamic sense of apostleship. This section has shown how Korean participation in mission and insistence on sending has been sustained, despite practical and theological pressures against it. Korean Christianity does not only consist of renewed forms of spirituality but is a

---

Slowdown and Maturation,« *International Bulletin of Missionary Research* 36, no. 2 (2012): 84–85.

[69] Korean Missionary Society, *2014 Introduction: Korean Missionary Society* (Seoul: Korean Missionary Society, 2014), 1.

[70] Bosch, *Transforming Mission*.

[71] For in-depth study of the origins of the *missio Dei* paradigm, see John G. Flett, *The Witness of God: The Trinity, Missio Dei, Karl Barth, and the Nature of Christian Community* (Grand Rapids, MI: Eerdmans, 2010).

movement that aims to serve personal, social, national and even international concerns.

10 Conclusion: Catholicity in the Context of Christians without Borders and Churches on the Move

The recent history of Korean Protestantism offers various manifestations of »Christians without borders and churches on the move«. The Korean churches moved due to persecution, migration and displacement. The challenges to national borders gave the church a desire to maintain its international links. It also gave a transnational self-understanding but for survival encouraged its primary expression in local congregations and even house-groups. The result today is, first, that Korean Christianity is not limited to Christianity in Korea and, second, that Korean churches continue to be mobile in the sense of both migration and (not unrelated) missionary sending. Korean Christianity is a dynamic global network: Korean denominations have developed diaspora expressions and Korean agencies are sending missionaries in multiple directions. The rise of Korean Christianity represents a further diversification of the faith in that over the last couple of centuries another global expression of Christianity has been added to the very many already existing. Furthermore, this new form of Christianity exists in multiple denominations.

The development of another form of Christianity may be seen as a blow by those who have been working toward structural unity which reduces the number of denominations. Furthermore, the mobile and boundary-crossing nature of Korean Christianity interferes with the settled ministry developed in Europe over centuries and with efforts for peace between religious communities in many parts of the world. However, as I have pointed out, »Christians without borders and churches on the move« is not a new pattern of Christianity. As I have indicated, this is a New Testament pattern that is replicated many times in church history. Since Pentecost, for various reasons both voluntary and forced, the church has been globally widespread and represented by many different ethnic identities that have often co-existed with each other in particular localities. Our theologies of unity and ecumenism should not bemoan such diversity but celebrate it, recognise other Christians and reflect on the implications of these developments.

The history of Korean Christianity raises important questions about the meaning of catholicity and at the same time it suggests some theological tools for understanding it. First, from its history, it poses a significant challenge to theologies which prioritise structural unity in inter-church relations. It shows that although structurally unified churches may be desirable, they are not practicable everywhere. The reality for many Christians globally is that, for reasons of survival in hostile situations, churches exist as small underground independent groups, possibly networked with one another. Therefore, if the church is catholic, then this reality must also be an expression of it. Furthermore, the experience of the Korean churches under the latter part of Japanese colonial rule shows how structural unity is not necessarily the result of reconciliation between Christians but may be the result of political pressure or even be forced on churches by government authorities. True catholicity, therefore, must be more than structural in its expression. It must arise from Christian freedom and love within which difference and diversity is expressed without fear.

A second historical question is that the growth of Korean Christianity, and of world Christianity in general, shifts interest away from viewing Christian diversity primarily in terms of doctrine and polity toward the ethnic and/or geographical diversity, which was the primary sense in which the first councils of the church experienced it. Therefore the catholicity envisaged is not mainly across denominations but more across cultures and regions. The ecumenism of the colonial period, which gave birth to the World Council of Churches, tended to assume that overcoming the doctrinal and liturgical differences between the churches of Europe and the denominations they fostered would unite Christians globally. Now that we have other globally connected churches emerging from different centres, new models of ecumenism are needed and our understanding of catholicity must include global interconnectedness. For historical reasons, Korean churches include a diaspora expression and they have also developed global mission activities. While this may be problematic for inter-church relations, it is a repeated historical pattern (the Anglican Communion, to name but one example). Nor is it only a matter of lack of respect; in contexts of denominational plurality, it may not be clear which is the legitimate local church with which to work. Perhaps there is a need for more informal means of mutual recognition that allow for working together until the more complex structural, liturgical and doctrinal issues can be addressed.

As well as raising historical questions for catholicity, Korean Christianity has some theological tools to suggest, particularly in regard to pneumatology and to mission. Korean theology draws attention to pneumatology, particularly in the narrative of Pentecost and mission in the book of Acts. This biblical perspective suggests a border-crossing and dynamic understanding of the church as it participates in the *missio Spiritus*. It suggests that catholicity must allow for a missional understanding of church and for eschatological expectation. The church's catholicity is still being discovered and expressed. Furthermore, the repeated Pentecosts of Acts give weight to theological conviction that there are no second- or first-class Christians – God shows no partiality. This theological insight of the first Christians is echoed in the conviction of Korean theologians that the Holy Spirit has been present and active in Korean history and has been outpoured on the nation. This is ground for the legitimacy of Korean Christianity as one among many expressions of the faith and for mutual respect between these to be a necessary aspect of catholicity. The gift of discernment of spirits is given to Koreans as much as to others who have been Christian for longer, therefore discernment should be an »ecumenical endeavour« and a truly »global conversation«.[72]

Regarding mission, Korean church leaders have a theology of sending and sharing motivated by both gratitude and obligation. If catholicity includes reciprocity, which it surely does, then it must accommodate this desire to »repay the debt« in appropriate ways. Only by all churches being both givers and receivers can the Korean church and other churches be affirmed in their maturity. In a world of »Christians without borders and churches on the move«, where Christians read the Acts of Apostles and see themselves as part of it, missionary sending activity will continue in varied directions. It should be recognised as a valid and valuable expression of faith. The challenge to catholicity is to ensure that missionary activity is done in an ethical and responsible way with regard both to other Christians and people of other faiths and none.[73] »Mission in the Spirit« will be mutually up-building and contribute to the growth of the kingdom.[74]

---

[72] Stanley Samartha, »The Holy Spirit and People of Other Faiths,« in *To the Wind of God's Spirit: Reflections on the Canberra Theme*, ed. Emilio Castro (Geneva: World Council of Churches, 1990), 50–63, at 58; Kim, *The Holy Spirit in the World*.

[73] For an important step in this direction, see the joint statement by the Roman Catholic Church, WCC and World Evangelical Alliance, »Christian Witness in a Multi-Religious World: Recommendations for Conduct« (2011).

[74] Samuel Rayan, »A Spirituality of Mission in an Asian Context,« SEDOS (1999), para. 11. Available at http://sedosmission.org/old/eng/rayan2.htm (accessed August 1, 2014). See also Kirsteen Kim, *Mission in the Spirit: The Holy Spirit in Indian Christian Theologies* (Delhi: ISPCK, 2003).

Einheit und Verschiedenheit von Religionsgemeinschaften in sozialwissenschaftlichen und theologischen Perspektiven

Wolfgang Lienemann

Einleitung

Einheit und Verschiedenheit (unity and diversity) sind für praktisch alle bekannten menschlichen Gesellschaften unvermeidlich und eine immer neu zu bearbeitende Herausforderung. Thomas Hobbes hat den Naturzustand der Menschen als ein *bellum omnium contra omnes* beschrieben, welches nur durch die Errichtung einer unwiderstehlichen Zwangsordnung überwunden werden kann. Jean-Jacques Rousseau hat als *problème fondamentale* des *Contrat Social* die Frage formuliert, wie eine gesellschaftliche Form gefunden werden kann, bei der »jeder, indem er sich mit allen vereinigt, nur sich selbst gehorcht und genauso frei bleibt wie zuvor«.[1] Immanuel Kant hat den Ausdruck der »ungeselligen Geselligkeit« unter den Menschen geprägt,[2] welche unvermeidlich ist und als solche nicht überwunden, wohl aber gebändigt und geregelt werden kann durch eine allgemein zustimmungsfähige rechtliche Ordnung, eine Verfassung. In den Sozialwissenschaften von Comte bis

---

[1] Œuvres complètes, Bd. III (Bibl. Pléiade), Paris 1964, 360.
[2] Idee zu einer allgemeinen Geschichte in weltbürgerlicher Absicht (1784), zit. nach: WEISCHEDEL (Hrsg.), Werke in sechs Bänden, Darmstadt 1964, Bd. VI, 37. Vgl. dazu ALLEN WOOD, Ungeselige Geselligkeit. Die anthropologischen Grundlagen der kantischen Ethik, in: DIETER HÜNING/BURKHARD TUSCHLING (Hrsg.), Recht, Staat und Völkerrecht bei Immanuel Kant, Berlin 1998, 35–52.

Marx, Weber bis Habermas, Durkheim bis Luhmann und Bourdieu ist unstrittig, dass Gesellschaften – von kleinen Gruppen bis zur »Weltgesellschaft« – durch Konflikte geprägt, herausgefordert und verändert, bisweilen revolutioniert werden. Auf der anderen Seite ist ebenso unverkennbar, dass es eine menschliche Fähigkeit zu friedlicher Arbeitsteilung, Kooperation, Interessenausgleich und zur Integration, vor allem durch Errichtung einer übergreifenden Rechtsordnung, gibt. Es muss, schreibt Kant, die Errichtung einer solchen Ordnung möglich sein, »selbst für ein Volk von Teufeln, wenn sie nur Verstand haben«.[3] Einheit und Verschiedenheit sind mithin ein übergreifendes Thema jeder Gesellschaftsanalyse, und zwar anscheinend zu allen Zeiten in allen Kulturen. Das gilt für politische wie für religiöse Gemeinschaftsbildungen.

Meine Leitfrage der folgenden Überlegungen lautet: Können die Kirchen der Christenheit im Blick auf (interne und externe) Konflikte und Kooperationen, ihre ekklesiologischen Konzepte und ihr Verhalten in Konflikten und Kooperationen etwas von den Sozialwissenschaften und der Sozialphilosophie lernen? Diese leitende Frage enthält eine empirische und eine normative Seite: Wie werden Einheit und Verschiedenheit wahrgenommen? Welche Konzepte und normativen Erwartungen kommen dabei ins Spiel?

Ich gehe bei den folgenden Überlegungen von einigen grundlegenden Erfahrungen und Auffassungen von Pluralität und Pluralismus,[4] Konflikten und Kooperationen in der heutigen Weltgesellschaft aus und skizziere exemplarisch einige Probleme von Differenzierung und Integration, externem und internem Pluralismus in religiösen Gemeinschaften (1). Anschließend erörtere ich prominente ekklesiologische Einheitskonzepte, mittels derer jeweils versucht wird, Erfahrungen von Einheit und Verschiedenheit im Binnen- wie im Außenverhältnis religiöser Gemeinschaften reflektierend zu verarbeiten (2). Danach wird der Blick auf einige normative Herausforderungen gelenkt, die sich aus einem internen und externen Pluralismus ergeben (können) (3).

---

[3] Zum ewigen Frieden (1795), a.a.O., 224.
[4] Die Verwendung des Pluralismus-Begriffs stößt auf mannigfache Schwierigkeiten, ist aber wohl unvermeidlich. Ich spreche in diesem Beitrag von »Vielfalt« im Sinne von tatsächlicher Pluralität und Mannigfaltigkeit, von »Pluralismus« überwiegend dann, wenn damit mehr oder weniger eine gedeutete kollektive Erfahrung und teilweise ein Konzept oder sogar eine normative Konzeption gemeint sind. Ganz trennscharf lässt sich diese Begrifflichkeit indes nicht durchhalten.

Schließlich interessiert mich, ob und was Theologien[5] und Sozialwissenschaften im Blick auf dieses (viel zu) weite Feld möglicherweise voneinander lernen können, ob es vielleicht sogar etwas wie eine Komplementarität oder Konvergenz der Perspektiven geben kann (4) und auf welche Grenzen man dabei stoßen kann (5).

1   Pluralität, Konflikt und Kooperation in der Weltgesellschaft

1.1 Drei Prämissen

Zu Beginn möchte ich drei Prämissen nennen, ohne die meine weiteren Ausführungen in der Luft hängen würden. Man kann diese Voraussetzungen problematisieren, aber man kommt schwerlich umhin, mit ein paar anfänglichen Unterscheidungen zu beginnen.

Die heutige *Weltgesellschaft* ist in einer historisch-qualitativ neuen Art *vereinheitlicht* und zugleich durch eine ungeheuer differenzierte *Pluralität* unterschiedlichster Arten auf zahlreichen Ebenen bestimmt.[6]

Dass die Welt *eine* ist, betrifft zuerst die global entschränkte und zeitlich simultane *Kommunikation*, wobei Kommunikation nicht bloß auf der Ebene von Information und Desinformation geschieht, sondern alle gesellschaftlichen Funktionsbereiche betrifft: des Verkehrs, der Medien (einschließlich Geld und Kapital), der Produktion, des Wissens, des Handels, des Konsums, der Mobilität, der Religiosität sowie aller damit einhergehenden möglichen Konflikte.[7]

---

5   Ich beziehe mich durchgehend nur auf Theologien im Kontext christlicher Kirchen, gehe also auf jüdische oder islamische Theologien nicht ein. Zum dabei vorausgesetzten Theologiebegriff vgl. WOLFGANG LIENEMANN, Wahrheit und Freiheit der Religionen, in: WALTER DIETRICH/WOLFGANG LIENEMANN (Hrsg.), Religionen – Wahrheitsansprüche – Konflikte. Theologische Perspektiven, Zürich 2010, 9–42 (hier 15f).
6   Kant hat als erster die »Kugelfläche« der Erde als Inbegriff der Nötigung zur Bildung einer inklusiven Weltordnung verstanden und von daher sein Konzept einer Völkerrechtsordnung und die Idee einer Weltrepublik entwickelt; siehe: Zum ewigen Frieden, a.a.O., 208–217.
7   Zum modernen Begriff der Weltgesellschaft unter dem konstitutiv-umfassenden Aspekt der Kommunikation siehe besonders NIKLAS LUHMANN, Die Gesellschaft der Gesellschaft, Frankfurt a.M. 1997, Bd. 1, 145–171. Pointiert: »Weltgesellschaft ist das Sich-Ereignen von Welt in der Kommunikation.« (150) Vgl. zur weiterführenden Differenzierung dieses Ansatzes RUDOLF STICHWEH, Die Weltgesellschaft. Soziologische Analysen, Frankfurt a.M. 2000.

Die Weltgesellschaft zeichnet sich durch eine *mehrdimensionale, konfliktträchtige Pluralität* aus, die ethnische, politische, wirtschaftliche, soziale und – nicht zuletzt – religiöse und weltanschauliche Antagonismen und daraus resultierende Kämpfe einschließt und immer wieder neu hervorbringt.

Für die plural verfasste Weltgesellschaft ist nicht nur die globale Entschränkung von Kommunikationen charakteristisch, sondern ebenso die Tatsache, dass zugleich alte und neue Konflikte auf vielen Ebenen entfacht worden sind und dass die globalen Strukturen zunehmend multipolare Formen angenommen haben. Im Blick auf die politische Weltordnung ist das offenkundig: An die Stelle einer mehr oder weniger bipolar ausgeprägten Ordnung, wie sie nach 1945 für die relativ kurze Zeit der Ost-West-Konfrontation und des Kalten Krieges, der vielfach auch in die südliche Hemisphäre getragen wurde, typisch war, ist erneut ein System von dominanten und peripheren Machtzentren getreten.

Für die heutige Weltgesellschaft sind zudem zahlreiche gegenläufige Tendenzen bemerkenswert: Einerseits tiefgreifende Konflikte, antagonistische Strukturbildungen, insbesondere Machtkonflikte von Gruppen, Ethnien und sozialen Klassen, andererseits entstehen neue Koalitionen und Kooperationsformen (man denke an die Erweiterung der EU, die Entwicklung von Freihandelszonen wie in Südostasien in Gestalt der ASEAN, aber auch an soziale Netzwerke, die staatliche Grenzen übergreifen). Der modernen Weltwirtschaft und den von dieser hervorgebrachten Konflikten steht, wie Immanuel Wallerstein[8] und viele andere gezeigt haben,[9] nicht in vergleichbarer Weise ein politisches und ökonomisches Ordnungssystem gegenüber, wie das (vielleicht) früher für manche rechtsstaatlich geregelte Volkswirtschaften gelten mochte. Die »global player« der Real- und vor allem der Finanzwirtschaft unterliegen trotz internationaler Institutionen wie dem Internationalen Währungsfonds und der Weltbank nur schwachen

---

[8] Sein umfassendes Werk über »The Modern World-System«, seit 1974 in mehreren Bänden erschienen, liegt in zahlreichen Sprachen vor. Vgl. zur Einführung WALLERSTEIN, Geopolitics and Geoculture. Essays on the Changing World-System, Cambridge MA 1991; ders., World-Systems Analysis. An Introduction, Durham, NC 2000.

[9] Eine gute Übersicht aus der Zeit vor der Finanzkrise von 2008 bietet der Abschlussbericht der Enquetekommission des Deutschen Bundestages »Globalisierung der Weltwirtschaft – Herausforderungen und Antworten« (BT-Drucksache 14/9200 v. 12.06.2002).

staatlichen und überstaatlichen Kontrollen.¹⁰ Verschärfend kommt hinzu, dass in sehr vielen Staaten und Regionen der Gegenwart die internen gesellschaftlichen Heterogenitäten und die entsprechenden Spannungen teilweise dramatisch zugenommen haben, wenn sich beispielsweise weltmarktorientierte Zentren und archaische Produktions- und Verkehrsformen innerhalb eines wenig entwickelten oder in einem Schwellenland gegenüber stehen, Konflikte, die nicht selten in ihrem verheerenden Antagonismus durch Korruption, vielfältige Gewaltformen und hochgeputschte religiöse Konflikte verschärft werden.¹¹

Teil dieses zugleich vereinheitlichenden und spaltenden Weltsystems sind auch die Religionsgemeinschaften, deren Mitglieder auf vielfache Weise als Akteure, Opfer, Nutznießer oder Gegner in die angedeuteten Antagonismen und Verwerfungen unweigerlich einbezogen werden.¹² Polyzentrische Strukturen und Institutionen prägen inzwischen nicht nur die globalen wirtschaftlichen und politischen Beziehungen, sondern auch die Religionslandschaften der Weltgesellschaft. Die

---

10   Die klassische Kritik der Bretton-Woods-Institutionen hat JOSEPH E. STIGLITZ geschrieben: Globalization and Its Discontents, New York 2002 (deutsch: Berlin 2002).

11   Besonders Länder mit wichtigen, großen Rohstoffressourcen wie die DR Kongo sind bis heute unfähig geblieben und unablässig von außen daran gehindert worden, ihren potentiellen Reichtum zugunsten der gesamten Bevölkerung zu nutzen. Zugleich wirken sich die internen und externen Ausbeutungsverhältnisse auch verschärfend auf interreligiöse Konflikte aus, wie man besonders am Beispiel Nigerias sehen kann.

12   Zum Verhältnis von großen Religionsgemeinschaften zu Globalisierungsprozessen siehe, in ausdrücklichem Anschluss an Niklas Luhmann PETER BEYER, Religions in Global Society, London/NewYork 2006. Dass Globalisierungsprozesse in den Religionsgemeinschaften sehr unterschiedlich wahrgenommen und beurteilt werden, machen die Beiträge in HEINRICH BEDFORD-STROHM u.a. (Hrsg.), Jahrbuch Sozialer Protestantismus, Bd. 3: Globalisierung, Gütersloh 2009, exemplarisch deutlich. Dabei ist als sozialethische Grundtendenz in der ökumenischen Bewegung und im (deutschen) Protestantismus zu erkennen, dass die Globalisierungskritik nicht in völlig illusionäre Forderungen nach einer De-Globalisierung mündet, sondern auf eine politische, menschenrechtlichen Kriterien unterliegende und kulturelle Differenzen berücksichtigende Gestaltung von Prozessen und Strukturen in der Weltgesellschaft zielen muss. Das konvergiert mit den Positionen der römisch-katholischen Soziallehre und ihren Aktualisierungen in zahlreichen Ortskirchen auf allen Kontinenten; vgl. für die »Wissenschaftliche Arbeitsgruppe für weltkirchliche Aufgaben der Deutschen Bischofskonferenz« die umfassende internationale Bestandsaufnahme von MATTIAS KIEFER, Kirchliche Stellungnahmen aus Partnerkirchen zum Thema Globalisierung, Münster 2005.

Christenheit, ihre Kirchen und insbesondere ihre missionarischen Aktivitäten und Institutionen waren zwar von Beginn an polyzentrisch und tendenziell global ausgerichtet,[13] aber die weltgeschichtliche Realisierung derartiger Intentionen erfolgte erst in der Epoche der europäischen Expansion und Kolonialisierung seit dem 18. und 19. Jahrhundert.[14] Es ist kein Zufall, dass seit geraumer Zeit Untersuchungen zu den Weltreligionen allgemein[15] sowie zur »Weltchristenheit« (world christianity) im Besonderen einen lange Zeit vorherrschenden Eurozentrismus in der historischen Analyse einer scharfen Kritik unterzogen haben.[16]

Diese politisch-soziale, religiöse und rechtliche Mannigfaltigkeit lässt danach fragen, ob es in der Weltgesellschaft universale Normen geben kann, soll oder muss, oder ob die Verschiedenheit, die Relativität und womögliche Unvereinbarkeit partikularer Ordnungen und Überzeugungen unüberwindbar sind, und ob (möglicherweise) universale Normen auch für Selbstverständnis und Handeln von Religionsgemeinschaften einschließlich der Kirchen relevant sind oder werden können.

---

[13] Siehe ADOLF MARTIN RITTER, Polyzentrismus als Merkmal der frühen Christentumsgeschichte, in: CIPRIAN BURLACIOIU/ADRIAN HERMANN (Hrsg.), Veränderte Landkarten. Auf dem Weg zu einer polyzentrischen Geschichte des Weltchristentums (FS Klaus Koschorke), Wiesbaden 2013, 15–25.

[14] Siehe dazu KLAUS KOSCHORKE, Polyzentrische Strukturen der globalen Christentumsgeschichte, in: RICHARD FRIEDLI u.a. (Hrsg.), Intercultural Perceptions and Prospects of World Christianity, Frankfurt a.M. u.a. 2010, 105–126; sowie die Fallstudien in KLAUS KOSCHORKE/ADRIAN HERMANN (Hrsg.), Polycentric Structures in the History of World Christianity. Polyzentrische Strukturen in der Geschichte des Weltchristentums, Wiesbaden 2014. Siehe ferner die beiden letzten Bände der »Cambridge History of Christianity«: SHERIDAN GILLEY/BRIAN STANLEY (Hrsg.), World Christianities c. 1815 – c. 1914, Cambridge 2006; HUGH MCLEOD (Hrsg.), World Christianities c. 1914 – c. 2000, Cambridge 2006.

[15] Hilfreich zur Beobachtung aktueller Entwicklungen sind die umfassenden Daten, Materialien und Interpretationen des Pew Research Center (The Pew Forum on Religion & Public Life), hier vor allem: The Global Religious Landscape. A Report on the Size and Distribution of the World's Major Religious Groups as of 2010, Dezember 2012, und Global Christianity. A Report on the Size and Distribution of the World's Christian Population, Dezember 2011. Weiteres unter: http://www.globalreligiousfutures.org (Stand: 20.02.2015).

[16] Vgl. dazu CHRISTINE LIENEMANN-PERRIN, *World Christianity* als Erfahrungsfeld und theoretisches Konzept, in: Theologische Zeitschrift 69 (2013) 1/2, 118–145; dies., »World Christianity« – A New Concept Challenging the Understanding of »Catholicity« (in diesem Band), WOLFGANG LIENEMANN, Die Christenheit in der Weltgesellschaft. Kommentar und Fragen zu einem Forschungsprogramm, in: KOSCHORKE/HERMANN, Polycentric Structures, 385–393.

1.2 Interner und externer Pluralismus als Problem und Chance von Religionsgemeinschaften und Kirchen

Unabhängig davon, ob einzelne Kirchen oder Denominationen der Christenheit für sich überzeugt sind, dass sie (allein) in umfassendem Sinne katholisch sind, insofern sie (allein) die Fülle des Heils und der geistlichen Vollmacht repräsentieren, bilden sie gleichwohl, empirisch-historisch gesehen, jeweils nur eine unterschiedene Größe im Pluriversum der Kirchen und Konfessionen und existieren in immer mehr Ländern und Regionen zudem neben zahlreichen weiteren nichtchristlichen Religionsgemeinschaften. Dieser Pluralismus der Kirchen nicht nur in einzelnen Ländern, sondern in der Weltgesellschaft verdankt sich internen und externen Konstellationen und Ursachen, ist er doch selbst eine geschichtliche Folge von kulturellen, religiösen, sozialen, wirtschaftlichen und politischen Differenzierungsprozessen. Insofern unterscheide ich zwischen internem und externem Pluralismus, der binnen- und der zwischenkirchlichen Differenzierung sowie dem Miteinander und bisweilen Gegeneinander von Religionsgemeinschaften in einer Gesellschaft.[17]

Interner Pluralismus von Gemeinden, Traditionen, Kirchen und »Konfessionen« begleitet die Christenheit indes seit ihren Anfängen,[18] auch wenn der spezifische frühneuzeitliche Konfessionsbegriff im Sinne bekenntnismäßiger Unterschiedenheit erst ein Kind der Reformation des 16. Jahrhunderts ist. Soziologisch kann man die bemerkenswerte Formulierung 1Kor 11,19 (δεῖ γὰρ καὶ αἱρέσεις ἐν ὑμῖν εἶναι, ἵνα [καὶ] οἱ δόκιμοι φανεροὶ γένωνται ἐν ὑμῖν – lat. *nam oportet haereses esse ut et qui probati sunt manifesti in vobis*: denn es müssen auch Spaltungen unter euch sein, damit die Bewährten/Rechtschaffenen unter euch offenbar werden) auch dahingehend verstehen: Konfliktträchtige Differenzierungen, Gruppenbildungen und Pluralisierungen sind erwartbar

---

[17] Zu den zahlreichen Aspekten eines umfassenden Pluralismus-Verständnisses vgl. CHRISTOPH SCHWÖBEL, Art. Pluralismus II. Systematisch-theologisch, TRE 26, 724–739; EILERT HERMS, Pluralismus aus Prinzip, in: ders., Kirche für die Welt, Tübingen 1995, 467–485, sowie den breit angelegten Kongressband: JOACHIM MEHLHAUSEN (Hrsg.), Pluralismus und Identität, Gütersloh 1995.

[18] ERNST KÄSEMANN hat 1951 im Blick auf die damalige ökumenische Debatte über die Einheit der Kirche die Titelfrage seines Aufsatzes »Begründet der neutestamentliche Kanon die Einheit der Kirche?« mit der These beantwortet: »Der nt.liche Kanon begründet als solcher nicht die Einheit der Kirche. Er begründet als solcher, d.h. in seiner dem Historiker zugänglichen Vorfindlichkeit dagegen die Vielzahl der Konfessionen.« Abgedruckt in: ders., Exegetische Versuche und Besinnungen, Bd. 1, Göttingen ⁴1965, 214–223, hier 221.

und unvermeidlich – sie wurzeln gleichsam in der natürlichen Ordnung menschlich-religiösen Verhaltens, dessen Krisen und Abgrenzungserfordernissen.[19] Fragen der Lehre, der Sakramente und Rituale, des Ethos sowie des Rechts – und in allen diesen Hinsichten auch immer Legitimitätsfragen von Autoritäten, Herrschaftsansprüchen, Befehl und Gehorsam – können zu Anlässen, Ursachen und Gründen von internen Konflikten und insofern zum Motor von interner Differenzierung werden.[20] Darin liegen gleichzeitig Chancen zu Innovationen: Strittige Lehren können korrigiert und präzisiert werden, an Prägnanz und Kohärenz gewinnen, das Ethos kann – prinzipienfest oder opportunistisch – unter veränderten Umständen neu konkretisiert werden, das Religionsrecht lässt sich auf neue Herausforderungen einstellen, nicht zuletzt durch Rezeptionsvorgänge im Verhältnis zum weltlichen Recht, wobei es dabei erneut zu Pluralisierungen und Polarisierungen kommen kann.[21]

[19] FRIEDRICH SCHLEIERMACHER hat von den »natürlichen Ketzereien am Christentum« gesprochen: »die doketische und nazoräische, die manichäische und pelagianische«: Der christliche Glaube. Nach den Grundsätzen der evangelischen Kirche im Zusammenhange dargestellt, 2. Aufl., Ausgabe MARTIN REDEKER, Berlin 1960, 129–134. Er hat diese vier Grundformen gegenüber der historischen Mannigfaltigkeit von Häresien als »allgemeine Formen« (130) behandelt, methodisch durchaus vergleichbar der späteren Bildung von Idealtypen bei Max Weber.

[20] MAX WEBER hat in seiner Religionssoziologie im Rahmen der Studien, die lange unter dem Titel »Wirtschaft und Gesellschaft« vorlagen, religiöse Gemeinschaften stets auch unter dem Aspekt ihrer Konfliktbildung und -bearbeitung in herrschaftssoziologischer Perspektive betrachtet (5. Aufl. hg. v. JOHANNES WINCKELMANN, Tübingen 1972, 654–726, jetzt ders., Wirtschaft und Gesellschaft. Herrschaft, Max Weber Studienausgabe = MWS I/22-4, Tübingen 2009, 132–171 und 172–216), und Niklas Luhmann hat, in ausdrücklichem Anschluss an Weber, immer wieder die Aufmerksamkeit auf interne Differenzierungsprozesse von Religionen, verstanden als spezifische gesellschaftliche Funktionssysteme, gerichtet; vgl. LUHMANN, Die Ausdifferenzierung der Religion, in: ders., Gesellschaftsstruktur und Semantik Bd. 3, Frankfurt a.M. 1989, 259–357. CHRISTOPH DINKEL, Kirche gestalten. Schleiermachers Theorie des Kirchenregiments, Berlin/New York 1996, 59, weist zu Recht in dieser Hinsicht auf eine bemerkenswerte sachliche Nähe Luhmanns zu Schleiermachers Häresien-Typologie hin.

[21] Als Beispiel sei nur die Auseinandersetzung mit den neuzeitlichen Menschenrechtskonzepten genannt: in Teilen des Protestantismus schon früh einsetzend, in der römisch-katholischen Kirche erst mit der Enzyklika »Pacem in Terris« von JOHANNES XXIII. (11.04.1963) und der Erklärung über die Religionsfreiheit »Dignitatis humanae« des Zweiten Vatikanischen Konzils (07.12.1965) wegweisend. Die russische orthodoxe Kirche hat 2000 in ihrer neuen »Sozialdoktrin« die Menschenrechte erstmals positiv gewürdigt, diese Position später aber teilweise wieder revidiert. Vgl. dazu DAGMAR HELLER, Menschenrechte, Menschenwürde und sittliche Verantwortung im kirchlichen Dialog zwischen Ost und West, in:

Insbesondere im Blick auf die kirchliche Rechtsgeschichte lassen sich vielfache Wechselwirkungen zwischen internem und externem Pluralismus erkennen.

Externe Einwirkungen auf Religionsgemeinschaften können Diffusions- und Differenzierungsprozesse auslösen, und dies wiederum besonders im Zuge von politischen Interventionen, gesellschaftlichen Umbrüchen und freiwilligen oder aufgezwungenen Migrationen. Wenn beispielsweise in der Spätantike der Kaiser sich in interne und/oder externe Religionsstreitigkeiten einmischte und höchste Vollmacht in Reichssynoden in Anspruch nahm,[22] oder wenn in der Reformationszeit Reichstage über Religionsangelegenheiten berieten und entschieden,[23] oder wenn eine Volksvertretung eine radikale Trennung von Religionsgemeinschaften und Staat verfügt, dann wird damit auch in die inneren Verhältnisse und die interreligiösen Beziehungen eingegriffen und dann wurden und werden damit Einigungen *und* Ausgrenzungen intendiert und bewirkt – Zwang zu Einheit und Eindeutigkeit durch Anerkennung oder Aberkennung im Bezug auf den wahren, orthodoxen Glauben, Ausgrenzung im Bezug auf tatsächliche oder vermeintliche Schismatiker und Häretiker, Ermöglichung oder Beschränkungen der freien religiösen Selbstorganisation. Nicht zuletzt waren die strikte Unterscheidung (nicht: beziehungslose Trennung) von geistlichem und weltlichem Regiment bei den Reformatoren für eine sorgfältige und historisch folgenreiche Differenzierung von kirchlichen und weltlichen Kompetenzen bahnbrechend.[24] In den frühneuzeitlichen Bürgerkriegen in Europa überlagerten sich auf mannigfache Arten dann erneut religiöse und politische Konflikte, bis – nach der Einsicht in die Irreversibilität der eingetretenen religiösen Spaltungen *und* die Notwendigkeit einer politisch-rechtlichen Friedensordnung[25] – das Vertragssystem des

---

ÖR 59, 2010, 308–329; STEFAN TOBLER, Menschenrechte als kirchentrennender Faktor? Die Debatte um das russisch-orthodoxe Positionspapier von 2008, in: ZThK 107, 2010, 325–347.

22 Vgl. dazu ADOLF MARTIN RITTER, Reich und Konzil, in: GERHARD RAU u.a. (Hrsg.), Das Recht der Kirche. Bd. II: Zur Geschichte des Kirchenrechts, Gütersloh 1995, 36–57.

23 Siehe THOMAS KAUFMANN, Geschichte der Reformation, Frankfurt a.M./Leipzig 2009, 570–581. 613–623.

24 Vgl. dazu WOLFGANG LIENEMANN, Art. Zwei-Reiche-Lehre, in: EKL, Bd. 4, ³1996, 1408–1419.

25 Siehe EIKE WOLGAST, Religionsfrieden als politisches Problem der frühen Neuzeit, in: HZ 282 (2006), 59–96.

Westfälischen Friedens die religiösen Konflikte in Europa hinreichend stillstellen konnte.[26]

Für die Gegenwart haben etliche dieser Entwicklungen und Entscheidungen freilich seit langem ihre gesellschaftlich prägende Bedeutung verloren. Alle Menschen, unerachtet ihres Glaubens oder Unglaubens, genießen heute in liberalen Rechtsstaaten im allgemeinen eine umfassende Glaubens- und Religionsfreiheit und können sich ohne spürbare negative Folgen einer auf Einheitswahrung programmierten religiösen und/oder politischen Herrschaft entziehen. Doch wäre der Eindruck einer umfassenden religiösen Indifferenz und »Säkularisierung« sowie einer durchgehenden Abdrängung der Religionen in die Privatsphäre falsch.[27] Zudem haben in den letzten Jahrzehnten die großen Migrationsbewegungen der Gegenwart nicht nur in Europa und Nordamerika die politischen und religiösen Landkarten erneut von Grund auf verwandelt, sondern auf der anderen Seite sind durch religiöse Differenzierungs- und Pluralisierungsprozesse traditionelle religiöse Homogenitäten gesprengt worden, auch und besonders in der südlichen Hemisphäre. Zugleich haben die Migranten die religiösen Felder in den Zuwanderungsländern verändert, mit Wechselwirkungen wiederum auf die Herkunftsländer.[28] In der Schweiz, gleichsam einem

---

[26] Vgl. dazu exemplarisch CHRISTOPH LINK, Die Bedeutung der Westfälischen Friedens in der deutschen Verfassungsentwicklung, in: Juristen Zeitung 53, (1998) 1, 1–9; KARL-HEINZ ZIEGLER, Die Bedeutung des Westfälischen Friedens von 1648 für das europäische Völkerrecht, in: Archiv des Völkerrechts 37, (1999), 129–151; MARTIN REPGEN, Dreißigjähriger Krieg und Westfälischer Frieden. Studien und Quellen, FRANZ BOSBACH UND CHRISTOPH KAMPMANN (Hrsg.), Paderborn 1998; MARTIN HECKEL, Konfessionalisierung in Koexistenznöten. Zum Augsburger Religionsfrieden, Dreißigjährigem Krieg und Westfälischem Frieden in neuerer Sicht, in: HZ 280 (2005), 647–690; HEINZ SCHILLING, Zwang zum Krieg und Fähigkeit zum Frieden. Der Westfälische Friede in deutscher und europäischer Perspektive, NZZ 247, 24./25.10.1998, 67. Für die Schweiz hat damals der Basler Bürgermeister Rudolf Wettstein erfolgreich die Verhandlungen mit dem Ziel der völkerrechtlichen Anerkennung der Souveränität der Eidgenossenschaft geführt.

[27] Auf die neueren Debatten zu Begriff und empirischen Befunden der »Säkularisierung« kann ich hier nicht eingehen. Vgl., leider nur überwiegend im Blick auf Europa, für die historischen Befunde HARTMUT LEHMANN (Hrsg.), Säkularisierung, Dechristianisierung, Rechristianisierung im neuzeitlichen Europa. Bilanz und Perspektiven der Forschung, Göttingen 1997, sowie aus soziologischer Sicht DETLEF POLLACK, Säkularisierung – ein Mythos?, Tübingen 2003.

[28] Im Blick auf afrikanische Kirchen siehe JEHU J. HANCILES, Beyond Christendom. Globalization, African Migration, and the Transformation of the West, Maryknoll, NY 2008; FRIEDER LUDWIG/J. KWABENA ASAMOAH-GYADU (Hrsg.), African Christian Presence in the West. New Immigrant Congregations and

mitteleuropäischen Mikrokosmos religionspluraler Entwicklungen, haben sowohl orthodoxe Kirchen als auch früher weitgehend unbekannte Kirchen und Religionsgemeinschaften mit außereuropäischen Wurzeln in den letzten Jahrzehnten enorm zugenommen, am stärksten, ganz ähnlich wie in Deutschland oder Frankreich, durch die Zuwanderung von Muslimen.[29] Nach den Zugehörigkeitszahlen bilden Muslime, Buddhisten und Hindus in der Schweiz inzwischen größere Gemeinschaften als die Juden.[30] Etliche der von Migranten gebildeten christlichen oder nicht-christlichen Gemeinschaften sind oder waren in ihren Herkunftsländern hochgeachtete Mehrheitsreligionen oder privilegierte »Staatskirchen«, während sie in den neuen Umgebungen oft nur marginale Minderheiten sind, die sich zugleich bemühen, die Kontakte zur alten Heimat aufrechtzuerhalten. Dass sie zugleich örtlich gebundene Personalgemeinden und Teil eines globalen Netzwerkes sind,

Transnational Networks in North America and Europe, Trenton NJ 2011. Eine kurze Darstellung im Blick auf Europa: REINHARD HEMPELMANN (Hrsg.), Leben zwischen den Welten. Migrationsgemeinschaften in Europa, Berlin 2006; weitere Angaben in: DARRELL JACKSON/ALESSIA PASSARELLI, Mapping Migration. Mapping Churches' Responses. Europe Study, Brüssel 2008. Zur Schweiz: SIMON RÖTHLISBERGER/MATTHIAS D. WÜTHRICH, Neue Migrationskirchen in der Schweiz, Bern 2009. Leicht zugängliche Daten und Publikationen zu aktuellen Migrationsprozessen findet man über die Homepage der Internationalen Organisation für Migration (IOM); siehe besonders die interaktive App zu den Migrationsströmen: http://www.iom.int/cms/en/sites/iom/home/about-migration/world-migration.html (19.02.2015) oder bei der deutschen Bundeszentrale für politische Bildung, dort die »Länderprofile«: http://www.bpb.de/gesellschaft/migration/laenderprofile (Stand 19.02.2015).

[29] Vgl. dazu die Studien des Nationalen Forschungsprogramms (NFP) 58 über »Religionsgemeinschaften, Staat und Gesellschaft«; eine Darstellung und Auswertung der wichtigsten Ergebnisse nebst einer Liste der einzelnen Projekte und Veröffentlichungen findet man in: CHRISTOPH BOCHINGER (Hrsg.), Religionen, Staat und Gesellschaft. Die Schweiz zwischen Säkularisierung und religiöser Vielfalt, Zürich 2012. Nähere Informationen zu Mitgliederzahlen und räumlicher Verteilung findet man bei MARTIN BAUMANN, Religionsgemeinschaften im Wandel. Strukturen, Identitäten, interreligiöse Beziehungen, in: BOCHINGER, a.a.O., 22–75; ders./JÖRG STOLZ (Hrsg.), Eine Schweiz – viele Religionen. Risiken und Chancen des Zusammenlebens, Bielefeld 2007 (frz. Genf 2009).

[30] Man schätzte für das Jahr 2000 den Anteil der Muslime an der Wohnbevölkerung der Schweiz auf 4,3%. (vgl. BAUMANN, Religionsgemeinschaften, 39); in Deutschland zwischen 5 und 7% (Stand 2012), wobei die Zahlenangaben von muslimischen Verbänden, säkularen Forschungseinrichtungen und staatlichen Stellen erheblich differieren.

muss kein Widerspruch sein; das gilt insbesondere für pentekostale oder charismatische Gemeinschaften.[31]

Um die Frage zu beantworten, inwieweit sich die Religionen der Migranten in einer relativ stark säkularisierten Gesellschaft wie der Schweiz in späteren Generationen verwandeln, ist es noch viel zu früh. Man kann beobachten, dass in der ersten und zweiten Generation die Zugehörigkeit zur angestammten religiösen Gemeinschaft eine wichtige soziale und kulturelle Unterstützung darstellt, individuell und kollektiv Halt gibt, zugleich an die Üblichkeiten der neuen Heimat heranführt und damit insgesamt eine starke Integrationsfunktion hat,[32] aber ob das in Zukunft so bleiben wird, ist nicht prognostizierbar. Auf der anderen Seite haben die traditionellen großen Volkskirchen in der Schweiz genauso wie in anderen großstädtischen Ballungsgebieten Europas inzwischen ihre frühere oligopolartige Stellung eingebüßt, einerseits durch den wachsenden Anteil der Konfessionslosen,[33] andererseits durch die zunehmende Zahl der nicht am Gemeinschaftsleben partizipierenden, distanzierten Mitglieder, welche teilweise bei sich bietenden Gelegenheiten austrittsgeneigt sind.

2 Ekklesiologische Einheitskonzepte unter Bedingungen des Pluralismus

Wie gehen Kirchen in Europa mit den hier nur knapp skizzierten Herausforderungen einer pluralistischen Religionslandschaft und den internen sowie externen Differenzierungen um? Gibt es in den Kirchen der Christenheit gemeinsam geteilte, zumindest konvergierende Verständnisse von Einheit und unvermeidlichem, legitimem, vielleicht sogar sachlich notwendigem Pluralismus? Welches sind die Merkmale entsprechender normativer Konzeptionen?

---

[31] Siehe MICHAEL BERGUNDER/JÖRG HAUSTEIN (Hrsg.), Migration und Identität. Pfingstlich-charismatische Migrationsgemeinden in Deutschland, Frankfurt a.M. 2006.

[32] Die äthiopische orthodoxe Tewahedo-Kirche in Bern zeigt in ihrem neuen Gottesdienstraum im Berner »Haus der Religionen«, den sie mit der Brüdergemeine teilt, die äthiopische und die Schweizer Fahne.

[33] BOCHINGER, Religionsgemeinschaften, 58. Ob und inwiefern Muslime, die keine erkennbaren religiösen Aktivitäten zeigen (Gebete, Moscheebesuch usw.) als »konfessionslos« bezeichnet werden können, ist umstritten. Scharf geschnittene Alternativen formaler Mitgliedschaft wie die christlichen Kirchen kennt der Islam im allgemeinen nicht. Ähnliches gilt für buddhistische und hinduistische Gemeinschaften.

2.1 Traditionelle großkirchliche Konzeptionen

Zuerst stößt man hier auf eine Paradoxie: Die meisten Kirchen der Christenheit nehmen für sich selbst unter Aufnahme der altkirchlichen Symbole von Nicäa 325 und Konstantinopel 381 die Katholizität als eines der vier Merkmale der Kirche (*una, sancta, catholica et apostolica ecclesia*) in Anspruch, verstehen aber keineswegs unter Einheit und Katholizität dasselbe oder bestreiten einander sogar die Legitimität einer solchen Selbstauffassung. Katholizität begegnet seit den Kirchenspaltungen des 11. und 16. Jahrhunderts in differenten konfessionellen Traditionen und Selbstbeschreibungen.[34] Man kann die Katholizität der Kirche sehr verschieden verstehen: a) als ein historisch-empirisch beschreibbares Merkmal ihrer umfassenden räumlichen und zeitlichen Verbreitung auf der bewohnten Erde, b) als die universale Bedeutung der Verkündigung von Jesus Christus für alle Welt, c) als die geistliche und rechtliche Einheit von Kirchenvolk und Bischöfen unter dem römischen Papst oder einem Patriarchen oder d) als die in Christus schon gegebene und geglaubte, aber erst am Ende der Zeiten offenbar werdende Allgemeinheit (Inklusivität) der wahren Kirche. Diese Bestimmungen sind offenkundig teils deskriptiver, teils normativer (kontrafaktischer) Art. Der historischen Beschreibung im Sinne einer globalen Ausbreitung christlicher Kirchen wird man nicht widersprechen können, auch wenn die länderspezifischen Befunde die ganze Breite zwischen marginalisierten Diaspora-Situationen auf der einen Seite, religiös-kultureller Dominanz anderseits umfassen. Der »Sendungsbefehl« der Verkündigung des Evangeliums (Mt 28,18–20) impliziert einen globalen Auftrag[35] und hat entsprechende weltweite missionarische Aktivitäten hervorgebracht, aber die universale Bedeutung des Evangeliums, welche den Glaubenden und Verkündigenden gewiss ist, ist nicht eine allgemein einsehbare Tatsache, sondern Verheißung und von außen bestreitbarer Anspruch.

---

[34] Siehe dazu BERND OBERDORFER, Art. Katholizität der Kirche, RGG⁴, Bd. 4, 902–905. Grundlegend zum Verständnis der Katholizität WOLFGANG BEINERT, Um das dritte Kirchenattribut. Die Katholizität der Kirche im Verständnis der evangelisch-lutherischen und römisch-katholischen Theologie der Gegenwart, 2 Bde., Essen 1964.

[35] Auch wenn er keineswegs immer so verstanden worden ist! Zur Wirkungsgeschichte vgl. ULRICH LUZ, Das Evangelium nach Matthäus, 4. Teilband (EKK I/4), Düsseldorf/Zürich/Neukirchen-Vluyn 2002, 444–459.

Strittig war und ist vor allem die Katholizität im römisch-katholischen und orthodoxen Verständnis einerseits, in der Auffassung der Reformatoren andererseits. Während für das Lehramt der römisch-katholischen Kirche nach wie vor gilt, dass die wahre »katholische« Kirche in ihrer Fülle nur in der sichtbaren, bischöflich geleiteten und rechtlich geordneten römisch-katholischen Kirche unter und mit dem Papst wirklich besteht,[36] waren die Reformatoren selbstverständlich ebenso von der Katholizität ihrer Kirchen überzeugt und vermochten zugleich eine katholische Kirche überall dort anzuerkennen, wo und sofern die reine Verkündigung des Evangeliums und die Feier der Sakramente stiftungsgemäß erfolgten und erfahrbar waren, also auch in mit dem Papst verbundenen Kirchen.

Es geht hier nicht darum, die fundamentaltheologischen, ekklesiologischen und kirchenrechtlichen Bemühungen um die Einheit der Kirche und das Verständnis ihrer Katholizität näher zu erörtern. Wichtig ist vor allem, dass zahlreiche Auffassungen von gegebener und/oder aufgegebener kirchlicher Einheit sowie ökumenische Zielvorstellungen sehr wohl vereinbar sind mit einer Verschiedenheit hinsichtlich der individuellen und gemeinschaftlichen Äußerungsformen des christlichen Glaubens, in der Glaubenslehre, in den Ordnungen der Kirchen und in einem Pluralismus kirchlicher Lehrbildungen.[37] Aber dem als

---

[36] Lat. *subsistit*. In der amtlichen deutschen Übersetzung »ist verwirklicht« (DSH 4119). Diese berühmte Formulierung der dogmatischen Konstitution »Lumen Gentium« (8) des Zweiten Vatikanischen Konzils ist seither immer wieder diskutiert worden, ohne dass zu erkennen wäre, dass das Lehramt damit eine wirkliche Anerkennung anderer Kirchen als Kirchen (im Vollsinne) intendieren würde, was jedoch nach Ansicht vieler und m.E. theologisch durchaus möglich, ja geboten wäre.

[37] Siehe dazu HARDING MEYER, Ökumenische Zielvorstellungen, Göttingen 1996. Quellen: HARDING MEYER/HANS JÖRG URBAN/LUKAS VISCHER (Hrsg.), Dokumente wachsender Übereinstimmung, bisher drei Bände, Paderborn/Frankfurt a.M. 1983ff. – CHRISTOPH SCHWÖBEL betont zurecht, dass die Wahrheitsgewissheit von Christenmenschen im Blick auf ihren Glauben unaufhebbar plural ist, weil für sie die Glaubensfreiheit in dem menschlicher Verfügung entzogenen und gegenüberstehenden »Wort Gottes« ihren Grund hat. Darum ist der sanktionierende Zugriff auf den Glauben anderer ein illegitimer Übergriff. »Wird der Pluralismus aus der Perspektive des christlichen Glaubens begriffen, ist er im strengen Sinne als *Pluralismus aus Glauben* zu begreifen.« (Art. Pluralismus II, 732) Wie eine derart »notwendig plurale Gestalt des Glaubens« indes einen »universalen Wahrheitsanspruch impliziert«, ist nicht leicht zu sagen (ebd., 733). Man kommt hier nur weiter, wenn man a) zwischen Wahrheit und Wahrheits*anspruch* (Ansprüche sind fehlbar und bestreitbar) und b) zwischen dem unverfügbaren *Inhalt* und den menschlichen Zeugnissen darüber unterscheidet.

legitim angesehenen internen Pluralismus entspricht oft keine Anerkennungsbereitschaft in den Außenbeziehungen zu sachlich nahestehenden, gleichsam familienähnlichen Gemeinschaften. Die normative Zielvorstellung, die am ehesten einer komplexen Einheit Rechnung zu tragen vermag, welche von der der Kirche geschenkten Einheit einerseits, von der Verschiedenheit von Ritus, Lehre, Ordnung und Ethos andererseits, ausgeht, ist das Konzept bzw. »Modell gegenseitiger Anerkennung«.[38] Es hat seine Grundlage in der Einsicht und Überzeugung, dass die in Jesus Christus der Kirche aller Zeiten geschenkte und vorgegebene Einheit eine Vielfalt historischer Verwirklichungen freisetzt, die je auf ihre Weise die Fülle der Verheißungen Gottes aufnehmen und auf menschliche Weise repräsentieren, nicht kraft menschlicher Anstrengungen, sondern allein aufgrund der gnädigen Erwählung und Rechtfertigung aller Geschöpfe durch Gott. Daraus ist besonders in den lutherischen Kirchen das Konzept der »versöhnten Verschiedenheit« hergeleitet worden. Der Lutherische Weltbund hat schon 1984 in Budapest in diesem Sinne als »Ziel der Einheit« formuliert:

> Die Vielfalt in dieser Gemeinschaft (sc. konfessionell verschiedener Kirchen, WL) ergibt sich aus der Verschiedenheit der kulturellen und ethnischen Situationen, in denen sich die eine Kirche Christi verwirklicht, und aus der Vielzahl der kirchlichen Traditionen, in denen der apostolische Glaube durch die Jahrhunderte hindurch bewahrt, weitergegeben und gelebt worden ist. Indem diese Verschiedenheiten als Ausprägungen des einen apostolischen Glaubens und der einen allgemeinen christlichen Kirche anerkannt werden, verändern sich kirchliche Traditionen, werden Gegensätze überwunden und wechselseitige Verwerfungen aufgehoben. Die Verschiedenheiten werden versöhnt und umgewandelt in eine legitime und lebensnotwendige Vielfalt innerhalb des einen Leibes Christi.[39]

Diese Formulierungen machen sehr schön die Verschränkungen eines internen (Gemeinschaft unterschiedlicher Kirchen) und externen (kulturelle und ethnische Situationen) Pluralismus deutlich und sind zugleich

---

Doch auch dann bleibt die Koinzidenz von Anspruch und Inhalt eine weiter begründungsbedürftige Behauptung.

[38] Dazu MEYER, Zielvorstellungen, 106–111.
[39] In: Budapest 1984. Bericht der Siebenten Vollversammlung des Lutherischen Weltbundes (LWB-Report Nr. 19/20, 1985, 183). Schon 1977 hatte der LWB in Daressalam für ein Konzept der »Einheit in versöhnter Verschiedenheit« plädiert; siehe MEYER, Zielvorstellungen, 67.

geeignet, die Engführungen einer eurozentrischen Perspektive hinter sich zu lassen. Dem korrespondiert auf römisch-katholischer Seite zwar nicht die bisherige Position des Lehramtes, wohl aber etlicher Theologinnen und Theologen, wie beispielsweise Johannes Brosseders Verständnis der *communio* selbständiger Kirchen in der Ökumene.[40]

2.2 Pfingstlerisch-charismatische Positionen

Die bisherigen Beobachtungen beziehen sich durchweg auf Kirchen oder Kirchengemeinschaften, die sich als Institutionen durch einen hohen Organisationsgrad auszeichnen (rechtliche Ordnung, Ämter, Professionalisierung, Regeln der Lebensführung, Mitgliedschaftsrollen, klare Eintritts-/Austrittsregelungen etc.), also auf einen anstaltlichen Kirchentypus.[41] Anders sieht es in freien, nicht-anstaltlichen religiösen Gemeinschaften aus, die Weber – nicht wertend! – als »Sekten« typisiert und zu denen man die unübersehbare Fülle von freien religiösen

---

[40] Siehe seinen Vortrag: Ökumene baut Brücken. Ökumene auf dem Weg zum Reformationsjubiläum 2017 (Wir sind Kirche, März 2014). Vgl. ders./JOACHIM TRACK, Kirchengemeinschaft jetzt! Die Kirche Jesu Christi, die Kirchen und ihre Gemeinschaft, Neukirchen-Vluyn 2010.

[41] Vgl. dazu MAX WEBER, Wirtschaft und Gesellschaft, a.a.O., 692–708; ders., Wirtschaft und Gesellschaft. Herrschaft (MWS I, 22-4), a.a.O., 172–195; ders., »Kirchen« und »Sekten« in Nordamerika. Eine kirchen- und sozialpolitische Skizze (zuerst 1906), in: ders., Asketischer Protestantismus und Kapitalismus. Schriften und Reden 1904–1911 (MWG I/9), Tübingen 2014, 436–462. Für die Ausgabe seiner Gesammelte(n) Aufsätze zur Religionssoziologie, Bd. I, hat Weber den Text stark überarbeitet (Tübingen 1920 = ⁶1972, 207–236; soll in MWG I/18 erscheinen). Webers klassische Definition lautet: »Eine ›Kirche‹ will eine ›Anstalt‹ sein, eine Art göttlicher Fideikommißstiftung zur Seelenrettung der Einzelnen, die in sie *hineingeboren* werden und für sie prinzipiell *Objekt* ihrer an das ›Amt‹ gebundenen Leistung sind. Eine ›Sekte‹ – nach der hier ad hoc geschaffenen Terminologie, die selbstredend von den ›Sekten‹ selbst nicht verwendet werden würde – ist dagegen eine freie Gemeinschaft lediglich religiös *qualifizierter* Individuen, in welche der Einzelne kraft beiderseits freier Entschließung *aufgenommen* wird.« (MWG I/19, 448) An Weber anknüpfend PIERRE BOURDIEU, Religion, Berlin 2011: »Die Konstituierung eines religiösen Feldes ist das Ergebnis der Monopolisierung der Verwaltung von Heilsgütern durch ein *Korps von religiösen Spezialisten*« (45). NIKLAS LUHMANN hat zwar gesehen, dass man mit dem Konzept der »Anstalt« bei weitem nicht alle relevanten kirchlichen Organisationstypen erfassen kann und gefordert, »auf die Vielgestaltigkeit des Vorkommens von Organisationen im weltgesellschaftlichen Religionssystem zu achten«, hat dergleichen aber selbst nicht behandelt (Die Religion der Gesellschaft, Frankfurt a.M. 2000, 229f). Siehe aber die Luhmann-Rezeption bei PETER BEYER, Religions in Global Society, London/New York 2006.

Gemeinschaftsbildungen rechnen muss. Ihre typische frühneuzeitliche Gestalt bilden jene Gruppen und Bewegungen wie die Täufer (Mennoniten, Amish People, Hutterer, Brethren usw.), die, zahlreichen Verfolgungen zum Trotz, sich als staatsfreie Gemeinschaften aufgrund individueller Zugehörigkeitswahl gebildet haben und, obwohl zuerst ganz binnenorientiert und von der Außenwelt abgesondert, enorme Außenwirkungen gewonnen haben. Sodann sind die weiteren freikirchlich organisierten, oft durch den Pietismus in seinen vielen Formen geprägten Gemeinschaften zu nennen, die das der Entwicklung des persönlichen Glaubens dienende Gemeinschaftsleben mit weit nach Übersee ausgreifenden missionarischen Aktivitäten verbunden haben, wie beispielsweise die Herrnhuter. Seit dem 18. und insbesondere im 20. Jahrhundert traten im Anschluss an ältere Entwicklungen die weltweit sich ausbreitenden pfingstlerischen und charismatischen Gemeinden mitsamt ihren globalen Netzwerken hervor, welche in den letzten Jahrzehnten die größten Zuwachsraten aller christlichen Gemeinden zu verzeichnen haben, insbesondere in der südlichen Hemisphäre.[42] Ihre Sozialgestalten reichen von kleinsten Garagengemeinden mit einer einzigen Leiterin oder einem Leiter bis zu Megachurches, die wie moderne Großkonzerne geführt werden. Teilweise zeichnen sich diese Gemeinschaften durch Merkmale aus, wie sie schon Max Weber herausgestellt hat (persönliche Berufung durch Geisterfahrungen, Bedeutung führender Charismatiker, Einbeziehung breiter sozialer Schichten, Gemeindeautonomie, Überwindung der Trennung von Klerikern und

---

[42] »The Southern Shift of Christianity« ist die Kurzformel einer Diagnose, die in Europa bisher nur ganz unzureichend zur Kenntnis genommen worden ist; siehe den Beitrag dieses Titels von PAUL GIFFORD, in: BURLACIOIU/HERMANN, Veränderte Landkarten, 189–205. Zur Geschichte und Verbreitung der Pfingstbewegung, die auch als »die Religion der Globalisierung« bezeichnet wurde (STEFAN REIS SCHWEIZER, NZZ v. 17.05.2013), siehe ganz knapp MARCO FRENSCHKOWSKI, Art. Pfingstbewegung/Pfingstkirchen, in: RGG[4], Bd. 6, 1232–1235; ALLAN H. ANDERSON, The Pentecostal and Charismatic Movements, in: MCLEOD (Hrsg.), World Christianities, 89–106. Umfassend angelegt: WALTER J. HOLLENWEGER, Charismatisch-pfingstliches Christentum. Herkunft – Situation – Ökumenische Chancen, Göttingen 1997; PETER ZIMMERLING, Charismatische Bewegungen, Göttingen 2009; ALLAN H. ANDERSON u.a. (Hrsg.), Studying Global Pentecostalism. Theories and Methods, Berkeley 2010. Zur Kritik der USA- und Europazentrierten Geschichtsschreibung der Pfingstbewegung vgl. ALLAN H. ANDERSON, Pfingstliche Geschichtsschreibung in globaler Perspektive. Eine Revision, in: JÖRG HAUSTEIN/ GIOVANNI MALTESE (Hrsg.), Handbuch pfingstliche und charismatische Theologie, Göttingen 2014, 135–159; im Blick auf Asien siehe ders./EDMOND TANG (Hrsg.), Asian and Pentecostal. The Charismatic Face of Christianity in Asia, Baguio City (Philippinen) 2005.

Laien, ethischer Rigorismus etc.), aber in der Weltgesellschaft der Gegenwart sind noch viele weitere, kontextspezifische Merkmale hinzugekommen, welche selbstverständlich keineswegs für alle diese Gemeinschaften gelten: politisches Engagement,[43] überlappende Zugehörigkeiten[44] und durchaus auch theologische Gespräche zwischen traditionellen Kirchen und wachsenden pfingstlerischen Gemeinschaften.[45] Die weltweiten, soweit ich sehe: überwiegend nichthierarchischen Kooperationen und Kommunikationen zwischen diesen Gemeinschaften haben ihre globale Ausbreitung beflügelt.[46]

Vertreten die pfingstlerisch-charismatischen Gemeinden spezifische Konzeptionen kirchlicher Einheit, in denen womöglich ausdrücklich auf Erfahrungen und Herausforderungen des sozialen, kulturellen und religiösen Pluralismus Bezug genommen wird? Eine Antwort ist mir aus etlichen Gründen schwierig bis unmöglich. Erstens sind diese Gemeinden als Teil einer weltweiten Bewegung selbst ursprünglich pluralistisch verfasst. Zweitens ist es immer wieder zu Trennungen, Spaltungen, aber auch zu Annäherungen und Betonung von Gemeinsamkeiten gekommen. Drittens scheint diesen Gemeinden eine übergreifende, repräsentative Autorität, womöglich in Verbindung mit bürokratischen Strukturen, wesensfremd zu sein. Viertens sind sie durch die jeweiligen gesellschaftlichen Kontexte so nachhaltig geprägt, dass es ziemlich unwahrscheinlich ist, dass allgemein konsensfähige ekklesiologische Auffassungen intendiert und gebildet werden. Und fünftens scheint die Betonung der Geisterfahrung und der individuellen

---

[43] Einen Überblick gibt PAUL PRESTON, Evangelicals and Politics in Africa, Asia and Latin America, Cambridge 2001. Zu Brasilien siehe RUDOLF VON SINNER, The Churches and Democracy in Brazil. Towards a Public Theology Focuzed on Citizenship, Eugene, OR 2012, 240–274. Dieser Befund widerspricht MAX WEBERS Behauptung, dass eine »Sekte« ein »spezifisch antipolitisches oder doch apolitisches Gebilde« sei (Wirtschaft und Gesellschaft, 724; MWS I/22-4, 214). Ob die von Weber diagnostizierte »Wahlverwandtschaft mit der Struktur der Demokratie« »auf der Hand liegt«, ist ebenfalls heute zu relativieren.

[44] Zu Ghana siehe CEPHAS OMENYO, Pentecost Outside Pentecostalism. A Study of the Development of Charismatic Renewal in the Mainline Churches in Ghana, Zoetermeer 2002.

[45] Siehe VELI-MATTI KÄRKKÄINEN, Die Pfingstbewegung und der Anspruch auf Apostolizität. Ein Essay zur ökumenischen Ekklesiologie, in: HAUSTEIN/MALTESE, Handbuch pfingstliche und charismatische Theologie, 430–448.

[46] Die sozialen Gestalten pfingstlerisch-charismatischer Gemeinschaften sind inzwischen so bunt und heterogen, dass man sie mit den von Max Weber gebildeten Typen nicht mehr hinreichend erfassen kann, so nützlich diese in heuristischer Absicht bleiben mögen.

Berufung und Bekehrung in Spannung zu stehen zur Ausbildung einer übergreifenden, integrierenden theologischen Lehre und zur Bildung einer Art bürokratischer Organisation.

Angesichts der internen Vielfalt dieser Bewegungen wird man Generalisierungen vermeiden wollen. Immerhin sehe ich jedoch mindestens vier Tendenzen ekklesiologischer Reflexion und Verständigung nach innen wie nach außen: Erstens ist nicht in allen, aber in sehr vielen charismatisch-pfingstlichen Gemeinden ein starkes soziales Engagement zu beobachten.[47] Die Gemeinde weiß sich sozial verantwortlich. Das korreliert mit der sozialen Herkunft zahlreicher Mitglieder, kann sich freilich im Zeitverlauf und durch soziale Mobilität auch wieder ändern. Zweitens scheinen sehr viele dieser Gemeinschaften zunächst einem kongregationalistischen Kirchenverständnis mit der Betonung der Selbständigkeit jeder Einzelgemeinde zu folgen, aber es ist unübersehbar, dass damit koordinierte, gemeinsam verwaltete und finanzierte Aktivitäten (Presse, Schule, Medien) vereinbar sind.[48] Drittens gibt es allerdings auf der anderen Seite längst Mega-Churches pentekostaler Herkunft und Prägung, die wie ein expansionsfreudiger Medienkonzern geführt werden, mithin von ihren Ressourcen in genau der Weise Gebrauch machen, wie es in ihrer gesellschaftlichen Umwelt durchaus üblich ist.[49] Und viertens finden seit geraumer Zeit (1978) Gespräche zwischen Pfingstlern und Katholiken zu ekklesiologischen Fragen statt, bei denen nicht die kontroversträchtigen Merkmale der Einheit, Heiligkeit und Katholizität der Kirche im Zentrum stehen, sondern die weit weniger strittige Apostolizität, diese wieder in einem

---

[47] MAX WEBER hat bei »Erlösungsreligionen« eine »antikapitalistische Gesinnung und Sozialpolitik« erkennen wollen (Wirtschaft und Gesellschaft, 717; MWS I/22-4, 206), aber heutzutage gibt es auch charismatische Gemeinschaften, die die Förderung des innerweltlichen Reichtums verheißen und primär zu dessen Erlangung Askese fordern und praktizieren.

[48] HOLLENWEGER, Charismatisch-pfingstliches Christentum, erwähnt, dass unter schwedischen Pentekostalen zeitweise »die Ideologie der Nicht-Organisation ... den Status eines Glaubensbekenntnisses« hatte, aber dann doch organisatorische Formen entwickelt wurden (290f). Hollenweger meint, dass, was Weber die »Veralltäglichung des Charisma« genannt habe, etwas qualitativ Anderes bezeichne als der Begriff des »charisma« bei Paulus.

[49] Als Beispiel steht mir die »Yoido Full Gospel Church« in Südkorea vor Augen. Sie wurde 1958 gegründet, hatte 2012 in Südkorea 780.000 Mitglieder und weltweit nach eigenen Angaben zudem über eine Million Anhänger. Ihr Zentrum liegt in Seoul auf der Insel Yoido im Han-Fluss, dort, wo Parlament und zahlreiche Konzernzentralen errichtet sind, oder wie manche sagen: Koreas Wallstreet.

doppelten Sinne, nämlich der Orientierung aller Kirchen am gemeinsamen Ursprung des apostolischen Zeugnisses und ihrem gemeinsamen Sendungsauftrag in alle Welt.[50]

3 Pluralismus als normative Herausforderung

Um mit tatsächlichen Differenzierungen und Pluralisierungen umgehen zu können, gibt es wahrscheinlich nicht sehr viele Grundalternativen mit normativem Gehalt. Wenn man grundsätzlich bereit ist, einen internen oder externen Pluralismus als unvermeidlich und/oder legitim zu akzeptieren, stellen sich Fragen nach den zustimmungsfähigen Möglichkeiten und Grenzen einer wechselseitigen Anerkennung der unterschiedenen Größen.

Ich möchte fünf Grundformen des Umganges mit interner Vielfalt unterscheiden, die normative Elemente enthalten:

- die Durchsetzung einer meist »hierarchischen« Herrschaftsordnung[51] (Rangordnung sowie häufig Monopolisierung von Herrschafts- und Entscheidungskompetenzen), häufig unter Rezeption analoger weltlicher Strukturen,
- die Institutionalisierung geordneter Funktionen, Ämter und Regelwerke innerhalb einer Gemeinschaft aufgrund von Wahlen und (zwanglosem) Konsens aller intern Beteiligten und Berechtigten,
- die Institutionalisierung einer partizipationsfreundlichen Verfahrensordnung zur konsensorientierten Konfliktbearbeitung (multizentrale Organisation, konziliare bzw. synodale Vertretungen),
- die Entwicklung charismatischer und tendenziell eher egalitärer, bisweilen jedoch auch autoritärer Gemeinschaftsbeziehungen mit

---

[50] Siehe KÄRKKÄINEN, Die Pfingstbewegung und der Anspruch auf Apostolizität. Er umschreibt ein anerkennungsfähiges ekklesiologisches »Minimum« von sieben Merkmalen der Apostolizität, dass von Pfingstlern wie von Katholiken (und selbstredend auch von vielen Protestanten) geteilt werden kann (444).

[51] Das Verständnis und die Begriffe von »Hierarchie« enthalten zahlreiche Probleme, die hier nicht weiter verfolgt werden können. MAX WEBER spricht von »hierokratischer Herrschaft« in einem soziologisch-deskriptiven, nicht normativen Sinn (Wirtschaft und Gesellschaft, 688–726, MWS I/22-4, 172–216; dort speziell zur Entwicklung der Kirche zur Hierokratie 692f bzw. 177f), während in Ekklesiologien und Kirchenrecht konfessionell geprägte und folgerichtig teilweise unterschiedliche, teilweise unvereinbare Auffassungen von Hierarchie begegnen; siehe SIEGFRIED WIEDENHOFER u.a., Art. Hierarchie, RGG⁴, Bd. 3, 1724–1726.

horizontalen Vernetzungen, verbunden mit einer großen Gestaltungsflexibilität und bisweilen erheblicher Ferne zu weltlichen Rechtsordnungen,
- einen normativ weitgehend entleerten, unter Umständen wachsenden Indifferentismus gegenüber Ordnungen, Kompetenzen und Verfahren (Neutralisierung von Geltungsansprüchen durch faktische Nicht-Beachtung von Unterschieden und Gleichgültigkeit gegenüber Abweichungen).

Diese Grundformen, als Idealtypen verwendbar, haben wiederum Ursprünge oder zumindest Analogien in weltlichen Ordnungskonzepten. Sie können selbstverständlich konkret in Mischformen auftreten, beispielsweise wenn auf der einen Seite, etwa von Amtsträgern, Urteils- und Entscheidungskompetenzen beansprucht werden, die etliche Betroffene auf der anderen Seite durch schlichte Nichtbefolgung leerlaufen lassen können.[52] Sodann begegnen Mischformen, z.B. von Hierarchie und Egalität in charismatischen Gemeinschaften, und dies wiederum sowohl als tatsächliche, empirisch feststellbare Gegebenheiten wie als normativ-kontrafaktische Unterstellungen.[53] Schließlich gilt für alle fünf Typen, dass sie historischen Veränderungen und Fortbildungen unterliegen.

Diese Typen von interner Pluralitäts-Bewältigung in religiösen Gemeinschaften wiederum können aufgrund freier geistlicher Einsichten, theologischer Reflexionen und interner Entscheidungen der Mitglieder der entsprechenden Gruppen oder Institutionen, aber auch unter dem Einfluss nicht-religiöser, externer Kräfte (politische Machtverhältnisse, Prinzipien, Urteile und Verordnungen innerhalb einer Rechtsordnung, emanzipatorische Ansprüche, finanzielle Anreize usw.) oder aufgrund einer Mischung von verschiedenen dieser Elemente zustande kommen. Dieser letzte Aspekt ist insofern wichtig, weil es dabei um Relationen zwischen Ordnungsformen unterschiedlicher Art und Herkunft geht, so wie das kirchliche Recht in seiner Geschichte zwar zahlreiche eigenständige religiöse Wurzeln hatte und nach wie vor hat, aber im guten Sinne opportunistisch auch nicht-religiös begründete Rechtsnormen

---

[52] So vielfach im Blick auf die normativen Geltungsansprüche kirchlicher Sexualethik.
[53] Zum orthodoxen Verständnis von Hierarchie ist zu lesen: »Jede Ebene der Hierarchie hat als Grundprinzip die Struktur primus inter pares, d.h. den Primat innerhalb der Kollegialität, die gegenseitige Abhängigkeit und Verantwortung.« So DANIEL CIOBOTEA, Art. Hierarchie 2., RGG⁴, Bd. 3, 1726. Wie es mit der Entstehung von (charismatischen) Hierarchien in Pfingstgemeinden aussieht, entzieht sich meiner Kenntnis, aber ich halte dergleichen für wahrscheinlich.

der jeweiligen Gesellschaften, Epochen und Ordnungen aufnehmen, umformen und inkorporieren konnte.

Auf die Fälle der externen Pluralität, d.h. im Außenverhältnis verschiedener Religionsgemeinschaften in einem Staat, in einer rechtlich geordneten Staatengemeinschaft oder in der Weltgesellschaft können die fünf Typen der internen Pluralitäts-Bewältigung nur in modifizierten Formen übertragen werden. Das aber ist möglich. Dabei kommt im Zuge der neueren Globalisierungs- und Migrationsprozesse eine wichtige weitere Komplikation hinzu, die in gewisser Weise gegenüber dem Dualismus von »extern – intern« eine dritte Variante hinzufügt. Diese zeigt sich darin, dass die interne plurale Differenzierung von Religionsgemeinschaften diese dazu veranlassen muss, zwischen dem (legitimen) Pluralismus von Mitgliedern einer Konfessions- oder Kirchenfamilie einerseits (Kirchen der Reformation, Kirchen und kirchliche Gemeinschaften der Christenheit) und der faktischen, in ihrer Bedeutung strittigen Pluralität unterschiedlicher Weltreligionen (Buddhismus, Hinduismus, Judentum, Christentum, Islam) zu unterscheiden, die beide wiederum einem säkularen Pluralismus gegenüber stehen können. Hier kann man bei den Konfessionsfamilien der Christenheit vielfach eine Entwicklung von feindlicher Ab- und Ausgrenzung zu geschwisterlicher Anerkennung beobachten, nicht selten unter dem Druck externer Kräfte, während zwischen den Weltreligionen bisher – abgesehen vom Verhältnis Judentum – Christentum – eher Abgrenzung und mehr oder minder friedliche Koexistenz, aber nicht wirkliche Anerkennung (von Gleichen) zu beobachten ist. Indes zeigt gerade die Christentumsgeschichte, dass die Überführung von externen Abgrenzungen (scharfe Konfessionalisierung) in interne Differenzierungen (»versöhnte Verschiedenheit«) möglich ist.

Der äußere Rahmen der Regelung pluralistischer Verhältnisse kann freilich nicht von einer einzelnen Größe, konkret: einer bestimmten Religionsgemeinschaft in diesem Feld bestimmt werden, wenn Gleichheit und Freiheit aller anderen religiösen Gemeinschaften gewahrt werden sollen. Genau dies wurde und wird aber immer wieder versucht, insbesondere dann, wenn eine Religionsgemeinschaft zahlenmäßig dominiert und erfolgreich eine Position überlegener oder monopolartiger Deutungs- und Entscheidungsmacht beansprucht. Das war der Fall in zahlreichen Konstellationen der Geschichte der Christenheit (Staatskirchen) ebenso wie dort, wo der Islam oder der Hinduismus Alleingeltungsansprüche erhoben haben, allenfalls verbunden mit Toleranzgewährung für prinzipiell nicht gleichgestellte Angehörige anderer Religionen. Ein entscheidender Test dafür, ob eine Religionsgemeinschaft im säkular-normativen Sinne pluralismusfähig ist, ist die Beantwortung der Frage, ob sie in Achtung der Religionsfreiheit eines jeden Menschen eine Konversion bzw. einen Religionswechsel sowohl als Zuwendung wie als Abwendung zulässt, nicht behindert, sondern zumindest akzeptiert, wenn nicht sogar als legitim anerkennt.[54]

Es scheint nun vielfach so zu sein, dass nur eine externe, religionsneutrale, überlegene Macht die Freiheit jeder Religionsausübung[55] und zugleich einen Pluralismus der Gleichheit und Nicht-Diskriminierung zwischen Religionsgemeinschaften dauerhaft durchsetzen und sichern kann, obwohl es grundsätzlich auch möglich, wenngleich historisch überaus selten ist, dass Religionen aufgrund der freien Anerkennung eines allgemeinen, weltlichen, von ihnen geteilten Verständnisses von Religionsfreiheit aus eigener Einsicht eine solche Form gegenseitiger Anerkennung praktizieren.[56] Anerkennung aber heißt weder Gleichgültigkeit noch Versöhnung. Aufgrund religiöser Überzeugung bejahte Anerkennungsverhältnisse sind sicher nicht von der Art, dass nunmehr alle Gegensätze religiöser Überzeugungen, der Riten, der Lehre und des Ethos angeglichen oder aufgehoben würden, sondern sie müssen mit bleibenden, äußerst scharfen Konflikten vereinbar sein. Zugespitzt gesagt: Externe Pluralität muss mit unversöhnten Wahrheits- und praktischen Geltungsansprüchen vereinbart werden, und die erste Bedingung dafür ist, dass der harte Kampf zwischen religiösen und weltanschaulichen Überzeugungen ohne jede Gewalt ausgetragen wird.

---

[54] Zu diesem historisch und aktuell äußerst schwierigen Problem im interreligiösen Verkehr siehe CHRISTINE LIENEMANN-PERRIN/WOLFGANG LIENEMANN (Hrsg.), Religiöse Grenzüberschreitungen. Studien zu Bekehrung, Konfessions- und Religionswechsel/Crossing Religious Borders. Studies on Conversion and Religious Belonging, Wiesbaden 2012.

[55] Wie andere Freiheitsrechte unterliegt auch die individuelle und kollektive Religionsfreiheit bestimmten Grenzen, insbesondere solchen, die aufgrund der Gewährleistung anderer Menschenrechte unabdingbar sind, aber auch jener Grenzen, die durch die für alle Bürger verbindlichen Gesetze bestimmt sind. Zu dieser »Schrankenklausel« siehe für Deutschland WOLFGANG BOCK, Das für alle geltende Gesetz und die kirchliche Selbstbestimmung, Tübingen 1996. Unter Bedingungen einer religiös pluralistischen Gesellschaft müssen diese Grundsätze auf alle Religionsgemeinschaften angemessen angewendet werden; siehe dazu JOST-BENJAMIN SCHROOTEN, Gleichheitssatz und Religionsgemeinschaften, Tübingen 2015 (im Druck).

[56] Das ist z.B. dann der Fall, wenn eine Religionsgemeinschaft *aufgrund* ihrer eigenen religiösen Überzeugung, theologischen Argumentation und konkreten Entscheidung zu dem Schluss kommt, dass ein rein weltlicher Staat von Gott geboten, ein *mandatum Dei* ist, wie es der V. Barmer These von 1934 entspricht.

4 Faktische Verschiedenheiten und normative Integrationskonzepte in der Weltgesellschaft

Nicht erst für die heutige Weltgesellschaft ist das Zugleich von Vereinheitlichung und Zerfall, zentralistischen Bestrebungen und zentrifugalen Kräften, Integration und Desintegation, Inklusion und Exklusion charakteristisch. Die aktuelle Lage und Entwicklung der Weltchristenheit zeigt ähnliche ambivalente Tendenzen der Differenzierung und Pluralisierung, nicht selten unter Schwächung oder Verlust übergreifender Einheitsvorstellungen. Auf der globalen politischen Ebene ist die Debatte über Universalismus und Partikularismus der Menschenrechte, damit zugleich über die Wünschbarkeit und Möglichkeit einer globalen Friedensordnung, ein analoges Schlüsselthema.[57] Ob die UN in ihrer derzeitigen Gestalt den Erfordernissen einer globalen Friedensordnung auch nur ansatzweise gerecht zu werden vermögen, ist ebenso eine offene Frage[58] wie die nach der künftigen institutionellen Integration der EU[59] und der denkbaren, womöglich notwendigen Entwicklung hin zu einer »Konstitutionalisierung des Völkerrechts«[60] – Entwicklungen, die in ihrer Interdependenz geeignet sind, gewaltarme, friedliche Formen eines globalen Pluralismus zu fördern und zu sichern – diesseits geteilter Rechtsauffassungen, jenseits neokolonialer Bevormundungen.

Damit sind der Bezugsrahmen und die Ebene angesprochen, hinsichtlich derer ich theologische Konzepte von Einheit und Verschiedenheit und sozialwissenschaftliche und sozialphilosophische Überlegungen zu Möglichkeit und Wünschbarkeit einer Weltordnung nach Rechtsprinzipien in Beziehung setzen möchte. Dabei ist durchgehend wichtig, zwischen empirischen Befunden und normativen Konzepten zu unterscheiden.

---

[57] Vgl. GEORG LOHMANN u.a. (Hrsg.), Die Menschenrechte – unteilbar und gleichgewichtig?, Potsdam 2005.
[58] Zu Reformvorschlägen für das System der UN siehe ERNST-OTTO CZEMPIEL, Die Reform der UNO. Möglichkeiten und Mißverständnisse, München 1994.
[59] Vgl. JÜRGEN HABERMAS, Zur Verfassung Europas. Ein Essay, Berlin 2011.
[60] Wie sie JÜRGEN HABERMAS im Anschluss an Kant diskutiert hat: Eine politische Verfassung für die pluralistische Weltgesellschaft?, in: ders., Zwischen Naturalismus und Religion, Frankfurt a.M. 2005, 324–365, hier 326.

4.1 Funktionale Differenzierung der gesellschaftlichen Subsysteme von Politik und Religion

In den Sozialwissenschaften gibt es äußerst unterschiedliche Versuche, religiöse Gemeinschaftsbildungen wie Kirchen, »Sekten« oder »Bewegungen« zu analysieren und zu würdigen. Ich greife wenige Beispiele heraus. In der Religionssoziologie Max Webers wird vor allem die Bedeutung der religiösen Prägungen von Weltbildern und Wirtschaftsgesinnungen betont. Daneben und vielleicht noch wichtiger ist, dass Weber Religionsgemeinschaften immer auch unter herrschaftssoziologischen Aspekten und im Gegenüber zu staatlicher Herrschaft analysiert.[61] Exemplarisch betont Weber beispielsweise die Konflikte zwischen amtskirchlicher Hierarchie und Ordensgemeinschaften sowie diejenigen zwischen Propheten und Priestern im Kampf um die Herrschaft über die Laien.[62] Insgesamt hatte er ein gutes Gespür für die vielfältigen internen Konflikte von religiösen Gemeinschaftsbildungen und deren Folgen, insbesondere im Falle des »Puritanismus« und der entsprechenden »Gesinnungen«.

Eine systemtheoretisch begründete, normativ ganz enthaltsame Diagnose von gesellschaftlicher »Evolution« stellt Niklas Luhmanns Theorie der funktionalen Differenzierung dar,[63] die vor allem die relative Verselbständigung gesellschaftlicher Subsysteme wie Politik, Wirtschaft, Wissenschaft, Recht, Kunst etc. betont und in diesen Rahmen auch die Entwicklung von Religionssystemen einzeichnet. Religionsgemeinschaften sind danach relativ autonome soziale Subsysteme in einer komplexen Umwelt, die sich mit anderen Subsystemen austauschen und zugleich weitgehend selbständig reproduzieren.[64]

Demgegenüber ist die Theorie gesellschaftlicher Kommunikation, wie sie Jürgen Habermas vertritt, dadurch ausgezeichnet, dass sie die Prozesse gesellschaftlicher Differenzierung berücksichtigt, aber zugleich und insbesondere auch die normativen Gehalte konkurrierender Wahrheits- und Geltungsansprüche in der Sphäre sozialer und politischer Beziehungen, damit tendenziell auch im Verhältnis der Kirchen, Konfessionen und Religionsgemeinschaften untereinander und im

---

61 Wirtschaft und Gesellschaft, 688–726, MWS I/22-4, 172–216.
62 Wirtschaft und Gesellschaft, 275–279, jetzt: ders., Wirtschaft und Gesellschaft. Religiöse Gemeinschaften (MWS I/22-2, 35–40).
63 Die Gesellschaft der Gesellschaft, 413–594.
64 Die Religion der Gesellschaft, 210–216. 250–277, wo am Schluss ausdrücklich von »Weltreligionen« die Rede ist, ohne diese in der Sache weiter zu berücksichtigen.

Gegenüber zur politischen Öffentlichkeit und zu einer weltlichen Rechtsordnung als möglichen Gegenstandsbereich vernünftiger (Selbst-) Aufklärung der Menschen – und nicht nur der Glaubensgenossen – betont.[65] In ihrem Kern setzt diese Theorie auf die Möglichkeiten allgemeiner Regeln der Kommunikation, auf rationale und gemeinsam geteilte Rekonstruktionen von differenten Weltsichten und ihren elementaren Grundlagen sowie auf die Chance, über divergente Anschauungen und Konzepte zu einem argumentativ offenen Austausch von Gründen für Geltungsansprüche zu kommen, verbunden mit entsprechend rational ausweisbaren Forschungsverfahren.

So unterschiedlich diese Theorien konturiert sind, so gehen sie doch gemeinsam davon aus, a) dass Religionsgemeinschaften konstitutiv bezogen sind auf ihr gesellschaftliches Umfeld und sich in Wechselwirkungen mit diesem verändern – teils aus eigenem Antrieb, teils dazu extern veranlasst; b) dass es rationale Verfahren religionswissenschaftlicher und theologischer Forschung gibt oder geben kann/sollte, die zur Binnen- und Außenkommunikation von Religionsgemeinschaften in aufklärerischer Absicht beitragen können. Dabei ist allerdings c) umstritten, in welchem Verhältnis religiöse und säkulare (philosophische) Sprache zueinander stehen oder stehen sollten.[66] In dieser Konstellation ist es nicht angemessen und vertretbar, der religiösen Sprache, die ihrerseits unlösbar verbunden ist mit einer bestimmten Praxis, darauf bezogener Lehre und einem institutionellen Rahmen, lediglich ein apartes gesellschaftliches Funktionssystem zu reservieren, sondern es ist für diese Sprache, genauso wie für die philosophisch-säkulare Kommunikation, wesentlich, auf den Gesamtzusammenhang gesellschaftli-

---

[65] Siehe vor allem JÜRGEN HABERMAS, Vorpolitische Grundlagen des demokratischen Rechtsstaates?, ders., Religion in der Öffentlichkeit. Kognitive Voraussetzungen für den »öffentlichen Vernunftgebrauch« religiöser und säkularer Bürger, beides in: ders., Zwischen Naturalismus und Religion, Frankfurt a.M. 2005, 106–118 und 119–154; ders., Religion und nachmetaphysisches Denken. Eine Replik; ders., Ein Symposium über Glauben und Wissen. Replik auf Einwände, Reaktion auf Anregungen, beides in: ders., Nachmetaphysisches Denken II, Berlin 2012, 120–182 und 183–237.

[66] HABERMAS, Religion und nachmetaphysisches Denken. Eine Replik, hat seine Position in dieser Frage gegenüber einer ganzen Reihe von teils divergierenden, teils konvergierenden Auffassungen präzisiert. Darauf kann hier nicht weiter eingegangen werden außer mit zwei Hinweisen: Es ist im Verhältnis von jüdischen und christlichen Überlieferungen zur (säkularen) Philosophie wichtig, bei gänzlich verschiedenen religiösen und säkularen Ausgangspunkten immer wieder auf grundlegende Texte der Bibel zu *hören*, und es ist nötig, darüber miteinander zu *sprechen*.

cher Verhältnisse zu zielen, auch wenn die einzelne Rede oder Theorie ein derartiges Kohärenzpostulat nur annäherungsweise erfüllen kann. Unter diesen Voraussetzungen sind sowohl Streit zwischen beiden »Sprachen« als auch die Entdeckung von Analogien oder Wahlverwandtschaften möglich.

Ein klassisches Beispiel für solche (hypothetisch-veranschaulichenden) Analogie-Beobachtungen ist die Parallel-Konstellation im Titelblatt von Thomas Hobbes' »Leviathan« (1651), welches in der Doppelgestalt eines »Commonwealth Ecclesiasticall and Civill« dargestellt ist.[67] Natürlich lässt sich Hobbes' typisierende Zuordnung nicht auf eine rechtsstaatliche, demokratische Gesellschaft und eine föderalistisch verfasste, »Kantische« Weltrepublik übertragen, aber sie kann dazu anregen, nach heutigen analogen Beispielen zu fragen.

---

[67] Siehe dazu die Beiträge in PHILIPP MANOW/FRIEDBERT W. RÜB/DAGMAR SIMON (Hrsg.), Die Bilder des Leviathan. Eine Deutungsgeschichte, Baden-Baden 2012.

Non est potestas Super Terram quæ Comparetur ei Iob. 41. 24
LEVIATHAN
Or
THE MATTER, FORME and POWER of A COMMON-WEALTH ECCLESIASTICALL and CIVIL.
By THOMAS HOBBES of MALMESBURY.
London
Printed for Andrew Crooke
1651

In der unteren Hälfte des Leviathan-Titelblattes stehen sich jeweils fünf Symbole der weltlichen und der kirchlichen Macht gegenüber (ich gehe hier nur auf diesen Aspekt ein und blende den komplexen Zusammenhang des oberen Blattteiles ganz aus): Der Burg des Landesherrn steht der geschlossene Bau einer Kirche gegenüber; der weltlichen Krone korrespondiert die päpstliche Mitra; den Kanonen antworten die Blitze der exkommunizierenden, inquisitorischen Kirche; den Kampfsymbolen der Schlacht entsprechen die spitzen Waffen der Logik; der blutigen Schlacht im Felde ist die streng disziplinierte Disputation gegenübergestellt.

Hier soll nur die Form der Analogiebildung interessieren, um zu fragen, ob es möglich ist, im Blick auf Herausforderungen des Umganges zwar nicht mit ungebändigter Gewalt, sondern mit einer konfliktträchtigen, antagonistischen, dabei zur Gewalt hin offenen Pluralität vergleichbare korrespondierende Elemente (Institutionen, Prinzipien und Verfahren) zu bezeichnen, die der friedensfördernden Bearbeitung einer latent oder manifest konfliktreichen Pluralität zu dienen vermögen. Unter heutigen Bedingungen muss man selbstredend die Hobbes-Tafel der geistlichen und weltlichen Gewalt (*potestas*) mit anderen Merkmalen und Symbolen auszeichnen. Vielleicht so:

Politische Öffentlichkeiten und ihre Repräsentationen		Lebendige Gestalten von Kirche in *communio*
Prinzipien der Gewaltenteilung		Konziliare und/oder synodale Gremien und Verfahren
Rechtserhaltende Gewalt Polizei und völkerrechtlich legitimiertes Militär		Vom Kirchenvolk bestimmte Ordnungen und korrekte Verfahren
Öffentliche politische und rechtliche Auseinandersetzungen		Freie theologische Disputationen; argumentative Begründungspflichten
Internationale Gerichtshöfe mit Sanktionsvollmachten gegenüber Verletzern grundlegender Rechte		Konzilare/synodale Entscheidungen über Bedrohungen und Grenzen der Einheit wie der Vielfalt

4.3 Anerkennung legitimer Vielfalt und Durchsetzung fundamentaler Normen

Im Zuge der europäischen Religionskriege, deren Erfahrung das Werk des Thomas Hobbes geprägt hat, sind wenigstens drei übergreifende Einsichten gereift, die einen harten normativen Kern enthalten:

– Gesellschaftliche Konflikte, nicht zuletzt solche religiöser Art, sind unvermeidlich, aber sie können und müssen durch einen den Religionen gegenüber unabhängigen, an Recht und Gesetz gebundenen Staat bzw. eine religionsunabhängige Rechtsordnung mit der Kompetenz zur Durchsetzung eines legitimen staatlichen oder überstaatlichen Gewaltmonopols eingegrenzt werden.

– Glaubens- und Religionsfreiheit sowie religiöse Verschiedenheit werden kontextspezifisch ermöglicht, geschützt und begrenzt, soweit sich die Religionsgemeinschaften in ihren Handlungen und ihrer öffentlichen Wirksamkeit an die Grundregeln der geltenden politischen Ordnung halten.

– Interner Pluralismus von Religionsgemeinschaften ist als Gestalt religiöser individueller und gemeinschaftlicher Religionsfreiheit gegen externe Eingriffe geschützt, und zwar so weit, dass a) Individuen ihre verpflichtende Zugehörigkeit frei wählen können und b) soweit Pluralismus nicht die für alle Bürger und Menschen geltenden Rechte und Pflichten verletzt.[68]

– In welcher Form Religionsgemeinschaften und Kirchen wiederum ihrerseits auf die gesellschaftliche und staatliche Ordnung einwirken können und dürfen, hängt weitgehend von den jeweiligen gesellschaftlichen Traditionen, Kräften und Strukturen ab. Grundsätzlich müssen sie sich an öffentlichen Diskursen frei, paritätisch und ohne Diskriminierungen beteiligen können.

Zwar hat es Jahrhunderte gebraucht, bis diese und verwandte Grundsätze nach und nach in Staaten und Religionsgemeinschaften Anerkennung gefunden haben. Diese Anerkennung ist in der heutigen Staatenwelt freilich alles andere als universal und bildet insofern ein durchaus unvollendetes Projekt der Moderne aus dem Geist der Aufklärung, mit zahlreichen Wurzeln in der vor allem europäischen Geistes- und

---

[68] Zur Verdeutlichung: Auch wenn in einem liberalen Rechtsstaat grundsätzlich die rechtliche Gleichheit von Frauen und Männern gewährleistet ist, impliziert das nicht ein Recht oder eine Pflicht des Staates, diese Gleichheit auch innerkirchlich notfalls mit Sanktionen durchzusetzen, *sofern* es den Einzelnen freisteht, die entsprechende Gemeinschaft ohne Nachteile zu verlassen.

Sozialgeschichte. Die Grundtendenz ist, nicht nur im Blick auf europäische Entwicklungen, hinreichend eindeutig: Ein Konsens über fundamentale, unverzichtbare, rechtliche Normen des Zusammenlebens bei gleichzeitiger Anerkennung und Förderung legitimer Vielfalt von kulturellen Besonderheiten, Religionen, moralischen Überzeugungen und entsprechenden Lebensformen. Einen normativen Kern dieser (politisch-rechtlichen) Einheit von Verschiedenheit und Einheit bildeten in früheren Zeiten naturrechtliche Konzepte.[69] An ihre Stelle sind heute weithin die grundlegenden Menschenrechte getreten.[70] Diese fundamentalen Rechte werden durch Verfahren einer grundsätzlich freien und egalitären Kommunikation und Gewährleistungen sozialer Subsidiarität untermauert.

Eine offenkundige Grenze solcher normativen Konzepte mit universalem Anspruch besteht nun freilich darin, dass der Bezugsrahmen für die konkreten politisch-rechtlichen Integrationsmöglichkeiten durch historisch-partikulare staatliche Ordnungen bestimmt und begrenzt ist. Ermöglichung und Begrenzung von Pluralismus bedürfen staatlicher Regelungen, solange die Weltgesellschaft einer föderativen Verfassung mit basalen religionsverfassungsrechtlichen Elementen entbehrt. Viele schreckt genau diese letztere Vorstellung und Möglichkeit ab, allerdings aus unterschiedlichen Gründen. Während die einen Machtverlust durch Recht befürchten, sehen die anderen die Gefahren einer globalen »Ordnung«, die alle kulturellen Besonderheiten von Lebensformen unter sich begräbt. Das gilt nicht zuletzt für Religionsgemeinschaften, die tiefe Wurzeln in ihren Herkunftskulturen haben. Immanuel Kant hat mit seinem Konzept einer Völkerrechtsordnung und eines Kosmopolitismus die Grenzen einer globalen Rechtsordnung einerseits nüchtern analysiert, andererseits in normativer Absicht künftige Möglichkeiten

---

[69] Vgl. zu antiken und mittelalterlichen Positionen J. RUFUS FEARS, Natural Law. The Legacy of Greece and Rome, in: EDWARD B. MCLEAN (Hrsg.), Common Truths. New Perspectives on Natural Law, Wilmington, DE 2000, 19–56; JOHN JENKINS, Aquinas, Natural Law, and the Challenges of Diversity, in demselben Buch, 57–71.

[70] Inwiefern nicht-europäische Konzepte damit konvergieren, ist eine vielfach diskutierte Frage. Siehe dazu HEINER BIELEFELDT, Philosophie der Menschenrechte. Grundlagen eines weltweiten Freiheitsethos, Darmstadt 1998. Eine instruktive Studie im Blick auf die Bedeutung der konfuzianischen Tradition für moderne, pluralistische Gesellschaften ist JOSEPH CHAN, Confucian Perfectionism. A Political Philosophy for Modern Times, Princeton NJ 2014; ders., Confucianism and Human Rights, in: JOHN WITTE JR./M. CHRISTIAN GREEN (Hrsg.), Religion and Human Rights, New York/Oxford 2011, 87–102.

und Notwendigkeiten politisch-rechtlicher Art skizziert. Max Weber hat in zahlreichen Studien, nicht nur in jenen zur Wirtschaftsethik der Weltreligionen, eine global komparative Sicht der Weltreligionen und eine Typologie ihrer Grundgestalten entwickelt. Habermas und Luhmann haben ihre Sozialtheorien angesichts der Globalisierungsprozesse konsequent auf die Perspektive der Weltgesellschaft ausgerichtet und dabei in unterschiedlicher Weise auch die Rolle und Zukunft der Religionsgemeinschaften thematisiert – Habermas in einer besonders im Anschluss an Kant entwickelten, explizit normativen, menschenrechtlich fundierten Völkerrechtskonzeption, Luhmann in einer weitgehend normativ indifferenten Theorie der sozialen Evolution, die stark durch funktionale Differenzierungen bestimmt ist.

Diese Hinweise sollten darauf aufmerksam machen, dass es auf der Ebene (der Theorie) internationaler Beziehungen sehr wohl Institutionen und Verfahren gibt, die es erlauben, den konfliktträchtigen Pluralismus von Religionen, Traditionen, Interessen und Machtpositionen in einer übergreifenden Einheit nach Maßgabe fundamentaler Rechtsprinzipien anzuerkennen und zu begrenzen. Dieses Modell erinnert nicht zufällig an Immanuel Kants Grundprinzipien für einen »ewigen Frieden«, der keine irreale Utopie, sondern eine vernünftig kalkulierte politisch-republikanische Option darstellt. Es liegt an den Bürgern selbst, ob diese Möglichkeit realisiert wird.

4.4 Konvergenz von sozialwissenschaftlichen und theologischen Einheitsperspektiven?

Johannes Brosseder hat in seinem oben erwähnten Vortrag, der wohl als eine Art theologisch-ökumenisches Vermächtnis verstanden werden muss, analysiert, dass die meisten Kirchen der heutigen Weltgesellschaft und ihren Herausforderungen das Entscheidende schuldig bleiben, wenn sie nicht in der Lage sind, ihren Glauben gemeinsam zu bezeugen und konziliar zu verantworten. Er hat geschrieben:

> Im Unterschied zur Alten Kirche sind die Kirchen heute nicht in der Lage, angesichts bestimmter Herausforderungen den Glauben zu formulieren, der ›allgemein‹ geteilt wird, weil sie das Instrument des universalen bzw. ökumenischen Konzils nicht mehr haben. Katholizität und Ökumenizität der Kirche Jesu Christi sind dann wiedergewonnen, wenn die selbständigen und selbständig bleibenden Kirchen ihre Gemeinschaft, communio wieder aufnehmen. Dann können die Kirchen – z.B. auf einem Konzil – gemeinsam

Sorge tragen, angesichts bestimmter Herausforderungen einen Glauben zu formulieren, der tatsächlich ›allgemein‹ geglaubt wird. Das, was nicht alle glauben, gehört nicht in den katholischen Glaubensbegriff.[71]

Brosseder hat die der Kirche geschenkte Einheit als *communio* im Blick, und zwar in der Weise, dass er sie auf die Herausforderungen des Glaubens in der heutigen, pluralistischen Welt bezieht. Die Kirchen, so ergänze ich, haben der »Welt« gegenüber die Chance und die Pflicht, deutlich zu machen, dass und inwiefern ihre Einheit auch für die gewaltlose Integration einer pluralistisch bleibenden Weltgesellschaft von Bedeutung ist oder Bedeutung bekommen kann. Zugleich muss man sehen, dass die getrennten und zur *communio* berufenen Kirchen der Christenheit immer wieder erst von den »Weltkindern« lernen mussten, wie man unter Bedingungen gesellschaftlicher Pluralität auf gewaltfreie Weise Einheit und Frieden gewinnen und erhalten kann. Zu fragen ist also: Können Religionsgemeinschaften und Kirchen von den empirisch-historischen Entwicklungen eines modernen politisch-sozialen Pluralismus lernen, dabei leitende normative Traditionen rezipieren und zugleich ihren internen, als theologisch legitim anerkannten Pluralismus bewahren, womöglich sogar kommunikativ-einladend entfalten? Und was sind die bleibenden Hauptunterschiede zwischen einer weltlichen Unterscheidung von Einheit und Verschiedenheit einerseits, der theologischen Unterscheidung zwischen dem Grund der Einheit der Kirche und den vielfältigen kirchlichen Sozialgestalten und ihrer möglichen Gemeinschaft und Einheit, andererseits? Welche unterschiedlichen menschlichen Aufgaben sind dadurch konstituiert?

Man könnte auf den ersten Blick vielleicht meinen, dass es die Kirchen in Fragen der Einheit leichter haben als politische Entitäten. Denn ihre Einheit ist, zumindest einem breiten ökumenischen Konsens zufolge, von den Anfängen bis zur Vollendung *extern konstituiert*: Die Kirche *ist* eine, sie *ist* die *una, sancta, catholica et apostolica ecclesia*, weil und soweit sie sich mit diesen sie bestimmenden Eigenschaften nicht selbst konstituiert, sondern von ihrem Grund, Ursprung und Ziel in Jesus Christus als die *eine Gemeinschaft derer, die ihrem Herrn nachfolgen*, konstituiert und geschaffen, erhalten und geleitet wird. Die Kirche muss ihre Einheit nicht aus eigener Kraft schaffen, sondern als Geschenk wahrnehmen und verantworten. Sie ist *communio* selbständiger Kirchen,

---

[71] BROSSEDER, Ökumene baut Brücken.

in denen das Evangelium verkündet und die Sakramente gefeiert werden. Aber mit dem Vertrauen in die tragende Kraft dieser vorgegebenen Einheit scheint es immer wieder nicht weit her zu sein. Statt dass die Kirchen in ihrer Unterschiedenheit sich wie Planeten auf Jesus Christus als die eine Sonne, der sie alles Licht verdanken, beziehen und sich in dieser Funktion gegenseitig wahrnehmen und anerkennen, scheinen sie immer wieder sich selbst an die Stelle der Sonne zu drängen.[72]

Demgegenüber ist die politische Einheit in der Weltgesellschaft angesichts der »ungeselligen Geselligkeit« der Menschen eine notwendige, durch und durch menschliche, säkulare Aufgabe, zu deren Lösung es des menschlichen Verstandes und keiner klerikalen Bevormundung bedarf. Immer wieder überfordert diese Aufgabe zwar die Fähigkeiten der Menschen, aber hier »rettet (uns) kein höheres Wesen, kein Gott, kein Kaiser, kein Tribun«, wie es in der »Internationale« heißt. Man muss selber verhandeln, Verträge schließen, verbindliche Menschenrechtskonventionen ratifizieren, über Krieg und Frieden entscheiden und sich, wenn es wirklich gut geht, in eine übergreifende Völkerrechtsordnung, die Dissidenztoleranz praktiziert und Platz für die Gegner hat, einreihen und auf jede Form eines waffengestützten Unilateralismus aus Einsicht und aufgrund nüchterner Interessenkalkulation verzichten. Das ist schwierig und eine unendliche Aufgabe, aber, wie die europäische Vereinigung gezeigt hat, nicht einfach unmöglich.

Die »selbständig bleibenden Kirchen« (Brosseder) können und sollten in diesem Bezugsrahmen eine Form der *communio* suchen und sichtbar darstellen, welche auch für die Gestaltung und Durchsetzung von Recht und Frieden im innerstaatlichen wie im zwischenstaatlichen Verkehr insbesondere dann von höchster praktischer Bedeutung ist, wenn es bei den kirchlichen Positionsbezügen nicht um partikular-plurale religiöse bzw. kirchliche Interessen geht, sondern um das – hier darf man den zum Schlagwort herunter gebrachten Begriff nicht scheuen – Gemeinwohl in einer pluralistischen Weltgesellschaft geht.[73]

Dabei werden Kirchen den höchst partikularen Ursprung ihrer Einsichten nicht verschweigen und in einer rein säkularen Sprache gleich-

---

[72] Das Bild von Sonne und Planeten hat EDMUND SCHLINK betont (Ökumenische Dogmatik, Göttingen 1983, 696); analog hat DOROTHEA SATTLER (in diesem Band) die Metapher des Rades mit der offenen Nabe und den festen Speichen aufgerufen.

[73] Zu einer realistischen Gemeinwohlkonzeption *à jour*, welche Mindestanforderungen jenseits von lediglich prozeduralen Bestimmungen und umfassenden materialen Kriterien formuliert, siehe CHRISTIAN BLUM, Die Bestimmung des Gemeinwohls, Berlin/New York 2015.

sam verbergen, sondern offen legen und einer freien Urteilsbildung mit vernünftig nachvollziehbaren Argumenten anbieten. In alten reformierten Synoden soll man auf den Stuhl des Vorsitzenden keinen Menschen gesetzt, sondern eine aufgeschlagene Bibel gelegt haben. Das ist ein ganz anderes Bild von Repräsentation der Einheit als es in den orthodoxen Kirchen oder der römisch-katholischen Kirche begegnet. Die aufgeschlagene Bibel symbolisiert den unverfügbaren Ursprung sowohl kirchlicher Verschiedenheit als auch Einheit, und recht verstanden können und dürfen auch Patriarchen, Päpste und charismatische Massenapostel genauso wie jeder Christenmensch, der zur Weitergabe des Evangeliums berufen ist, jeweils nur in ihrer je besonderen Zeugenfunktion gegenüber diesem einheitsstiftenden Ursprung wirken. Diese Dienstfunktion – und keinen Herrschaftsanspruch – in weltlichen Angelegenheiten bringt die Bezeichnung der *politischen Diakonie* immer noch gut zum Ausdruck.

5 Grenzen eines legitimen Pluralismus

Ist die hier entwickelte Sicht einer spannungsreichen, hinreichend[74] gewaltfreien Komplementarität von unverzichtbaren, übergreifenden säkularen Rechtsprinzipien einerseits, der Existenz einer Vielzahl von Religionsgemeinschaften und damit einer unaufhebbaren Konkurrenz unterschiedlicher bis gegensätzlicher religiöser (und weltanschaulicher) Grundüberzeugungen und Wahrheitsverständnisse andererseits eine Illusion? Ist es naives Wunschdenken, wenn man meint, es ließen sich Integrations- und Inklusionsregeln mit der Anerkennung dauerhafter und womöglich unüberwindbarer Differenzen vereinbaren? Die alteuropäische Bearbeitung dieses fundamentalen Problems stand im Zeichen der »chalkedonensischen« Lösung: Die Sphären des Religiösen und des Politischen »unvermischt und ungetrennt« zu halten,[75] und dies nicht im Sinne einer statischen Kompetenzzuordnung und dauerhaft fixierter Grenzen, sondern als ein geschichtlich sich entwickelndes

---

74 Ich betone »hinreichend«, weil ich eine gewaltfreie Gesellschaft in einem uneingeschränkten Sinne nicht für menschenmöglich halte – aus Gründen einer fundamentalen Ungeselligkeit und damit verbundenen Gewaltfähigkeit von Menschen, was immer die Ursprünge dessen sein mögen.
75 Das Konzil von Chalkedon (451) hat die Einheit der göttlichen und menschlichen Natur in Jesus Christus u.a. mit diesen Worten ausgesagt (DH 302: unvermischt, unveränderlich, ungetrennt und unteilbar).

und zu gestaltendes Spannungsfeld. Thomas Hobbes' Entwurf einer staatlich-integrativen Rechtsordnung, die freilich wesentlich eine Unterwerfungsordnung war, entstand vor dem geschichtlichen Hintergrund der konfessionellen Bürgerkriege, die in Grundzügen durch die Westfälische Friedensordnung von Münster und Osnabrück überwunden wurden. Immanuel Kants Entwurf griff darüber weit hinaus auf die notwendigen Bedingungen einer globalen Friedensordnung nach allgemein zustimmungsfähigen Rechtsprinzipien. In beiden Fällen stellte sich historisch die Frage nach den Grenzen dieser Konzeptionen, nicht zuletzt im Blick auf die Grenzen der Gehorsamspflichten der Bürger und ein denkbares Recht, wenn nicht, unter Umständen, einer Pflicht zum Widerstand.[76] In einer gewissen Ähnlichkeit stellt sich diese Frage in heutigen demokratischen Rechtsstaaten in der Form, welches die Stellung und die Rechte derer sind oder sein sollten, die einen solchen Staat, der gleiche Rechte für Alle hinreichend erfolgreich zu gewährleisten versucht, prinzipiell ablehnen. Während sehr viele Formen von Dissens bis hin zu organisiertem Widerstand durchaus ins Recht gefasst werden können, stösst das Recht auf eine qualitative Grenze bei jenen, die Recht überhaupt negieren. Bisweilen in einer generalisierten Ablehnung »des (bestehenden) Systems« schlechthin. Mit anderen Worten: Gibt es so etwas wie »absolute Feindschaft« als Negation der Minimalbedingungen eines legitimen Pluralismus?

Der auf den Ideen Lenins und der brutalen Praxis Stalins beruhende Bolschewismus hat, zumindest in der offiziellen Ideologie, eine solche Position absoluter Unvereinbarkeit bzw. Feindschaft gegenüber »dem« Kapitalismus vertreten, sich davon aber im Zeichen einer notwendigen Koexistenz unter den Bedingungen wechselseitiger nuklearer Vernichtungsdrohung nach und nach verabschiedet. Der deutsche Nationalsozialismus hat im Zeichen des »totalen« Staates und seiner Expansion ebenfalls Menschen zu »absoluten« Feinden gemacht, versklavt und vernichtet und die Idee einer rechtsstaatlichen Ordnung in seiner Ideologie und Praxis von Grund auf negiert. In der Gegenwart gibt es Indizien dafür, dass unter den führenden Ideologen des radikalen muslimischen Jihad ein durchaus vergleichbares Denk- und Verhaltensmuster begegnet. In seiner sorgfältigen Analyse schreibt dazu Behnam T. Said:

---

[76] Zu Hobbes vgl. QUENTIN SKINNER, Eroberung und Einverständnis. Hobbes und die Kontroverse um die Gehorsamspflicht, in: ders., Visionen des Politischen, Frankfurt a.M. 2009, 224–251; zu Kant KENNETH R. WESTPHAL, Kant on the State, Law, and Obedience to Authority in the Alleged »Anti-Revolutionary Writings«, in: Journal of Philosophical Research 17 (1991/92), 383–426.

Ein Grundkonsens zwischen diesen Gelehrten [sc. des radikalen Jihad, WL] besteht in der gemeinsamen Ablehnung säkularer Gesetzgebung, der Feindschaft gegenüber dem Westen und gegenüber den arabischen Herrschern sowie der Übereinkunft, dass islamische Staaten errichtet werden sollen und der bewaffnete Kampf zur Erreichung diese Zieles notwendig ist.[77]

Es ist zwar ziemlich wahrscheinlich, dass die Gruppen, die solchen und ähnlichen Überzeugungen anhängen, sehr klein sind und bleiben werden, aber die grundsätzliche Feindschaft gegenüber menschlichem Recht, welches nicht – und exklusiv – auf Koran und Scharia basiert, und demokratischen Institutionen und Verfahren als Gestalten eines schlechthin verwerflichen und mit allen Mitteln zu bekämpfenden Götzendienstes kann man nicht anders denn als »absolute Feindschaft« bezeichnen – »absolut« auch in dem ganz spezifischen Sinne, dass Selbstmordattentate gegen völlig unbeteiligte Zivilisten durch ihre Form einer bewusst selbstzerstörerischen Gewalt zeigen, dass der definitive Kommunikationsabbruch gewollt ist. Said zitiert eingehend in seinem Buch das Bekenntnis eines radikalen Jihadisten, in dem der religiös-apokalytische Grundzug dieser Haltung zum Ausdruck kommt,

---

[77] BEHNAM T. SAID, Islamischer Staat, IS-Miliz, al-Qaida und die deutschen Brigaden, München 2014, 92. Demgegenüber wird die alleinige »Souveränität« Allahs proklamiert, die eine grundlegende »Ablehnung der weltlichen Autorität«, welche nicht exklusiv dem Koran und der darauf gegründeten Scharia gehorsam ist, impliziert; so der sehr einflussreiche SAYYID QUTB, Zeichen auf dem Weg (zuerst 1965, kurz vor seiner Hinrichtung 1966), aus dem Englischen deutsch von Mohammed Shukri, Köln 2005, 49, 102, 104, 125 u.ö. In den vom Islam geprägten Staaten der Gegenwart gibt es sehr unterschiedliche Versuche, weltliches Recht und Scharia vereinbar zu machen, aber eine starke Tendenz geht dahin, dass staatliches (positives) Recht nur soweit Legitimität beanspruchen kann, als es mit den anerkannten Rechtslehren des Islam, basierend auf der Scharia, übereinstimmt, d.h. dass die spezifisch schariatrechtlichen Bestimmungen im Sinne einer Leges-Hierarchie die oberste Instanz bilden. So schreibt Miklos Muranyi im Blick auf die von der Orthodoxie vertretene Auffassung in Ägypten: »Die Reformierung geltender Gesetze im Sinne der *shari'a* ist also, abgeleitet aus der Verfassung selbst, eine verfassungsrechtliche Notwendigkeit.« In: WERNER ENDE/UDO STEINBACH (Hrsg.), Der Islam in der Gegenwart, München ²1989, 344–358, hier 349. Es liegt auf der Hand, dass eine solche Position nicht ohne weiteres mit einer vorbehaltlosen Anerkennung von Menschenrechten zusammen gehen kann; siehe dazu näher Gudrun Krämer, Gottes Staat als Republik. Zeitgenössische Muslime zu Islam, Menschenrechten und Demokratie, Baden-Baden 1999.

wenn die jetzigen Kämpfe als aktive Herbeiführung des Endes dieser Zeit und des Tages des Wiederauferstehung gepriesen werden.[78] Erschwerend kommt dabei hinzu, dass radikalisierte Jihadisten häufig insbesondere andere Muslime als »Ungläubige« brandmarken, ausgrenzen und bekämpfen,[79] dass die meisten Opfer radikal-jihadistischer Anschläge Muslime sind und dass es anscheinend zwischen den sich bekämpfenden Richtungen und Schulen des Islam kaum Ansätze zu einer Art innerislamischer Ökumene gibt.

Unter solchen Voraussetzungen ist es nicht verwunderlich, wenn faktische oder bloß mögliche Pluralität und theoretischer Pluralismus von radikalen Jihadisten uneingeschränkt zurückgewiesen werden. Ist das automatisch das Ende eines legitimen, um des irdischen Friedens und Rechtes willen möglichen und notwendigen Pluralismus? Nicht dann, wenn und soweit eine freiheitliche Rechtsordnung in einer Weise und mit Mitteln verteidigt wird, dass auch ihre ausgemachten Gegner, unerachtet ihrer Verbrechen, als Rechtssubjekte anerkannt bleiben. Auch Verbrecher können und müssen ins Recht gefasst werden – sie können sich selbst zu *outlaws* machen, aber der Rechtsstaat kennt keine *outlaws*. Ob und wie die Religionsgemeinschaften ihrerseits einen säkularen, die Religionsfreiheit garantierenden Pluralismus verstehen und verteidigen, sagt Entscheidendes über ihr Rechtsverständnis und ihre Friedensfähigkeit.

---

[78] SAID, Islamischer Staat, IS-Miliz, al-Qaida, 148–151.
[79] Eine derartige Erklärung (»Takfir«) eines Menschen oder einer Gruppe als »ungläubig« entspricht teilweise der (traditionellen) Häresie-Feststellung im Kontext christlicher Kirchen; vgl. den Art. »Takfir« in: The Encyclopedia of Islam, New Ed., Bd. X, 122.

Is Catholicity Still an Appropriate Concept in a Postmodern World?

Henk Witte

In his discussion of sections 14–16 of *Lumen gentium* – the well-known sections of the dogmatic constitution on the Church, in which the Second Vatican Council expressed the Catholic position on salvation and the religious »other« – the American Catholic ecclesiologist Paul Lakeland accounts for the results of ecumenical and interreligious dialogue. In the ecumenical realm he notices a great deal of *rapprochement* in the years since the Council. However, there have also been difficulties and ambiguities.

> In ecumenism we have seen major dialogues especially with the Anglican Communion and with the Lutherans, with a growing understanding of questions of ministry and sacraments on the one hand, and of the meaning of justification on the other, but these developments have not led to any institutional movement forward. There has been no progress on intercommunion or on the recognition of the validity of one another's orders at the level of church organizations themselves. Rightly or wrongly, this is often considered to be because of reluctance or inertia on the part of the Catholic Church.[1]

---

[1] Paul Lakeland, *A Council That Will Never End:* Lumen Gentium *and the Church Today* (Collegeville: Liturgical Press, 2013), 115–116.

According to Lakeland, the main ecumenical problem is an institutional one. He is not the only one to make this diagnosis.[2] Indeed, the churches have not succeeded in translating the evolutions made in their (self-)understanding into a change of their organizations. Usually, this problem is discussed in terms of models of unity. While models of unity propose ideas on how to conceive unity and to achieve it, they do not effect changes in church organization or structuring. Lakeland observes »a shift away from talk on unity« in the field of ecumenism. Such talk is replaced by what he calls »the rhetoric of ›listening and learning‹.« In a footnote he refers to Paul Murray's program on »Receptive Ecumenism and Catholic Learning.«[3] But listening and learning, no matter how important they are, have little to no implications for organizational issues and changes.

Why such stress on the organizational factor? Should not the focus be, rather, on a discussion of how far catholicity and postmodernity can accord with one another? Indeed it should; yet the rapid digitalization of our world has brought about an awareness of some shifts in present-day life that have a major impact on the organization of the churches and on how they deal with catholicity. The trend toward digitalization can be considered as the technical foundation of socio-cultural developments. In a broad sense, culture was already developing in a postmodern direction; now the process of digitalization is having a catalysing effect. It renders processes typified as »postmodern« more visible and, unavoidably, swifter; these processes seriously affect church life. The main characteristics of postmodernity are well known: think of individualization, globalization, the predominance of particularities over unity, the failure of meta-narratives, and, consequently, the absence of a shared view of the past and a common hope for the future, the preference for experience and emotion, and the emphasis on spirituality rather than on institutionalized religion.[4]

---

[2] Cf. Thomas Bremer, »Ökumene und ökumenische Theologie im Umbruch,« in *Ökumene – Überdacht. Reflexionen und Realitäten im Umbruch*, eds. Thomas Bremer and Maria Wernsmann (Freiburg/Basel/Wien: Herder, 2014), 18–36.
[3] Lakeland, *A Council That Will Never End*, 116.
[4] There is an overabundance of literature on postmodernism. I rely in particular on Jean-Pierre Willaime, »L'ultramodernité sonne-t-elle la fin de l'œcuménisme?« *Recherches de science religieuse* 89 (2001): 177–204; Walter Kasper, *Theologie und Kirche,* vol. 2 (Mainz: Matthias Grünewald, 1999), 249–264; Gerard Mannion, »Postmodern Ecclesiologies,« in *The Routledge Companion to the Christian Church*, eds. Gerard Mannion and Lewis Mudge, (New York and London: Routledge, 2009), 127–152. See also Henk Witte, »From System

I will first explore the nature of digitalization and its impact on the current organizational model of the churches. In my opinion, we are facing a transition from a union-oriented organization model to a network-oriented model. I will discuss some difficulties caused by this shift in relation to the leadership style of the churches and their catholicity. I will then reflect on the notion of catholicity, and discuss the conditions required for this concept to deal with a postmodern context appropriately.

1 Digitalization and Its Ecclesial Impact

According to René Munnik, a philosopher of technology, the process of digitalization constitutes a socio-cultural development based on a technical invention. He names four characteristics of this process. The first concerns the unpredictability of its social and cultural implications, even when the technical aspects are based on predictable scientific processes. A second distinguishing mark is the phenomenon which Lewis Mumford has called »pseudo-morphism«, according to which we perceive technical innovations within the framework of what is familiar to us – and value them as an improvement – while tending to overlook their peculiarity. A classic example is the invention of the »coach-without-horse«, now known to us as the automobile. Notwithstanding all the positive appraisals this invention aroused, hardly anyone pondered the longstanding effects it would have, such as our current road system, the petrochemical industry, pollution, etc. A third characteristic is the invisibility of technical developments since, at some point, we uncritically accept them as »normal«. The fourth mark concerns their mediating function: technical inventions may disclose new perceptions of the reality which is known to us. An example of such an effect is the seventeenth century's comparison of God as creator with a watchmaker: likewise today we use computer metaphors to understand how the brain works.[5]

One such historic technical invention with a far-reaching influence on religion was the invention of the alphabet. This induced scripture-

---

Into Networking. The Social Shape of Ecumenism in the 21st Century,« *Exchange* 34 (2005): 386–396.

[5] René Munnik, »De digitalisering van de wereld,« *Collationes* 44 (2014): 5–22, esp. 6–11. See also his *Tijdmachines: Over de technische onderwerping van vergankelijkheid en duur* (Zoetermeer: Clement, 2013).

based religions, a culture of literacy with its special interest in history and reflective thinking, and juridical systems based on codification.[6] To a large extent Christianity, as »a religion of the book« like Judaism and Islam, owes its very existence, shape, and dissemination to the invention of the alphabet. Should we expect that the vast process of computerization and digitalization we are presently experiencing will produce an entirely *different* culture, based as it is on the binary system of the digits 1 and 0, instead of on 24 graphemes? Possibly this is already manifest in the growing influence of images as a vehicle for the transmission of messages.

Put more precisely, the question is: What is the impact of the ongoing digitalization of our daily life on the churches? This question raises a multitude of other questions.[7] Here I must confine myself to discussing the impact of the digitalization of our daily life on the organization and leadership of the churches, in relation to how they deal with catholicity.

Experts observing the use of social media agree that they advance horizontality in human communication. The use of such media displays a democratic pattern, inviting an active reply on an equal footing. In particular, those churches that build on forms of top-down communication will find themselves increasingly challenged by this development.[8] There is more to it. This shift surpasses the appeal for more democracy and more »say« because the digital world is polycentric by nature: with my iPhone at hand, I consider myself to be an autonomous centre of communication stretching out in a variety of directions. I can determine for myself with whom, when, and for how long I will be in contact. I can decide for myself which messages I either accept and reply to, or neglect and reject; and I can do so independently from time and space. Yet my autonomy is limited. It depends on the reliability of hardware and software, on the economic power of companies such as Apple, Microsoft, and Google. Nonetheless, whenever using modern

---

[6] Munnik, »De digitalisering van de wereld,« 11–16.

[7] Henk Witte, »Ecclesiologische kanttekeningen bij de digitale omwenteling,« *Collationes* 44 (2013): 73–86. For instance, the question of whether online church is possible. Cf. also Onderzoeksgroep virtuele zingeving, VU Amsterdam, »De (on)mogelijkheid van de digitale kerk,« http://www.handelingen.com/detailed-news/article/de-onmogelijkheid-van-de-digitale-kerk.htlm (accessed August 1, 2014). Also, ethical questions need to be addressed because the way churches present themselves on the internet asks for correspondence with their identity and values.

[8] Hans Geybels, »Theologie van de communicatie,« *Collationes* 44 (2014): 49.

communications media I experience myself as *a centre of power*. The digital world consists of an enormous number of such centres and, therefore, renders our world into a polycentric universe. Precisely on this level, postmodern tendencies such as individualization and the predominance of pluralism manifest themselves directly.

Polycentrism, however, poses serious challenges to the churches, challenges concerning their organization and corresponding leadership style as well as how they deal with catholicity. In particular, churches governed in a mono-centric way – whether or not they are hierarchically structured, for even congregationally structured churches may be subject to mono-centric types of government – have to face the challenges of polycentrism.

Mono-centrism characterizes, for instance, the model according to which the Roman Catholic Church considers its social shape. Up to the First World War, this church considered itself as analogous to a monarchic state, later on also as a union. Both models intertwined in the *societas perfecta* terminology, which stressed the church's juridical independence over and against other authorities. This image of the church needs to be understood in the context of the nineteenth and early twentieth centuries, where it was coined in opposition to the Protestant collegial system (*Kollegialsystem*), and where it sought to resist the claims of emerging European nation-states. This model also articulated the church's superiority: its origin, structure, and aim were said to be instituted by Christ.[9] As a state, a union was understood as a gathering of people with a common objective, governed by a common authority, and embraced by both. Here the central position and strong voice of church leadership was remarkable, with its focus on being in control and on building up the divine underpinning of its authority as grounded in Christ's institution of the church. Just as remarkable was the description of its members, holding their proper rights and, above all, their duties, and taking for granted their full identification and full participation in the body of their church. One became a member by

---

[9] Joseph Listl, *Kirche und Staat in der neueren katholischen Kirchenrechtswissenschaft* (Berlin: Duncker & Humblot, 1978), esp. 107–112; cf. Henk Witte, »›*Ecclesia, quid dicis de teipsa?*‹ Can Ecclesiology be of Any Help to the Church to Deal with Advanced Modernity?« in *Towards a New Catholic Church in Advanced Modernity,* eds. Staf Hellemans and Jozef Wissink, Tilburg Theological Studies 5 (Münster: Lit, 2012), 123–134; Michael J. Lacey, »Leo's Church and Our Own,« in *The Crisis of Authority in Catholic Modernity*, eds. Michael J. Lacey and Francis Oakley (Oxford/New York: Oxford University Press, 2011), 57–92.

baptism and remained a member for life. Mutual relations were ordered juridically, and gained universal validity; degrees in identification, belonging, or participation were almost impossible.

It is exactly this type of the churches' social order which has increasingly lost its credibility in a digitalized world. Bit by bit the prevailing union-oriented paradigm is being replaced by a network model. Nowadays, network organizations respond to the postmodern atmosphere of polycentrism, based on the assumption of free choice.[10] In part they replace those groups that individuals usually cannot avoid, for instance, family and religion. The principle of group building in networks relies on a shared interest or a common affinity. These interests can vary considerably: a health problem or a hobby can be a reason for entering a network, as well as a philosophical, religious, or spiritual affinity. Access is open to all, and engagement varies from core membership, via regular visiting, to sympathy and support of common values; sharing an outspoken opponent is also welcome. Partiality, plurality, and fluidity characterize contemporary network organizations. The nuances are important: partiality indicates the participants' identification (or conscious *non*-identification) with a network's identity; plurality indicates the range of varieties of engagement; fluidity refers to the often-limited duration of participation in a network.

Although each unit of a network gains autonomy, this autonomy would be impossible without »facilitating« and »moderating« functions (as they are called in computer terminology). Both functions refer to the exercise of authority, the first enabling exchange as such and the second determining and watching over the content of exchange, by establishing rules of conduct, decency, and – put theologically – orthodoxy. These notions are comparable with the governing and teaching functions of the churches. Their authority, however, is less visible and is less often experienced as an obstacle than is the case in the union model.

In addition, a new type of authority comes to the fore in the world of the internet: the iconic or symbolic leadership of persons with an identity-determining role within a network. Cyber gurus and cyber imams are examples of this, but persons such as Pope Francis may just as well fit this role. Iconic leaders can be recognized by the number of

---

[10] Cf. Liliane Voyé, »Het kerkinstituut uitgedaagd,« in *Geloven in de kerk: Een multidisciplinaire benadering,* ed. Jef Stevens (Averbode: Altiora, 2000), 69–97, esp. 85–92; Michael Hochschild, »Networking: Eine Chance des ständigen Diakonats für die Kirche,« *Diaconia Christi* 38 (2003): 6–10.

»followers« and »friends« they have; here the pontifical »Twitter-account« may serve as an example. Their leadership prevailingly consists of connecting their followers, and keeping them connected, through often very short yet personal messages. This appears to be a necessary condition for transmitting traces of the Gospel today. Instead of an authoritarian and control-oriented leadership style, iconic leadership requires an inspiring and stimulating style. At the same time, however, it is a risky endeavour: a computerized world never forgets a slip of the tongue, and lacks a hermeneutical consciousness.

In short, a network organization inevitably follows its own leadership style. Yet the transition from a union model to a network model will be accompanied by misunderstandings and conflicts, involving leaders as well as the faithful. Contemporary leaders who remain »stuck« within the union model, and define their position and competencies accordingly, will rapidly be misunderstood – and tacitly ignored – by those other leaders, and those faithful, to whom the network model is a self-evident framework.

Network organization implies more challenges to the churches. Given the key role of open access to networks in our present-day society, churches are facing the major challenge of voicing and maintaining their orthodoxy. The autonomy of the »players« on the one hand, and the context of religious pluralism on the other, creates ambiguity or even hybridity in the mind-sets of individuals interested in religion. Moreover, orthodoxy cannot be demonstrated by pressing a »like« or »dislike« button.

In this situation the notion of catholicity appears to be challenging. My key point is that networks in an ecclesial context are based on affinities. Although, in principle, network participation may display varying degrees of loyalty and disloyalty, any network easily tends to develop into an instrument of mutual affirmation of the like-minded – and, in our case, the like-minded *faithful*. When, for instance, such participants consider themselves as »true Catholics«, their claim will raise questions regarding their representativeness. And, in the end, it will raise questions about the nature of the grace-filled mystery of God. Assuming – from within the Christian tradition – that catholicity is at once a divine gift and a commission to the church, the question becomes: does the truth-claim of a group to be »truly orthodox Catholics« imply that catholicity consists only in the repetition of their like-mindedness?

The next issue emerging is the question whether God has a preference for sameness, or if God advocates, rather, for the value of the otherness of others? It is well known today that multiplication of sameness risks leading to exclusion, under the brands of colonialism and fundamentalism. Here the notion of catholicity is important, given its awareness of being part of a larger and more diverse whole. This striving for wholeness requires the art of renouncing exclusivism. It requires the art of balancing both identification and non-identification at the same time. It induces a plea, as Paul Lakeland advocated, for a humble church.[11] The question now is whether humility and openness to other voices are imbedded in the concept of catholicity.

2 Catholicity

The Nicene Creed mentions catholicity as the third of the four marks of the Church.[12] In Latin we speak of *notae* or *proprietates ecclesiae*. The

---

[11] Lakeland, *A Council That Will Never End*, 101–154.

[12] Yves Congar, »Die Wesenseigenschaften der Kirche,« in *Mysterium salutis: Grundriß heilsgeschichtlicher Dogmatik*, vol. IV/1: *Das Heilsgeschehen in der Gemeinde*, eds. Johannes Feiner and Magnus Löhrer (Einsiedeln/Zürich/Köln: Benziger, 1972), 478–487; Avery Dulles, *The Catholicity of the Church* (Oxford: Clarendon Press, 1985); Hermann Joseph Pottmeyer, »Die Frage nach der wahren Kirche,« in *Handbuch der Fundamentaltheologie*, vol. 3: *Traktat Kirche,* eds. Walter Kern, Hermann Joseph Pottmeyer and Max Seckler (Freiburg: Herder, 1986), 212–241; Wolfgang Beinert, »Ökumenische Leitbilder und Alternativen,« in *Handbuch der Ökumenik*, vol. 3/1, eds. Hans Jörg Urban and Harald Wagner (Paderborn: Bonifatius, 1987), 129–131; Max Seckler, *Die schiefen Wände des Lehrhauses. Katholizität als Herausforderung* (Freiburg: Herder, 1988), 178–197; Peter Steinacker, »Katholizität,« in *TRE* 18, 72–80; Henk Witte, »Katholieke identiteit. Op zoek naar nieuwe oriëntatie,« in *Vitaliteit van geloof en kerk,* Piet Leenhouwers, Henk Meeuws, Henk Witte (Aalsmeer: Dabar/Luyten, 1992), 63–85; Peter De Mey, »Is the Connection of ›Catholicity‹ and ›Globalization‹ Fruitful? An Assessment of Recent Reflections on the Notion of Catholicity,« *Bulletin ET* 13 (2002): 169–181; Henk Witte, »Orthodoxie en katholiciteit,« in *Orthodoxie en belevend geloven,* F.A. Maas, H.P.J. Witte and P.A. Nissen (Tilburg: Theologische Faculteit Tilburg, 2006), 25–49; Richard R. Gaillardetz, *Ecclesiology for a Global Church: A People Called and Sent* (Maryknoll: Orbis, 2008), 35–84; Peter De Mey, »Eenheid in verscheidenheid. Het katholiciteitsbegrip van Vaticanum II«, in *De K van Kerk: De pluriformiteit van katholiciteit,* eds. Peter De Mey and Pieter De Witte (Antwerpen: Halewijn, 2009), 31–46; Lawrence S. Cunningham, *An Introduction to Catholicism* (Cambridge: Cambridge University Press, 2009), 3–8; Walter Kardinal Kasper, *Katholische Kirche. Wesen – Wirklichkeit – Sendung* (Freiburg: Herder, 2011), 225–238, 254–265; Marcel Sarot, »Confessing the Catholicity of the church,« *International Journal of Philosophy and Theology* 74 (2013): 154–168.

Latin noun *nota* is related to the verb *notare*.[13] *Noto* means »I mark, I note, I observe«. The significance of this is revelatory: it opens up the observer's point of view. It is *to an observer* that catholicity appears to characterize the church. The other traditional term, *proprietas*, also helps to clarify our point. *Proprietas* means »quality«, »peculiarity«, »ownership«, »property«.[14] The term may just as well denote the proper quality of an object, as an exclusive ownership. From this perspective, catholicity refers to a peculiar quality of the church – one which, however, may easily turn into an exclusive possession. Catholicity then ends up in a competitive ecclesial context, in which it will be used as a criterion for legitimizing a specific church as the »true church«.[15]

Considered as a quality of the church, catholicity appears to be a divine gift and a commission at the same time. Qualities are precious. They do not disclose their meaning and impact immediately but require patient reception: the transcendent nature of catholicity implies that an attitude of respectful receiving is crucial to grasp its meaning. It has to be discovered, or rather, it slowly discloses itself to us in ever-changing contexts. Its concretization is co-dependent on the verbal and instrumental tools a context offers. The governmental form of the Roman Empire, for instance, offered a model for governing the Latin Church in Late Antiquity, just as Greek philosophy helped crucially to articulate Christian faith in Hellenistic milieus. But this is not without risk: contextual concretization of a God-given value risks over-concreteness on the one hand, and under-concreteness on the other. Over-concreteness tends to offer soteriological value to contextual data too easily; this will require purification in the end. Under-concreteness denotes a lack of interest for the changing course of history, and the concrete lives of individuals and communities; it reveals our unavoidably incomplete knowledge and understanding of a divine gift and requires continuing discernment and shaping. Both pitfalls affirm the necessity of openness for dialogue with other voices and the need for ecclesial humility.[16]

---

[13] It relates to the Greek *gignosko*.
[14] It is related to *proprius* (special, own, very own, individual) which comes from *pro privus*: for the individual, in particular.
[15] Cf. Pottmeyer, »Die Frage nach der wahren Kirche,« 221–225.
[16] During the discussions on ecumenism at the Second Vatican Council, Cardinal Paul-Émile Léger, Archbishop of Montréal, pleaded for an attitude not only of love for the truth and charity, but also of humility in investigating, together with our separated brethren, the unfathomable divine mysteries. In his plea for humility, he did not advocate a false modesty, but opposed the possessive

It is well known that the word »catholic« is absent in the New Testament. Ignatius of Antioch's statement: »Wherever the bishop appears, there let the people be; as wherever Jesus Christ is, there is the Catholic Church«[17] is mentioned as the first sentence in which the notion *katholikos* was coined in Christian discourse. Still, the fact that the word is first found in a post-Biblical text does not imply an absence of the reality of catholicity in Sacred Scripture. According to Richard Gaillardetz, the Church's catholicity was inherent in its sense of mission.[18] The Hebrew Bible anticipates it, for instance, in Deutero-Isaiah's more open response to the Babylonian captivity, understanding it as a chance for a

---

attitude of what he called »doctrinal immobilism«, an attitude which refuses to investigate truth. See *Acta synodalia* II, VI, 10–12. *Unitatis redintegratio* 10, paragraph 3, reflects his intervention.

[17] *Letter to the Smyrnaeans* VIII; translation taken from John R. Willis, *The Teachings of the Church Fathers* (San Francisco: Ignatius Press, 2002), 53–54. The interpretation of Ignatius' saying is much discussed. According to some scholars, Ignatius makes a comparison between the local church and the universal church (for instance, Seckler, *Die schiefen Wände des Lehrhauses*, 195; other references in De Mey, »Is the Connection of ›Catholicity‹ and ›Globalization‹ Fruitful?,« 173). This analogy, however, breaks down, as Christ does not exercise leadership in the universal church in the same way as a bishop does in a local church. Other scholars make a connection with the end of chapter 1 of Ephesians, where the church is said to be Christ's body, »the fullness of him who fills all in all«. Referring to this Christological *pleroma*, Ignatius would have preferred *katholikos* in order to avoid a term which was also beloved among Gnostics (Beinert, »Ökumenische Leitbilder und Alternativen,« 130). In a (neo-)platonic framework, the bishop could be understood as the earthly representation of Christ in heaven. As Christ is the fullness of truth for salvation, the bishop represents him on earth in questions of certainty and reliability concerning truth and salvation; cf. Peter Stockmeier, »Zum Begriff der καθολικὴ ἐκκλησία bei Ignatius von Antiochien,« in *Ortskirche – Weltkirche*, FS Kardinal Döpfner, ed. Heinz Fleckenstein et al. (Würzburg: Echter, 1973), 63–74. The Orthodox Churches emphasize the connection of the local Eucharistic gathering, presided by a bishop or his representative, and Christ's full presence in the Eucharistic communion; cf. De Mey, »Is the Connection of ›Catholicity‹ and ›Globalization‹ Fruitful?«, 172–176, referring to John Zizioulas, *Being as Communion: Studies in Personhood and the Church* (Crestwood: St. Vladimir's Press, 1985). Walter Cardinal Kasper, *Katholische Kirche*, 255, remarks that the christological fullness in which the individual local churches participate is connected to the church's episcopal structure and the unity of episcopacy. Attention to the role of the bishop in relation to the validity of being church is also expressed in the sentence, following the one quoted from Ignatius' Letter: »It is not lawful without the bishop either to baptize or to celebrate a love-feast; but whatsoever he shall approve of, that is also pleasing to God, so that everything that is done may be secure and valid.«

[18] Gaillardetz, *Ecclesiology for a Global Church*, 35.

new beginning in contrast to a more closed and exclusive response which considered the captivity as a punishment for Israel's mixing with other nations. In particular the Book of Acts, Gaillardetz continues, illustrates how catholicity had a missionary ring to it from the start. It begins with the programmatic and all-encompassing assignment to the apostles to »be my witnesses ... to the ends of the earth« (1:8) and assumes the Church's increasing missionary awareness and activity as a development of the gift of the Holy Spirit, a gift which unifies differences without destroying them (2:8–12).[19]

Mission implies the encounter with otherness: other groups, other peoples, other languages, and other cultures. Catholicity, according to Gaillardetz, is the theological expression of the reality »that God's love is neither divisive nor oppressive but gathers up genuine difference in an inclusive wholeness«.[20] From the biblical missionary perspective, catholicity even appears as prior to the value of the church's unity because the discovery of unity usually follows a confrontation with what is perceived as other, as non-identical. Thus the notion of unity stands as a qualifier to the concept of catholicity, and not the other way around. From the Roman Catholic perspective this is important: the expression »catholic unity« is often used in the documents of the Second Vatican Council.[21] It suggests (somewhat unfortunately) a priority for unity and cannot avoid entirely the suggestion that catholicity, because it implies diversity, is perceived as a concession.

From an historical theological perspective, the idea of »orthodoxy« soon developed into a twin-concept of catholicity.[22] The almost-universal geographical spread of the church, and the soundness and reliability of the orientation of its beliefs, rooted in apostolic witness, balanced one another. Increasingly, universality was deemed to be an affirmative token of orthodoxy; just as orthodoxy was regarded as a

---

[19] Ibid., 36–39.
[20] Ibid., 35.
[21] Cf. *Lumen gentium* 8: »These elements, as belonging to the Church of Christ, are impelling toward catholic unity.« *Lumen gentium* 13: »All men are called to be part of this catholic unity of the people of God ...« *Ad gentes* 6: »Thus it is plain that missionary activity wells up from the Church's inner nature and spreads abroad her saving Faith. It perfects her Catholic unity by this expansion.« On this vocabulary, cf. De Mey, »Eenheid in verscheidenheid. Het katholiciteitsbegrip van Vaticanum II«.
[22] Congar, »Die Wesenseigenschaften der Kirche,« 478–487; Witte, »Orthodoxie en katholiciteit,« 29–38; Cunningham, *An Introduction to Catholicism*, 4–7; Kasper, *Katholische Kirche*, 254–256.

condition for genuine universality. In a sermon on Ezekiel 34:6, Augustine of Hippo meditated on the theme of the sheep of the Lord scattered over the whole earth. Although heretics, he said, can be found all over the world, not all heretics will be found everywhere: *alii hic, alii ibi, nusquam tamen desunt*. Moreover, they do not know each other. Some sects exclusively live in Africa, such as the Donatists. Others prevail in the East, such as the Eunomians, yet are absent in Africa. Augustine claims this to be in contrast to the presence of the catholic church all over the world.[23] This needs to be nuanced: based on the understanding of the church of the *doctor gratiae*, the universality of the church's presence does not point to a geographical spread in a quantitative sense; rather, it refers to a worldwide communion in which love is the principle of togetherness. Separation occurs where love is absent.[24] Heretics refuse to be part of a whole. The fundamental co-existence of catholicity and orthodoxy is summarized in St. Vincent of Lérins' well-known maxim, *quod ubique, quod semper, quod ab omnibus creditum est.*

The confessional era of Christianity caused important changes in the understanding of catholicity. Most of these changes occurred in the second millennium, although similar tendencies were already present in the Codex Theodosianus (438), the Codex Justinianus (529–534), and the Holy Roman Empire of the German Nation, which all claimed imperial recognition for the Orthodox Church only.[25] Nowadays, these tendencies are understood as a narrowing[26] or a reduction[27] of the genuine concept of catholicity.

Max Weber's concept of »elective affinity« (*Wahlverwandtschaft*) may help to clarify some aspects of the confessional reduction of catholicity.[28] Elective affinity defines the congruency of social developments

---

[23] Augustin, *Sermo* 46, 18.
[24] Kasper, *Katholische Kirche*, 255.
[25] Ibid., 256.
[26] Ibid., 256–258.
[27] Gaillardetz, *Ecclesiology for a Global Church*, 42–47.
[28] Michael Löwy, »Le concept d'affinité élective chez Max Weber,« *Archives de sciences sociales des religions* 49 (2004):93–104. Cf. Henk Witte, »The Future of Christian Confessions in Europe: Response from a Catholic Perspective« in *Religiöse Bindungen – neu reflektiert: Ökumenische Antworten auf Veränderungen der Religiosität in Europa / Reimagining Religious Belonging. Ecumenical Responses to Changing Religiosity in Europe*, eds. Ivana Noble, Ulrike Link-Wieczorek and Peter De Mey, Beihefte zur Ökumenischen Rundschau 90 (Leipzig: Evangelische Verlagsanstalt, 2011), 104–111.

and developments in the field of knowledge. A separation between groups is not only a social event, but it also constitutes a mental event with regard to the experience and articulation of truth.[29] The social and the epistemological realms are intertwined here. Elective affinity implies that a specific group will prefer, emphasize, and deepen well-determined aspects of the truth and neglect other aspects. When churches are unable to enter into encounter, they cease to share their theological and spiritual insights mutually. Spiritual and theological growth becomes an inner group process. A doctrinal confession, therefore, can be understood as the articulation of the Christian truth in the particular timbre and emphasis of a particular Christian group.

From a bird's eye view, a rough sketch of this development reveals that the adjective »catholic« was included in the name of the latin church of the West, and »orthodox« in the name of the churches in the East. This nominal scission between the notions of »catholicity« and »orthodoxy« is quite interesting. The »Catholic« church experienced Christ's incarnation as the centre of its faith, while the »Orthodox« churches emphasized the paschal-pneumatological core of the divine mysteries. The pre-Vatican II liturgical experience of the creedal statement about the incarnation may well illustrate this Western emphasis on incarnation; it was sung more slowly than other parts of the creed, with the faithful kneeling down in devotion, while they sang the other parts standing upright.[30] Likewise, an example of the Eastern stress on Easter can be seen in the presence of the *anastasis* icon on an ambo; the words of the Gospel reach the faithful primordially via the mystery of Christ's death and resurrection.

A similar process of terminological and theological reduction and selective emphasizing happened between Roman Catholicism and Protestantism. While Protestants stressed the salvific core of the Christian faith in its *Christus solus*, the cross, and the *sola fide, sola gratia, sola Scriptura,* Catholics emphasized the elements through which the

---

[29] The clarification of the relation between sociality and truth was introduced in ecumenism by Peter Lengsfeld and his collaborators. See Peter Lengsfeld (ed.), *Ökumenische Theologie: Ein Arbeitsbuch* (Stuttgart/Berlin/Köln/Mainz: Kohlhammer, 1980). Recently, this approach is revisited in Thomas Bremer and Maria Wernsmann (eds.), *Ökumene – Überdacht. Reflexionen und Realitäten im Umbruch* (Freiburg: Herder, 2014).

[30] This was a general practice in Roman Catholic liturgy until the liturgical renewal after the Second Vatican Council. The Catholic tradition rediscovered the centrality of the Easter mystery in Catholicism over the course of the twentieth century, in the context of the liturgical movement.

content of the faith was mediated: the sacraments, the church, ministry, the saints, among them, Mary in particular.

This confessional tendency, therefore, implied not only a narrowing down but also a selective emphasis, resulting in a reciprocal and symbiotic »no« to the identity of the other confession. What was lost was the idea that the value of catholicity is not co-extensive with the shape of Roman Catholicism.

The Second Vatican Council aimed at overcoming confessionalism. It articulated its view on the value of catholicity in *Lumen gentium* 13. The aforementioned biblical and missionary motif of all humankind's call to the new people of God frames this doctrinal text.[31] On the one hand, it expresses the spread of the church throughout the whole world and in all ages in order to gather God's scattered children together. On the other hand, it gives expression to the legitimate diversity of the new people of God. Whereas the Council called the spread of the church all over the world »the characteristic of universality (*universalitatis character*) which adorns the people of God«, it used the term »catholicity« (*catholicitas*) to pay attention to the diversity that cannot be dissociated from the church's unity.[32] The text mentions three diversifying factors: the church as made up of different peoples who bring their own cultures; its inner structure of being composed of different ranks; and the rightful place of particular churches that enjoy their own traditions.[33]

Fifty years ago, the idea of diversity slowly gained ground in the Catholic Church's self-perception. The Council stressed its legitimacy, as did post-conciliar reception. During the fifty years following the Council, more and more differentiated contexts championed their legitimate place within the unity of the church, often with an emancipative purpose. In the beginning differentiation was made according to continents (Latin America, Asia, and Africa – Europe was yet to discover its particularity); later on also according to race, gender, sexual preference, and spiritual affinities.

---

[31] Cf. its first and its last sentence: »*Ad* novum *populum Dei* cuncti *vocantur homines*« and »*Ad* hanc igitur catholicam *Populi Dei* unitatem ... omnes *vocantur homines.*« Italics HW.
[32] Cf. De Mey, »Eenheid in verscheidenheid,« 34–37.
[33] The Vatican website translates (as Abbott and Flannery do) *proprii traditionibus fruentes* as »retain their own traditions«. »Enjoy«, in my opinion, retains the Augustinian connotation that *fruere* has.

Lumen gentium 13, however, pursued another aspect of that diversity: the sharing of gifts. »In virtue of this catholicity each individual part contributes through its special gifts to the good of the other parts and of the whole church.« Through sharing, the whole and each of the parts increase. »For the members of the people of God are called to share ….« The idea of sharing is important here, since it implies dialogue in both word and deed. The Council, in other words, unfolded a communicative and dialoguing concept of catholicity. Properly understood, catholicity implies the reciprocal in-between among particularities, their mutual effort to stay in contact, and to share spiritual riches, temporal resources, and human capital.[34]

3 Appropriate in a Postmodern World?

Let us return to the starting point of this contribution, namely, the contemporary situation of a society in which postmodern networking models prevail. Is catholicity an appropriate concept in a postmodern world? In principle, my answer would be »yes«. The nature of catholicity as a divine gift and a value implies a re-discovery and re-shaping in ever-changing contexts. I cannot imagine that, in the end, a context – even a postmodern one – could appear to be stronger than a gift from God. Therefore, in principle, catholicity and post-modernity need not exclude one another. Each context is an invitation to disclose, and give shape to, new aspects of a value. And the same is true for the context of postmodernity.

However, the underlying question is: Under which conditions does the notion of catholicity appear to be a fruitful concept to the churches in dealing with postmodern polycentrism? By way of conclusion, I will mention three conditions.

First, it is not so much catholicity but, rather, the refusal of particularities to communicate with others that causes the problem. It is true that network organizations bear the risk of stimulating closed-minded attitudes; yet they only do so by virtue of a reduced perception of today's reality. The openness that marks networks also permits alternative voices to interfere. Catholicity invites polycentric worlds to interconnect. This implies that the social meaning of catholicity, the awareness of being part of a whole and the capacity of dialogue, has priority.

---

[34]   *Lumen gentium* speaks about »apostolic workers«.

Still, conversation and encounter without content will remain meaningless chatter. Thus it is evident that the proclamation of the Gospel, as well as orthodoxy, will be included – but secondarily, and as a common design for investigation and shaping the discourse, rather than as an untouchable »given« for convincing or even overruling others.

A second condition concerns the awareness and skills needed for being a part of a whole. It is the church of Christ as a *whole* that is believed to be catholic. The notion cannot be exclusively claimed by a certain group, let alone by an individual believer. John Zizioulas underlines the fact that »being a person is basically different from being an individual or ›personality‹ in that the person cannot be conceived in itself as a static entity, but only as it *relates to*.« Personhood implies an openness or *ek-stasis* of being, that is, he says, »a movement towards communion«. It leads to a transcendence of the boundaries of the »self« and reveals the person's »being in a *catholic*, that is, integral and undivided, way.«[35] This may be extended to ecclesial groups and networks as well.

Finally, a third condition concerns the spiritual ability to let go of familiar and beloved concepts and forms which we think embody catholicity – without, however, losing their underlying value. To a great extent, listening and learning imply *un*learning.

Ecumenical encounter, and ecumenical experiences, can provide a valuable help to realize these conditions in a postmodern world. The postmodern, networked world can help ecumenism regain its original identity as a movement, and stimulate the churches to be on the move, even on the level of their organizations. This will be a work for the long term.

---

[35] John D. Zizioulas, *Communion and Otherness: Further Studies in Personhood and the Church*, ed. Paul McPartlan (London: T&T Clark, 2006), 212–213.

CATHOLICITY – GLOBAL AND LOCAL

KATHOLIZITÄT – GLOBAL UND VOR ORT

»World Christianity« – a New Concept Challenging the Understanding of »Catholicity«

Christine Lienemann-Perrin

»The most pressing issues
in twenty-first century Christianity
are ecumenical«
                (Andrew F. Walls)

Introduction

At New Delhi in 1961, the World Council of Churches (WCC) articulated the ecumenical vision with these words: »We believe that the unity ... is being made visible as *all in each place* who are baptized in Jesus Christ and confess him as Lord and Savior are brought ... into one fully committed fellowship ... and who at the same time are united with the whole Christian fellowship *in all places and all ages*.«[1] That great vision has driven the modern ecumenical movement up until today. Unity of all in each place, as well as in all places and all ages, has been at the core of the prayers and hopes of ecumenically minded churches throughout the 20th century.

Indeed, ecumenical awareness and practice has increased in many ways during this period. Yet despite this progress, the gap between ecumenical vision and reality has not diminished – on the contrary, it is greater today than ever before in the history of Christianity. Worldwide diversities and divisions have reached new dimensions in the last thirty years – a trend that will continue in the years to come. The ecumenical movement has been bypassed by the accelerated increase of myriads of newly established churches and movements generating new splits and divisions in contemporary Christianity. The problem is that, on the one

---

[1] W.A. Visser 't Hooft, *The New Delhi Report: The Third Assembly of the World Council of Churches, 1961* (New York: Association Press, 1962), 116 (italics: CL-P).

hand, the new branches are generally not »on the radar screens« of the ecumenical movement. On the other hand, ecumenical structures are more stumbling blocks than suitable spaces for newly established churches to participate in ecumenism. Due to the so-called *studies on World Christianity*, ecumenical scholars have become aware of these failures and have begun to rethink ecumenism based on the results of these studies.

My paper questions how World Christianity as a concept challenges the understanding of ecumenism in general, and catholicity in particular. After a brief overview of studies on World Christianity (Section 1), I address core affirmations and normative implications as observed in some of these studies (2). My conclusion is that the understanding of catholicity needs to be extended (3), and that European ecumenism has to be scrutinized within the global context (4 und 5).

1   Studies on World Christianity: A Brief Overview

(1) *Subject*: Scholars of World Christianity have undertaken the huge task of investigating – at least in principle – all expressions of Christianity worldwide. This includes all kinds of past and contemporary expressions of faith, teachings, of liturgy and rites, organizations and structures, moral codes and relationships with other Christian churches, other religions and other realities in world society. Special attention is given to the global dimensions of Christianity, e.g. the cross-cultural, cross-continental and global communication between churches, movements, organizations and groups (therefore: *World* Christianity). No phenomena within Christianity were to be excluded on normative grounds from such studies. So far, there is no consensus on the definition of World Christianity. Where are the boundaries with other religions, and other spheres of reality, to be drawn? This particular question was debated at the first World Christianity Forum in Boston, in October 2013. Jonathan Bonk, one of the participants, described the term »World Christianity« as a cognitive domain that is still under construction. Scholars are using it, he said, as a rough, broad term without defining it. For purposes of empirical research, many scholars agree with the statement: »who claims to be Christian *is* a Christian«.[2]

---

[2] World Christianity Forum, Boston University, October 16–18, 2013; notes by S. J. Lloyd of the session »World Christianity? Just what is this thing we're studying?,« October 18, 2013 (statements of Jonathan Bonk, 1; 8).

(2) *Aims*: At first glance, studies on World Christianity are aimed at enlarging the story of Christianity and overcoming wide spread myopia in regard to the worldwide spread of Christianity. A closer look shows that studies on World Christianity are also aimed at widening the awareness of intra-Christian dissemination, of cultural diversities and the seismic shifts Christianity has undergone in the last few decades. The implicit or explicit motives for undertaking such research are to enlarge the »we« in the self-understanding of Christians, and to pave the way for an enhanced interrelatedness among the churches locally and globally, as well as to recognize the multi-polarity of Christianity worldwide. Hand in hand with these motives, critical questions are raised not only with regard to »traditional« ways of doing theology, but also in view of the modern ecumenical movement.

(3) *Centres and chairs for the study on World Christianity*: The bulk of research centres and chairs are located in the USA.[3] So far, only a few have been established in Europe and other parts of the world. Among the scholars involved are many former missiologists with experiences in the global South, together with colleagues mainly from Africa and Asia. English is the dominant language used in studies that focus on the following fields of research:

a. Statistical investigation on the growth and decrease of Christian churches, movements and organizations in all continents and all countries around the globe.[4] The purpose is to describe and characterize new forms of Christianity in the last 100 years, as well as to categorize phenomena and to reflect on the taxonomies behind the descriptions.

b. History of Christianity with the focus on the cross-cultural transmission and appropriation of the Christian faith. The historiography of Christianity is based on a missionary perspective, and affirms that the church is cross-cultural by nature.

c. Critical stance over against certain facts and trends in contemporary Christianity in the West, namely in Europe. Critical comments are based on normative assumptions and expressed by antonyms to World

---

[3] A leading research centre is the Boston Theological Institute, a consortium of ten theological schools and seminaries in the Boston area including the Gordon-Conwell Theological Seminary, South Hamilton, MA.

[4] World Christian Database, see http://www.worldchristiandatabase.org/wcd (accessed July 14, 2014); David B. Barrett, George T. Kurian and Todd M. Johnson (eds.), *World Christian Encyclopedia: A Comparative Survey of Churches and Religions in the Modern World,* 2 volumes, 2nd edition (Oxford: Oxford University Press, 2001); Todd M. Johnson and Kenneth R. Ross (eds.), *Atlas of Global Christianity 1910–2010* (Edinburgh: Edinburgh University Press, 2009).

Christianity; terms with negative connotations, such as »Christendom« and »post-Christian West« are used frequently.

2 Conceptual Implications of Studies on World Christianity

Three basic assumptions shared by many scholars of World Christianity can be uncovered and illuminated by delving into the *oeuvres* of Andrew F. Walls and Lamin Sanneh, two of the founding fathers of recent studies on World Christianity.[5] These assumptions are:

(1) *Translatability of the gospel*: In principle the gospel can be transmitted across all cultures, translated into all human languages, and therefore communicated to all societies in all contexts of all times. The addressees of the gospel which is communicated can appropriate it wherever, and whenever, they live. Lamin Sanneh, originating from Gambia and professor emeritus of Missions and World Christianity at Yale Divinity School, has elaborated that assumption in his famous essay, »Whose Religion is Christianity? The Gospel beyond the West«.[6] He writes: »Christianity seems unique in being the only world religion that is transmitted without the language or originating culture of its founder.« (98) »The fact of Christianity being a translated, and translating, religion places God at the center of the universe of cultures, implying free coequality among cultures and a necessary relativizing of languages vis-à-vis the truth of God. No culture is so advanced and so superior that it can claim exclusive access or advantage to the truth of God, and none so marginal or inferior that it can be excluded.« (105f.)

Studies on World Christianity are an attempt to come to terms with the growing plurality and disparities in Christianity around the globe. Global changes and »seismic shifts« in contemporary Christianity are estimated, in principle, as legitimate expressions of the translatability of the gospel: the plurality of languages, cultures and structures in Christianity »is not a failure of the religion but the triumph of its translatability« (130). Throughout mission history (Western) Christianity

---

[5] Forerunners of the recent studies on World Christianity were Henry P. van Dusen and Kenneth Scott Latourette in the first half of the 20th century.

[6] Lamin Sanneh, *Whose Religion is Christianity? The Gospel beyond the West* (Grand Rapids, MI: Eerdmans, 2003). For an extended reflection on his basic assumptions, see also: Lamin Sanneh, *Disciples of All Nations: Pillars of World Christianity* (Oxford: Oxford University Press, 2008). For a relativizing comment on that assumption, see Kirsteen Kim, *Joining in with the Spirit: Connecting World Church and Local Church* (London: SCM Press, 2012), 46–48.

has obscured that assumption time and again, but not expunged it completely from its memory. The »three self«-principle has been coined by Protestant missionaries, affirming that churches in foreign lands should become self-supporting, self-governing and self-propagating.[7] But the principle revealed a fundamental paradox inherent in the missionary movement: Wherever the »three self«-principle is applied, the process easily spins out of missionary control.

That is what happened in Africa when Africans began to establish independent forms of Christianity, starting a missionary dynamic in a form much greater than all the missionary initiatives launched by Westerners before the end of the Second World War. Scholars of World Christianity plead for acknowledging and honouring the translatability of the gospel as manifested in the proliferation of *local* answers to the transmitted Christian faith. They object to hasty condemnations of these as »deviant« forms of faith.

(2) *Cross-culturality of the Christian faith*: As a consequence of the translatability of the gospel, scholars of World Christianity affirm that the community of believers in Jesus Christ across diverse cultures is an essential mark of the church. Christian faith is cross-cultural by nature, states the Scottish missiologist, Andrew F. Walls, professor emeritus at the Akrofi-Christaller Institute of Theology, Mission and Culture (Ghana).[8] The council of the apostles at Jerusalem (Acts 15) is of eminent importance in Walls' concept of World Christianity. It is perceived as the birth certificate of the cross-cultural, universal church. From a nucleus of Jewish and Greek believers, the new faith community of the first century extended itself continuously by including more people who, in turn, contributed new perspectives to the church's self-understanding. Enriched – and at the same time challenged – by the neophytes and their appropriation of the Christian faith, the extended

---

[7] Rufus Anderson (1796–1880) and Henry Venn (1796–1873). On the Roman Catholic side, the Spiritan priest J. Vincent Donovan has coined and implemented similar ideas during his missional journey with the Masai; see idem, *Christianity Rediscovered*, 25th anniversary edition (Maryknoll, NY: Orbis Books, 2003).

[8] Andrew F. Walls, *The Cross-Cultural Process in Christian History: Studies in the Transmission and Appropriation of Faith* (Maryknoll, NY: Orbis Books; Edinburgh: T&T Clark, 2002); idem, »Christianity across Twenty Centuries,« in Johnson and Ross, *Atlas*, 48f.

community was time and again challenged to re-think its previously understood ways of being a church.[9]

As a consequence of this process believers in Christ gradually emerged as a community distinct from its mother religion, Judaism, on the one hand, and from the other religions of the time on the other. Walls concludes that the church preserves its vitality and capacity to grow only as long as the gospel is communicated cross-culturally. He is convinced that any given church is stagnating or even dying if that capacity is abandoned or, even, declared as illegitimate. More explicitly, he opines that Latin Christianity had turned away from cross-culturality in the 7th century and later developed its dogmas, church structures and canonical laws aloof from – if not explicitly against – other parts of Christianity outside Latin Europe.[10] The loss of cross-culturality is, according to Walls, the real Fall or Original Sin (*Sündenfall*) of Western Christianity, which has to be challenged and overcome by returning to the fold of cross-cultural *World* Christianity.

(3) *Catholicity recovered*: World Christianity as a concept is no alternative to the notion of catholicity, but an attempt to overcome shortcomings in the interpretation of catholicity and to recover it in its widest possible dimension. Kevin J. Vanhoozer and Charles E. Van Engen underline that aim in the volume »Globalizing Theology. Belief and Practice in an Era of World Christianity«.[11] Vanhoozer writes:

> On the one hand, what the church over time and across space has always believed provides an important check and balance to new developments. On the other hand, local theologies become great performances when they respond to specific cultural contexts and to new problems in ways that contain lessons for the whole church. (118).

---

[9] Andrew F. Walls »Converts and Proselytes? The Crisis Over Conversion in the Early Church,« *International Bulletin of Missionary Research* 28, no. 1 (January 2004): 2–6.

[10] Andrew F. Walls, »World Christianity and the Early Church,« in *A New Day. Essays on World Christianity in Honor of Lamin Sanneh,* ed. Akintunde E. Akinade (New York: Peter Lang, 2010), 17–30.

[11] Vanhoozer, »›One Rule to Rule Them All?‹ Theological Method in an Era of World Christianity,« in *Globalizing Theology: Belief and Practice in an Era of World Christianity,* eds. Craig Ott and Harold A. Netland (Grand Rapids MI: Baker Academic, 2006), 85–126; Charles E. Van Engen, »The Glocal Church: Locality and Catholicity in a Globalizing World,« in *Globalizing Theology,* eds. Ott and Netland, 157–179.

As the ecumenical creeds of antiquity are already a consensus between aspects of a multicultural communion, they have to be respected today in the sense of a *regula fidei*, but Vanhoozer continues: »There are many theological issues, however, that the rule of faith does not address.« (119) As the story of Christian communities continues and expands in new cultures and contexts, the ecumenical creeds of former times have to be widened by the insights and faith expressions coined in new languages. What has been an adequate rule of faith in a particular time and space may become too narrow when the faith community has grown across further spaces in later times. Shortcomings in the understanding of catholicity are often unveiled when new faith witnesses occur in response to new situations. Vanhoozer further writes: »Learning how Africans and Asians read Scripture, then, helps us better to see the beam in our own Western eyes.« (119) To point out the problem of theology trapped in a particular culture, Andrew F. Walls confronts »Western« with »African« models of theology.

> Western models of theology are too small for Africa. Most of them reflect the worldview of the Enlightenment, and that is a small-scale worldview ... to fit a small-scale universe. Since most Africans live in a larger, more populated universe, together with entities that are outside the Enlightenment worldview, such models of theology ... have no answers for some of the most desolating aspects of life – because they have no questions. They have nothing useful to say on issues involving such things as witchcraft or sorcery, since these do not exist in an Enlightenment universe.[12]

What Walls writes about Western theology applies also to the concept of catholicity, as far as it has been interpreted within the framework of Western theology. Catholicity in its embracing dimension can be recovered if there is trust in a paradox that has been coined by Walls as follows: »It is a delightful paradox that the more Christ is translated into the various thought forms and life systems which form our various national identities, the richer all of us will be in our common Christian identity.«[13]

---

[12] Andrew F. Walls, »Globalization and the Study of Christian History,« in *Globalizing Theology*, eds. Ott and Netland, 70–82, quotation on p. 75f.
[13] Andrew F. Walls, *The Missionary Movement in Christian History: Studies in the Transmission of Faith* (Maryknoll, NY: Orbis Books, 1996), 54.

3 Challenges in Understanding Catholicity

»The most pressing issues in twenty-first century Christianity are ecumenical.«[14] Andrew F. Walls' statement challenges contemporary ecumenism, in general and the understanding of catholicity in particular. While translating the message cross-culturally has been a feature of Christianity throughout its history, it has reached a new quantitative dimension during the last century, particularly in the last three decades. Globalization and the revolution of the media have accelerated that process tremendously, and led to a never-ending inner differentiation within Christianity. Facing the new level of globalization, the intrinsic paradox between growing diversities and holding fast the concept of oneness is at stake. According to the *World Christian Encyclopedia* about 40'000 different Christian »denominations« existed worldwide in 2010.[15] It is no wonder that World Christianity is in danger of losing sight of what the myriads of churches, movements, theologies and traditions have in common. Facing such diversity, the church risks losing its catholicity.

One reason why the modern ecumenical movement is facing a serious crisis is that it has failed to keep up with the accelerated changes within World Christianity; indeed it has been overrun by them. The never-ending process of inner differentiation may either end up in power-games among competing groups, or continue until the complete dissolution. One prediction is that Christianity may become more and more privatized and individualized, to the point that it finally could disappear as an organization. The crucial question, therefore, is how the oneness of *ecclesia* can be identified, and made visible, in the midst of the never-ending differentiation occurring in the widened horizon of World Christianity.

---

[14] Walls, »World Christianity and the Early Church,« 28.
[15] Information by Todd M. Johnson, Center for the Study of Global Christianity, Gordon-Conwell Theological Seminary, South Hamilton, MA (October 17, 2013). The term *denomination* is defined as: »Any agency consisting of a number of congregations or churches voluntarily aligning themselves with it. As a statistical unit in this survey, a ›denomination‹ always refers to one single country. Thus the Roman Catholic Church, although a single organization, is described here as consisting of 236 denominations in the world's 238 countries including countries not recognized as states by the United Nations.« See http://www.worldreligiondatabase.org/esweb.asp?WCI=Results&Query=2032&PageSize=25&Page=1 (accessed July 14, 2014).

What can be learned from this analysis? I mention three points that are currently being discussed in ecumenical fora:[16]

(1) *Border-crossing*: Ecumenism has given to the last century the epithet »ecumenical«. Confessional families developed their visions, strategies and structures to fulfill the expectations and needs of their time. For a considerable period, these were based on the growing communication and interrelations between Protestants, Anglicans, Orthodox and Roman Catholics in the global North, and in the mainline churches in the global South that have emerged from the missionary movement stemming from Europe and North America.

The crisis of that form of ecumenism became obvious, however, when the seismic shift within World Christianity dramatically changed the global religious landscape.[17] On the one hand confessional churches are confronted by a decrease in membership, and a loss of public attention paid to their ecumenical endeavours. On the other hand new visions, structures and strategies of commonality are emerging from among those sections of Christianity with only casual – or no – relation to the churches that had initiated and developed modern ecumenism. Additionally, some communities from the growing sections of Christianity have no ecumenical awareness at all and live on their own, if not against the other Christian groups of which they have any knowledge.

What do we imply, in terms of perspectives, strategies and structures, by crossing borders to join hands with groups outside the ecumenical fold? To illustrate the problem, let us consider the recent document on growing convergence and consent elaborated by the Faith and Order commission of the WCC, »The Church: Towards a Common Vision«.[18] First of all, the tradition of producing convergence documents

---

[16] Michael Kinnamon, *The Vision of the Ecumenical Movement and How It Has Been Impoverished by Its Friends* (St. Louis, MO: Chalice Press, 2003); Mélisande Lorke and Dietrich Werner (eds.), *Ecumenical Visions for the 21st Century: A Reader for Theological Education* (Geneva: WCC Publications, 2013). For the presentations at the Global Ecumenical Theological Institute (GETI) on ecumenical visions for the 21st Century in Busan, October 2013, see: http://www.globethics.net/web/ecumenical-visions/collection-articles?collection=DT5* (accessed July 14, 2014).

[17] However, a positive aspect of the changed ecumenical scene can also be mentioned: many aims of the ecumenical movement have been achieved and documented; see *Growth in Agreement. Reports and Agreed Statements of Ecumenical Conversations on a World Level*, 3 vols.; 4th vol. in preparation (Geneva: WCC,1984–2007).

[18] The document is available electronically: http://www.oikoumene.org/en/resources/documents/wcc-commissions/faith-and-order-commission/i-unity-

is not familiar in churches that have mainly a tradition of oral communication. Here church leaders, charismatics or ordinary church members receive »the truth« when filled by the Holy Spirit. There is also a problem of concepts and languages. This Faith and Order document on ecclesiology uses a terminology deriving from Greek and Latin. It will hardly be understood outside the historical ecumenical fold. In some parts of Christianity the terms »church« and »denomination« are not used at all; instead »fellowship« and »ministries«, among other terms, replace traditional ecclesiological language. Some groups practice rebaptism while others don't baptize at all. In contrast to the threefold ministry explained carefully in this document, African churches, and Pentecostals in Asia and Latin America, focus on many further ministerial roles such as those of prophets, apostles, healers and exorcists.

A special problem for established ecumenism are new forms of networking and communication among churches across countries and continents. These forms are popular in migrant churches and Christian groups in Africa, which add to their names the epithet »international«. The growing coexistence of *parallel ecumenisms*, with no interrelations among them, is a sign that catholicity needs to be broadened so that new shapes of ecumenism and catholicity can be embraced.

(2) *Discernment*: In a separate conversation, scholars on World Christianity continue to debate whether their discipline is essentially descriptive or whether it is also normative. »Should all those who claim to be Christians be counted as Christians?« is the crucial question. Scholars like Todd M. Johnson, Jonathan Bonk, Jehu J. Hanciles and Rodney L. Petersen favour a descriptive understanding of the discipline, while for some like Jim Miller, it is a sociological discipline. Yet others, including Dana L. Robert, raise concerns that a purely descriptive approach would not leave open the possibility for theological and normative reflections on World Christianity.[19] In any case, whatever studies in ecumenism World Christianity is concerned with, it cannot abstain from using normative criteria in some areas of discussion, especially in matters of catholicity. Nevertheless, even a purely descriptive concept of World Christianity challenges an understanding of catholicity; for even »normativity« has to be scrutinized again and

the-church-and-its-mission/the-church-towards-a-common-vision (accessed July 14, 2014).

[19] Notes on the World Christianity Forum (Boston, October 17–19, 2013) by S. J. Lloyd of the session »World Christianity? Just what is this thing we're studying?,« unpublished, October 18, 2013.

again in particular times and places. In theology unbiased description of phenomena (in our case, people calling themselves »Christians«), and critical discernment between claim and reality, are bound together in tension. They form a paradox. Catholicity is at stake if *all* phenomena labelled »Christian« are recognized, without reserve. But before theological scrutiny can begin, the criteria for catholicity have to be explored anew together with groups outside the established ecumenical fold. This is what scholars on World Christianity expect from ecumenical scholars.

To what extent, and how, is diversity a legitimate and necessary feature of the body of Christ today? That question has to be dealt with anew. The term »catholicity« has been coined by W.A. Visser 't Hooft, first General Secretary of the WCC, to describe the interconnection and interrelation between all local congregations at one place, as well as the togetherness between local churches at all places within the whole *oikoumene*. Catholicity is also expressed and explained by the metaphor of the many members of the one body (1Cor 12; Eph 4): Members of a body can live only as an integral part of an organism, not as separate selves. They are only part of the whole, not identical with the body as a whole. They are interdependent in their diverse functions; they play their roles for the well-being of the whole, renouncing a life for themselves. There may be no hierarchy of stronger over against weaker members, of more over against less important roles. Members are not to become the same as other members; instead they are to remain diverse and distinct from each other.

How these biblical guidelines need to be applied in World Christianity today is a matter for cross-cultural discourse about the cross-cultural character of the one, holy, catholic, and apostolic Church. This needs to be done by looking at the non-denominationals, Pentecostals, renewalists, independent churches, ministries, fellowships, groups and movements outside the ecumenical fold, all as members of the body of Christ. There is a need to explore together with them new forms and structures of ecumenism, aiming at a wider model of ecumenism. Discernment is urgently needed in questions of ethics, bible reading and culturally distinct expressions of faith.

(3) *Coherence*: In ecumenical studies, discernment and coherence together form another paradoxical tension that needs to be maintained. Discernment focuses on critical examination and differentiation between that which is acceptable and unacceptable in questions of faith. Its virtue is to draw boundaries over against unlimited openness. By contrast, coherence aims at unveiling unanimity in the midst of the

diversities in expressing the Christian faith. Coherence means mutual recognition of what is shared by Christians throughout time and space despite the diverse languages, notions and symbols used to express the common faith. Coherence in questions of faith deserves a method of translating and re-translating creeds forward and backward, and in all directions.

Unless the ecumenical movement is successful in translating and appropriating the message multilaterally, it loses the core of its existence. This would give way to continuing fragmentation, affecting the catholicity of the Church and ending up in separately existing Christianit*ies* or even separate religions. How can the diversities visible in the myriads of groups, movements and denominations worldwide be bridged in contemporary Christianity? How can ecumenism move ahead from the limited complexities for which it has been designed in the 20th century, to the multiplied complexities it faces today? In search for coherence, it probably needs to step back from ambitious formulations like the Faith and Order document *The Church: Towards a Common Vision* and return to basic and elementary statements, hoping that they can then be developed further, step by step. A synopsis of diverse expressions of basic statements could help raise the awareness of the cross-culturality and translatability of the gospel. An example to test this approach could be Christology. A synopsis of Asian, African, Latin American, North American and European interpretations, or »faces«, of Christ could be a starting point from which new commonalities may be explored in the midst of diverse languages, cultural expressions and socio-political contexts.

4 Consequences for a European Approach to Catholicity

The overall intention of the concept of World Christianity is to move away from a Euro-centred perspective on Christianity. Such a perspective implies that Europe is allotted a position apart from the rest of the world. As an association of ecumenical institutes and ecumenists in Europe, the Societas Oecumenica must analyse this matter precisely *because* the notion of World Christianity addresses European Christianity directly, on the basis of some provocative assumptions. I confine myself to three crucial – and controversial – statements, with reference to Andrew F. Walls, Jehu J. Hanciles and Lamin Sanneh.

(1) Europe is given a special position as the heartland of *Christendom*, with the term bearing a negative connotation, something from which *Christianity* has to be liberated and positively distinguished. There are no terminological equivalents in other European languages to this Christendom/Christianity antagonism – and perhaps no equivalents in languages of other continents.[20] That probably explains why the Christendom/Christianity debate has little resonance beyond the English-speaking world.[21]

Scholars of World Christianity identify the roots of »Christendom« in early medieval times. They reconstruct the history of the Latin church in a way that confirms their concept of Christendom as applied to contemporary Western Europe. That approach is best illustrated by Walls' and Hanciles' *oeuvres*. According to Walls, the historical roots of Christendom reach back to the times when Christianity was transmitted to the barbarian tribes in Northern Europe and appropriated by them on the demand of their kings.[22] It was continued by the churches of the Reformation and survived, in various modifications,

---

[20] The term *Christendom* was coined in late ninth-century Anglo-Saxon England as *Cristendome* when it had »no exact parallel in the Latin or Greek words used previously to designate Christian adherence, *Christianitas* or *oikoumene*.« The Anglo-Saxon concept of Christendom derives from the period, »when Charles the Great created a notion of Christian universality in his Holy Roman Empire«; Judith Herrin, *The Formation of Christendom* (Princeton NJ: Princeton University Press, 1987), 8. Later on, the many different kingdoms and cultures in the Western part of medieval Europe were bound together not exclusively, but mainly, by the Latin language and the Catholic church with its spiritual authority in Rome. This unified whole was called *Christendom*. – In the studies on World Christianity the English term *Christianity* is used today (1) for a religious system such as Hinduism or Buddhism, and (2) for ›true‹ expressions of the Christian faith. Distinct from Christianity, *Christendom* is used in a clearly pejorative sense. It mirrors the »medieval imperial phase of Christianity when the church became a domain of the state, and Christian profession a matter of political enforcement« (Sanneh, *Whose Religion*, 23).

[21] In German, Christen*tum* and Christen*heit* are not juxtaposed in the same way as in the English speaking discourse on World Christianity. There exists no literal equivalent in German to the English (pejorative) term *Christendom* – except the sometimes negatively connoted plural »*Christentümer*«. Likewise, other European languages as e.g. Dutch, French and Spanish give no equivalent terms to the English juxtaposition of positively or neutrally connoted *Christianity* over against negatively connoted *Christendom*.

[22] »[T]he northern peoples, with no easy way of dividing sacred and profane custom, produced territorial Christianity by their need to have a single body of custom. A single people must follow a single code.« (Walls, *Cross-Cultural Process*, 35).

until the 19th century, contends Walls. Christendom is seen as a problematic model based on the principle of territoriality. While the church is characterized as a captive of the state, the latter is perceived as the servant of the one and single *religio licita*. Walls argues that in former times all people within a territory were supposed to be members of the church – not out of free will, but as subjects of the state. Later on, the model of Christendom was expanded to – and imposed on – the non-European world by missionary movements and by settlers migrating from Europe to the Americas.[23] Christendom – while outdated even in the West – is conserved in its enduring structures and further nurtured by money and manpower.

But in the judgment of scholars of World Christianity, it is seen as a dead body. Today it can no longer serve as an ideal for Christian communities in other regions of the world. They may instead liberate themselves from it, or ignore it altogether. Jehu J. Hanciles, a scholar of World Christianity in Atlanta originating from Sierra Leone, declares Christendom bankrupt as an idea and a reality.[24] According to him, to Walls and many other scholars the future belongs to Christianity *without* Christendom. Walls again: »Christendom is dead, and Christianity is alive and well without it.«[25] Christianity is developed in Africa, Asia and Latin America where Western mission has only been an historical episode.[26]

(2) Europe is given a special position as the heartland of the *Post-Christian West* from which *Non-Western Christianity* is positively distinguished.[27] That assumption is derived from the extensive global statistics on long-term developments in church membership. Secularism in Western and Eastern Europe is perceived as a terminal threat to Christianity. Christian life is seen as affected in various ways: in terms of the constant decline in church attendance, decline of active

---

[23] »The natural objective was to incorporate the new lands within Christendom. The only known model of Christianity was territorial.« (Walls, ibid., 38).

[24] Jehu J. Hanciles, *Beyond Christendom: Globalization, African Migration, and the Transformation of the West* (Maryknoll NY: Orbis Books, 2008), and there especially chapter 4 on »The Birth and Bankruptcy of Christendom« (84–111).

[25] Walls, *Cross-Cultural Process*, 34.

[26] According to Walls, the impact of the Western missionary movement in Africa was not more than a detonator of an explosion that continued afterwards independently (ibid., 33).

[27] North America (Canada and USA) is seen as less affected by post-Christianity because of the permanent influx of Africans, Latin Americans and Asians who constantly introduce new forms of non-Western Christianity in the »West«.

participation in the church and in membership. Church authority is diminishing due to ignorance of the moral teachings of the churches. Knowledge by church members about their faith is diminishing rapidly. The public role of the church has given way to the privatization of faith. In short: »The massive de-Christianization in the old heartlands ultimately points to the provisional nature and ultimate failure of the Christendom model«.[28] By contrast, the vitality and unchallenged authenticity of non-Western Christianity seems to be self-evident: numbers tell about a constant increase of churches, accompanied by a high identification of members with their teachings. New models of Christianity are emerging everywhere, Hanciles writes. Hence in Western lands the Christian world supposedly has a future thanks only to the migrant churches, since they exist *in* the West without being *from* the West. As North America shows, Christianity in the West undergoes a qualitative transformation in this process.[29]

(3) Contemporary Europe is given an isolated position at the *periphery* of Christianity, due to the recent shift of its *centre of gravity* from Europe to the global South. That assumption is backed by historical cases from which the *serial* – or *sequential* – nature of Christian expansion is derived: Christianity is understood as being spread through a *series* marked by progress and decline. Throughout history, centres of missionary outreach later declined and became weak while the peripheries, the former targets of mission, were fuelled with a new interpretation of the Christian message, with new life and missionary energy.[30] Throughout mission history, Christianity survived thanks to its missionized peripheries and not due to its traditional centres. Walls opines »that the recessions typically take place in the Christian heartlands, in the areas of greatest Christian strength and influence ... while the advances typically take place at or beyond its periphery« (30). The energizing stimulus is a result of new challenges from missionary outreach into foreign lands across other cultures and languages. Where that challenge is lacking, the driving force decreases.

---

[28] Hanciles, *Beyond Christendom*, 110.
[29] Ibid., 276–302. According to Hanciles, the only hope for legitimate forms of Christianity in the West is the migrant churches in that they introduce non-Western forms of Christianity in North America. African American churches are praised for having never gone through Enlightenment experiences.
[30] Walls, *Cross-Cultural Process*, 27–48. To give an example (ibid. 31): »The Christian heartlands moved from the urban centers of Mediterranean civilization, with their advanced technology and developed literary tradition, to a new setting among peasant cultivators and semi-settled raiders.«

According to Walls: »the survival of the Christian faith as a major force in the world depended on its having crossed a cultural frontier« (31).

The problem with European Christianity is that over centuries it has cut itself off from cross-cultural exchanges and become monocultural and exclusivist in its self-understanding. Multi-linguality in theological thinking was lost. Furthermore, it developed a mission-less and even anti-missionary attitude that has been enforced by its adaptation to secularism. Walls concludes that »what the Christianity of the twenty-first century will be like, in its theology, its worship, its effect on society, its penetration of new areas, whether geographically or culturally, will depend on what happens in Africa, in Latin America, and in some parts of Asia« (32) – but not in Europe. To summarize bluntly: There is no hope for the »oxygen-starved Christianity of the West« (47) unless it is ready to learn from the diversity of Christian forms and expressions in the rest of the world.

5   Comments and Conclusion

Having bluntly presented the core criticisms against European Christianity I will briefly mention four aspects of the concept of World Christianity which, I think, need to be scrutinized. Then I will conclude with the challenges for rethinking catholicity in Europe.

(1) The concept of World Christianity aspires to a *comprehensive and integrated view* of all facets of Christian life all over the globe at all times. However, the related studies are still far from being all-inclusive, are even at times selective, and suffer from many *lacunae*. Their focus is Africa and Asia. Latin America and the Orthodox world in Eastern Europe rarely come to the fore, and Christianity in Western Europe and other secularized countries is of interest, at most, as a counter-narrative to their more valued forms of Christianity.

(2) The profile of the concept of World Christianity has been shaped mainly in reaction to – and as a critique of – Euro-centrism in church historiography and theology.[31] Unfortunately that critique has

---

[31]   In his essay »Whose Religion is Christianity?,« Lamin Sanneh deals with the impression of his interlocutor that »[t]he West is inclined to dismiss world Christianity by reducing it to Third World syncretism blended with vestigial paganism and spiced with exotic and implacable tribalism« (*Whose Religion*, 70).

ended up constructing the dichotomous *Christianity/Christendom paradigm*, more or less disconnected from reliable historical analysis. Since some historical aspects are selected while others are obscured or omitted, the critique does not do justice to the process of inculturation of Christianity in medieval Europe. In fact the criticisms made of so-called »Christendom« are, to a certain extent, congruent with criticisms expressed from *within* European Christianity.

I would even state that self-criticism, and the capacity for renewal, are features of European Christianity past and present. Already in medieval times, religious (reform-)orders have been founded precisely to overcome grievances in the church; likewise, various reformations of the church have been initiated and developed in the heartland of »territorial« Christianity. Thus the Enlightenment criticized, first of all, aberrations of certain Christian practices, not Christianity as such. Religious revivals in the 18th and 19th centuries emerged from European Christian soil. Some of the sharpest critics of bourgeois Christian religion in the 20th century have been, besides Friedrich Nietzsche, Karl Barth and Franz Overbeck in Basel.

(3) There is, of course, some evidence that Christianity's *centre of gravity has shifted* southwards in the last decades. However, scholars of World Christianity are often obsessed with figures. The »global shift« theory is based mainly on figures of church growth which neglect the paradoxical quality of the Christian message and life.[32] Figures are not the only thing that counts in Christian history; what is of more importance is if, and how, the impact of Christianity transforms the world. Paradoxically, success and failure in translating the message are sometimes disclosed as precisely the opposite of what they are supposed to be. In short, it would probably be more exact to speak of *multi-polarity* rather than the »southward shift« of World Christianity. At the least, Europe and North America continue to be powerful centres of academic theological research and financial capacity.[33]

---

[32] Sebastian C.H. Kim, »The Future Shape of Christianity from an Asian Perspective,« in *Global Christianity: Contested Claims,* eds. Frans Wijsen and Robert Schreiter (New York, Amsterdam: Rodopi, 2007), 69–93.

[33] Dietrich Werner, a vigorous promoter of theological education in the global South with knowledge of contemporary conditions of theological training worldwide, is concerned about the quality of newly established schools in Asia that »offer only light and ›fast food‹ theological education with impressive titles, but no libraries, developed curricula or common ecumenical framework«; see idem, »Perspectives on the Future of Theological Education in Asia,« in

(4) The problem with the theory of the *serial/sequential spread of Christianity* is that it is applied, so to speak, as a principle – if not a kind of natural law – when Christianity in Europe is analysed, and its future development predicted. The »serial spread« theory is made from selective historical analysis and given a normative quality. According to this theory, Europe is on the declining side of World Christianity and therefore of no significance for its contemporary self-understanding. European Christianity is disqualified as a stumbling block to World Christianity, rather than taken as part of it. This has far-reaching consequences for the understanding of catholicity. Within Christianity in continental Europe (though not in Great Britain), conversation on catholicity has become negligible. This is, of course, a great loss for ecumenism in Europe. But the strategy of non-communication also affects World Christianity's discourse outside Europe.

Having stated these four reservations as to the concept of World Christianity, the question remains as to challenges about the European understanding of catholicity. Here I have four observations:

Firstly, the challenge is to overcome every kind of naïve cultural idiocentrism in *church historiography* and theology in Europe. Instead of just reproducing for that purpose the Christendom/Christianity paradigm, the gaps between Europe and other parts of the world should be explored carefully *in each individual case*.[34] The historiography of World Christianity is possible only by a conscious interplay with the relativity of different perspectives – *including* those from Europe, not without them. This begs the correct perception and organization of a multitude of sources, questions and perspectives provided by micro-historical studies. My impression is that present attempts to write a history of World Christianity need to be further developed in that direction.

Secondly, *European theology* must be accepted as part of the catholic heritage of the church worldwide only on an equal basis with theologies from other parts, cultures and languages of the world. Claims of dominance and control over other theologies need to be surrendered. At the same time theologies characterized as *non*-Western, in the sense

---

Asian Handbook for Theological Education and Ecumenism, eds. Hope Antone et al. (Oxford: Regnum, 2013), 657–666, quotation on p. 658.

[34] The German historian Jürgen Osterhammel has reflected convincingly on the requirements of world history; see *Die Verwandlung der Welt: Eine Geschichte des 19. Jahrhunderts* (München: C.H. Beck, 2011 [1st ed. 2009]).

of »anything-*but*-Western«, are also not a suitable approach in a conversation on catholicity. As Kevin J. Vanhoozer has put it: »The way forward is not non-Western but *more*-than-Western theology.«[35] Mutuality of acknowledgement *and* critical challenge will lead to a renewed and extended understanding of catholicity.

Thirdly, globalization is significantly transforming religions in Europe, including Christianity. *Migrant churches* are gaining momentum in our religious landscape, introducing aspects of global Christianity in the heart of European Christianity. As they become an integral part of European Christianity it is necessary to conceptualize catholicity in dialogue with them. This requires a serious encounter and discourse with migrant Christianity at all levels.

Fourthly, labels like »post-Christianity«, »post-Christian West« and »post-Christendom Europe« all refer to long-term transformations of the Christian legacy in the direction of »*secularization*«. That process can, of course, be deplored as a great loss of the Christian faith. But the European scene could also be perceived as a space within which, and a proof of, how Christianity has experienced – and positively coped with – processes of secularization.[36] Could this not be a lesson to be learned by local churches in other parts of the globe?

---

[35] Vanhoozer, »One Rule«, 119.
[36] Frans J. Verstraelen, »Jenkins' *The Next Christendom* and Europe,« in *Contested Claims*, eds. Wijsen and Schreiter, 95–116. Verstraelen states that »European Christianity not only is surviving, but also has a significant contribution to make to the future of global Christianity« (ibid., 95). See also Ryan K. Bolger (ed.), *The Gospel after Christendom: New Voices, New Cultures, New Expressions* (Grand Rapids, MI: Baker Academic, 2012). Bolger is surprised to recognize that »fresh expressions« of faith emerge from the very heart of societies that have been shaped for centuries by »Christendom« and secularization. See also as a recent study on the same topic Gabriel Monet, *L'Eglise émergente: Être et faire Eglise en postchrétienté* (Berlin: LIT, 2014).

Catholicity as Communion
Three Moments of the Orthodox Experience

Dorin Oancea

The challenge in the title of this paper expresses the challenge of reality: in Asia, Africa and Latin America Christianity is growing so quickly, that the number of Christians living there will surpass the number of those living in traditional Christian areas. This process takes place in regions with an important ethnic and religious diversity and goes hand in hand with a corresponding inculturation, so that it leads not only to growth in numbers but also to growth in diversity and therefore enters the scope of ecumenical reflection.

The whole phenomenon is a major component of globalization and has been studied in this context quite thoroughly, if one remembers the debate around the important book of Philip Jenkins, *The Next Christendom. The Coming of Global Christianity*.[1] Jenkins offers almost startling statistics about the growth of Christianity with its various denominations in different parts of the world, mainly in Asia, Africa and Latin America. When reading this, I said to myself – »Dorin, you should be happy, because the name of the Lord is being praised by a much larger number of faithful.« But then I remembered a story from the *Paterikon* about an old monk, who had lived a lifetime all alone for

---

[1] Philip Jenkins, *The Next Christendom: The Coming of Global Christianity* (Oxford: Oxford University Press, 2002). As an example for the debate, see the contributions, including that of Philip Jenkins, in Frans Wijsen and Robert Schreiter (eds.), *Global Christianity: Contested Claims* (Amsterdam/New York: Rodopi, 2007).

himself on a remote mountain and now was visited by a young monk. He asked the young one to tell him something about the world, about faith in the world. The young monk had much to say about the end of the persecutions, the religious freedom Christians enjoyed and their overwhelming growth in number. But the hermit was a bit stubborn and interrupted him, quite harshly: »I am not interested in numbers, that kind of growth means nothing to me! Just tell me whether faith is still powerful enough to move the mountains.« That very moment the mountain started to shake and the young monk was terribly frightened, whereas the old one addressed the mountain quite calmly: »Stay still, I haven't spoken with you!« What happened? The mountain stopped shaking, of course.

This old story expresses two ways of understanding catholicity – one concentrating upon the extension of faith, the other on its intensity. Are the two aspects contradictory or should they be considered together? Should we rejoice about the growth in numbers of our faithful, associated with the term »Global Christianity«, or should we concentrate, as a positive alternative, upon the purity and the high standards of our identity, in a time when all real values are being washed up? Or should we better do both, rejoice about the growth and keep the standards? I shall try an answer looking at three ways of understanding catholicity in the early church.

My analysis is not dedicated so much to the historical circumstances related to these three situations as to the communion with Christ we find in them and which is, in my opinion, essential for Christian self-understanding.

1   Three Early Models of Catholicity

The All-embracing Catholicity: St Justin Martyr and Philosopher[2]

In his two Apologies St Justin refers to the universal presence of the Word, the second person of the Holy Trinity and identical with Jesus Christ. This presence is interpreted as a spermatic word (*logos spermatikos*, literally mentioned in the Second Apology XI) dwelling in each creature, including all humans (»He is the Word of whom every race of men were partakers«. First Apology, XLVI; »... he was and is the Word

---

[2]   St Justin, martyr and philosopher (100–165 A.D.).

who is in every man.«, Second Apology X). Christ is present as a seminal word in the whole of creation, irrespective of the complexity inherent to each individual creature: both in the most simple subatomic particle and in the so highly developed human being the seminal words of Christ are present, in different ways certainly, according to their complexity. In Justin's opinion certain specialists, like philosophers and lawyers, are able to identify these seminal words, but only to a certain extent. Full knowledge is given to those who receive it through revelation and who experience communion with Christ in the church.

It is not difficult to notice two levels of communion with Christ. The first one, with a maximal extension, includes the whole of mankind, actually every individual person and the social group to which he/she belongs, and is founded upon the seminal words specific to the group or/and to that or that person. We can notice here an all-embracing catholicity, on the one hand related to the creating Word, on the other to the saving Christ, because the two are identical, as long as Justin mentions the presence or absence of communion with Him in the case of people who »lived before Christ ... who lived reasonably ... (or) lived without reason«.[3] We could define this as *extensive catholicity*.

This extensive catholicity should not be looked at as something intended to be understood by philosophers and lawyers alone, because of their intellectual training. Philosophers and lawyers are representatives of humankind as such and if they are able to identify the seminal words, then the whole of mankind is. Potentially everybody is able to understand her/his belonging to this extensive catholicity, as long as she/he has an adequate training. With the insights of Justin the doors of seminal communion with Christ are opened for whole humankind, non-Christians and non-religious people included. They allow me to realize that everything happening in this world is related to God, to the creative work of Christ who is present in each of his creatures, in every human being, as we read in Mathew 10:30: »... even the hairs of your head are all numbered.« This is an important dimension of life in Christ:

---

[3] »[A]nd those who lived reasonably are Christians, even though they have been thought atheists; as, among the Greeks, Socrates and Heraclitus, and men like them; and among the barbarians, Abraham, and Ananias, and Azarias, and Misael, and Elias, and many others whose actions and names we now decline to recount, because we know it would be tedious. So that even they who lived before Christ, and lived without reason, were wicked and hostile to Christ, and slew those who lived reasonably.« (First Apology, XLVI)

to identify him everywhere in everybody, irrespective of religious or non-religious backgrounds and to act accordingly.

Extended Christianity on a seminal basis is a matter of interest with regard not only to non-Christians but also to Christians with a different denominational background. It is the first universal conviction all of them can share – that Christ is present in the whole of creation, in all its details, and that we are invited to meet him there, to meet him in the seminal words at work in all Christians, in everyone of us, for example. This way, when I meet a fellow Christian with an identity different from my own, I know that I meet Christ himself, who put the structures of a unique communion with him in each of us. When comparing gentile philosophers with Christian faithful, St Justin mentioned the advantage of Christians of being in life-communion with Christ, not only by means of the seminal words, but also without excluding them. As for inter-Christian relations, fundamentalists who refuse to acknowledge value to any Christian identity different from their own should honour the others at least the same way as St Justin did with regard to Gentile philosophers.

Narrow Catholicity: St Ignatius of Antioch[4] and St Cyprian of Carthage[5]

St Ignatius in his letters did not address Roman authorities, as St Justin did, but fellow Christians. Therefore he shows no interest in the possible relation of pagans to Christ and this way of understanding catholicity. Nevertheless he reveals a special content of the term when he considers the structure of the church.

As it is well known, the martyr bishop from Antioch understands catholicity in relation to the bishop, as image of Christ, and the community around him. The classic text can be found in his Epistle to the Smyrnaeans, chapter 8:

> See that you all follow the bishop, even as Jesus Christ does the Father, and the presbytery as you would the apostles; and reverence the deacons, as being the institution of God. Let no man do anything connected with the

---

[4] Born around 50, died between 98 and 117, possibly during the persecution of Trajan in 107. My option goes to 107 because in 107 Trajan martyred Christians in order to celebrate his victory upon the Dacia, on the nowadays Romanian territory.

[5] St Cyprian of Carthage (200/210–258).

Church without the bishop. Let that be deemed a proper Eucharist, which is [administered] either by the bishop, or by one to whom he has entrusted it. Wherever the bishop shall appear, there let the multitude [of the people] also be; even as, *wherever Jesus Christ is, there is the Catholic Church*. It is not lawful without the bishop either to baptize or to celebrate a love-feast; but whatsoever he shall approve of, that is also pleasing to God, so that everything that is done may be secure and valid.[6]

It is worth noticing that catholicity is defined by Ignatius also in relation with Christ, and this means it is defined in terms of communion, because he considers Christ in relation with His Church. He then offers a complex scheme of connections between Christ and the Church/congregation through the bishop, without excluding a direct communion with the individual believer by means of baptism. Addressing St Polycarp of Smyrna, St Ignatius specially mentions the sacrament, associated with faith in Christ: »Let your baptism endure as your arms; your faith as your helmet; your love as your spear; your patience as a complete panoply.«[7] Communion with Christ means here baptism together with right faith in everything he has done for the faithful, love of the neighbour and readiness to accept suffering for the sake of this relation with the Lord. According to the Antiochian bishop, catholicity is experienced in two ways: on the one hand there is a hierarchical structure with the bishop as its head, followed by the priests and deacons around him, and then the faithful, all of them professing the same homologated faith; on the other hand there is, I would say, a boot strap structure between all the members of one of the three levels and, possibly, intertwining the different levels. They are of equal importance and actually meet in the person of Christ himself. I underline this implicit complementarity because nowadays there is a tendency to keep in mind only the hierarchical structure with its homologated faith and to relativize the horizontal dimension of catholicity which is being shaped through the good works of love, so much present in the Epistles of St Ignatius.

The main feature of this model of catholicity, with its two complementary wings, is the archetype – image relation between Christ and the bishop, expressed through the right faith of the latter, through his »orthodoxy«. Therefore, if I do not have a rightful bishop, confessing and experiencing the right faith, I am not the image of Christ, I do not

---

[6] Emphasis by D.O.
[7] For an English translation, see http://www.newadvent.org/fathers/0110.htm (accessed August 1, 2014).

belong to the church, I experience no catholicity.[8] It is obvious that catholicity is equally conditioned by the right structure, right faith and right action. Absence or incomplete presence of one of these elements means there is no catholicity.

What about those Christians who do not fit into this model, for one of the three reasons, mainly for having a »false doctrine«[9]? They are not to be allowed in the community because they do not share the basic common elements of the doctrine as revealed by Christ himself: the dogma of the Holy Trinity and the christological dogma. All them are not part of the Christian catholicity and therefore of the Christian way of salvation. Almost 150 years later the idea was reiterated in an almost harsh, definitively exclusivistic form by another martyr bishop, Cyprian of Carthage, with his famous formula »extra ecclesiam nulla salus«.[10] At the same time Cyprian made it quite clear that the argument against the so called heretics also negates the possibility of any genuine communion with God in religions different from Christianity.

Ignatius, Cyprian and many others were not interested in the seminal communion with Christ, but very much in the question whether there is or not a possibility of communion with Christ outside the homologated church because of a not homologated faith. They did not deny the presence of some or even many Christian elements in the faith of groups outside the church but were not ready to acknowledge the presence of a real communion with the living Christ without the full confession of the homologated faith. Plenitude of homologated faith and full communion, or just partially homologated faith and no communion at all, these were the only options. No catholicity without plenitude of faith and by that of full communion. I think it is important to grasp the whole positive significance of such an attitude:

> Christian identity is not possible without well defined limits of communion with and in Christ, which are shaping at the same time an intensive Catholicity, willing to reject forms of communion which could relativize fundamental elements of life in faith, of life in Christ.

---

[8] Quoting John 6:33, *The Epistle to the Ephesians*, V, reads: »Let no man deceive himself: if any one be not within the altar, he is deprived of the bread of God.« To be in the altar means to be with the bishop, i.e. with Christ, provided the bishop confesses the homologated faith.

[9] Ibid., chapter IX.

[10] The classical text is the 72nd Epistle to Jubaianus, were we find a categorical denial of catholicity outside the Church: »nothing is lawful there outside the Church.«

As important as this is for Christian identity, this *intensive catholicity* taken alone reveals a shadowy side too, confronting us with several difficulties.

a. First of all, by rejecting everybody outside its boundaries it does not take into account the strong attachment to one's identity which is a seed everybody receives when she/he is created by God. This attachment is an essential part of my self-understanding and includes all conscious and unconscious levels of my being a person, so that it is impossible to me or anybody else to change it on command or according to my rationality alone. In my opinion, intensive catholicity ignores the idea of parallel catholicities as confessed by particular ecclesial groups.

b. Secondly it relativizes God's creative action who decides that a person is to be born and socialized in one family, in one spiritual environment or another. The person's attachment is directed towards a religious environment chosen for me by God himself. Ultimately God is held responsible for my not being able to give up my catholicity model and to adhere to yours.

c. Thirdly and in continuity of one and two, a plurality of catholicities, originating in human attachment to a spiritual and social environment received according to God's decision, are as many forms of communion with Christ. Therefore, whenever I meet a Christian with an identity similar with or different from mine, indirectly I meet Christ. Therefore, not accepting the catholicity of the other means to reject this form of indirect communion with Christ.

As a conclusion to this shadowy side of narrow Catholicity we might say that the exclusivistic interpretation of narrow Catholicity leads to ignoring one's attachment to a God given environment and to rejecting an indirect form of communion with Christ offered to human beings.

Dynamic Catholicity: The Debate on the Holy Spirit

The model of intensive catholicity dealt with problems which seemed to be more or less clear to the faithful and were just in need of a proper formulation, provided by the two fathers. The *lex orandi* of the Church seemed to be in perfect agreement with her *lex credendi*, formulated by gifted theologians. This was certainly true for a significant part of the church, but not for the whole of it, because Justin's vision of a communion with the seminal Christ was not an isolated oddity. Two hundred years later we can see it at work in St Basil's Long Rule, when he answers to the second question of his Long Rule that love for God cannot be learned, but has as source a seminal word received at creation. And soon after St Cyprian's Epistle to Jubaianus it became obvious that the content of faith itself was not as clear as the African father had believed, so that it had to be formulated by means of a generally accepted *lex credendi*. This happened during the Ecumenical Councils. I shall briefly mention here only the debate on the Holy Spirit.

It is a well known fact that the First Ecumenical Council in Nicea (325 A.D.) established the *lex credendi* for the relation between the Father and the Son, by saying that they are different persons with the same nature (*ousia*), that they are *homoousios*. About the Holy Spirit the *Ekthesis* of the Council affirmed only that He/She belongs to God and nothing more: »And (we believe) in the Holy Ghost«.[11] It was a lack of precision which was corrected 56 years later in Constantiople, during the Second Ecumenical Council. I am not interested as much in the history of the Council as in some aspects related to the faith confessed between the two Ecumenical Councils, at Constantinople and afterwards, for a certain while at least.[12]

The first difficulty Christians had to encounter was the Nicene *homoousios* formula, which had been suspect of Sabellianism to Orthodox eyes some time before the Council of 325 and remained so for almost a century. Without entering into any details about the Arian conflicts and their political dimension, one should not forget that the whole problem had remained unsettled until 378 when Theodosius became emperor and the Nicene Creed »was to come into full operation in all the sees of the East«.[13]

Which was the relevance of prolonged Arian uneasiness, to speak euphemistically, for the theology of the Holy Spirit? It was quite significant because: how could it have been possible to assert the *homoousiousness* of the Holy Ghost with the Father, as long as that of the Son was

---

[11] First Council of Nicea (A.D. 325). For the text, see http://www.newadvent.org/fathers/3801.htm (accessed August 1, 2014).

[12] On the first Ecumenical Council in Constantiople, see Jaroslav Pelikan, *Credo: Historical and Theological Guide to Creeds and Confessions of Faith in the Christian Tradition* (New Haven: Yale University Press, 2003); Adolf Martin Ritter, *Das Konzil von Konstantinopel und sein Symbol* (Göttingen: Vandenhoeck & Ruprecht, 1965).

[13] Philip Hughes, *The Church in Crisis: A History of the General Councils, 325–1870* (New York: Doubleday, 1961), 42.

still in dispute? This means that for 56 years at least the *lex credendi* had not received that homologated form able to properly express the *lex orandi* and to give it the necessary certitude. What about catholicity under these circumstances? Who was inside and who was outside the church with regard to the right doctrine, in order to meet the criteria of St Ignatius and St Cyprian? The answer to this difficult question came from one of the great masters of the century, from St Gregory of Nazianz.

In his Oration 21.33, *On the Great Athanasius, Bishop of Alexandria* from 373, St Gregory praises the right trinitarian faith of St Athanasius, »when all the rest who sympathised with us were divided into three parties, and many were faltering in their conception of the Son, and still more in that of the Holy Ghost, (a point on which to be only slightly in error was to be orthodox) and few indeed were sound upon both points.«[14] It is worth noticing, on the one hand, that the »Orthodox« party had three different understandings in basic elements of doctrine. This can happen at times! One of the three, regarding the Son, was obviously false and the only excuse of those adhering to it was their hesitating attitude, or faltering. Nevertheless they are counted amongst those »who sympathised with us«, »who belonged to us«, provided such a paraphrase is permitted. On the other hand, the attitude of the Cappadocian Father is definitely more understanding in relation to those faltering in the conception of the Holy Ghost, because this was »a point on which to be only slightly in error was to be orthodox«. Why so? Because there had not been a synodal decision on the Holy Spirit.

What is the significance of St Gregory's point of view for our understanding of catholicity? He makes clear that under special circumstances it is possible to accept different levels of catholicity as long as the basic elements of faith are shared. One could speak of a mutual acceptance of catholicities which move towards a single one.

Oration 21, On the Great Athanasius, was not intended to settle the theological problem of the Holy Spirit but might have contributed to St Gregory being called to Constantinople two years later. There, in the capital of the empire, with St Gregory as first president, the Second Ecumenical Council was convened in 381, to give a final form to the lex credendi, which resulted in the Nicene-Constantinopolitan Creed. The agreement was reached by 150 bishops from the Eastern part of the Empire, I dare say those St Gregory had in mind in his Oration 21. I

---

[14] For an English translation, see http://www.newadvent.org/fathers/310221.htm (accessed August 1, 2014).

don't think that things had changed spectacularly from 373 to 381 – there were more or less the same persons with almost the same convictions. Some of them were resolute in defending the oneness of the Triadic God, some may have been faltering in their conception of the Holy Spirit, but were willing to accept a compromise agreement formula.[15]

Beyond the intentions of a compromise aiming at achieving religious peace there are two realities: the definitive article on the Holy Ghost, as the lex credendi formulated by the Council, and the individual ways the participants understood and shared it which may have differed from one another. Each of these particular forms of understanding was an individualized lex credendi, largely shared by the signing bishops with their faithful too. After a certain while the differences in understanding vanished and the credal formula on the Holy Ghost, »who with the Father and the Son together is worshipped and glorified« actually expressed the homoousios idea, as St Basil had imagined it. These original differences in understanding were not forgotten but overcome in the Holy Spirit as part of the indirect communion with Christ. Sharing and deepening their lex orandi and lex credendi during their life in Christ, the above mentioned bishops, their flocks and their descendants gradually noticed that no hidden differences separated them, that they share one and the same homologated faith.

As regards catholicity, it is obvious that the formula meets the all-known requirements of an intense catholicity. The individual understandings of the faltering bishops and their dioceses take part in it, but in specific ways which lead in time to a common understanding. The two dimensions are consistent, both of them, because they express an authentic communion with Christ, with many convergences and on the way to an undoubted consensus, which conveyed to the Council its ecumenical character. The history of these convictions is the history of a dynamic experience of a catholicity which is faithful to revelation, to the communion with Christ, and at the same time willing to deepen its own understanding of revelation, to find new ways of expressing it, not in order to meet a political or any other worldly expectation but to share the experience of being together in communion with Christ beyond differences which seem to be impossible to overcome at times.

---

[15] For the different positions represented and the compromise agreement, see Leo Donald Davis, *The First Seven Ecumenical Councils (325-787): Their History and Theology* (Wilmington: Glazier, 1980), 124-126.

Dynamic catholicity is both faithful to one's own identity and looking for sharing life in Christ with Christians of different identities because this the most excellent way of experiencing the indirect communion with Christ.

2 The Three Models of Catholicity and Global Christianity

These three moments in early Christian history were able to illustrate that catholicity is nothing else but communion with Christ which is experienced differently under particular circumstances and from different points of view. It takes cosmic dimensions when considered in terms of seminal communion. It is concentrating upon a definite shape as experienced in the homologated structure and faith of the church. Within this definite shape it reveals its process character, as vivid as the life in the Spirit, enduring uncertainty, hoping and striving for the certainty of the lex credendi and its equivalence with the lex orandi.

All-embracing Catholicity. As regards Global Christianity, actually all the faithful who could be associated with these formula, it is obvious that we share with them the seminal communion with Christ, not only in the anonymous or unconscious way St Justin spoke about, but as Christians perfectly conscious of their identity, of their being created and sustained in life by the Divine Logos who is identical with Jesus Christ. It is a comprehensive, all-embracing catholicity which should not be underestimated, because our belonging to this or that church is not a merit of ours but a free gift of God who decides for each human person to be born and socialized in a certain environment. It offers the possibility of seminal communion with Christ to everybody and this is an opportunity as real as and as significant as the Eucharistic communion.

Narrow Catholicity. This model is vital for understanding the necessity of a clear Christian identity and assuming it in different spiritual contexts. Most of the contemporary Orthodox would not be as exclusive as St Ignatius or St Cyprian, mainly because they live in a completely different context and a long Christian history has a lot to say against one-sidedness. But they equally would appreciate the importance of God's decision for them to live in a certain spiritual environment and not in another. They emphasize the importance of honouring God by knowing one's identity and being attached to it. The participants in the ecumenical dialogues have learned the importance of discussing with partners who know the structure and the relational nuances of their own Christian confession well enough. This is the primary condition of an honest dialogue which can lead to experiences of life in Christ they hold in common. When dealing with the reality/realities of Global Christianity it is important for everybody who she/he is and who is the partner and this is possible only by seriously considering one's own catholicity, not in order to exclude the other but to share with him/her.

This leads me to the last model:

Dynamic Catholicity. The deeper meaning of the consensus formula from Constantinople is that the broader limits of homologated faith express a common communion with Christ, experienced differently but moving towards unity – a unity given to us already now or only in the Eschaton,[16] but given to each of us as a possibility. Therefore, when meeting a person belonging to a different way of experiencing life in Christ, first of all I am asked to meet the Lord and only after that to reflect upon the differences. At the same time I am asked to reveal to him/her my own way to be in communion with Christ, not in order to enter into a competition but in order to praise together the Father in heaven, as we were urged to do by the Lord himself.

Praying or praising together is not an easy thing to do, especially when the worlds of social and religious life are so different. I learn that the different formulas of Global Christianity are as different as the spiritual territories were they take birth and grow, that inculturation may change basic elements of the Christian way of expressing the faith and of living in Christ. This perspective should not be ignored because it could be a real threat against catholicity. But were the Christians of the first centuries not facing similar problems, similar threats? Did the so many inculturation forms of Christianity have no impact upon the unity of the church in the first centuries? They certainly did, but they were at the same time the instrument chosen by the Holy Spirit to foster the same unity they seemed to undermine. This happened by activating the seminal words put inside each of the Christians living at that time, by striving for communion with Christ under the guidance of the Holy Spirit. The result was, for example, the Nicene-Constantinopolitan Creed we use in our liturgical life, with new ways of articulating the life in Christ, already experienced in the lex orandi and waiting for a corresponding lex credendi. It is my strong belief that our meeting of new forms of Christian life summed up under the collective name

---

[16] It is not the right moment to explore this possibility, a quite familiar contemporary Orthodox reflection. See Georges Khodr, »Christianity in a Pluralistic World: The Economy of the Holy Spirit,« *ER* 23, no. 2 (1971): 118–128.

»Global Christianity« happens in the Spirit calling for new and mutually acceptable ways of communion with Christ. Nobody could ever predict how long this process may last or if it will reach its finality during our earthly or eschatological life. What we do know is that this final end will be reached eventually and all Christians will meet in the framework of a homologated, generally accepted and individually experienced catholicity.

Praying and praising together despite of the so many differences, this is an objective almost impossible to attain, as some developments in the recent history of the ecumenical movement seem to suggest. Enmity and conflicts dominate the world scene or parts of it, nowadays unfortunately in the immediate neighbourhood of Hungary and Romania. Is there any place left for praying and praising together, of discovering Christ in the neighbour who is different from me, of helping him to fulfil the calling to communion she/he received when created? Probably not, according to the law of this world, most certainly yes, if we live in Christ. Catholicity can be experienced only by life in Christ and therefore it is first of all a matter of Christian spirituality. It is a challenge to Orthodox spirituality to find new ways of communion with other Christians, most certainly ways for a theology of the Eucharist, able to share even in the absence of a consensus upon homologated faith. A thorough reflection upon the developments around the first two Ecumenical Councils, might be of inspiring help.

CASE STUDIES – HUNGARY

FALLSTUDIEN – UNGARN

Interpreting the Epithet »Catholic«
Living Catholicity: A Case Study in Hungary

Mihály Kránitz

For many people in Hungary the epithet »catholic« is inseparable from the epithet »Roman«. At the same time the word »catholic« is connected inseparably to the word »church« in the Apostle's and in the Nicene-Constantinopolitan Creed.

The original Greek word »katholikos« means *regarding the whole, all-embracing, wholeness in all parts*[1]. In Christian terminology the word »catholic« has been used in various ways: it describes the universal church as distinct from local Christian communities, and quite early it was used to distinguish the »orthodox« faith from »heretical« or »schismatic« faith. After the schism between East and West in the 11th century, the Western church referred to herself as »catholic«. And since the Reformation Roman Catholics have come to use it exclusively for themselves. Nowadays, in order to avoid the epithet »catholic« it is often replaced by other words of similar meaning, e.g. universal, general, common.

What does catholicity mean in Hungarian context?

As each of the Christian denominations is attached to a bigger unit – the Reformed and the Lutheran churches to Protestantism, the Hungarian Roman Catholic Church to the Roman Catholic World Church, the different usages are supported by layers of theological and historic tradition. There are, of course, special local usages of the word, but in

---

[1] Cf. *Catechism of the Catholic Church*, 830.

general the usage is determined by belonging to a bigger unit viz. community. This present consultation gives us the opportunity to compare the general meaning of the word with Hungarian experience.

It is well known that the Reformation, – which soon celebrates its 500th anniversary – , in some ways turned away from doctrines of the Middle Age church and/or theologians determining them, and tried to reach back to the early church fathers. Only the ecumenical efforts of the last century made it possible that Protestants and Catholics see their common heritage together.

In this sense we can see that the epithet »catholic« is crucial, not because its usage or its non-usage would separate anybody – on the contrary, the ecclesiastical writers of major importance of the 1500 years preceding Reformation can give us indispensable help to an unbiased analysis of the word usage.

The idea of what the word »catholic« means reaches back to the Old Testament (Gen 12:3: »by you *all* the families of the earth shall bless themselves«) and can be found in the New Testament (Mt 28:19 »Go therefore and make disciples of *all* nations«). These verses make it apparent that the church, which carries Christ's work of redemption, must be, should be universal in space, time and content.

The church is not only »catholic« because of its worldwide presence and the huge number of Christians, but because catholicity is an essential element of the church – not only of the Roman Catholic Church. Catholicity does not belong to the realm of geography or numbers. It is not of material but of spiritual nature. Catholicity is the inner reality of the church.

But in Hungary a special attitude is prevailing (especially in certain Protestant circles) that does not use the word »catholic« because in their view it is linked with the epithet »Roman«. By narrowing the original meaning this way the outcome is the opposite. In other words: by avoiding or replacing the epithet »catholic«, which is referring to the whole, they stress particularity and alter the original creeds. At the same time the proper use of »catholic« is discredited.

In a certain sense the epithet »catholic« can be placed side by side with the word »universal«, because »universal« is one aspect of the meaning of »catholic«, but it is not its primary meaning. Though the word »catholic« cannot be found in the New Testament, it was included in the Creed by the early fathers. But *ecclesia catholica* does not refer to some or any kind of a denominational church. It must be mentioned here that in countries of Western or Eastern Europe the epithet »catholic« is not replaced by the word »universal«: Swedish Lutherans for example confess in their creeds and confessions the »catholic« church.

Thus, in Hungarian-populated territories the epithet »catholic« is »under pressure«. And there is still some time to pass for the new generation(s) not to see and hear particularity, a self-sufficient part or fraction in the adjective *catholic* but to bravely confess the words of the creed descending from the ancient church to this very day and to understand the whole church as such as »catholic« and not to identify exclusively the Roman Catholic Church with this epithet. This is very clear in the Second Vatican Council, which stated in Lumen Gentium 8 that the church subsists in the catholic church (*ecclesia subsistit in ecclesia catholica*).

It is possible, of course, to translate the epithet »catholic« with »universal«, as it was done by St. Cyril of Jerusalem (A.D. 313–387): The church is called catholic a) because it extends over all the world, from one end of the earth to the other; b) because it teaches universally and completely one and all the doctrines which ought to come to men's knowledge, concerning things both visible and invisible, heavenly and earthly; c) because it brings into subjection to godliness the whole race of mankind, governors and governed, learned and unlearned; and d) because it universally treats and heals the whole class of sins, which are committed by soul or body, and possesses in itself everyform of virtue which is named, both in deeds and words, and in every kind of spiritual gifts.[2]

The »catholic church« originally meant, without controversy, the *whole*, the integrated church as opposed to the local churches. The first occurrence of the epithet »catholic« can be found in St. Ignatius of Antioch's Epistle to the Smyrnaeans: »Wherever Jesus Christ is, there is the Catholic Church.«[3] Another occurrence can be found in St Cyprian's (A.D. 200–258) work on the unity of the catholic church. This is of special importance to us as it establishes the closest contact between unity and catholicity:

> The Church also is one, which is spread abroad far and wide into a multitude by an increase of fruitfulness. As there are many rays of the sun, but one light; and many branches of a tree, but one strength based in its tenacious root; and since from one spring flow many streams, although the

---

[2] Cf. Bishop St Cyril of Jerusalem, Catechetical Lectures, in *Az imaórák liturgiája* (Liturgy of the Hours) III (Budapest, 1992), 480.
[3] Ignatius, Ep. ad Smyrn., 8,2.

multiplicity seems diffused in the liberality of an overflowing abundance, yet the unity is still preserved in the source. Separate a ray of the sun from its body of light, its unity does not allow a division of light; break a branch from a tree, when broken, it will not be able to bud; cut off the stream from its fountain, and that which is cut off dries up. Thus also the Church, shone over with the light of the Lord, sheds forth her rays over the whole world, yet it is one light which is everywhere diffused, nor is the unity of the body separated. Her fruitful abundance spreads her branches over the whole world. She broadly expands her rivers, liberally flowing, yet her head is one, her source one; and she is one mother, plentiful in the results of fruitfulness: from her womb we are born, by her milk we are nourished, by her spirit we are animated.[4]

The missionary characteristic of the church directly originates from its catholicity. Mission is the task of the church to take Christ to everybody and to take everybody to Christ.[5] The missionary characteristic of the church originates in the will of God »who desires all men to be saved and to come to the knowledge of the truth« (1 Tim 2:4).[6] Mission entrusted to the church evokes the emotion of catholicity in every Christian who is deeply committed to pass the gospel on.

It is a key task of the ecumenical movement to expound and use the word »catholic«, as the clarification of the word can bring the churches closer to each other. The *catholic* church can of course be easily associated with the Roman Catholic Church, but as John Paul II initiated, by way of dialogue the often mistakable concepts can be clarified. Among them one of the most important words is the epithet »catholic«, which is preserved by the *Roman Catholic Church* with humility, striving for mutual understanding that should serve unity.

As baptism is the sacrament of admitting and belonging to the church, and the constant epithet of the church is *catholic*, we can say that the baptised are the children of the catholic church. »All those justified by faith through Baptism are incorporated into Christ. They

---

[4] St Cyprian, On the Unity of the Church, 5.
[5] Cf. the Decree on the Mission activity of the church (Ad Gentes), 2: »The pilgrim Church is missionary by her very nature, since it is from the mission of the Son and the mission of the Holy Spirit that she draws her origin, in accordance with the decree of God the Father.«
[6] Cf. Ad Gentes, 36: »Therefore, all sons of the Church should have a lively awareness of their responsibility to the world; they should foster in themselves a truly catholic spirit; they should spend their forces in the work of evangelization.«

therefore have a right to be honoured by the title of Christian, and are properly regarded as brothers and sisters in the Lord by the sons and daughters of the *Catholic* Church.«[7]

In his encyclical letter on ecumenism *Ut unum sint* (1995), John Paul II. outlines the path towards visible unity when he explains that we can achieve »catholic« unity in the community of one single church, which is according to the will of Christ: »The Churches may truly become a sign of that full communion in the one, holy, *catholic* and apostolic Church«.[8]

The Hungarian Catholic Church reflects together and progresses together with the Roman Catholic Church and is able to show the decisive aspects of catholicity. Ecumenical activity – which is regarded by the Second Vatican Council as the mercy of the Holy Spirit[9] – has been practised by the Protestant churches since 1943, joined by the Orthodox churches in 1961. Ecumenical efforts had had an impact on the Roman Catholic Church by the time of the establishment of the World Council of Churches in 1948, so that the Roman Catholic Church was ready to effectuate real Catholicism, the final goal of which is Christ's will »that they may all be one« (John 17:21).

Also the events of the Hungarian revolution and the war of independence in 1956 rallied Christians to unity when they took a stand for the freedom of all churches. It is almost beyond comprehension that during the time of existing socialism and communism the state promoted Hungarian ecumenism from a certain point of view, for reasons of transparency and equal (mis)handling. The state promoted Hungarian churches to form a whole, a »catholic« unity, by, for instance, controlling the participation in the ecumenical week of prayer.

During the time of oppressive communist dictatorship (1948–1963) each church had her martyrs, and this fact fortified Christ's only gospel and its influence through the churches in the world. In a small country any step taken in the field of ecumenism creates a stir and becomes widely known. So Hungarian Christians received with interest the Hungarian translation of the documents of the Second Vatican Council published in 1975. The Roman Catholic Church's commitment to ecumenism became more and more comprehensible as its Decree on Ecumenism stated: »The divisions among Christians prevent the Church from attaining the fullness of catholicity proper to her, in those of her

---

[7] Ut unum sint, 13.
[8] Ut unum sint, 78.
[9] Unitatis redintegratio, 1.

sons who, though attached to her by Baptism, are yet separated from full communion with her. Furthermore, the Church herself finds it more difficult to express in actual life her full catholicity in all her bearings.«[10] In the commentary prepared for the 40th anniversary of the opening of the Council a Lutheran and a Catholic professor wrote the notes. This is also a result of the progress towards catholicity.[11]

A similar result in the pursuit of catholicity was the signing of the *Joint Declaration on Justification* (Augsburg, October 31, 1999) and its reception in Hungary, which sets a promising example to both churches, and is also exemplary to other Hungarian churches for the deepening of bilateral dialogues.

The not yet complete but in some kind of form existing catholicity was strengthened again by the ecumenical translation into Hungarian of the *Charta Oecumenica* (April 22, 2001) and its acceptance by 8 Hungarian churches (October 1, 2002). Hungarian churches were second in signing this document after the Netherlands, which again showed a common urgent desire for unity. The European Ecumenical Assemblies (1989: Basel; 1997: Graz, 2007: Sibiu) meant joining of the forces of Hungarian churches both in preparation and realization. This was a special form of catholicity, because the delegates of Hungarian churches had to present themselves with one voice.

At the events organised by the Ecumenical Council of Churches in Hungary, at the Week of Prayer for Christian Unity each year in January, at the worship celebrated for the nation preceding the state holiday of 20th August the »recurrent« moments of mutual attentiveness, respect and seeking for better ways of cooperation form and approach the »whole«-ness as it is included in the epithet »catholic«.

Exactly 50 years ago, on 21st November 1964, the Roman Catholic Church accepted the Decree on Ecumenism, *Unitatis Redintegratio,* and cleared the way for fruitful dialogues, joint documents, shared acts of atonement and reconciliation, which mark the way to unity for the churches as milestones. All churches are now under a certain pressure that is »pushing« them towards the achievement of catholicity, which

---

[10] Unitatis redintegratio, 4.
[11] M. Kránitz and K. Hafenscher, »Unitatis redintegratio: Határozat az ökumenizmusról (1964) [Unitatis redintegratio. A Decree on Ecumenism (1964)],« in *A II. Vatikáni Zsinat dokumentumai negyven év távlatából 1962–2002: A zsinati dokumentumok áttekintése és megvalósulása* [The Documents of the Second Vatican Council from the Perspective of 40 years 1962–2002. A Survey and the Realization of the Documents], ed. M. Kránitz (Budapest: SZIT, 2002), 135–159.

cannot be disregarded. After all, the name »Christian« obliges us not only to speak about the fact that Christ founded one church, but also to live accordingly as it was put by Pope Francis in *Evangelii gaudium* (2013): »The credibility of the Christian message would be much greater if Christians could overcome their divisions and the Church could realize the fullness of catholicity proper to her.«[12]

Walking along this way we should always be aware that we belong together and should overcome our prejudices in order to find the complete, the whole i. e. the *catholic* church, which is not our church, but Christ's:

> We must never forget that we are pilgrims journeying alongside one another. This means that we must have sincere trust in our fellow pilgrims, putting aside all suspicion or mistrust, and turn our gaze to what we are all seeking: the radiant peace of God's face.[13]

When Pope John XXIII announced the Second Vatican Council as the 21st ecumenical council of the Roman Catholic Church, Willem Visser't Hooft, General Secretary of the World Council of Churches said that this council was also the affair of the Protestant Churches (*nostra res agitur*). What concerns Christians is in fact manifest in the realm of catholicity.[14] With the Second Vatican Council the Roman Catholic Church ceased to be withdrawn into herself and to be self-centred. She opened up towards the »non-Roman Catholic churches«. For the catholicity of the church is her specific vocation, i.e. to represent and give Christ to all people in all circumstances. The catholicity of the church is understood only in a limited sense if we examine it only in an ecclesiological context. The expression »catholic church« has also an ecumenical meaning in the relationships of different churches, as they are all dependent on the catholicity of Christ's church. It is the real ecumenical challenge, to interpret the churches in their catholic diversity. Church-centeredness draws away from catholicity because it disconnects the church from her correlative two aims, i.e. from the kingdom of God on the one hand and from the populated earth (in the original sense of *oikoumene*) on the other, and thus in the cosmos from the whole of mankind. So catholicity

---

[12] Pope Francis, *Evangelii gaudium*, 244.
[13] Ibid.
[14] Art. »Catholic,« in *The Concise Oxford Dictionary of the Christian Church,* ed. E. A. Livingstone (Oxford: Oxford University Press, 2006), 105.

has a much wider ecumenical meaning, which reaches beyond the church, and from the churches towards all things.[15]

The church is not catholic in itself and for itself but exclusively for her relationship to Christ and as a witness of Christ's catholicity. Consequently the catholicity of the church is essentially a serving catholicity. The demand for the catholicity of the church and the determination in it is in fact a denial of the self and counter witnessing. Catholicity essentially pertains to Christ and to the kingdom of God. The grand vision of John XXIII appears in the documents of the Council, which have preserved the power of renewal, but which often encounter fear, misunderstanding and difficulties. The Second Vatican Council was, as a matter of fact, an encounter with the Roman Catholic Church and with catholicity itself. New encounters are now taking place among all churches in an attentive attitude to the Holy Spirit.

We could study the »catholicity« of the Second Vatican Council under various complementary aspects. There is a turning point, from which there can be no return. In this sense Vatican II was a moment, when Roman Catholicism came to realize, that its very catholicity was in jeopardy. It became aware of the fact that it was faced with the temptation, (1) to treat its own particularities as absolutes; (2) to overemphasize the »supernatural« side of Christian faith; and (3) to consider Christians' experience of God extrinsic to the world and history.

Roman Catholicism discovered in Vatican II the privileged *kairos*, to go beyond these temptations, and attain a more truly »catholic« consciousness. The concept of »catholicity« could mistakenly be understood in a restrictive sense, limited to ecclesiology. But such ecclesiocentrism is quite the opposite of a catholicity which points to »all things«, the catholicity of the Triune God, and the catholicity of the Gospel. The church's catholicity is linked to humanity, not simply because the church is fully part of humanity, but above all because she is a model of humanity.

---

[15] Cf. G. Siegwalt, »Vatican II et l'enjeu de la catholicité,« *Irénikon* 85, no. 1 (2012): 5.

Catholicity and Ecumenism in Hungarian Reformed Perspective
Living Catholicity: A Case Study in Hungary

Ferenc Szűcs

The word »catholic« has been used in the Reformed vocabulary since the time of the Reformation because both the Apostolic Creed and the Nicene – Constantinopolitan Creed were regarded as the official confessional documents of the Reformed Churches. The preamble of the constitution of our church starts with the statement:

> The Reformed Church in Hungary is part of the universal Church of Jesus Christ, she is the body of Christ, therefore partaker of Christ's anointment and service.

There was no problem with the terminology until the Latin texts were used. The expression »catholic church« was translated into Hungarian in the sixteenth century with the expression »common Christian Church«. In 1988 a joint Roman Catholic and Protestant Committee produced a common translation of the Creeds and the Lord's Prayer which changed »catholic church« to »universal Church« in the Protestant usage, while in the Roman Catholic text the original word »catholic« was kept. The obvious reason of the Protestant cautiousness was the fear of misidentification of the word »catholic« with »Roman Catholic«. In the Reformed interpretations the word »Roman« has often been regarded as a narrowing down of the meaning of »catholic,«[1] however, none of the Creeds refers to it.

The sixteenth century Reformed confessions and theologians were very keen on emphasizing the catholicity of the church because they did not accept to be accused of separation from the universal church. The Second Helvetic Confession which was accepted in Debrecen in 1567, – in its introduction, – quotes the decree of the three emperors (Gratianus, Valentinianus, Theodosisus) (380), which defines who can be called »Catholic Christians«, differentiating them from the heretics. The word »catholic« was used here in the patristic sense: catholic teaching versus heresies. Chapter XVII has the subtitle »Of the Catholic and Holy Church of God.« The Confession emphasizes three aspects in the understanding of catholicity. The first one is the refusal of heresies in the etymological sense of the word: *haireo,* to cut off (the wholeness). The second is the catholicity in time which means the continuity and community of the church from the beginning to the end of the world. The third is the catholicity in space meaning the unity and oneness of the church all over the world (*kat'holen ten gen).* Time and space are clearly stated in the definitions of both confessions of the Reformed Church in Hungary. The Second Helvetic Confession says:

> It follows of necessity that there always was, and now is and shall be to the end of time, a Church, or an assembly of believers and a communion of saints, called and gathered from the world.

Almost the same is said in the 54th Q.A. of the Heidelberg Catechism:

> What do you believe concerning »the Holy Catholic Church«? – I believe that the Son of God through his Spirit and Word, out of the entire human race, from the beginning of the world to the end, gathers, protects and preserves for himself a community.

Probably it is unique and characteristic for the Reformed ecclesiology to emphasize the oneness of the church with the *qahal/ekklesia* of the Old Testament Israel, or even of the patriarchs. The covenant of the fathers is substantially the same as ours, it differs only in its forms and methods, according to Calvin.[2] The historic continuity is expressed even

---

[1] László Ravasz, *Kis dogmatika* (Budapest: Reformatus Zsinati Iroda Sajtóosztálya, 1990), 116.
[2] Calvin, *Institutes* II.10.2.

by the Greek word *ekklesia* which is borrowed from the Septuagint. Lukas Vischer has justly identified the *covenant* as a constant, uniting the variables of Reformed confession and doctrine.³

Unfortunately this clear statement« of the two covenants had been forgotten concerning the present Israel and Jewish people because of the so called »substitution idea« which became dominant in Hungarian Reformed theology. Only in 1956 a new voice could be heard in a study paper which was sent to the World Council of Churches. This was a continuation of the process of the committee work which had started after the Evanston Assembly (1954). The authors rejected the substitution model and urged to change the arrogant ecclesiological attitude within the Jewish Mission. It stated that »Israel and the church share the heritage of the same promise.«⁴

The rediscovery of the »Reformed Catholicity« started after the Uppsala Assembly of the WCC in 1968. The main theme of the fourth assembly was *The Holy Spirit and the Catholicity of the Church.* The discussion was inspired by Paul Minear, professor of Yale University, who was the moderator of the Faith and Order Commission at that time. He wanted to avoid the polemic character of the word *catholic* and emphasized instead the original meaning of *kat' holon* – concerning the whole, the fullness.⁵ The Pauline word *pleroma* (Eph 1:19-23; Col 1:19) connects Christology and ecclesiology together. The fullness of Christ means an inseparable unity of the head and the body. This ecclesiology was inspired by Barthian theology which was dominant at that time. In the Systematic Department of the *Doctoral College* the ecclesiological research came into prominence. 1 Cor 12:12 became an important text and argument of the identification of the *soma tou Christou* with the fullness of Christ. The parallelism used by Paul illustrates the plurality and unity of the body, but he changes the word »church« to »Christ«. »For just as the body is one and has many members, and all the members of the body, though many, are one body, so *it is with Christ.*« The structure of the sentence shows that Paul does not use here »the body« as a metaphor but rather as an analogy.⁶ A great debate

---

3   Quoted by Alan E. Lewis, »Catholicity, Confessionalism and Convergence,« *Reformed World* 38, no. 8 (1985): 423.
4   Ferenc Szűcs, »Church and Israel: Church and the Jews in Hungarian Reformed Theology and Practice,« in *Strangers and Pilgrims on Earth: Essays in Honor of Abraham van de Beek,* ed. Eddy van der Borght (Leiden: Brill, 2012), 186.
5   Paul S. Minear, »Catholicity in Practice,« *Ecumenical Review* 15 (1962): 39-44.
6   Sándor Szathmáry, »Az úrvacsora ekkléziológiai értelme,« *Theol. Szemle* 16 (1974): 1-2, 24-28.

started about this identification refusing the idea of a reciprocal identity. The church is not a *Christus prolongatus* and the order cannot be changed: *ubi Christus ibi ecclesia*. This *pleroma* theology expressed the inner dynamics of catholicity. There is one Christ, so there is »one faith and one baptism« (Eph 4:4–5). Karl Barth is probably right when he speaks of a kind of interrelatedness of the four attributes of the church: oneness, holiness, catholicity and apostolicity. The church remains identical to itself through the whole history.[7] In this sense he is right: the church is either catholic or she is not a church.[8]

The famous teaching of Calvin about the *unio mystica cum Christo* deepened this ecclesiological idea, which is explained in his teaching of the Lord's Supper. In contrary to a general misunderstanding, the Lord's Supper is not the mystical union of the individual souls with Christ, but the union with his body and through it, with the head of the body.[9] This union is expressed also in the Heidelberg Catechism in rather materialistic terms:

> Through the Holy Spirit, who lives both in Christ and us, we are united more and more to Christ's blessed body. And so, although he is in heaven and we are on earth, we are flesh of his flesh and bone of his bone.[10]

The body of Christ in the Pauline usage has a double meaning. It is the bread of the Eucharist (*touto mou estin to soma – this is my body*; 1 Cor 11:24) and also the church (v. 29 in the same chapter). Those who initiate divisions in the church do not respect the body of Christ and will be guilty of profaning the Eucharist itself.

We have to mention here a recent stumbling-block around the interpretation of the Eucharist which has poisoned the ecumenical climate between the Roman Catholic and the Reformed churches. This appeared with the new translation of the Heidelberg Catechism which raised the possibility of omission of the 80th question which condemns the Roman Catholic Mass as »basically nothing but denial of the one sacrifice and suffering of Jesus Christ and a condemnable idolatry.«[11]

---

[7] Karl Barth, *Kis dogmatika* (Budapest: Országos Református Missziói Munkaközösség, n.d.), 116.
[8] Karl Barth, KD IV/1, 784ff.
[9] C. Werk, »Das Abendmahl,« in *Calvin Handbuch,* ed. Herman Selderhuis (Tübingen: Mohr Siebeck, 2008), 345.
[10] Heidelberg Catechism, Q.A. 76.
[11] Heidelberg Catechism, Q.A. 80.

Apart from the fact that this question is altogether absent from the first edition of the catechism, it expresses errors concerning the present interpretation of the eucharist in Roman Catholic dogmatics. It refers to the so called Damiani Document which is out of use in the present theology. Unfortunately the Synod of the Reformed Church in Hungary accepted the full text in 2012, in spite of the earlier oppositions of some Reformed theologians.[12] It can also been regarded as a technical mistake of the Synod because only the translation was on the agenda and not the revision or the evaluation of the text. Yet, it was an unnecessary debate which obviously sinned against the ecumenical spirit and the hermeneutics of the *regula charitatis.*

During the socialist regime there was a temptation of misusing the *soma* ecclesiology. The *kenosis* in Christology (Phil 2:6–11) was applied to the ecclesiology which later led to the term of the *serving church.* (In the Lutheran church the theology of diaconia was its parallel development.) Formally the argumentation contained some truth because the church as the body of Christ can be identified with the humiliated and crucified Christ, yet it was often misused against resistance towards the totalitarian regime. At the same time it was a one-sided identification because the church is the body of the risen Lord as well. The same can be said about the Lord's Supper which was interpreted as a *sacrament of service.*[13] This also has true aspects from the point of view of John 13, where the story of the footwashing is situated in the chronology of the Last Supper. But the story does not show Christ only as an example of service but it presents Christ who is acting among his disciples. Baptism is unrepeatable while the Eucharist is his continuous action.

One of the advantages of the participation of the Reformed Church in Hungary in the ecumenical movement was the discovery of the richness of the sacraments and the worship. After the puritan influence or rather the effects of the Enlightenment and liberal theology, our liturgical life, – if there had been any, – became very colourless and simple. Sermons became the centre of the worship identifying this one aspect of the Word with the whole Word of God. János Pásztor described this situation in an article of the Reformed World as follows: »the Lord's Supper (and also Baptism) has been pushed into a peripheral position. Holy Communion is celebrated very infrequently – be-

---

[12] Károly Fekete, *A Heidelbergi Káté magyarázata,* (Budapest: Kálvin Kiadó, 2013), 357–367.
[13] Bartha Tibor, »A keresztyén szolgálat ekkléziológiai összefüggései,« *Theol. Szemle* 15 (1973): 1-2, 11 (7–12).

tween 6 to 10 times a year in most cases. Even then it is celebrated as a ›second service‹ following the service of the Word. Secondly, many biblical elements have been omitted from our Communion liturgies – most of them were part of the pre-Reformation tradition, and most of them tested and found to be evangelical by the Reformers. Thus, for example, the great Eucharistic prayer and the recitation of Nicene – Constantinopolitan Creed were abandoned in the middle of the nineteenth century. In the first half of the last century litanies, the Te Deum and other forms were in living use.«[14] Attempts for renewal of the worship were made by the new Hymnbook in 1948. Its editors gave attention to the »catholic« heritage of hymnology and selected hymns from the whole church history. They followed the European tradition keeping the 150 Geneva Psalms which connect to the Old Testament worship, seven hymns were taken over from the Ambrosian and Gregorian heritage, the majority were selected from the material of the sixteen century Hungarian hymnbooks and from the German and Anglo-Saxon traditions.

Yet, the liturgical renewal could not have been successful because Bishop László Ravasz, who prepared the new liturgy alongside with the hymnbook was put aside for political reasons. Now, a committee of the General Convent of the Reformed Churches in the Carpathian Basin is working on the new understanding of the theological and practical dimensions of the worship and prepares a common liturgy and hymnbook. One of the new discoveries is the old prayer of Calvin which is still alive in the Transylvanian services. It starts with the following words: »We are gathered here in the company of the angels and the glorified saints«. This forgotten dimension of the worship reminds us to the true catholicity of the church. We are in one company »with all those who in every place call on the name of our Lord Jesus Christ, both their Lord and ours« (1 Cor 1:2) and with all those who are partakers of the heavenly worship. According to the popular hymn of John Stone and Samuel Wesley »Yet she on earth hath union / With God the Three in One / And mystic sweet communion / With those whose rest is won.«

The Trinitarian dimension of the poetry has not been followed in the ecclesiology for a long time. This »lost dimension« has been discovered in the different traditions by the middle of the 20th century. Therefore in the Hungarian theology the translation of the book of Miroslav

---

[14] János Pásztor, »The Lima Text (Eucharist) in the Hungarian Context,« *Reformed World* 38, no. 6 (1985): 345.

Volf *After our Likeness* can be called an ecumenical turning point because it starts a dialogue between the three main traditions: the Roman Catholic, Orthodox and Protestant, including even the free churches as the author used to belong to it.[15] We can deeply agree with Volf on his honest and realistic conclusion: every church wants to be Catholic but each in its own way.[16] Does it mean that we cannot go beyond the 24 points of the Uppsala Assembly which emphasized the plurality in catholicity?[17] It is true that catholicity does not mean homogenization but simple pluralism either. If we come back to the patristic understanding of catholicity we have to agree with the community of the catholic faith. It is not necessary to agree with all the dogmatic developments of the church history but we have to remain in the apostolic foundation, i.e. Christology and the Trinitarian Creeds. This *homo logia* keeps the unity of the Spirit in the bondage of peace. In it we have more common than what divides us. When we confess our common faith either with the same words of the Apostle's Creed or with the Nicene Creed we give testimony of the catholicity of the church.

The existence of the church roots in the unity and the relationship of the persons of the Holy Trinity (John 17:6–26). The true image of the church is the love relationship inside the Triune God. This relational community can overcome the two bad extremes of our age: the collectivity and individuality as well as the universality and the locality .Our churches and our society survived the time of collectivism and we are suffering now from a growing individualism. The churches could show an alternative to the community. A community which has an eschatological character waiting for the Kingdom of God when this broken world will whole, *holon* again. Until that we will have been partakers of God's mission to the end of this earth (Acts 1:8; Matt 28:20). Mission is »catholic« because it is embracing the whole humanity: all nations, cultures and languages.[18]

Locality and universality, national identity and Christian faith have always been a great issue in the Hungarian churches. Last week we celebrated St Stephan's Day, the foundation of the Christian Hungarian

---

[15] Miroslav Volf, *Képünkre és hasonlatosságunkra* (Budapest: Harmat, 2013).
[16] Ibid., 337.
[17] Lajos Bakos, »A Szentlélek és az egyház katholicitása,« *Theol. Szemle* 11 (1968): 9–10, 264–265.
[18] Jürgen Moltmann, *Kirche in der Kraft des Geistes* (München: Kaiser, 1975), 374–375.

state and monarchy in the year 1000. King Stephan joined the Latin part of the still unbroken Catholic Church before the schism, however there was also a significant Byzantine mission in the South-Western part of the historic Hungary. We can see this double origin of Hungarian Christianity in the religious vocabulary where terminology comes from both sources.[19] So, the beginning of our Christianity can be called fully catholic. This festivity is also a national event, but it has a strong connection to the Roman Catholic liturgy. The Medieval symbols, like the crown and the so called »Holy Right Hand« of the king are national and ecclesiastical objects at the same time. It is obvious that we Protestants and Reformed share our common heritage of Christianity and the Reformed Church can also acknowledge that our Western tradition created the possibility for spreading the Reformation in the country. We are also reminded that the Christian church did not start in 1517. Reformed congregations sometimes tend to forget this continuity.

Since the sixteenth century the Hungarian culture has had a double face: a Roman Catholic and a Protestant. Calvinism is often called a Hungarian religion because it mostly spread among the Hungarian ethnicity of the historic Hungary. This tradition has given a rich cultural contribution to developing Hungarian language and literature and has also continuously supported the independence fights of the nation parallel with the fights for religious freedom. All these shaped our identity and both Catholics and Reformed are convinced that our Christian identity does not exclude our other identities. We must be aware of the temptation of nationalism as well as denominationalism. But saving our values by telling our Eastern European memories may enrich both the ecumenical family and the larger human communities.

---

[19] Feriz Berki, »Az ortodox kánonjog,« in *Felekezeti egyházjog*, ed. Lajos Rácz (Budapest: HVG-ORAC, 2004), 118.

Catholicity
Case Study: Hungary – from a Lutheran Perspective

Péter Szentpétery

1 From Christian State to Lost World Wars[1]

Hungary has been an organic part of Western Christianity since its first king Stephen (István) the Saint (997–1038). He was canonized not only by Rome in 1083, but also by the Ecumenical Patriarchate of Constantinople in 2000 and by the Russian Orthodox Church in 2007.

If one thinks of the canonized members of the Árpád Dynasty, of whom Saint Elisabeth of Thuringia/Marburg is the most popular, one can gain an idea of the catholicity of the Church. She embodied what it means to be a follower of Christ in His whole Church.[2] On the other hand, catholicity had to mean that the role of the church and the primacy of the pope should never be questioned, as we see in the measures

---

[1] For Hungarian history, see e. g. Miklós Molnár, *A Concise History of Hungary* (Cambridge: Cambridge University Press, 2001, 2013). For a short overview: István Lázár, *A Brief History of Hungary* (Budapest: Corvina, 2012).

[2] See e.g. András Korányi, »Nostra enim Elisabeth: Die Gestalt der heiligen Elisabeth im ungarischen Geistesleben des 19. und 20. Jahrhunderts,« in *Elisabeth von Thüringen: Eine europäische Heilige (Katalog der 3. Thüringer Landesausstellung, Aufsätze)*, eds. Dieter Blume and Matthias Werner (Petersberg: Michael Imhof Verlag, 2007), 603–609. Wolfgang Breul, András Korányi and Lothar Vogel, »Elisabeth von Thüringen (1207–1231): Wissenschaftliche Beiträge zum Jubiläumsjahr 2007,« in *Hessisches Jahrbuch für Landesgeschichte* 59 (2009): 179–205. On Hungarian saints, see www.katolikus.hu/hun-saints (accessed May 1, 2015), and www.hungariancatholicmission.com/faith/hungariansaints.htm (accessed May 1, 2015).

taken against the Waldensians, Wiclyffians, Hussites etc. The universality of the church was often overwritten by particular interests as it has been throughout her history.

When Reformation arrived in Hungary, the Hungarian National Assembly passed a law against Lutheranism in 1523 in the city of Buda. All Lutherans and their patrons were sentenced to decapitation and to forfeiture of property. Everyone was regarded as »Lutheran« who turned against the Church of Rome even if (s)he had never heard of Luther and his writings. Two years later at the Assembly of Rákos (Pest) the noble orders expressed their threat in harsher terms: »All Lutherans ... should be burnt alive ... and their possessions should be confiscated by the Treasury or the landowners.« This famous »Lutherani omnes comburantur« Act of 1525 was even more short-lived than the decapitation order. The Reformation brought a spiritual renewal to the country as a whole where people – as throughout the Church – were fed up with the luxurious, hedonistic life of the Roman hierarchy. The rapid spread of the Reformation in Hungary was due mostly to those urban intellectuals who graduated from foreign universities or from famous Hungarian schools.[3] – Luther and Melanchthon had maybe more than one thousand students from Hungary, nobody knows their exact number.[4] The Reformers saw in the lost battle of Mohács, Southern Hungary (1526) and later the Turkish occupation (from 1541 onward) a divine punishment for the sins of the nobles and, indeed, of the people as a whole. By the middle of the 16th century 75–80 % (some scholars put the figure higher, up to 90 %) of the population had joined the Reformation.[5] The first complete Hungarian translation of the New Testament

---

[3] Tibor Fabiny, *A Short History of Lutheranism in Hungary* (Budapest: Magyarországi Evangélikus Egyház Sajtóosztálya, 1997), 3ff. For further reading: Zoltán Csepregi, »Die Anfänge der Reformation im Königreich Ungarn bis 1548,« in *Die Reformation in Mitteleuropa. Reformacija v sredjni Evropi. Prispevki ob 500-letnici rojstva Primoža Trubarja, 2008*, eds. Vincenc Rajšp, Karl W. Schwarz, Boguslaw Dybaś and Christian Gastgeber, Mitteleuropäische Bibliothek 4 (Ljubljana: Zalozba ZRC – Wien: Österreichische Akademie der Wissenschaften, 2011), 127–147.

[4] More than one thousand matriculated. Katalin Keveházi, »Die Quellen der Rezeption Philipp Melanchthons in Ungarn. Melanchthon Fülöp magyarországi recepciójának forrásai,« in *Philipp Melanchthon: Briefe für Europa. Levelek Európának. Internationale Wanderausstellung zum 500. Geburtstag Philipp Melanchthons. Nemzetközi Vándorkiállítás Melanchthon Fülöp születésének 500. évfordulója alkalmából Katalog*, ed. Melanchthonhaus Bretten (Bretten: Melanchthonhaus, 1999).

[5] Tibor Fabiny, *A Short History of Lutheranism in Hungary*, 4f., 11.

by Lutheran preacher János Sylvester was printed in 1541, in Sárvár (Western Hungary) and the complete Bible was translated in 1590 by the Reformed dean Gáspár Károli at Vizsoly (Northern Hungary).[6] In 1568, for the first time in Europe, the National Assembly of Torda (Thorenburg) in Transylvania declared the freedom of the four main religions: Catholic, Reformed, Lutheran and Unitarian in the principality. In so doing, it provided a lesson to the rest of Europe on the catholicity of the church, showing that unity and diversity are not mutually exclusive. This new dispensation was not, however, wholly catholic, as the Orthodox were not included. (The Orthodox were not persecuted, but in case of mixed marriage the Orthodox party was obliged to convert.)[7]

The Catholic Habsburgs could not tolerate this new spirit and used the Jesuits as a battering-ram in the Counter-Reformation. It is true that there were highly educated theologians among them, without Protestant counterparts educated to the same level at the end of the 16th century. One should mention firstly the Archbishop of Esztergom and Primate, the Jesuit Péter Pázmány (1570–1637) who came from a Protestant family and was a great writer in the Hungarian language at that time.[8] He founded the University of Nagyszombat (today Trnava, Slovakia), in 1635 (today Pázmány Péter Catholic University), which was moved to Buda in 1777. He supported the first complete Catholic Bible translation by his fellow Jesuit György Káldi in 1626, who also came from a Protestant family. Bible translations (mostly that of Gáspár Károli) had a very important impact on the later development of the literary language as it was the case in many other nations.

Unfortunately, the Counter-Reformation did not stop at the level of theological controversies, and it was not lacking in bloody events. Two important ones should be mentioned. The first is the so-called bloodbath of Csepreg. In 1621 the Lutheran church of this village in Western Hungary was burnt with the villagers inside who were prevented from

---

[6] János Bottyán, *A magyar Biblia évszázadai* [Centuries of the Hungarian Bible] (Budapest: Kálvin Kiadó, 2009).

[7] On the historical circumstances, see Susan Ritchie, »Lecture Two of the Series. Children of the same God: European Unitarianism in Creative Cultural Exchange with Ottoman Islam,« Minns Lectures, 2009, www.minnslecture.org/archive/Ritchie/RitchieLecture2pdf (accessed January 16, 2015).

[8] On Pázmány, see e.g. the Encyclopedia of World Biography, 2004: www.encyclopedia.com/topic/Peter_Pazmany.aspx (accessed January 16, 2015).

fleeing by military force. There were 1223 people burnt or killed.[9] The second event is the history of the galley-slaves, the attempted forced conversion of Protestant pastors. In 1674 Protestant pastors from Royal Hungary and even from the Turkish occupied territories were ordered to Pozsony (today Bratislava) to the Royal Court by the Catholic Primate to withdraw their convictions. The Turkish Pasha of Buda forbade the attendance of those living in the occupied territories, furnishing us today with a sign not of the catholicity of the church but with that of humankind. The Muslim enemy was often more friendly to the Protestants than the Roman Catholic royal Habsburg dynasty of their country who should have protected them from the Turks. Thus 336 Protestants – 284 Lutherans and 52 Calvinists went to Pozsony. In case of refusal they were offered only two choices: execution after a period of prison, or exile. At the end, ninety of them refused to convert. They were sent to several prisons where many died within a year while others yielded to the pressure to comply. The rest (42 people, 24 Reformed and 18 Lutherans) were sold to Spanish galleys at Naples as slaves. They were liberated on the intercession of the Swedish and the Dutch rulers and military in 1675, because Emperor Leopold I (1657–1705) needed the help of the Netherlands against France.[10]

Hungarian Protestants secured the achievements of the Reformation with successive wars of independence. The Viennese Court had to be forced with weapons to respect the relative liberty of Protestants. The tactic of openly bloody persecution changed to social harassment during the 18th century, e. g. in mixed marriages the Protestant party was compelled to convert.[11]

---

[9] Mihály Tóth-Szöllős (ed.), *Csepreg 1621–1996* (Budapest: Evangélikus Sajtóosztály, 1996).

[10] Cf. Fabiny, *A Short History of Lutheranism in Hungary,* 13 ff.; cf. also to note 7: Péter Szentpétery, »Heilung der Erinnerungen: Zeichen und Versuche in den Kirchen Ungarns,« in *Mission und Einheit: Gemeinsames Zeugnis getrennter Kirchen? / Mission and Unity: Common Witness of Separated Churches?,* eds. Peter de Mey, Andrew Pierce and Oliver Schuegraf, Beihefte zur Ökumenischen Rundschau 91 (Leipzig: Evangelische Verlagsanstalt, 2012), 271–282, quotation on p. 275f.

[11] Cf. Fabiny, *A Short History of Lutheranism in Hungary,* 15 ff.; cf. Zoltán Csepregi, »Das königliche Ungarn im Jahrhundert vor der Toleranz (1681–1781),« in *Geheimprotestantismus und evangelische Kirchen in der Habsburgermonarchie und im Erzstift Salzburg (17./18. Jahrhundert),* eds. Rudolf Leeb, Martin Scheutz and Dietmar Weikl, Veröffentlichungen des Österreichischen Instituts für Geschichtsforschung 51 (Wien, Oldenburg, München: Böhlau, 2009), 299–330.

A decisive turn occurred in the life of the Protestant churches in Hungary with the issuing of the Edict of Tolerance in 1781. Emperor Joseph II (1780–90) allowed public worship in all towns and villages where at least one hundred Protestant (or Orthodox) families lived. The church had to be built without a steeple so that it should not be conspicuous. On the other hand, the Emperor dissolved the monastic orders in spite of the Pope's personal intervention in Vienna.[12]

Let us make a big leap to the Civic Revolution and War of Independence of 1848–49. Representatives of different churches played an important role in the events, and full religious freedom was declared. In a sense, then, catholicity of the church was promoted from outside.[13] With the peace treaty of Grand Trianon Palace, Versailles, signed on 4th June 1920, both Catholic and Protestant Churches lost a great number of their members. Lutheranism suffered the greatest proportional losses amongst all the denominations, losing about two thirds of its members. In the history of the Lutheran Church three languages have been in use: Hungarian, Slovak and German. After WW I most of the Slovak and a great part of the German Lutherans in Hungary were attached to the neighbouring countries – so one could say, Lutheranism became in a sense less »catholic«. Given these losses it is little wonder that churches supported the governments in trying to ameliorate or put an end to the injustices of the peace.

In 1944 church leaders stood up in protest against the deportation of the Jewish people and tried to help them according to their limited possibilities. After WW II, half of the population of German origin, including many Lutherans, had to leave the country, and many of Slovak origin moved to Czechoslovakia to the place of driven away Hungarians, under the framework of the so-called Population-Exchange Agreement of 1946.[14]

---

[12] Cf. ibid., 19.
[13] Cf. ibid., 20 ff.
[14] Cf. ibid., 26 ff.

2 From Communist Takeover to System Change[15]

After WW II, another lost war, as the communists came to power they made all efforts to eliminate the churches with all their marks including catholicity. They nationalized church schools in 1948 in the teeth of opposition from Church leaders. Lutheran Bishop Lajos Ordass (1901–1978) was arrested on a false charge of offending against currency regulations and sentenced to two years of prison. In the prison he was in a single cell with 15 Roman Catholic priests, for whom he preached on occasions such as Christmas in 1949. He could return to his office only during the revolution in 1956 but as he continued to withhold full loyalty from the communist state, he was deprived of his office for the second time in 1958. The house in which he lived was kept under observation by the police for years and pastors were warned against visiting him and even to participating in his funeral service in 1978. Ironically, the catholicity of the church was expressed in a special way when he was called by state authorities »the Lutheran Mindszenty«.[16] The Archbishop of Esztergom and Primate József Cardinal Mindszenty (1892-1975) was arrested at Christmas 1948 and tortured at the headquarters of the State Defence Authority (ÁVH). Before that, as Bishop of Veszprém, he had been kept in prison during the Nazi-friendly regime, too. The Cardinal was seen as an emblematic figure of the fight for the independence of the church, let us say, the one, holy, catholic and apostolic church, regardless of actual church affiliation. Although the attacks, imprisonment and show trials against the churches, first of all against the Roman Catholic Church, its bishops, priests, monks and nuns – frightened a great part of the clergy and their parishioners. There were a number of them who did not compromise with the system and took upon themselves the burden of heavy punishment. In case of necessity such action belongs to the *pleroma*, the NT word for

---

[15] Cf. Péter Szentpétery, »Yhteiskunta, kirkot ja haasteet Unkarissa ensimmäisen maailmansodan jälkee: luterilainen näkökulma [Society, Churches and Challenges in the Post-I World War Hungary],« *Ortodoksia* 51 (2010): 217–235.

[16] Lajos Ordass, *Önéletrajzi írások* [Autobiographical Writings], ed. István Szépfalusi, vols. 1–2 (Berne: Európai Protestáns Magyar Szabadegyetem, 1985 and 1987). Cf. Lajos Ordass, *Válogatott írások* [Selected witings], ed. István Szépfalusi (Berne: Európai Protestáns Magyar Szabadegyetem, 1982), 287. László Terray, *He Could Not Do Otherwise: Bishop Lajos Ordass, 1901–1978* (Grand Rapids: Eerdmans, 1997); H. David Baer, *The Struggle of Hungarian Lutherans Under Communism* (Collage Station: Texas A&M University Press, 2013).

catholicity (cf. Dagmar Heller's opening address of this Consultation) of the church. Mindszenty was sentenced to life in prison, but liberated during the revolution on 30st October 1956. His freedom lasted only a few days, because he had to flee to the U. S.-Embassy from the Soviet troops on 4th November and had to stay there until 1971 when he could leave the country for Rome. Pope Paul VI declared the archiepiscopal seat of Esztergom vacant in 1974 when Mindszenty was over 80. The new archbishop, László Lékai (1910–1986) was nominated only one year after Mindszenty's death, in 1976. Mindszenty did not want to be buried in Hungary as long as it was under Soviet occupation; Accordingly, he was buried first in Mariazell, and his mortal remains were taken to the crypt of the Esztergom Basilica only in 1991.[17]

The Protestant churches, for their part were forced to sign agreements with the state in 1948. In the agreements, the state promised the maintenance of obligatory religious instruction, a decree which was annulled the following year. Religious instruction became voluntary, i.e. participating children had to be registered in the schools by their parents. These children were either discriminated against or commissioned teachers tried to prevent the parents from registering their children saying that they would not be admitted to grammar school, not to mention higher education. If this propaganda did not work, there was often no room available for the priests or pastors who were to impart the instruction. But confirmation or chrism education, and Sunday school for children in the congregation were never prohibited officially, although the parents had to reckon on certain disadvantages. The communist authorities left only eight grammar schools run by the churches, six Catholic, one Reformed and one Lutheran (this latter was closed in 1952). From this point of view we had a feeling of being less »catholic« than the other two churches, although maintaining schools does not belong to the marks of the church. The state guaranteed a subsidy for pastors for a period of twenty years as compensation for the nationalisation of church property. Thus, effectively they gave 20 years to the churches with all their marks including catholicity to become an extinct species. Nevertheless, the subsidy was extended several times until the system change, even if its sum was only slightly increased. This does not alter the fact, however, that the communist state never gave up the elimination or liquidation of the churches as one of its main goals. They founded the State Office for Church Affairs in

---

[17] József Cardinal Mindszenty, *Memoirs* (London: Macmillan, 1974).

1951 as an administrative organ for controlling the churches. But the churches were in fact controlled by the secret police as well as the State Office. After the Stalinist era and the revolution of 1956, the means became less and less brutal, but the »party state« continued to regard the church as an alien body. Having seen that they could not uproot the church through brutal persecution, they stressed more and more that religion would become unnecessary and extinct in the developed socialist society on the way to communism. A very characteristic example of this is a sentence from party leader János Kádár at a press conference on the occasion of Kádár's visit to Italy and to the Vatican on June 9 1977: »Personally it is my conviction that the Socialist Hungarian state, the Hungarian People's Republic will continue to exist through many-many generations and the churches will still exist through generations, too« – he said.[18] Conclusively the difference of endurance between the Socialist state and the Churches is between »many-many generations« and simply »generations«. But the People's Republic passed away 12 years later. The Vatican had signed a partial agreement with the Hungarian state in 1964 which made the occupation of vacant Episcopal seats possible, »of course« with the consent of the state. In the Catholic Church the so called »peace priests« were favoured by the state, preaching that the churches must make their contribution to world peace, i.e. »pax sovietica«.

Protestant church leaders went further and laboured out a contextual theology. In the Reformed Church it was the »theology of the servant church«, while the Lutherans adopted the »theology of diakonia«. While theological in its reflection, this kind of contextual theology clearly contradicted the catholicity of the Church, expecting her to support a partial and hostile ideology. Apart from openly supporting the atheism of the party state, pastors were called upon or forced to speak out in favour of the social justice allegedly embodied in it.[19]

---

[18] Viktor Attila Soós, »Hírszerző szervezte Kádár pápai audienciáját [Papal Audience for Kádár Was Organized by an Intelligence Agent],« Múlt-Kor Történelmi Portál, May 26, 2012, http://mult.kor.hu/cikk.php?id=28117 (accessed August 3, 2015).

[19] Cf. Erzsébet Horváth, »History of the Hungarian Reformed Church Communist Era (1945–1989),« in *Die ungarischen Kirchen: Ihre jüngste Geschichte und aktuelle Probleme. Internationales Staat-Kirche-Kolloquium, 15/16. November 2004* (Berlin: Gesellschaft zur Förderung Vergleichender Staat-Kirche-Forschung, 2005), 44f; cf. Gábor Orosz, »An der Schwelle zweier Epochen: Zur Rolle der Evangelisch-Lutherischen Kirche in der postkommunistischen Zeit,« in ibid., 89–98. For further reading: András Korányi, »Diakonische Theologie:

The dissolution of the socialist system, however, could not be held up, it could only be slowed down a bit. The state made more and more concessions and the extinction of the churches in the communist utopia was postponed to a far off future. In the middle of 1989 the State Office for Church Affairs was dissolved, it became simply unnecessary – if, indeed, it was ever needed.

3   System Change (»Wende«)

In September 1989 the world famous grammar school of the Lutheran Church (Fasori Gimnázium), which gave two Nobel-Prize winners and a range of famous scientists to the world, and which had to be given up in 1952, was reopened.[20] In the following years more and more schools were given back to the churches. A law was passed on the restitution of church real estates in 1991. The state made an agreement with the Vatican (1997) and with other churches on their financing, including the settlement of the problem of former church property. The churches could claim back their former real estates up until 2011.

As the financial basis for the maintenance of educational and health institutions was ceased due to the nationalisation of church-owned land in 1948, the state gives an annual subsidy in the form of a percentage of the budget to them. At present more than 220 thousand children and youngsters learn in church schools. All the churches, and because of its size mostly the Roman Catholic, play an important role in the service of the country, in the areas of religious life, education, health care and culture.

Although the churches were more or less involved in their inner problems, in which restitution or reparation of former real estates

---

Weg oder Irrweg zwischen Staat und Kirche in der Kirchengeschichte Ungarns?,« *Zeitschrift für Bayerische Kirchengeschichte* 74 (2005): 23–27; András Korányi, »Sondern dass er diene ... Die Kirchenpolitik im Sozialismus unter János Kádár (1956–1988) und die Bischofszeit von Zoltán Káldy (1958–1987),« in *Die evangelische Diaspora in Ungarn. Jahrbuch des Gustav-Adolf-Werks* 79 (Leipzig: Gustav-Adolf-Werk, 2010), 48–59; András Korányi: »The Church between Socialist Isolation and the Global Context of Cold War World,« in *Christian World Community and the Cold War (International Research Conference)*, ed. Julius Filo (Bratislava: EvangelicalTheological Faculty of the Comenius University, 2012), 106–119.

[20] These Nobel-Prize winners were: Jenő (Eugene Paul) Wigner (physics, 1963) and János (John C.) Harsányi (economy, 1994).

played an eminent and often overemphasized role, a number of very important symbolic events took place not long after the change. On 18th August 1991 there was an ecumenical service in the main Reformed church of Debrecen on the occasion of the visit of Pope John Paul II, who, after the service laid a wreath at the monument to the galley-slaves of 1674–1675 near the church. On 20th January 1993 there was another ecumenical service in the Archiepiscopal Basilica of Esztergom in memory of the three Catholic martyrs of Kassa (today Košice in Slovakia) who were murdered by the soldiers of the Reformed prince of Transylvania in 1623. On 6th January 1996 an ecumenical service was held in the church of Csepreg, Western Hungary in memory of the victims of the massacre which took place there.[21]

The Ecumenical Council of Churches in Hungary was established in 1943 by the Reformed and the Lutheran Churches, (the already mentioned Lajos Ordass, later Bishop, was its Lutheran secretary), i.e. during WW II and five years before the foundation of the WCC in Amsterdam. The Orthodox and Free Churches also joined in 1954. The Council was able to represent ecumenism in Hungary more and more after the consolidation of the sixties, not only in the WCC but also in the Conference of European Churches (CEC), and in more and more interdenominational organisations and associations. The 14th Assembly of CEC was held in 2013 in Budapest. [22]

Hungarian Lutherans have always been active in the ecumenical movement, though space forbids a fuller discussion of all the persons playing an active role in international organisations. Vilmos Vajta, founder of the Ecumenical Institute of the Lutheran World Federation in Strasbourg, was an official observer at the Second Vatican Council. Károly Hafenscher Sen. was a member of the LWF-Vatican Joint Commission between1973–1984. The holding of the VIIth Assembly of the Lutheran World Federation in Budapest, 1984 with more than thousand taking part, gave our church members a taste of catholicity in the geographical sense. Bishop Béla Harmati was co-chairman of the Joint Commission from 1995 to 2006 and the final text of the Joint Declaration on Justification was accepted at the meeting in Dobogókő, northwest of Budapest, in 1997. He always stressed that Lutherans are Catholic, too, although not Roman but Wittenberg Catholics. The text and the accompanying documents were jointly translated by Catholic

---

[21] See note 9.
[22] See the Ecumenical Council's homepage www.meot.hu

and Lutheran theologians. Hungarian Lutherans did not overestimate the Declaration, but hoped that something new and better was taking shape in inter-Church relations. But in the following year we experienced the Dominus Iesus Declaration, especially in its fourth chapter a cold shower. During a conference in November 2000, Károly Hafenscher Sen. vehemently protested against regarding Lutherans as a third-rank church or not even a church but only an »ecclesiastical community«. Fortunately, this rhetoric has not been heard any more in the last few years.

Béla Harmati and Attila Kovách, subsequently a Reformed Bishop played a significant role in the formulation of the Concorde of Leuenberg in 1973. The Community of Protestant Churches in Europe (CPCE) held its 6th Assembly in Budapest, 2006. The Lutheran, Reformed and Methodist churches jointly celebrated its 40th anniversary at the Lutheran Theological University (Church Seminary). [23]

The ecumenical Week of Prayer for Christian Unity has been celebrated among Protestants since the fifties, officially and openly with the Catholics only since 1987. This breakthrough was initiated by Károly Hafenscher Jr., pastor of the Lutheran congregation of Csengőd, about 100 km south of Budapest. He had the courage to invite the archbishop of Kalocsa, László Paskai (later cardinal and Archbishop of Esztergom) to the occasion. Before that such initiatives were not looked upon kindly by the state and Protestant bishops were charged with rebuking pastors celebrating it with a Catholic colleague. Now the study booklet for the Prayer Week is jointly translated and used year by year. The Year of the Bible was jointly celebrated by the Ecumenical Council and the Roman Catholic Church in 2008. The Hungarian Evangelical Fellowship was founded in 1936 and members of all churches take part in the Alliance Week of Prayer, too. The YMCA has been active again since 1991.

Of course representatives of the Churches from Hungary, including us Lutherans, actively took part in all the three European Ecumenical Assemblies in Basle 1989, Graz 1997 and Sibiu 2007. The joint translation of the Lord's Prayer and the Apostle's Creed were accepted before that, in 1990. A joint Wedding Liturgy was introduced in 2001.

---

[23] Lutherans and Reformed in Hungary had already made agreements in 1830 (Northern part) and 1833 (Western part) and renewed the second one in 1900. Mihály Márkus (ed.), *Három egyezmény. Drei Abkommen. 1830–1833–1900* (Budapest: Kálvin Kiadó, 2006). The book was published to the honour of the CPCE Assembly.

Hungarian Churches were the second (after those in the Netherlands) in Europe who signed the Charta Oecumenica on 1st October 2002, and this was an act in which the catholicity of the Church was tangibly experienced. Catholic, Reformed and Lutheran bishops meet regularly, at least twice a year, to discuss problems of common interest.

Currently we are preparing for the 500th jubilee of the Reformation with a new selection of translations of Luther's work, trying to show as much as possible that he worked for the truly catholic church.[24]

4 Summary and Conclusions

1. Lutheranism in Hungary as everywhere has regarded itself as the successor of the one holy catholic and apostolic Church. Unfortunately, although not rejected, this view was eclipsed after the Enlightenment, and denominational identity was more and more defined by distancing oneself from Roman Catholicism.
2. Ecumenism for a Hungarian Protestant, either Lutheran or other, means above all contacts with the Roman Catholic Church. Catholicity must be defined and experienced in this contact, making our Protestant church members conscious that catholicity and (Roman) Catholicism are not the same.
3. Being Lutheran has often meant over the centuries sharing a common fate with the people in hard times, and this we may deem catholicity or *oikumene* in the broadest sense. In the elevating moments of national cooperation, e. g. in 1848 and 1956; particular, denominational aspects and interests could be pushed into the background.
4. The influence of the churches in Hungary is very limited, in spite of all their social activities. This is the truth contrary to all other opinions. Accordingly, regarding themselves and relating to each other as parts of the whole, i. e. The catholic church of Christ is in their interest and renders their service more effective as experience has shown.
5. Not only is the church universal but – unfortunately – the sins and human weaknesses of its servants are, too. All the churches in Hungary including the Lutherans have to draw conclusions from the faults and omissions of the past, ecumenically not to yield and resolve to any anti-Christian, anti-human ideology.

---

[24] Selected Works of Luther in 12 volumes; since 2011 four have been published.

CATHOLICITY IN THE FUTURE /
THE FUTURE OF CATHOLICITY

**KATHOLIZITÄT IN DER ZUKUNFT /
DIE ZUKUNFT DER KATHOLIZITÄT**

Catholicity – Exclusive or Inclusive?

Friederike Nüssel

When theologians speak of catholicity, it is mostly in the context of ecclesiology to explain the nature of the Church as described in the Creed of Nicea and Constantinople and in the Apostle's Creed. The attribute of »catholicity«, in distinction from the other attributes of »unity«, »holiness«, and »apostolicity«, emphasizes the universal character of the Church as embracing all times and all spaces. In this meaning the ecclesial attribute of catholicity is not just a given quality of the church, but is grounded in the catholicity of the Gospel of Jesus Christ that addresses all humankind. Accordingly, one of the major challenges of Christian teaching and particularly dogmatic theology is to interpret and defend the catholicity of the Christian faith in its various dimensions. In fact, this challenge is one of the reasons why dogmatic theology as a discipline is an important part of theological education. From my teaching experience I can say that in almost any course students are particularly attentive and alert when we discussed dogmatic topoi that in one way or another involve some sort of exclusivism, e.g. the doctrine of election and vocation, the doctrine of salvation through Jesus Christ and the question whether there is salvation outside of the Christian Church, regulations about the admission to sacraments, and the doctrine of the final judgment and of eternal condemnation. These topics consistently evoke a discussion about inclusivism and exclusivism. Even those students who are not too interested in dogmatics or systematic theology will show interest and engagement when discussion turns to these topics and they realize that prominent Christian theologians in one way or another have taught and defended exclusivist ideas. It would be interesting to hear from teaching experiences in other denominations.

To my understanding this is not surprising, but rather natural. When students have difficulties with exclusivist parts of Christian teaching, this reflects their conviction about the universal outreach of the Gospel of Jesus Christ through which God the Father in the power of the Holy Spirit offers his unconditioned grace to all mankind. Certainly students know that the New Testament writings envisage the final judgment of works, and the possibility of eternal condemnation, and describe faith in Jesus Christ as a necessary condition for eternal salvation without which there is no hope for eternal life. However, in discussions about those topics they point to the overwhelming power of God's love revealed in the death and resurrection of Jesus Christ, and in line with the first letter of Timothy rely on a God »who desires all people to be saved and to come to the knowledge of the truth« (1 Tim 2:4). Since the Gospel of Jesus Christ addresses all peoples at all times and all places, the Gospel really is the source of the notion of catholicity in Christianity. The message of the Gospel is inclusive and not exclusive. Hence, it is natural in Christian religiosity and theology to be concerned about the exclusivist parts of Christian doctrine and try to reflect on those parts in light of the overriding idea of God's universal love rather than the other way round.

1 The Catholicity of Christian Faith and Sympathy

Friedrich Schleiermacher has beautifully analyzed this Christian feeling in the eschatological chapter of his dogmatics »The Christian Faith« (1821/1831).[1] In a paragraph on eternal condemnation – which he relegates to an appendix – Schleiermacher argues that for a Christian believer »there are great difficulties in thinking that the finite issue of redemption is such that some thereby obtain the highest bliss, while others (on the ordinary view, indeed, the majority of the human race) are lost in irrevocable misery.«[2] Even if the two realms of eternal damnation and eternal bliss »were quite separate, yet so high a degree of bliss is not as such compatible with entire ignorance of others' misery, the more so if the separation itself is the result purely of a general judgment, at which both sides were present, which means conscious each of the other«.[3] Moreover, the idea of personal survival in some form or other »includes memory of our former state, in which it will always happen some of us

---

[1] Friedrich Schleiermacher, *The Christian Faith* (Edinburgh: T&T Clark, 1999).
[2] Ibid., 722.
[3] Ibid., 721.

were associated with some of them in a common life; and sympathy will be all the stronger because in that earlier time there was a point when we were as little regenerate as they.«[4]

Schleiermacher's argument involves a strong and profound notion of Christian sympathy. In his Enlightenment perspective on the history of humankind Schleiermacher understands humanity to gain more and more perfection in the process of history, and the evolution of sympathy is part of this process. He claims: »If the perfecting of our nature is not to move backwards, sympathy must be such as to embrace the whole human race, and when extended to the damned must of necessity be a disturbing element in bliss, all the more that, unlike similar feelings in this life, it is untouched by hope.«[5] Eternal damnation, »if it should exist at all«, could only be just, because »the vision of God embraces also His righteousness.«[6] But even the idea of divine righteousness, in Schleiermacher's view, cannot rule out sympathy. Rather, sympathy will persist over and against the idea of justice. Schleiermacher also claims that »in this life we rightly expect a deeper sympathy to be shown to merited than to unmerited suffering,«[7] if one includes the »pains of conscience«[8] added to the suffering. Therefore, Schleiermacher concludes concerning the idea of eternal damnation that »(w)e ought not to retain such an idea without decisive testimony to the fact that it was to this that Christ Himself looked forward; and such testimony is wholly lacking«.[9]

Schleiermacher's argument that the hope for eternal bliss is not compatible with the idea of eternal damnation not only emphasizes the role of sympathy, but also the intimate relation between individual and communal salvation. It is impossible for individuals to leave behind their social relationships and memories of others when they enter the state of eternal bliss, because in Schleiermacher's view it is impossible to »separate communal life from man's nature as such.«[10] For a Christian it is even more unthinkable to »conceive himself apart from such a life; for the fellowship of believers with each other and that of each with Christ are one and the same thing«.[11] Accordingly, the eternal fruit of Christ's redemption not only allows for the salvation of individuals, but will

[4] Ibid.
[5] Ibid.
[6] Ibid.
[7] Ibid.
[8] Ibid., 720.
[9] Ibid., 722.
[10] Ibid., § 163, 718.
[11] Ibid., 718.

culminate in the fulfillment of the Church. For Schleiermacher the telos of the Christian religion, the kingdom of God, includes the idea of humanity existing in a community that is no longer disturbed by sin as the characteristic feature of the world. Hence, the state of eternal bliss would not be a state of solitude, but a state in which all broken relationship is reconciled and healed. While Schleiermacher is usually accused of having fostered subjectivism and anthropocentrism, he explains the fundamental role of the church for shaping real human community as based on the general role community has in human flourishing. The essential bond of this community is love and sympathy for each other, and, therefore, it is impossible to imagine that parts of humanity should be definitively excluded from this. Schleiermacher's reflections on eternal bliss and damnation point to the existence of a catholic feeling of Christians as part of Christian faith. Hence, it would be not surprising at all for Schleiermacher to see students react to exclusivist ideas in Christian teaching in a critical way. Rather, he could take this as a sign of their living Christian faith in the redemption of Jesus Christ. Yet, the idea of redemption involves an exclusivist element, as Christ's redemption is meant to overcome sin, which determines this world. While Schleiermacher interprets the proclamation, life, and work of Jesus as the effective event that over the course of history will develop universal outreach, he is clear about a strict distinction between the realm of sin and the realm of grace and faith. Thus, there is an exclusivist element in Christian teaching, and the difficulty is to explain this element in a way that will not resolve the universal and catholic character of the Christian message. But before I say something about this, I will further explore some essential aspects of the catholicity of the Christian faith.

2   Issues for a »Catholic« Ecclesiology

As I have indicated already, the Gospel of Jesus Christ is not only universal in the sense that it addresses all peoples, but it is catholic in the sense that it is meant to reach all human beings in their lifetimes and at their places. The catholicity of the Gospel is grounded in the hope for God's eternal kingdom, which was the central topic of Jesus' proclamation. In giving hope for participation in the community of God's eternal, yet near kingdom, especially for those who were outsiders of the society, the Gospel message of Jesus broke with various exclusivist ideas of religious groups that surrounded him. The catholicity of the Gospel depends on its eschatological outreach. Only if there is hope for a universal fulfillment of human destiny and eternal reconciliation, the idea of eternal beatitude is attractive. It includes the hope for an abolition of the manifold ways in which human beings exclude each other from sharing community and in which they prevent each other from peacefully sharing the material and spiritual resources needed for human flourishing.

The New Testament writings relate to Jesus' proclamation of God's near kingdom in various, even diverse ways. Yet, they all make clear that the catholicity of the Gospel is intimately connected with the notion of God's eternal and universal kingdom, which only He himself can and will eventually fully realize. For example, in John 1:15f we find John's witness to reflect the incarnation of the Son and his presence in the world at all times when he says »This was he of whom I said, ›He who comes after me ranks before me, because he was before me.‹« The »fullness« of the Son through the Spirit in this time dwelling and time embracing sense is the condition for receiving »grace upon grace«. Hence, real catholicity is grounded in God's eschatological promise and his future as the Father of the Son in the power of the Holy Spirit. While eschatological expectation underwent a significant transformation in early Christianity, it remained the dominant perspective as we can see in the eschatological passages in Apostle's Creed and especially in the Nicene-Constantinopolitan Creed. The ecclesiological confession in the one, holy, catholic and apostolic church is embedded in the reflection on the work of the triune God in fulfilling his creation and the expectation of the world to come. Only in the light of this hope we may be able to believe in the catholicity of the church. The church is not catholic in itself. Rather the catholicity of the church is dependent on God's eschatological promise and powerful governance of the Father through the Son in the power of the Holy Spirit. Ecclesiology, therefore, has to be developed in light of Eschatology, as a number of Systematic Theologians across different denominations argued in the 20th century. Among them in the Protestant tradition were Jürgen Moltmann[12] and Wolfhart Pannenberg.[13]

From Wolfhart Pannenberg's Systematic Theology, I would like to recall and highlight two important theses for our topic. The first refers to the understanding of eschatological fulfillment as the consummation

---

[12] Cf. Jürgen Moltmann, *Theology of Hope: On the Ground and the Implications of a Christian Eschatology* (London: SCM Press, 1967).

[13] Wolfhart Pannenberg, *Systematic Theology*, vol. 3 (Grand Rapids, Mich.: Eerdmans, 1997).

of all creation in the kingdom of God. As Pannenberg argues, there is no human fulfillment only on the individual level. Rather, a Christian hope for human fulfillment necessarily includes the hope for a community of all human beings with God[14] and among one another that is no longer ruled by human law but by God's love.[15] The second thesis refers to the nature and mission of the church, which, according to Pannenberg, can only be understood in light of this eschatological vision. The church's mission is to be a witness and sign of God's future kingdom in its liturgical and communal life.[16] This mission requires that the church thoroughly distinguishes itself from the eternal kingdom of God, since »the church cannot transform the world into the kingdom of God«.[17] Only in this way can the church can appropriately serve as an anticipation and sign of the future kingdom that has been promised in the life, death, and resurrection of Jesus Christ. Pannenberg sees the same eschatological role of the church expressed in the Second Vatican Council's Dogmatic Constitution *Lumen Gentium* that »the Church is in Christ like a sacrament [Latin: veluti sacramentum] or as a sign and instrument both of a very closely knit union with God and of the unity of the whole human race« (LG 1). When »we may justifiably take *sacramentum* in *LG* 1 to mean ›sacrament of the kingdom of God‹,«[18] it is in Pannenberg's view not problematic to speak of the church as »*veluti* sacramentum«. Yet, Pannenberg in analyzing the church's interpretation as »sign and instrument« is cautious of the term *instrument*, because this can easily be misunderstood as if the Church itself would promote the future

---

[14] Cf. Pannenberg, *Systematic Theology*, vol. 3, 546–555, 580–586. See especially 585f: »Without all the members of the race participating in the fulfillment of its destiny as this is expressed in Christian eschatology by the linking of the consummation of the kingdom of God to the resurrection of the dead, there would be no reconciliation of the individual and society in the concept of a fulfillment of human destiny. For this reason eschatology of society that thinks only in this-worldly terms falls short of the concept of a fulfillment of human destiny. Even if we ignore the question whether a state of eternal peace such as Kant had before him as the goal of history, or Marx, in the form of classless society, envisioned as the goal and standard of political action, is really attainable at all, in any case only the individuals who live in the relevant generation could have a share in it«.

[15] One can find this argument already in Pannenberg's early theses on the theology of the church, cf. Wolfhart Pannenberg, *Thesen zur Theologie der Kirche*, 2nd edition (München: Claudius, 1974).

[16] Cf. Pannenberg, *Systematic Theology*, vol. 3, 38–48, see especially 45.

[17] Pannenberg, *Systematic Theology*, vol. 3, 48, cf. 37.

[18] Ibid., 39. Pannenberg approves of Jürgen Moltmann's suggestion to call the church a »sacrament of the kingdom,« cf. ibid., 46.

kingdom. Therefore, he restricts the instrumental role of the Church strictly to its role as a sign.[19]

It would be interesting to debate in greater detail how the notion of sign or the notion of instrument need to be related appropriately to meet the major concerns of ecclesiology. But what is more important here is to define those major concerns themselves:
- to explore the nature and mission of the church in strict relation to the eschatological *telos*;
- to distinguish the church's catholicity as preliminary from the future kingdom of God as the realization of real (i.e. full) catholicity;
- to be realistic about the fact that the church can and will only be an imperfect sign and to reflect all proclamation and ecumenical encounter in light of this;
- to avoid worksrighteousness and self-justification in the self-presentation of the church(es).

When I suggest these concerns to be major points in any reflection on catholicity, I am not saying that they will help us a to develop a full-fledged understanding of the catholicity of the Church. Rather, I see them only as necessary conditions for not only confessing the catholicity of the church but also for living out what it means to be a catholic church. In my view these reminders are important in light of current developments in ecumenism, at least in the encounter and dialogues between the established denominations/churches, which have been the major protagonists of the modern ecumenical movement up to know. While the beginning of the ecumenical movement was inspired by the idea of global evangelization and the vision of an ever-expanding religion, churches in the northwestern hemisphere are in a quite different situation today as they face two major challenges: the progress of secularization on the one hand and, on the other hand, the shift of religious inclinations and desires into non-Christian forms of spirituality or new religious movements and organizations. In this situation churches seek to explain, defend and even reconstruct their identity. In my view, this creates new dynamics and tensions in ecumenical or interdenominational conversations. While ecumenical formation and ecumenical institutions were meant to support mutual learning processes, growth in doctrinal agreement, and joint engagement for justice and peace, there is a growing tendency to use those structures for interpreting one's own identity. Hence, catholicity is under new pressure.

---

[19] Ibid., 48.

Is the major goal in ecumenical conversations still to reconcile diversity? It seems to me, at least, that in some constellations dialogues are being used more and more to explain, defend, and even reconstruct one's own identity.

Ecumenical dialogues should certainly help to clarify and affect the identities of ecumenical partners. The goal, however, in dialogues – at least as they were designed in the last decades – was not to shape or refresh denominational identities, but to get to know the other, to discover agreement beyond disagreement, to overcome condemnations, to explore ways of worshiping together, and to witness and act together in situations of social and political challenge. When interdenominational conversations, however, are used to reconstruct or even construct one's own identity, this is problematic for two reasons. First, identity processes – even if they have inclusive elements – are meant to clarify and define one's own identity and as such incorporate some sort of exclusivism. In most cases they are driven by a need for self-assertion and accordingly tend to be self-centered. However, this is not only counterintuitive to the idea of ecumenism, but also to the idea of Christian faith and life. Second, in identity processes catholicity tends to be explored as an *element* of one's own ecclesial identity, rather than the character, origin and *telos* of the Gospel of Jesus Christ, which is the *source* of all Christian identity and catholicity.

The way to avoid these two severe problems is to reflect on the eschatological hope as the horizon of Christian identity and its impact on conceiving Christian catholicity. It is notable that even secular thinkers like Jürgen Habermas point to the semantic potential of eschatological language in religion. In his book »Between naturalism and religion«,[20] Habermas explains in a very interesting essay on Kant why Kant in his purely philosophical approach to practical reason became interested in the idea of the kingdom of God.[21] According to his analysis this concept helped to rule out defeatism as the core challenge for pure practical reason. The idea of a future kingdom, however, provides a motivation for moral behavior and solidarity among citizens that cannot be enforced by law. As Habermas states, the democratic, liberal, and secular state depends in the long run on mentalities that it cannot produce

---

[20] Jürgen Habermas, *Between Naturalism and Religion: Philosophical Essays* (Cambridge, UK; Malden, MA: Polity Press, 2008).

[21] Jürgen Habermas, »The Boundary between Faith and Knowledge: On the Reception and Contemporary Importance of Kant's Philosophy of Religion,« in Habermas, *Between Naturalism and Religion,* 209–247.

from its own resources. But these resources are to be found in religious language. Accordingly, it is »in the interest of the constitutional state to conserve all cultural sources that nurture citizens' solidarity and their normative awareness«.[22] Eschatological language and imaginary is one of those resources, if it supports the idea of a universal kingdom of God in which human beings will be reconciled over and against all sorts of divisions, oppositions, and discriminations.

From a theological perspective it is important to add that religious language is only performative when it is *not* presented and understood in a functional way. If one takes the notion of the kingdom of God as an image or utopia that is *meant* to motivate and support civil societies, this instrumental or functional understanding will not serve the purpose, but, on the contrary, compromise religious language and the hope for future fulfillment of humanity in a reconciled community.

3   Ecumenism in Service of Catholicity

The power of Christian religious language is not limited to the spoken word, but includes the sacraments as visible signs of God's grace. While baptism enacts the regeneration to a new life by uniting the baptized with the death and resurrection of Jesus Christ and by incorporating him or her into the church as the body of Christ, the celebration of the Lord's Supper affirms assures believers of God's justification and allows them to experience fellowship with Jesus Christ and with fellow Christians.[23] In this way the Lord's Supper gives a foretaste of the future kingdom that God has promised in and through Jesus Christ. The celebration of the Lord's Supper is in fact the strongest symbol of the catholicity of God's church. In the words of institution, Christ promises his presence to those who assemble around his table according to his command. Although this takes place in local congregations, each local celebration shares depends upon the universal outreach of the Gospel of Jesus Christ and his Supper. In celebrating the Lord's Supper, the local community becomes a visible part of the universal church of Jesus

---

[22]   Ibid., 111.
[23]   According to Pannenberg, *Systematic Theology*, vol. 3, 238, the communal meal »depicts both the common fellowship of all communicants in the one Lord Jesus Christ and the fellowship of the church on this basis«. Moreover, the Lord's Supper »renews the church's fellowship by representing and repeating its grounding in the supper of the Lord«, cf. ibid., 292.

Christ. Consequently, as Pannenberg points out, the fellowship among local congregations »is essential to the integrity of each congregation as a form and manifestation of the one universal church of Christ«.[24] To celebrate the Lord's Supper includes the commitment »to the fellowship of all Christians beyond the confines of a local congregation«.[25]

While in the celebration of Lord's Supper God grants the experience of forgiveness and reconciliation to individuals and churches, the division between churches and exclusions at the Lord's table contradict this gift of God. In the 20th century ecumenical movement, churches have come to realize together the destructive character of the divisions between them. One of the strongest expressions can be found in the statement of the Decree on Ecumenism Unitatis redintegratio that »(s)uch division openly contradicts the will of Christ, scandalizes the world, and damages the holy cause of preaching the Gospel to every creature« (UR 1). The Decree also points to the constitutive role of the Lord's Supper »by which the unity of His Church is both signified and made a reality« (UR 1). Similarly, the Faith and Order Document *Baptism, Eucharist and Ministry*[26] by the World Council of Churches states: »The Eucharistic communion with Christ who nourishes the life of the Church is at the same time communion within the body of Christ which is the Church. The sharing in one bread and the common cup in a given place demonstrates and effects the oneness of the sharers with Christ and with their fellow sharers in all times and places. It is in the eucharist that the community of God's people is fully manifested. Eucharistic celebrations always have to do with the whole Church, and the whole Church is involved in each local Eucharistic celebration. In so far as a church clams to be a manifestation of the whole Church, it will take care to order its own life in ways which take seriously the interests and concerns of other churches.«[27]

The catholic dimension of the Lord's Supper is, however, obscured by the fact that divided churches, which cannot celebrate the sacrament together, exclude members of other denominations from taking communion together with them. Thus, the Lord's Supper becomes a sign of separation and exclusion, when it is meant to be a symbol of catholicity and inclusion. Moreover, exclusion disturbs the reconciling experience

---

[24] Ibid., 103.
[25] Ibid.
[26] *Baptism, Eucharist & Ministry: 1982–1990; Report on the Process and Responses*, Faith and Order Paper 149 (Geneva: WCC Publ., 1990).
[27] Ibid., cf. the chapter on Eucharist, par. 19.

that the celebration of the Lord's Supper is to convey. In ecumenical dialogues especially after the Second Vatican Council churches have discussed the theological differences, which give the reason for separation at the Lord's Table. It has become evident by now that in many interdenominational relations it is not the understanding of the Lord's Supper as such that prevents churches from sharing it, but differences in ecclesiology and particularly in the order of ministry.[28] Today we know that different understandings of ministry divide traditional denominations more than anything else. This is not only the case between Protestant churches on the one hand and the Roman-Catholic Church and Orthodox Churches on the other hand, but also between Protestant churches and churches of the Anglican Communion.

It is remarkable that in Europe – the home of *societas oecumenica* – there are now two church communions among churches who have adopted major principles of the Reformation – the *Community of Protestant Churches in Europe* (CPCE) and the *Porvoo Communion* of Anglican and Lutheran Churches in Northern Europe and the Iberian Peninsula. While some churches are members of both communions, and single CPCE churches are in communion with single Porvoo churches, the two communions are not in communion, because they significantly differ in what they require for achieving visible unity. CPCE understands ministry and episcope as essential for the existence of the church, but recognizes different ways of ordering the personal, communal and congregational elements of episcope.[29] The Porvoo communion, however, sees the threefold ministry and the episcopacy in historic apostolic succession as the adequate order and a condition of visible unity. Hence, »visible unity« – the goal of the ecumenical movement – is interpreted in different ways even among churches of the reformation.

While churches in the European and North-American context all struggle with the effects of secularization and religious pluralization and look for new ways to communicate the Gospel of Jesus Christ (cf. the Fresh Expressions), it is remarkable that when it comes to ecumenical

---

[28] Cf. Karl Lehmann and Wolfhart Pannenberg (eds.), *Lehrverurteilungen, kirchentrennend?*, vol. 1,1 (Freiburg im Breisgau; Göttingen: Herder; Vandenhoeck & Ruprecht, 1986). See also Friederike Nüssel, »Ist eine ›Gemeinsame Erklärung zum Herrenmahl‹ möglich und sinnvoll? Überlegungen aus evangelischer Sicht,« *Ökumenische Rundschau* 61 (2012): 429–439.

[29] Michael Bünker (ed.), *The Church of Jesus Christ: The Contribution of the Reformation towards Ecumenical Dialogue on Church Unity,* Leuenberg Documents 1 (Leipzig: Evangelische Verlagsanstalt, 2012), 117–120.

relationship visible unity *in* the order of ministry is the dominant topic. In the perspective of episcopal churches the order of ministry is decisive for the Apostolicity of the Church and for their authenticity, integrity and identity as churches. As a Lutheran I support the order of episcope in Lutheran churches. Yet, with regard to current ecumenical conversations and developments, I wonder whether the focus on apostolic ministry as a means of authenticity tends to jeopardize/overcast/compromise the concern about catholicity. It is important to reflect the mutual relationship and interdependence between apostolicity and catholicity. The striving for apostolicity and authenticity should not be driven by the desire to preserve one's own ecclesial identity, but by the proclamation of the Gospel in a way that highlights its telos to reconcile all humanity with God and by the support of visible expressions of the catholicity of the church. For the interpretation of catholicity, the eschatological vision of the universal Kingdom of God is fundamental, in which human community will be fulfilled over and against all discrimination and division we experience in this world. Since the Church is catholic and not confined to human borders between communities, »Christians and churches are faced with the task of making this gift of God recognizable in the shaping of their lives, in transcending boundaries of nation, race, society, culture and gender. In its catholicity the church is the promise of a community that comprehends all humankind.«[30] Consequently, the constant task of theology as the doctrine of God and his household is to reflect and interpret the catholicity of God's Gospel that is meant to include all peoples (Matt 28:19f). Exclusivist elements in Christian teaching and practice need thorough explanation and justification not only in interdenominational encounter and ecumenical formation but also in academic theological education. Therefore, it is important to encourage students in their sense of catholicity and to reflect the ecumenical goal of visible unity in light of the fact that the church will only be apostolic when it is truly catholic.

---

[30] Ibid., 112.

Towards a Healthy Future of Catholicity in the Roman Catholic Church
Recommendations by Pope Francis

Peter De Mey

In this paper I focus on the understanding and implementation of catholicity in my own church as opened up in the reflections and reform plans of Pope Francis. Since Pope Francis bases his ecclesiology strongly on the documents of Vatican II, I start with a brief prelude on the paragraph on catholicity in the dogmatic constitution *Lumen Gentium (LG)*.

1 Remembering the Second Vatican Council and Its Understanding of Catholicity

As is well-known, the heavy critique on the first draft of the Dogmatic Constitution on the Church during the first session of the Council made it necessary for the theological commission to prepare a new draft in spring 1963. After some discussion the draft prepared by the Louvain professor Gérard Philips was accepted as basis. When the commission ended its preparatory work, four chapters were ready to be sent to the Council fathers. In this draft the chapter *De populo Dei et speciatim de laicis* still followed the one on the hierarchy. Already in July 1963 Cardinal Suenens made the proposal to Philips to divide this chapter in two parts and to treat the people of God as a whole before focussing on the hierarchy. During the second session, in autumn 1963, Yves Congar served as an expert in the subcommission that would draft the new chapter *De populo Dei*. That chapter would for the first time contain a paragraph entitled: »De universalitate seu catholicitate unius Populi Dei.« The day before the Council ended Congar admits in his council diary that it was he who wrote the first draft of LG 13, and material evidence for this claim can be found in his personal archive.[1]

It was logical that the redaction was entrusted to Congar, since he had written on this theme since his first book on ecumenism *Chrétiens désunis: Principes d'un »œcuménisme catholique«* (1937) At that time, however, Congar still defined catholicity exclusively in terms of the Church's universality and unity:

> Catholicity means universality: universality means a gathering together in one (unus, vertere). The Catholicity of the Church must therefore be conceived of in relation to her Oneness. The one Church cannot but be catholic: its unity comes from Christ and through Him from the Father.[2]

These convictions forced him to make a sharp distinction between catholicity and ecumenicity[3]:

> Apart from the embodiment of unity there might be »ecumenism,« but not true catholicity. For catholicity is the taking of the many into an already existing oneness. Whereas what is to-day called »ecumenism« is the introduction of a certain unitedness into an already existing diversity – oneness in multiplicity. ... In other words, there may be, and there is, a non-Roman »ecumenism« – there can indeed be no other. But there cannot be a »non-Roman Catholicity«.[4]

---

[1] Yves Congar, *Mon Journal du Concile*, vol. 2, ed. Eric Mahieu (Paris: Cerf, 2002), 511; Archives du Saulchoir, F. Congar, YC 0852–0855. This version was entitled: »De univeralitate populi Dei« and is accompanied by a *relatio*.

[2] Yves Congar, *Divided Christendom: A Catholic Study of the Problem of Reunion* (London: G. Bles, 1939), 93.

[3] In his article »Expanding Catholicity through Ecumenicity in the Work of Yves Congar: Ressourcement, Receptive Ecumenism and Catholic Reform«, *International Journal of Systematic Theology* 13 (2011): 272–302, Paul Murray, relying on earlier research by Jean-Pierre Jossua, makes it clear that Congar will present a much more positive account of »reconciled diversity« in his 1982 book *Diversités et communion*. Cf. also Jean-Pierre Jossua, »L'évolution œcuménique du père Congar,« *Cristianesimo nella Storia* 35 (2014): 251–278.

[4] Congar, *Divided Christendom*, 101.

If the French Dominican, in those years, unambiguously defended an ecumenism of return, luckily he already defended the idea that such a return would enrich the diversity of Catholic life:

> The goal of an authentic reunion movement must be Catholic unity; the unity, that is, of the fullness of the mystical Christ. It must therefore be concerned with reintegration in the Una Catholica. ... This is the distinctive mystery of the perfect Unity which is also Catholicity, which can embrace diversity without division and bind it in a unity which is not mere uniformity.[5]

Of course Congar was not supposed to edit the paragraph on catholicity out of the blue but could rely on interventions such as the one made by the Belgian White Father and archbishop of Burundi Antoine-Hubert Grauls during the general congregation of October 4, 1963, in the name of 55 bishops of Burundi and Rwanda. According to Grauls the new paragraph would have to take into account that »the Church is decorated both with wonderful unity and with diversity.« Apart from the one faith, the one baptism and the one Eucharist, he argued, the Church »is also outstanding through its diversity.« Thanks to the »economy of the incarnation« she is able to »imbibe all human values proper to each culture.« The archbishop also was convinced that »such diversity finds its origin in God« and he saw it as the mission of the Church to promote »unity in diversity and diversity in unity.« He also mentioned that it was not sufficient to make a distinction between the Church of the East and the Church of the West; in different regions Christians participate in a particular »religious, cultural and social patrimony.«[6]

In the final version of LG 13 it is easily to be seen that the paragraph develops two points. The opening and concluding line stress the *universality* of God's salvific will.

> All human beings are called to the new people of God. Therefore this people, while remaining one and unique, is to be spread throughout the whole world and through every age to fulfil the design of the will of God...[7] Therefore to this catholic unity of the people of God ... all are called.

---

[5] Ibid., 252.
[6] Acta Synodalia II/2, 69–70.
[7] The documents of the Second Vatican Council are quoted from *Decrees of the Ecumenical Councils*, ed. Norman P. Tanner S.J. (London/Washington D.C.: Georgetown University Press, 1990).

With a reference to a homily of John Chrysostom, the spiritual unity of the geographically diverse people of God is being stressed:

> For all the nations of the earth, therefore, there is one people of God since it draws its citizens from all nations, but the kingdom is not earthly in character, but heavenly. For all the faithful scattered throughout the world are in communion with the rest in the holy Spirit, and so »the person who lives in Rome knows that Indians are his members«.

Congar remains faithful to his conviction since *Divided Christendom* that this unity can embrace the particularities of diverse cultures, an idea which will be further developed in the missionary decree *Ad Gentes*:

> [T]he church as the people of God ... takes nothing away from the temporal well-being of any people. On the contrary, it takes up and encourages the riches, resources and customs of peoples in so far as they are good; and in taking them up it purifies, strengthens and raises them up.

This first part concludes with a definition of universality:

> This note of universality (hic universalitatis character), which adorns the people of God, is a gift of the Lord himself by which the catholic church effectively and continually tries to recapitulate the whole of humanity, with all its riches, under Christ the head in the unity of his Spirit.

The second part of the paragraph starts with a definition of »catholicity« praising the creative tension between unity and diversity in the Catholic church:

> By virtue of this catholicity (huius catholicitatis eius), the individual parts bring their own gifts to the other parts and to the whole church, in such a way that the whole and individual parts grow greater through the mutual communication of all and their united efforts towards fullness in unity.

As example geographical diversity within Catholicism is mentioned, the different »states« in which Catholics live their faith, and the existence of »lawfully particular churches which enjoy their own proper traditions.«

Precisely when making the transition between the two parts of the paragraph, the original draft of Congar laid more emphasis on the fact that the »unity of this people of God does not exist in uniformity,«[8] words not maintained in the final version of LG 13. In his *relatio* he used even stronger words: »this universality or catholicity despises uniformity.«[9] The final version of the *relatio* read to the Council fathers returns to the two parts or aspects of LG 13. Both »the unity of human nature« and its mission »by Christ, the Holy Spirit and the Church« first of all make it clear that God's people is »of a universal nature.« It reflects »a unity« which »transcends all particularities« and is therefore able »to be present among all the people of the earth.« Secondly, the Council wants to underline in unusually strong words that its understanding of »universality or catholicity« »despises uniformity« (*uniformitatem respuit*).« It is »at the service of diversity in unity (*diversitatem in unitate servat*), by promoting communion and cooperation among different peoples and different states in the Church.«[10]

2 Pope Francis on Catholicity as Missionary Outreach and as Unity in Diversity

I will now argue that both aspects of Vatican II's teaching on catholicity occupy a central place in the teaching of Pope Francis.[11] His first interest

---

[8] YC0854, l. 44–45: »Universalitas haec Populi Dei, sicut catholicitas Ecclesiae, non in mera numerositate membrorum consistit, sicut nec unitas in uniformitate.«

[9] YC 0853: »Haec universalitas seu catholicitas uniformitatem respuit.«

[10] Constitutio dogmatica de Ecclesia Concilii Vaticani II Synopsis in ordinem redigens schemata cum relationibus necnon patrum orationes atque animadversiones. *Lumen Gentium Synopsis*, ed. Francisco Gil Hellín (Vatican City: Libreria Editrice Vaticana, 1996), 103: »De indole universali Populi Dei, fundata in principiis huius Populi, nempe in unitate naturae humanae et in missione Christi, Spiritus Sancti et Ecclesiae. ... Haec unitas Populi simul transcendens et immanens exstat, et sic, quia est *supra particularia*, omnibus terrae populis inesse potest. Haec universalitas seu catholicitas *uniformitatem respuit*: diversitatem in unitate servat, procurando communionem et cooperationem inter diversos populos et diversus ordines in Ecclesia.«

[11] In a recent book on Pope Francis Church historian Massimo Faggioli specifies in which sense the heritage of Vatican II is safe with this Latin-American Pope. Cf. Massimo Faggioli, *Pope Francis: Tradition in Transition* (New York: Paulist Press, 2015), 11: »For a Latin American bishop like Bergoglio, Vatican II is an essential and obvious part of the experience of the Church.«; 34: »The Argentine Jesuit Bergoglio perceives Vatican II as a matter not to be reinterpreted or restricted, but implemented.« The opening speech of the October 2014 Synod of bishops on the family by Pope Francis was, according to Faggioli, »an unequivo-

is that his church rediscovers its missionary nature, and, because of its longstanding preoccupation with the centre it is especially the mission to the periphery that he wants to promote. Second, this requires an institutional reform which is not afraid of promoting the same »diversity in unity« willed for by the Council. To both aspects – catholicity as missionary outreach and catholicity as unity in diversity – I now turn, limiting myself to studying four important texts of Pope Francis:

- It is difficult to ignore the first encyclical of this papacy on faith, entitled *Lumen Fidei* and promulgated on June 29, 2013, the solemnity of the Holy Apostles Peter and Paul.[12] It is an exceptional document in that Pope Francis recognizes that his predecessor had »almost completed a first draft« – as the logical sequel of his encyclicals on »charity« and »hope« – to which he only »added a few contributions of his own.« (§ 7). Normally, however, popes conceive their first encyclical as a programmatic statement, as was e.g. the case with *Ecclesiam Suam* of Pope Paul VI and *Redemptor Hominis* of Pope Jean-Paul II. In the case of Pope Francis one even wonders whether he himself would fully subscribe to its rather closed teaching on tradition.[13] The apostolic exhortation *Evangelii Gaudium* carries much more the character of a maiden encyclical.

- An important address given by Pope Francis was the one at the General Coordination Meeting of the Consejo Episcopal Latinoamericano

cal act of reception of the council. Branded by the right-wing Catholics (and sometimes also by left-wingers) as a generational event only for those who were there, Vatican II is still the compass of the Church in modernity – a compass that the hierarchy of the Catholic Church seemed to have lost in recent times.« (ibid., 72) Cf. also Walter Kasper, *Pope Francis' Revolution of Tenderness and Love* (New York/Mahwah, NJ: Paulist Press, 2015), 19: »Thus in the pontificate of Pope Francis, the spirit of the Second Vatican Council is coming alive again in a new and fresh way. Pope Francis is the first pope who himself did not participate in the Second Vatican Council. With his pontificate we have entered into a new phase of the postconciliar age and of conciliar reception.«

[12] http://w2.vatican.va/content/francesco/en/encyclicals/documents/papa-francesco_20130629_enciclica-lumen-fidei.html (accessed August 1, 2014).

[13] See however Faggioli, *Pope Francis: Tradition in Transition*, 44: »Managing, without undue embarrassment, an encyclical like *Lumen Fidei*, ... testifies on the one hand to the precipitous nature of the resignation of Pope Benedict, and on the other hand, to the capacity of the whole Church to accept magisterial documents in the light of a *sensus ecclesiae*.« Cf. also Kasper, *Pope Francis' Revolution of Tenderness and Love*, 10: »The continuity is most clearly expressed by the fact that Pope Francis, with only two short additions adopted as his own the encyclical *Lumen fidei* (2013), which had been prepared by Pope Benedict. One cannot express the continuity more clearly than that.«

(CELAM) in Rio de Janeiro, 28 July 2013.[14] The meeting was devoted to study the reception and implementation of their 5th general conference, which had taken place in May 2007 under the guidance of Cardinal Bergoglio in the Marian shrine of Aparecida, Bresil.[15]
- Interviews seem to be an important communication means in this pontificate. In view of the fact that doubts have been raised on whether the two interviews published by Eugenio Scalfari, the atheist founder of the Italian journal *La Repubblica*, have rendered the pope's words in a reliable way[16] I limit myself to referring to the joint interview with Pope Francis published by a few leading Jesuit opinion journals in September, 2013.[17]
- Our final source is the pope's apostolic exhortation *Evangelii Gaudium*, released on the solemnity of Christ the King of the Universe, November 24, 2013. This reflection by the Pope was meant to harvest the fruits of the 13th Ordinary General Assembly of the Synod of Bishops on »The New Evangelization for the Transmission of the Christian Faith« (Rome, October 7–22, 2012). I will focus especially on the pope's broader ecclesiological reflections in chapter 1 and in the beginning of chapter 3.[18]

---

[14] An English translation has been published on the website of the Vatican: http://w2.vatican.va/content/francesco/en/speeches/2013/july/documents/papa-francesco_20130728_gmg-celam-rio.html (accessed August 1, 2014).

[15] See for the English translation of the final document: http://www.celam.org/aparecida/Ingles.pdf (accessed August 1, 2014).

[16] See, for the English translation of the first interview (September 2013), http://www.repubblica.it/cultura/2013/10/01/news/pope_s_conversation_with_scalfari_english-67643118 (accessed August 1, 2014). The second interview was published only in Italian on July 13, 2014: http://www.repubblica.it/cultura/2014/07/13/news/il_papa_come_ges_user_il_bastone_contro_i_preti_pedofili-91416624/?ref=HREA-1 (accessed August 1, 2014).

[17] I consulted the version published in America, 30 September 2013, 15–38. Cf. http://jesuits.org/Assets/Publications/File/USA_AmericaMag_2013-09-30.pdf (accessed August 1, 2014).

[18] Cf. http://w2.vatican.va/content/francesco/en/apost_exhortations/documents/papa-francesco_esortazione-ap_20131124_evangelii-gaudium.html (accessed August 1, 2014).

Catholicity I: The Missionary Outreach to the Peripheries of the Diverse People of God

In his short intervention during the general congregations preceding the last conclave, Cardinal Bergoglio is reported to have said the following:

> 1. Evangelizing implies apostolic zeal. Evangelizing pre-supposes a desire in the Church to come out of herself. The Church is called to come out of herself and to go to the peripheries, not only geographically, but also the existential peripheries: the mystery of sin, of pain, of injustice, of ignorance and indifference to religion, of intellectual currents, and of all misery.
> 2. When the Church does not come out of herself to evangelize, she becomes self-referential and then gets sick.[19]

At the end of his intervention he expressed the hope that the next pope would »help the Church to go out to the existential peripheries.« In fact the leitmotif in these four texts by Pope Francis is the necessity for the Catholic Church to rediscover its missionary nature, especially by focusing on the periphery.

I take the paragraph in *Lumen Fidei* thematising the outreach towards non-believers to have been an addition by Pope Francis to Pope Benedict's draft version: »Because faith is a way, it also has to do with the lives of those men and women who, though not believers, nonetheless desire to believe and continue to seek.« (§ 35) It seems typical for the inclusive view on catholicity of Pope Francis to claim that »any-one who sets off on the path of doing good to others is already drawing near to God.«

In the CELAM address the pope contrasts a church in which the emphasis is on the centre so that »she becomes increasingly self-referential and loses her need to be missionary« to a missionary discipleship oriented towards »the existential peripheries«, recalling that »the centre is Jesus Christ, who calls us and sends us forth.«

The same topic is addressed in even greater detail in the Jesuit interview. Here, Pope Francis invites the Church »to step outside itself and go to those who do not attend Mass, to those who have quit or are indifferent.« (24) Towards persons living in what the Church considers to be irregular situations, such as homosexuals, we should in the first

---

[19] Quoted from *Pope Francis: Tradition in Transition*, 4.

instance proclaim God's mercy. The missionary strategy is definitely not »to occupy spaces« but rather to »initiate processes.« (30) When a church leader is confronted with pastoral approaches which he does not share himself, it is advisable to have patience, since God may reveal himself through unexpected ways. Today church leaders should »have the courage to open up new areas to God« rather than being »a restorationist« or »a legalist.« (32) Christians have »to live on the border and be audacious« but not »fall into the temptation to tame the frontiers.« (36)

The same leitmotif finally also occurs in *Evangelii Gaudium*. As of the first chapter of the apostolic exhortation the pope expresses the hope that the entire Church will be transformed by becoming missionary. This implies the willingness of being enriched by the periphery: »Each Christian and every community must discern the path that the Lord points out, but all of us are asked to obey his call to go forth from our own comfort zone in order to reach all the ›peripheries‹ in need of the light of the Gospel.« (§ 20)

In the same exhortation he also indicates that this missionary attitude of the Church may have liturgical or sacramentological implications. He ends the ecclesiological opening chapter with expressing the hope that the Church should keep its »doors open.« (§ 46) His words, reminiscent of the teaching of Vatican II that communion in the Church is not an issue of all or nothing but allows for degrees, seem to envisage in the first instance an as open access to the sacraments as possible for Catholic faithful: »Everyone can share in some way in the life of the Church; everyone can be part of the community, nor should the doors of the sacraments be closed for simply any reason.«[20] (§ 47) When Pope Francis deplores, however, that in our canonical regulations we frequently »act as arbiters of grace rather than its facilitators«, his words also remind the ecumenically attentive reader of the distinction made in UR 8 between »bearing witness to the unity of the church, and second, the sharing in the means of grace. Witness to the unity of the

---

[20] In the same vein in his address pronounced upon the conclusion of the Third Extraordinary General Assembly of the Synod of Bishops on »The Pastoral Challenges of the Family in the Context of Evangelization« (Rome, 5–19 October, 2014), Pope Francis deplored a.o. the following temptation which he had experienced during the synod: »the temptation to transform the bread into a stone and cast it against the sinners, the weak, and the sick (cf Jn 8:7), that is, to transform it into unbearable burdens (Lk 11:46).« Cf. http://w2.vatican.va/content/francesco/en/speeches/2014/october/documents/papa-francesco_20141018_conclusione-sinodo-dei-vescovi.html (accessed August 1, 2014).

church generally forbids common worship, but the grace to be had from it sometimes commends this practice.« Therefore, implicitly the Pope maybe also expresses his concerns about the current norms on intercommunion valid within the Catholic Church.

The missionary program which Pope Francis proposes to his church also affects the content of its doctrinal and moral teaching. Reminding his readership of the paragraph of *Unitatis Redintegratio* dealing with the existence of a hierarchy of truths (§ 36) and of the distinction made by Pope John XXIII in his famous opening discourse of the Council between the deposit of faith and the way it is expressed (§ 41), the Pope asks the pastors of the Catholic Church »not to be obsessed with the disjointed transmission of a multitude of doctrines to be insistently imposed« but rather to »concentrate on the essentials.« (§ 35)

It is difficult to harmonize this teaching of Francis with the much more Ratzingerean concluding section of the chapter on tradition in *Lumen Fidei* dealing with »The unity and integrity of faith« (§§ 47–49). Does »professing the same faith« necessarily require that »we have a single insight into reality«? The pope – again probably Benedict XVI – continues: »Since faith is one, it must be professed in all its purity and integrity. Precisely because all articles of faith are interconnected, to deny one of them, even of those that seem least important, is tantamount to distorting the whole.« The concept of catholicity which follows from such a view seems to leave no room for unity in diversity: »Faith is thus shown to be universal, catholic, because its light expands in order to illumine the entire cosmos and all of history.« One wonders how one is to start the dialogue with other churches from such a doctrinal point of departure.

The third chapter of *Evangelii Gaudium* on »The proclamation of the Gospel« offers Pope Francis the occasion to show his faithfulness to the ecclesiological model of the people of God which occupied a central place in *Lumen Gentium*. It is his deep conviction that »The entire people of God proclaims the Gospel«. When characterising the people of God as »a people with many faces« the pope employs the term catholicity: »In the diversity of peoples who experience the gift of God, each in accordance with its own culture, the Church expresses her genuine catholicity and shows forth the ›beauty of her varied face‹.«[21] (§ 116)

---

[21] The citation is from the apostolic letter of Pope John Paul II *Novo Millenio Ineunte* (2001).

The pope knows that »cultural diversity is not a threat to Church unity« (§ 117) because it is a sign of the presence of the Holy Spirit.

> It is he who brings forth a rich variety of gifts, while at the same time creating a unity which is never uniformity but a multifaceted and inviting harmony. Evangelization joyfully acknowledges these varied treasures which the Holy Spirit pours out upon the Church. We would not do justice to the logic of the incarnation if we thought of Christianity as monocultural and monotonous. (ibid.)

After paying particular attention to popular piety (§§ 122–126) the pope exhorts the faithful to cherish the existence of different charisms among them and not to be afraid of diversity:

> Differences between persons and communities can sometimes prove uncomfortable, but the Holy Spirit, who is the source of that diversity, can bring forth something good from all things and turn it into an attractive means of evangelization. Diversity must always be reconciled by the help of the Holy Spirit; he alone can raise up diversity, plurality and multiplicity while at the same time bringing about unity. When we, for our part, aspire to diversity, we become self-enclosed, exclusive and divisive; similarly, whenever we attempt to create unity on the basis of our human calculations, we end up imposing a monolithic uniformity. This is not helpful for the Church's mission. (§ 131)

A similar idea, emphasizing the uniqueness of each believer's contribution in the Church, is found in *Lumen Fidei* and is therefore perhaps an addition by Pope Francis:

> The image of a body does not imply that the believer is simply one part of an anonymous whole, a mere cog in a great machine; rather, it brings out the vital union of Christ with believers and of believers among themselves (cf. Rom 12:4–5). Christians are »one« (cf. Gal 3:28), yet in a way which does not make them lose their individuality; in service to others, they come into their own in the highest degree. (§ 22)

b) Catholicity 2: Reforming the Church with Greater Attention to Inity in Diversity

Pope Francis' ideas on reform are also deeply rooted in Vatican II. It is highly meaningful that the first reference to the documents of the Council in *Evangelii Gaudium* is § 6 of the decree on ecumenism *Unitatis Redintegratio*, the only Council document admitting that the Church is not only in need of renewal, bus also of reform[22]: »Every renewal of the Church essentially consists in an increase of fidelity to her own calling... Christ summons the Church as she goes her pilgrim way... to that continual reformation of which she always has need, in so far as she is a human institution here on earth«. (§ 26) In the Jesuit interview the pope warns that reforming the Church takes time – time for discernment, and he also revealed his intention to follow the example of Pope John XXIII, who implemented his huge project of *aggiornamento* by making a few well-chosen small steps.[23]

Pope Francis' proposal of ecclesial renewal pertains to the entire Church. In a subsection of the first chapter of *Evangelii Gaudium* entitled »An ecclesial renewal which cannot be deferred« (§§ 27–33) the pope deliberately first pays attention to the smallest level of the parish, to end up with the papacy itself. I follow the same order, but I will regularly also refer to insights found in sources other than *Evangelii Gaudium*.

Pope Francis expresses the diversity of viewpoints at the level of the parish by speaking about the parish as »a community of communities.« (§ 28) Having lived so long in Latin-America, the pope, however, immediately also considers »other church institutions, basic communities and small communities, movements, and forms of association« as a Spirit-driven »source of enrichment for the Church« if at least some integration in the life of the particular Church takes place. (§ 29) Not only does the pope promote diversity at the level of the local Church, but, as the *relatio* of LG 13 did 50 years ago, he also clearly despises uniformity. As he states in *Evangelii Gaudium*:

---

[22] Cf. Peter De Mey, »Church Renewal and Reform in the Documents of Vatican II: History, Theology, Terminology,« *The Jurist* 71 (2011): 369–400.

[23] Cf. also the reflection on time and space in *Lumen Fidei* (§ 57) – »Time is always much greater than space. Space hardens processes, whereas time propels towards the future and encourages us to go forward in hope.« – and *Evangelii Gaudium* (§§ 222–225), where the Pope states a.o.: »Giving priority to time means being concerned about initiating processes rather than possessing spaces.« (§ 223)

It always pains me greatly to discover how some Christian communities, and even consecrated persons, can tolerate different forms of enmity, division, calumny, defamation, vendetta, jealousy and the desire to impose certain ideas at all costs, even to persecutions which appear as veritable witch hunts. Whom are we going to evangelize if this is the way we act? (§ 100)[24]

In his CELAM address the pope also pleads for a greater involvement of lay people in the mission of the Church. In both diocesan councils and parish councils lay people should »participate in pastoral consultation, organization and planning.« The Pope believes that, »on this score we are far behind.«[25] As one of the most important pastoral dangers in Latin America, he warns against clericalism, also in the form of clericalizing the laity and thus again not taking the voice of all church members seriously.

In the Jesuit interview he is also aware that our communities need to better respect the contribution of women. »The feminine genius is needed wherever we make important decisions.« (28)[26]

---

[24] Cf. also the 15 diseases described by Pope Francis in his Christmas Greetings to the Roman Curia on December 22, 2014: http://w2.vatican.va/content/francesco/en/speeches/2014/december/documents/papa-francesco_20141222_curia-romana.html (accessed August 1, 2014).

[25] Cf. also *Evangelii Gaudium*, § 102: »Lay people are, put simply, the vast majority of the people of God. The minority – ordained ministers – are at their service. There has been a growing awareness of the identity and mission of the laity in the Church. ... At the same time, a clear awareness of this responsibility of the laity, grounded in their baptism and confirmation, does not appear in the same way in all places.«

[26] In *Evangelii Gaudium*, § 104 the pope insists that the Church is not entitled to grant »the power to administer the sacrament of the Eucharist« to women. »This presents a great challenge for pastors and theologians, who are in a position to recognize more fully what this entails with regard to the possible role of women in decision-making in different areas of the Church's life.« Somme commentators ask attention for the symbolic actions of the pope in this regard. See e.g. Michel Dubost, »Sortir aux périphéries,« in *Le grand tournant: l'an I de la révolution du pape François* (Paris: Cerf, 2014), 49–72, 70: »En lavant les pieds le jeudi saint à deux femmes, il a probablement donné plus de rayonnement à la pensée de Jean-Paul II sur les femmes que la lettre apostolique *Mulieris Dignitatem*.« According to Gerard Mannion, Pope Francis could go further in this: »Following Francis' constant example, then, instead of getting bogged down in the sterile debates about women's ordination that have proved so divisive in recent decades, what if Catholicism instead looked to what Christian communities gain when ministry, authority and leadership is carried out by women in other churches?« (Gerard Mannion, »Reengaging the People of God:

When moving to the level of the diocese Pope Francis seems to be aware of the fact that it is better not to conceive of the diocese as a »part« of the universal Church:

> Each particular church, as a portion of the Catholic Church under the leadership of its bishop, is likewise called to missionary conversion. It is the primary subject of evangelization, since it is the concrete manifestation of the one Church in one specific place, and in it »the one, holy, catholic, and apostolic Church of Christ is truly present and operative.« (§ 30)

The pope is also willing to listen to the input of the bishops on the themes he is discussing in his exhortation:

> Nor do I believe that the papal magisterium should be expected to offer a definitive or complete word on every question which affects the Church and the world. It is not advisable for the Pope to take the place of local Bishops in the discernment of every issue which arises in their territory. In this sense, I am conscious of the need to promote a sound »decentralization«. (§ 16)

The exhortation is also a clear break with the past in that the pope often quotes from meetings of national (8 times) and continental episcopal conferences (12 times; understandably almost always referring to the 2007 CELAM general assembly in Aparecida which convened under his presidency) and twice from a document of the International Theological Commission.[27]

Pope Francis and Vatican II,« in *The Ecclesiology of Pope Francis*, eds. Richard R. Gaillardetz and Thomas P. Rausch [New York, forthcoming]).

[27] A few years ago my conclusion was different with regard to the 2003 postsynodal exhortation *Ecclesia in Europa* of Pope John-Paul II. Cf. Peter De Mey, »The Church in a European Perspective,« in *The Routledge Companion to the Christian Church*, eds. Gerard Mannion and Lewis S. Mudge (London: Routledge, 2007), 364–385; 367: »It should also be noted by way of critique that the footnote references in *Ecclesia in Europa* draw exclusively on the teaching of the universal magisterium of the Church, whereas there can be little doubt that valuable contributions from individual European bishops and theologians or from their collaborative gatherings are also available. In the present author's opinion, it is sad – and perhaps some indication of a lack of ecumenical engagement on behalf of the Catholic Church – that there is no single reference in *Ecclesia in Europa* to the *Charta Oecumenica* (2001), a major result of cooperation between a Roman Catholic body, the Council of European Bishops' Conferences (CCEE) and the Conference of European Churches.« Also Felix Wilfred, »*Evangelii gaudium* –

Of great ecumenical significance, finally, is the paragraph of *Evangelii Gaudium* dealing with the »conversion of the papacy.« Pope Francis reminds his readership of the invitation raised by Pope John Paul II in his 1995 ecumenical encyclical *Ut Unum Sint* to theologians and leaders of other churches and denominations to help him reflect on the mode of exercising the primacy. The judgement of Pope Francis is crystal clear: »We have made little progress in this regard.« (§ 32) Especially the institution of the episcopal conference in his opinion has to play an important role in the transformation of »the papacy and the central structures of the universal Church.« By stating that »a juridical status of episcopal conferences which would see them as subjects of specific attributions, including genuine doctrinal authority, has not yet been sufficiently elaborated«, and by referring in footnote to the 1998 motu proprio *Apostolos Suos* of John Paul II which precisely intended to determine the juridical status of this institution in a very narrow way, Pope Francis publically criticizes the decision of his two predecessors, since one can be sure that the president of the Congregation for the Doctrine of the Faith was the main drafter of this document. Most probably the following quotation by the former Archbishop of Boston, John Quinn, contrasting *Apostolos Suos* with the teaching of Vatican II, inspired Pope Francis a lot.

The Second Vatican Council, then, does not reflect the idea that there are only two divinely based expressions of the episcopal office, the relationship of the individual bishop to the pope and the formal united and collegial action of the bishops of the world in an ecumenical council. In addition to these, there is the providential development of episcopal conferences, which are not mere administrative conveniences

Reflections from Asia,« *Zeitschrift für Missionswissenschaft und Religionswissenschaft* 98 (2014): 138–142, 138, draws ecclesiological conclusions from this important move of the pope: »I have hardly found documents of bishops' conferences being quoted in papal writings, and was overjoyed to see a statement of the Catholic Bishops' Conference of India cited when the pope speaks of inter-religious dialogue, Brazilian Bishops' conference when he speaks of poor and poverty; and the Bishops' Conference of the Philippines, when speaking of environmental issues. ... In this way, it seems to me that Pope Francis is giving concrete expression to the truth that the universal Church is made up of local Churches whose voices need to be listened to. He is probably bringing to a close the discussion on the relationship of the local church and the universal Church in the interpretation of Vatican II which has been for some years now a hot point of debate. ... The position of Pope Francis seems to be that both local Church and universal Church exist simultaneously and there is no question of speaking about priority.«

but a reflection of the communion of the local churches in a region or country and a manifestation of the diversity and catholicity of the Church.[28]

Also the Jesuit interview contains much information on the Pope's plans concerning the government of the universal Church. Pope Francis knows from personal experience – since he was made provincial at too young an age – that an authoritarian style does not work. In his government of the universal Church he wants to pursue the same style he has practised since he became archbishop of Buenos Aires, when he had two-weekly meetings with his auxiliary bishops and regular meetings with the council of priests. At the level of the universal Church meetings with the consistories of cardinals and the synods of bishops should be »real, not ceremonial consultations.« (20) In the same vein, following an explicit desire of the pre-conclave general congregations he installed a council of cardinals.[29] It should again become clear that the curia is »at the service of pope and bishops.« (28) An investigation of doubts raised on the orthodoxy of certain writings better takes place »by the local bishops' conferences, which can get valuable assistance from Rome.« (28) The Catholic Church could learn much from the way synodality is exercised among the Orthodox churches. When asked about the way towards unity, the pope's response reflects the same understanding of catholicity: »We must walk united with our differences: there is no other way to become one. This is the way of Jesus« (28).[30]

[28] John R. Quinn, *The Reform of the Papacy: The Costly Call to Christian Unity* (New York: Herder & Herder, 1999), 105. For an account of the personal contacts between Archbishop Quinn and Pope Francis, cf. the article posted by Sandro Magister on his blog, on August 7, 2014: »Reform of the Papacy: A Work in Progress.« See http://chiesa.espresso.repubblica.it/articolo/1350857?eng=y (accessed August 1, 2014).

[29] Cf. Faggioli, *Pope Francis: Tradition in Transition*, 15: »From the historical point of view, this committee is very close to the idea already expressed by the Second Vatican Council between 1963 and 1965 of the need for a permanent ›board of bishops‹ surrounding the pope above the Roman curia – an idea that was absorbed and eventually scuttled by the creation of the Synod of Bishops by Pope Paul VI in his *motu proprio Apostolica Sollicitudo* on September 15, 1965.«

[30] In the interview book with Rabbi Abraham Skorka, Cardinal Bergoglio had already approvingly quoted from *Einheit durch Vielfalt*, a book by Oscar Cullmann, who had been an observer at the Council: »There is a quote from a German Lutheran theologian, Oscar Cullmann, that refers to how to bring together the Christian denominations. He says we should not seek that everyone, from the outset, affirm the same thing, but instead he proposes that we walk together in

3   The Reception of the Teaching of Pope Francis on Catholicity

The words and deeds of Pope Francis have in the meantime been widely commented upon in books and articles.[31] The first monographs on Francis were biographical by nature and pay great attention to the changes in his leadership style from being an authoritarian young provincial and, in the words of Paul Valley's *Pope Francis: Untying the Knots* »the scourge of Liberation Theology«[32], to becoming a much more pastorally sensitive Archbishop of Buenos Aires. According to this well-received book Jorge Mario Bergoglio will remain a »pope of paradox«. He is »a doctrinal traditionalist but an ecclesiastical reformer. He is a radical but not a liberal. He seeks to empower others and yet retains a streak of authoritarianism. He is a conservative yet was on the far left of his reactionary Bishops' Conference.«[33]

As could be expected, the first articles have appeared which praise Pope Francis for those statements in *Lumen Fidei* which are clearly in line with the tradition. In the English edition of *Nova et Vetera* Reinhard Hütter is thankful that *Lumen Fidei* has challenged »the contemporary ›dictatorship of relativism‹ that has invaded certain superficial interpretations of the ›hierarchy of truths‹.«[34] For her part Irene Alexander wrote an article with the telling title: »Faith Enlightens the Mind: Pope Francis's *Lumen Fidei* and Contemporary Errors on the Nature of Divine Faith.«[35] It contains the following words of praise: »In his first encyclical, *Lumen Fidei*, Pope Francis goes straight to the heart of the modern

---

reconciled diversity; he resolves the religious conflict of the many Christian denominations by walking together, by doing things together, by praying together. He asks that we not throw rocks at each other, but rather that we continue walking together. It is the way of advancing the resolution of a conflict with the virtues of all, without nullifying the diverse traditions or falling into syncretism. Each one, from their identity, seeking the unity of truth« Cf. Jorge Mario Bergoglio and Abraham Skorka, *On Heaven and Earth: Pope Francis on Faith, Family, and the Church in the Twenty-First Century* (New York: Image, 2013), 217–218. See also Kasper, *Pope Francis' Revolution of Tenderness and Love*, 56.

[31] In this section I limit myself to a number of issues of theological journals dedicated to Pope Francis, from his election until August 2014.

[32] Paul Vallely, *Pope Francis: Untying the Knots* (London: Bloomsbury Academic, 2013), 115.

[33] Ibid., xi.

[34] Reinhard Hütter, »Enlightenment: Reflections on Pope Francis's Encyclical Letter Lumen Fidei,« *Nova et Vetera. The English Edition of the International Theological Journal* 12 (2014): 1–11, here 6.

[35] Ibid., 11–24.

world's erroneous conception about the nature of divine faith and shows the falsehood and inadequacy of the contemporary disjunction between the light of faith and the search for truth.«[36]

The Belgian CICM father Lode Wostyn had pronounced a warning in this regard. In a recent article in the Maryhill School of Theology Review he observes »an unresolved tension« in the current papacy, »which hopefully will get some clarification in the near future.«[37] He especially pointed to the difference between the first encyclical and the Jesuit interview: »The self-referential theologian of *Lumen Fidei* becomes in the *Interview* a prophetic missionary at the periphery who seeks dialogue, discernment, frontiers. ... The evangelizer-pope, opening doors, also closes some doors as the guardian of the Church's doctrinal past.«[38] Since also *Evangelii Gaudium* contains »a few warnings that the Pope cannot change the Church's doctrinal heritage,« Wostyn leaves it to the future to tell »who will prevail, the ›self-referential theologian‹ or the evangelizer.«[39]

The start of the new papacy was an occasion for the journal *Concilium* to forget its usually critical attitude towards Rome. The third issue of 2013 on »Saints and Sanctity today« already ended with two small articles with best wishes on the occasion of the new papacy from liberation theologians Joao Batista Libanio and Leonardo Boff. The former is hopeful because Bergoglio »is well placed to be a Pope who is a prophet of social justice as understood by the Third World.«[40] Not without expressing the hope that the new pope would call »a new Council of representatives of the whole Christian world, lay people, men and women, others famous for their knowledge and example, and the other Christian churches«, the latter wished the pope: »May he not lack courage and the powerful breath of the Holy Spirit.«[41] Immediately

---

[36] Ibid., 24. The article by Keith Lemna and David H. Delaney, »Three Pathways into the Theological Mind of Pope Francis,« *Nova et Vetera. The English Edition of the International Theological Journal* 12 (2014): 25–56, probably was included in the same issue not so much because of its sketch of Pope Francis's Latin American liberation theology a.o. inspired by the Argentinian philosopher and friend of Bergoglio, Juan Carlos Scannone, or of the Aparacida document, but because the article defends a dependence upon the writings of Luigi Giusani, the founder of the ecclesial movement *Communio e liberazione*.

[37] Lode Wostyn, CICM, »The Church Today: Realities and Vision-Mission,« *MST Review* 16 (2014/1): 1–31, 19.

[38] Ibid., 22.

[39] Ibid., 28–29.

[40] Joao Batista Libanio, »Pope Francis,« *Concilium*, no. 3 (2013): 137–141, 141.

[41] Ibid., 142–145, 145.

after it became known that the pope had decided to install a council of cardinals, the editorial board of *Concilium* decided to dedicate a special issue of its journal to the Reform of the Roman Curia. Alberto Melloni for his part considers the announcement of the institution of a council of cardinals to be a decisive step in the direction of a true reform of the curia, since it is an expression both »of the *communio ecclesiarum* [communion of churches] and of the *communio episcoporum* [communion of bishops]« and thus »a senate of communion.« [42]

In his contribution to the *Concilium* issue, but also in his recent contribution to a collective volume by the bishop of Evreux Michel Dubost on the occasion of the first year of this papacy, the French Dominican Hervé Legrand stresses the same point. In the pope's writings but also in his self-designation as »bishop of Rome« he sees a clear revalorisation »both of the communion between churches and the collegiality of the bishops rooted in this communion of churches.«[43] Legrand is very much convinced, however, that »the reforms will hurt themselves, at all levels, at the letter and the spirit of the current canon law which has rather disarticulated the relationship between the Roman primacy and the communion of churches.«[44] If the Pope would still be looking for advice in how to reform his church, Legrand has enough concrete suggestions to make. The pope could exercise his primacy again as a final appeal and does not necessarily have to take care of the daily government of the Catholic Church. The curia could become an instrument at the service of pope and bishops and also be accountable to the bishops, for example on the occasion of a meeting of the synod of bishops. Episcopal conferences at the level of a continent should cease to be merely consultative bodies and could be granted the same role as the ancient patriarchates. It should no longer be necessary to ordain priests as bishops simply because of their administrative or honorary positions. The diocese should finally play a greater role in determining the list of candidates for the episcopate.[45]

---

[42] Alberto Melloni, »Senatus Communionis: A Senate of Communion,« *Concilium*, no. 5 (2013): 35–50, 41.

[43] Hervé Legrand, »Enjeux ecclésiologiques des réformes institutionnelles envisagées par le pape François,« in Dubost, *Le grand tournant*, 185–210, 188. See also Legrand, »Roman Primacy, Communion between Churches, and Communion between Bishops,« *Concilium*, no. 5 (2013): 63–77.

[44] Ibid., 190.

[45] Ibid., 195–209: »Quelques institutions que les projets de réforme du pape François pourraient revisiter«.

To my surprise several contributions to a recent issue of the German version of *Communio* with a thematic focus on *Kircheneinheit – Petrusdienst* are equally appreciative of the greater attention for intermediary structures in this papacy. The main editor Jan-Heiner Tück has the impression that the pope, »more than his predecessor, wants to exercise his Petrine ministry in the sense of a primacy of communion« and insists that this is not in contradiction with Vatican I. Among the »signals of reform« that become visible he especially is appreciative of the fact that the pope, by emphasising »the relative autonomy of continental episcopal conferences« has given »an also ecumenically relevant counterbalance against Roman centralism.«[46] According to bishop emeritus Peter Henrici one may hope on the basis of a few statements of Pope Francis in *Evangelii Gaudium* that he is in favour of a decentralisation of the Church in which episcopal conferences play an important role. He for his part is convinced »that such local bodies can better judge what is right in a particular situation and what is useful for the Church than the Roman curia, which judges only from a distance and usually is thinking in the European if not the Italian way.« Secondly, he considers it »wise not to leave important decisions to one single bishop but to tie him in the community of his fellow bishops, which, by means of an active exchange of opinions, can come to a more balanced judgement.«[47]

This is not to deny of course that the texts we studied in preparation of this chapter sometimes also contain critical remarks. In the forum on *Evangelii Gaudium* in the *Zeitschrift für Missionswissenschaft und Religionswissenschaft* the contributors from the Global South are particularly critical about the teaching on non-Christian religions in the apostolic exhortation. Paulo Suess finds it hard to believe that the pope himself wrote the statement that their »sacred expressions lack the meaning and efficacy of the sacraments instituted by Christ« (§ 254).[48] This is seconded by Felix Wilfred:

---

[46] Jan-Heiner Tück, »Communio-Primat: Von Benedikt XVI. zu Franziskus: Überlegungen zum Petrusdienst im dritten Jahrtausend,« *Internationale Katholische Zeitschrift Communio* 43 (2014): 126–141, here 128, 137.

[47] Peter Henrici, »Die Bischofskonferenzen: Ihr zukunftsträchtiger Beitrag zur Einheit der Kirche,« *Internationale Katholische Zeitschrift Communio* 43 (2014): 156–164, here 162.

[48] Paulo Suess, »Kirche im Aufbruch,« *Zeitschrift für Missionswissenschaft und Religionswissenschaft* 98 (2014): 127–132, here 132.

In short, while what Pope Francis has to say about the poor and poverty finds immediate resonance with Asian Christians, they would find the scant treatment of what for them is of an equally important concern, namely interreligious dialogue, as a serious limitation of this document.[49]

4 Conclusion

Even if this is only one of two denominational contributions to the subtheme »Catholicity in the Future / The Future of Catholicity«, the reader of this book, which is the fruit of an academic consultation by *Societas Oecumenica*, may wonder whether a reflection on the understanding of catholicity by Pope Francis is only meaningful for Catholics or whether it has also wider ecumenical relevance. In my opinion the latter is the case. Whether the Pope is speaking about the missionary outreach of his church to the peripheries or about the need to reform the Church ad intra, the theme of unity in diversity never is far away. The claim that »unity is never uniformity« was found in Congar's draft of LG 13 but did not make it into the final version of the Dogmatic Constitution on the Church. Pope Francis for his part does not hesitate to make Congar's words his own in his Apostolic Exhortation *Evangelii Gaudium* (§ 117; 131). He invites the Catholic Church to renew and reform itself, by being more attentive to the diversity of gifts of the Holy Spirit among the faithful. He understands his own office in the first instance as that of the bishop of Rome who cherishes and really makes use of the diversity of inputs from the local churches and their intermediary structures of unity.

Even if a dramatic progress in the many bilateral and multilateral dialogues in which the Catholic Church is involved is not expected within the coming years, the Pope has applied his motto of diversity in unity also to ecumenism, as could be noticed in the Jesuit interview: »We must walk united with our differences: there is no other way to become one. This is the way of Jesus.« (28) He brings this method into practice in warm and personal ecumenical contacts, a.o. with the Ecumenical Patriarch, with Evangelical pastors and Pentecostal Christians. In light of the Pope's interesting remark in *Evangelii Gaudium* that »the doors of the sacraments should not be closed for simply any reason« (§ 47) one dares to hope that the coming ordinary general

---

[49] Wilfred, »Evangelii gaudium – Reflections from Asia,« 141.

assembly of the Synod of Bishops on »The vocation and mission of the family in the Church and in the contemporary world« may address some of the pains of those living in inter-church families.

WORKSHOPS

Misconceptions regarding the Terms »Catholic« and »Protestant« and Their Implication in Ecumenical Relations in Africa

James N. Amanze

1 Introduction

This paper is about the misconceptions and misunderstandings regarding the words »catholic« and »protestant« and their implication in ecumenical relations in Africa. It is argued in the paper that while the original meaning of the word »catholic« in Christendom meant »universal« or »general« , after the 16th century Reformation Christians, who remained under the jurisdiction of the Pope in Rome, began to use the term »catholic« exclusively to themselves and began to consider »Protestants« as renegades. This practice continues to the present day. Consequently, in Africa a number of Protestant churches avoid using the word »catholic« for fear that they would be mistaken of being Roman Catholics thereby undermining their identity. Catholics look upon Protestants as being not really Christians. Protestants on the other hand look upon Catholics as people whose Christianity is shrouded with traditions of human beings, which are not supported by the Bible. In Africa these misconceptions and misunderstandings have become a source of conflict between Catholics and Protestants. The paper argues that this should not be the case and calls for a better understanding of the word »catholic« among Roman Catholics and Protestants. The paper proposes that since it is now widely acknowledged that it is not possible to achieve visible unity of the church in the short or medium term, »Receptive Ecumenism« is the best way forward to achieve meaningful cooperation among different churches. This is because it advocates that people of different church traditions should learn and receive from one another the gifts that are uniquely of the other for purposes of spiritual growth, mutual understanding and cooperation without expecting the other to come over to the other side.

2   The Historical Background: Christianity Comes to Africa

It is important to point out that when Christianity first came to Africa it was essentially one with Christ as its sole head and all Christians as members of the one Christian family. By most accounts, the presence of Christianity in Africa is traced back to AD 34 when St. Mark preached in the streets of Alexandria in Egypt.[1] Most historians consider this event as the beginning of Christianity in Africa. Eventually, it spread to other parts of North Africa on the wings of the Roman Empire. This early beginning was followed by the introduction of Christianity in Abyssinia as reflected in the story of the Ethiopian Eunuch described in the book of the Acts of the Apostles 8:26–40.[2] These early beginnings, however, did not have an impact in Africa south of the Sahara. The era of Christian missions in sub-Saharan Africa is traced back to the beginning of the 19th century when different Protestant Christian denominations in Europe and America planted churches in Africa as outposts of the mother churches in their country of origin thus undermining the unity that existed in the Apostolic Church.

Coupled with this, the Roman Catholic Church launched an unprecedented campaign of establishing churches in Africa through a number of religious orders such as the White Fathers, the Montfort Fathers, the Jesuits, the Franciscans and others.[3] Thus, within a short period of time much Africa was brought within the ambit of Christendom. Today Christianity in Africa is experiencing an explosive growth. Sub-

---

[1]   See Jonathan Hildebrandt, *History of the Church in Africa* (Achimota, Ghana: Africa Christian Press, 1981), 5–8 where the introduction of Christianity in North Africa has been discussed in detail.

[2]   See Geoffrey Parrinder, *Religion in Africa* (Harmondsworth: Penguin, 1969), 108.

[3]   James N. Amanze, *A History of the Ecumenical Movement in Africa* (Gaborone: Pula Press, 1998), 69.

Saharan Africa has recorded the fastest growth in number of Christians in the past century which has climbed from 9% in 1910 to 63% in 2010. It is estimated today that about one in every four Christians in the world lives in sub-Saharan Africa. It has been noted that while in 1910 sub-Saharan Africa had fewer than 9 million Christians this number increased to 516 million by 2010.[4]

In order to put this discussion in its proper historical context, it is important here to look briefly into the missionary activities of both the Roman Catholic Church and the Protestant Churches in Africa from the time of their inception to the present.

The Roman Catholic Church Comes to Africa

Historiographers have indicated that though several attempts were made to introduce Roman Catholicism in Africa in the 15th and 16th centuries through the efforts of the Portuguese explorers and missionaries, these attempts did not have long lasting results. It is true that the church enjoyed some success in the Congo Kingdom and moved into Central Africa but the collapse of the Congo Kingdom in the mid-17th century and the decline of Portuguese power undermined the success of these missionary attempts and by the 19th century the Catholic Church in Africa had virtually disappeared.[5]

It is held that the missionary era of Roman Catholicism in Africa began in earnest through the missionary activities of the White Fathers, a religious group that was founded by Archbishop Charles Lavigerie in 1868. This religious order established a number of missionary stations in East Africa in present day Tanzania and eventually moved into central Africa. It is reckoned that by 1900 there were some two million Catholics in Africa south of the Sahara. During the 20th century it improved its efforts in education and increased a number of African priests and bishops to minister to the faithful. Their numbers increased to nearly 140 million by the early 21st century.[6]

---

[4] http:// www.pewforum.org/2011/12/19/global-christian (accessed August 12, 2014).

[5] http://www.britannica.com/EBchecked/topic/507284/Roman-Catholicism/ 43773/Roman Catholicism in Africa-in-Africa-and-Asia (accessed August 3, 2010).

[6] Ibid.

The success of the Catholic Church is attributed, largely, to its help to independent African countries in their educational systems to such an extent that in the 1990s many governments turned to the church to help them run their educational institutions. Its success is also attributed to its efforts to Africanise the clergy. Again the use of vernacular languages which replaced the traditional Latin of the mass and the process of inculturation which involved the incorporation into the liturgy of African traditions in music and dance contributed tremendously to the growth of the church. It is maintained that by the beginning of the 21st century the Catholic Church in Africa became one of the most dynamic churches of postconciliar Catholicism and is now poised for continued growth and wider influence in the continent.[7] According to the Vatican newspaper *L'Osservatore Romano* of 18th May 2008, between the years 2000 and 2006 the number of Roman Catholics rose from 12.4% to 14% thus making the African region the place where the Roman Catholic Church is experiencing the biggest growth.[8]

Protestant Churches in Africa

The second major block of Christians in Africa consists of Protestant churches so called because their system of Christian faith and church practice is based on the acceptance of the teachings and principles of the Reformation. Historiographers have indicated that the history of Protestant churches in Africa goes back to 1652 when Dutch settlers brought the Dutch Reformed Church to Cape Colony. This was followed by the Moravian Church which was planted there by George Schmidt in 1737. This humble beginning was followed by the missionary work of the London Missionary Society through the activities of John Theodore Vanderkemp. Thus from Cape Colony Protestant work spread far and wide in Southern Africa covering such countries as South Africa, Lesotho, Swaziland, Botswana, Zimbabwe, Zambia, Namibia, and beyond. The colonial and imperial activities of the British Government provided further opportunities for the expansion of Protestant churches not only in Southern Africa but in other parts of the African continent.

---

[7] Ibid.
[8] http://m.christianpost.com/nws/catholic-church-reports-biggest-growth-in-africa--32469 (accessed August 5, 2014).

A barrage of missionary societies which were formed in Europe and America as a result of the evangelical revival such as the Paris Evangelical Missionary Society, the Wesleyan Missionary Society, the Berlin Missionary Society, the Church Missionary Society, the Hermannsburg Missionary Society, the Universities Mission to Central Africa, the Glasgow Missionary Society, to name a few, planted Protestant churches in many countries in Africa which continue to flourish to the present day. Through the activities of the missionary societies, Protestant churches were planted in many African countries such as Sierra Leone, Nigeria, Tanzania, Kenya, Uganda, Ghana, Mozambique, Ethiopia, Malawi, to name a few. Today Protestant churches form a gigantic Christian movement in Africa.[9] According to the Pew Study on Global Christianity, more than 1/3 of Protestants and evangelicals in the world live in sub-Saharan Africa. In terms of percentages of all Christians living in sub-Saharan Africa it is reckoned that 57% are Protestants. This includes members of the African Independent Churches.[10]

3 The Relationship between Catholicism and Protestantism in Sub-Saharan Africa

Right from the beginning of the missionary era in Africa the relationship between Roman Catholics and Protestants has been a savory one. Roman Catholics view themselves, officially, as *sui generis*. Since the 16th century Reformation the Catholic Church has made exclusive claim of catholicity and in Africa this claim has made other Christian denominations avoid associating themselves with the word »catholic«. This position has generated a great deal of controversy between Roman Catholics and Protestants to the extent that in some Protestant Churches the word »catholic« in the Nicene Creed as been replaced by the words »universal« or »general« or »of everywhere«.[11]

It is important to note that in the missionary field both Catholics and Protestants have emphasized what divides them rather than what

---

[9] http://protestantism.enacademic.com5/5/Africa%2C_sub-Saharan (accessed August 8, 2014).
[10] https://benbyerly.wordpress.com/2011/12/21/more-than-13-of-protestants-and-evangelicals-live-in-sub-saharan-africa-pew-study (accessed August 1, 2014).
[11] Personal observation.

unites them as Christians as they battle in the missionary field for converts. High on the agenda are issues that make them different from one another. The Roman Catholics tend to emphasize the idea that they are the true church and that by divine right the Pope has universal jurisdiction over the universal church. They also emphasize, among others, the doctrine of the papal infallibility, the immaculate conception of the virgin Mary, the doctrine of purgatory, the doctrine of the Lord's Supper as sacrifice and the like. Protestant Churches reject the supremacy of the Pope over the universal church and put a great deal of emphasis on the doctrine of justification by faith alone, the doctrine of sola scriptura, the universal priesthood of all believers, private judgment on the interpretation of Scripture and the existence of two sacraments instituted by Jesus Christ himself.

One of the consequences of this is that there is a great deal of misunderstandings between Roman Catholics on the one hand and Protestants on the other hand. These misunderstandings make both Roman Catholics and Protestants erroneously believe that Christians in the opposite side are not part of the true Christian family. Protestants generally view Catholicism as a type of Christianity covered by a thick layer of traditions of human beings and that it is a legalistic distortion of biblical Christianity to which has been added a substantial amount of detailed, technical rules that are applied mechanically. Roman Catholics, on their part, believe that the core doctrines of Protestantism cannot be found anywhere in the Bible therefore they are false and disprove themselves. Furthermore it is argued that there are many biblical texts that support the Catholic position related to matters such as the role of tradition in the Catholic Church and the condemnation of personal and private interpretation of the Bible.[12]

It seems to me that many of the accusations that both Catholics and Protestants trade on one another are based on misconceptions, ignorance and prejudice against what they do not understand. There is therefore an urgent need for ecumenical theological education that can assist both Roman Catholics and Protestants to understand that though they are different they are members of the one and same Christian family of God.

---

[12] http://catholickgnight.blogspot.i.e./20/2/06/heresy-of-protestants (accessed July 28, 2014).

4 The Origin of the Word »Catholic« and Its Use in Christendom

Church historians trace the origin of the word »catholic« hence »Catholicity« to the early church as a result of the controversies that emerged within the *ecclesia*. Reference is made to two types of Christianity that were represented by Gnosticism and Marcionism. Gnosticism offered an immense diversity of beliefs because of its openness to mixtures of doctrines while Marcionism offered a very well defined but restricted view of Christianity with very precise boundaries. What is important to note is that the Christianity that emerged in reaction to these two possibilities adopted the same strategy as Marcion's in that it sought to define and create a uniformity of belief and church practice. This demanded a concept of the church that is one wherever it is planted. This universal version of Christianity combined St. Paul's mission to the gentiles with the teachings of ancient Israel to express its wider unity. In order to express this form of Christianity, the Greek word *katholikos or katholike* meaning »general« or »whole« or »universal« was used.[13]

According to Diamaid MacCulloch, the first known person to use the word *katholike* was Bishop Ignatius of Antioch in his letter to the Christians of Smyrna where the word *katholike* meaning »the whole church« was used without providing an explanation of what it meant. He took for granted that his readers were familiar with its meaning.[14] In agreement with McCulloch, Alister McGrath has indicated that the first use of the phrase »the catholic church« occurs in the writing of Ignatius of Antioch who was martyred at Rome at around 110AD. He wrote: »Where Jesus Christ is, there is the catholic Church«. Other writings of the second century use the term catholic to refer to the existence of a universal church alongside local congregations.[15] It is also held that the word »catholic« originated when Christians wanted to make a distinction between the church and the synagogue and in order to have a distinguishing name for those embracing Judaic and Gnostic error. According to this theory, St Ignatius used for the first time the word *katholikos* in his writings to describe the universality of

---

[13] Diarmaid MacCulloch, *Christianity* (New York: Penguin, 2009), 127.
[14] Ibid., 127.
[15] Alister E. McGrath, *Christian Theology: An Introduction* (Oxford: Blackwell, 2001), 500.

the church established by Christ.[16] Be that as it may, there is a general understanding that the term »catholic« is as old as the church itself and that its usage was never restricted to the church in Rome.

McGrath has indicated that in modern English the term »catholic« is often confused especially in non-religious circles with »Roman Catholic«. He has noted that the term »catholic« derives from the Greek phrase *kath'holou* which refers to »the whole«. These Greek words finally found their way into the Latin word *catholicus* which came to mean »general« or »universal«.[17] In its general sense, the word »catholic« embodies the meaning of »totality«. The idea behind this term is that while the *ecclesia* or the church locally is not the church in its totality, it nevertheless shares in that totality. It is in this sense of sharing in the totality of the Church of Christ that the word »catholic« is used to describe the church locally.[18]

McGrath has noted that the meaning of the term »catholic« changed fundamentally with the conversion of Constantine. By the end of the fourth century the term »*ecclesia catholica*« (the catholic church) came to mean »the imperial church« which was the only legal religion within the Roman Empire. Any other forms of Christian beliefs, which diverged from the mainstream Christianity were declared illegal.[19] By the beginning of the 5th century, as a result of the church's spread and its establishment throughout the entire Mediterranean world, the term »catholic« came to be interpreted as »embracing the entire world«.[20] In terms of its development McGrath has identified three stages of the meaning of the word »catholic«, namely (a) a universal and all-embracing church which underlies and undergirds individual local churches, (b) a church which is orthodox in its theology – contrasted with »schism« and (c) a church which is geographically extending throughout the world.[21] The writings of Cyril of Alexandria, cited by McGrath, capture this all. He writes:

> The Church is thus called »catholic« because it is spread throughout the entire inhabited world (oikoumene) from one end to the other, and

---

[16] http://www.americancatholictruthsociety.com/whycath.htm (accessed August 5, 2014).
[17] McGrath, *Christian Theology*, 500.
[18] Ibid., 500.
[19] Ibid., 501.
[20] Ibid.
[21] Ibid.

because it teaches in its totality (katholikos)and without leaving anything out of every doctrine which people need to know relating to things visible and invisible, whether in heaven and earth. It is also called »catholic« because it brings to obedience every sort of person –whether rulers or their subjects, the educated and the unlearned. It also makes available a universal (Katholikos) remedy and cure to every kind of sin.[22]

Thomas Aquinas in agreement with Cyril of Jerusalem says as follows in relation to the catholicity of the church:

> The church is catholic, i.e. universal, first with respect to place, because it is throughout the entire world (per totum mundum)...Secondly, the church is universal with respect to the condition of people, no one is rejected, whether master or slave, male or female...Thirdly, it is universal with respect to time...because this church will last to the end of the world..And after the close of the age it will remain in heaven.[23]

Thus in the writings of the ancient times the catholicity of the church was understood in terms of geographical, complete proclamation and explanation of the Christian faith, sociological and chronological universality.[24] Interestingly enough in post-Reformation Christianity the term »catholic« is closely associated with the Roman Catholic Church with its headquarters in Rome to the extent that other Christians in Christendom do not associate themselves so easily with this term. This has prompted McGrath to argue that it is not right to apply the notion »catholic« only to Roman Catholics.[25] He observed that many Protestant Churches, possibly because of uneasiness with the word »catholic« in the Creed, replaced the word »catholic« with the word »universal«. It is argued that the use of the word »universal« brings greater intelligibility to the belief in the »one holy universal and apostolic church«.[26]

One of the arguments advanced by the Roman Catholics, regarding the exclusive use of the word »catholic« by themselves, is that by revolting against Rome the Reformers destroyed the catholicity of their churches. However, the general understanding among

---

[22] Ibid., 501.
[23] Ibid., 502.
[24] Ibid.
[25] Ibid., 500.
[26] Ibid.

Protestants regarding this issue is that though it seemed as if catholicity was abrogated during the Reformation in the sense of »that which is believed everywhere, at all times and by all people«[27], the Reformers remained catholic, despite having broken away from the medieval church. This is because they retained the central and universally recognized elements of Christian doctrine. In this context, historical and institutional continuity was secondary to doctrinal fidelity. As a result, the mainstream Protestant Churches insist that they are simultaneously catholic and reformed – that is, they have maintained continuity with the apostolic church at the level of teaching having eliminated non-biblical beliefs and practices[28] that were prevalent in the church before the Reformation. McGrath has noted that in recent years the notion of »catholicity« as »totality«, which has come to the fore after the Second Vatican Council, is the oldest one. Local churches and particular denominations are »catholic« in the sense that they are manifestations or representations or embodiments of the one universal church as we know it today.[29] Hans Küng one of the most celebrated theologians of our times puts it succinctly thus:

> The catholicity of the church, therefore, consists in a notion of entirety, based on identity, and resulting in universality. From this it is clear that unity and catholicity go together, if the church is one, it must be universal, if it is universal, it must be one. Unity and catholicity are two interwoven dimensions of one and the same church.[30]

Interestingly enough this view is not shared by all the Roman Catholics.[31] As a result, Roman Catholics and Protestants have so far failed to find a common denominator on which they can establish a common identity as constituting the whole church of God. Instead they continue to view one another as rivals in the vineyard of the Lord and not as partners in mission under the banner of Christ.

---

[27] Vincent of Lérins, cited by McGrath, *Christian Theology*, 502.
[28] McGrath, *Christian Theology*, 502.
[29] Ibid., 503.
[30] Ibid.
[31] F. L. Cross (ed.), *The Oxford Dictionary of the Christian Church* (London: Oxford University Press, 1971), 251.

5 Quest for Church Unity: Past and Present

The quest for church unity is as old as the church itself. Our Lord Jesus Christ himself desired his church to be one as expressed in his Great Prayer (John 17:21) in which he prayed to his Father saying »that they all may be one. As you, Father, are in me and I in you, may they also be in us, so that the world may believe that you sent me«. St. Paul in his letters devoted much of his time urging his followers to be one. In 1 Cor. 1: 10–13 Paul writes:

> Now I plead with you, brethren, by the name of our Lord Jesus Christ that you all speak the same thing, and that there be no divisions among you, but that you being perfectly joined together in the same mind and in the same judgment. For it has been declared to me concerning you, my brethren, by those of Cloe's household, that there are contentions among you. Now I say this, that each of you says, »I am of Paul«, or »I am of Apollos« or »I am of Cephas«, or »I am of Christ«. Is Christ divided? Was Paul crucified for you? Or were you baptized in the name of Paul?

Similarly, in Ephesians 4:1–6, Paul urged his followers to »keep the unity of the Spirit in the bond of peace. There is one body and one spirit, just as you were called in one hope of your calling; one Lord, one faith, one baptism, one God and Father of all, and through all, and in all«. In Roman 16:17 Paul urged the faithful to avoid those who were intent in serving their own bellies and not the Lord Jesus Christ, cause divisions by smooth words and flattering speech thereby deceiving the hearts of the simple. St. Paul was not alone in this attempt to quell divisions in the church. During the patristic period St Cyprian in *De catholicae ecclesiae unitate* (On the unity of the Church) emphasized the indivisibility of the church and urged Christians to live by it. He writes:

> The church is one which with increasing fecundity extends far and wide into the multitude, just as the rays of the sun are many but the light is one, and the branches of the tree are many but the strength is one founded in its tenacious root, and, when many streams flow from one source, although a multiplicity of waters seems to have diffused from the

abundance of the overflowing supply nevertheless unity is preserved in their origin.[32]

And to drive his point home he adds:

> God is one, and Christ is one, and His Church is one, and the faith is one, and the people are joined into a substantial unity of body by the cement of concord. Unity cannot be severed; nor can one body be separated by a division of its structure, nor torn into pieces, with its entrails wrenched asunder by laceration. Whatever has proceeded from the womb cannot live and breathe in its detached condition, but loses the substance of health.[33]

St. Augustine of Hippo, for one, saw the unity of the church spelt out clearly in the eucharist. Referring to the unifying properties of the eucharist he says:

> However many loaves there may be on Christ's alters throughout the world, it is one loaf. ... As bread is made from many grains mixed together in water, so too we are made one in baptism through the water. When the Chrism is placed on our heads, we receive the Holy Spirit as the fire that bakes us. The bread we receive is one body. Through the one bread, we are continually brought together as the body of Christ. The bread is made of many grains. The church is made up of many people who become one in Jesus.[34]

It should be noted that on the basis of the teachings of Christ himself, St. Paul, and the Church Fathers as quoted above, there is a general consensus among theologians that one of the authentic marks of the church is to be one. The urgent need for church unity as we know it today became more apparent during the missionary era in the second half of the 19th century. The arrival of the divided church in Africa and indeed in many other parts of the world created unparalleled conflict between Protestants and Roman Catholics the roots of which are traced back to the time of the Reformation. Sometimes such conflicts

---

[32] De catholicae ecclesiae unitate, 23; see http://www.americancatholictruthsociety.com/whycath.htm (accessed on August 5, 2014).
[33] Ibid.
[34] Jeffrey S. Tunnicliff, »The Eucharist Makes the Church: A Look at St. Augustine and the Unity of the Church«, unpublished manuscript, October 2006, 3.

resulted in open battles with guns between the two rival missionary powers as was the case in Kampala, Uganda.[35] This necessitated an ecumenical action that would bring the warring parties together and establish a sense of common purpose and church unity.

The 1910 World Mission Conference at Edinburgh opened a new chapter in the history of church relations among Protestant Churches and among these churches on the one hand and the Roman Catholic Church on the other. The formation of the World Council of Churches in Amsterdam in 1948 opened new opportunities for dialogue between Protestant Churches and the Roman Catholic Church although the latter opted to remain outside of this very important ecumenical body. Unfortunately the long standing differences between Roman Catholics and Protestants persist to the present day with the issue of catholicity high on the agenda. Thus misconceptions and misunderstanding surrounding the meaning of the word »catholicity« continue to be a stumbling block on the road to church unity. If this impediment is ever to be surmounted, new ways of achieving church unity must be found and implemented.

The last section of this paper shall examine what has come to be known in recent years as »receptive ecumenism« whose philosophy of ecumenical relations among the churches is believed to be able to produce positive results in a situation where people found themselves in protracted antagonistic positions.

6 Receptive Ecumenism as a Way Forward to Achieving Church Unity

In view of the fact that both Catholics and Protestants have adopted a fixed posture in regard to their doctrines, practices and structures many people have come to conclude that the visible unity of the church on earth will possibly not be achieved. The issue at stake is that the churches seem to have reached a stalemate in their negotiations on church unity after more than one hundred years of dialogue. It is in this context that »receptive ecumenism« is being proposed as a way forward towards achieving unity among churches. There is a general awareness that despite the many ecumenical initiatives and activities that have been taken by many people, ecumenical organizations and churches in response to Jesus' prayer for unity, at present

---

[35] Amanze, *A History*, 124–125.

there is little movement on the ground towards achieving visible unity of the church.

Paul D. Murray in his article »Introducing Receptive Ecumenism« has indicated that the central aim of this new approach is to make people aware that it is now widely recognized that the possibility of visible structural and sacramental unity is not likely to be realized in the mid and long term of the life of the Church.[36] The new approach advocates that Christians of different church traditions – Catholics and Protestants alike should aim less at asking what it is that another church tradition needs to understand better about one's own tradition and to be aimed instead at asking what it is that one's own church tradition has to learn and needs to learn from other church traditions.[37] At the heart of Receptive Ecumenism is the assumption that further progress towards visible church unity will only be possible if each tradition moves away from asking other church denominations to change their traditions and focus instead on its own difficulties and tensions and the consequent need to learn, or receive, from the best visible practices associated with other church traditions«. [38]

At the core of this question is the realization that both Catholics and Protestants are not perfect. In the words of Murray, »Receptive Ecumenism represents ecumenism of the wounded hands: of being prepared to show our wounds to each other, knowing that we cannot heal or save ourselves; knowing that we need to be ministered to in our need from another's gift of grace; and trusting that as in the Risen Lord in whose ecclesial body these wounds exist, they can become sites of our redemption, jewels of transformed ecclesial existence.«[39]

Receptive Ecumenism starts from the awareness that some beliefs, practices, or processes within one's own church tradition may be inadequate or may lack the fullness of the Trinity.[40] Receptive Ecumenism invites Christians of different denominations, through the spirit of humility and a desire for healing, to share the pain, the woundedness and the felt-absence of God's presence with other churches. It encourages Christians to create space for learning, for

---

[36] Paul D. Murray, »Introducing Receptive Ecumenism,« *The Ecumenist* 51, no. 2, (Spring 2014): 1.
[37] Ibid., 3.
[38] Ibid., 4.
[39] Ibid., 5.
[40] *Healing Gifts for Wounded Hands,* South Australian Council of Churches, May 2014, 1.

receiving the giftedness of the other for conversion and for growing more fully and become more authentically what God has called them to be. It is argued that this approach offers the potential for change across the beliefs, practices and structures of the various church traditions and even the way people serve the Lord. Such changes may be the gateway towards the realization of the unity of the church in accordance with the Lord's prayer for unity (John 17:21).[41]

Receptive Ecumenism involves self-examination and inner conversion rather than convincing the other. Catholics and Protestants can help one another to grow in faith, life and witness to Christ if they are open to be transformed by God's grace mediated through each other. It has been observed that receptive ecumenism will help different church traditions to let the light of Christ shine on those parts of the church – people, practice, processes, systems, beliefs and structures – where people may feel shame, sorrow, confusion or absence. According to Murray, Receptive Ecumenism is, properly speaking, a matter of the heart before it is a matter of the head; a matter of falling in love with the experienced presence of God in the people, practice, even structures of another church tradition and being impelled thereby to search for ways in which all impediments to closer relationships may be overcome. This approach in ecumenical relations does not involve telling the other person to come to one's side in order to achieve visible unity rather, it involves receiving and giving, in the power of the Holy Spirits, the different gifts that we have in different churches with a spirit of humility, gentleness, forbearance with one another and love.[42] This approach, it seems to me, will liberate both Roman Catholics and Protestants from the unnecessary worries of who is catholic or not and strive for a meaningful church unity as willed by the Father of our Lord Jesus Christ and the Creator of all.

---

[41] *Healing Gifts*, 1.
[42] *Healing Gifts*, 2.

Unity in Diversity and the Perspective of Baptism

Augustinos Bairactaris

1 Introduction

As academic society but mostly as group of Christians coming from different countries and diverse ecclesial traditions, we came to reflect on the theme »Catholicity under Pressure. The ambiguous relationship between Diversity and Unity«.

Firstly I have to say that I liked the title. I think it is very dynamic and a promising one. Secondly, I realized that the reason for our gathering, here these days, is actually our difference. Have we ever thought that, if we were united, maybe we wouldn't know each other? So, the existing disunity brings us together today. But also, we gathered in order to declare our unity besides our diversity. Most of the times unity is considered to be synonymous to uniformity and diversity is mostly understood as the opposite to unity. But is that so? Does diversity really threaten catholicity? What does unity actually mean? According to the Princeton proposal for unity »The Unity of the Church does not reduce difference to uniformity«.[1]

From the Orthodox perspective allow me to say that diversity and unity are notions linked to each other. Someone easily could find much diversity even among the churches belonging to the Orthodox family, not in the doctrinal teaching, but in the structure of ecclesial life, what

---

[1] C. Braaten and R. Jenson, *In One Body through the Cross: The Princeton Proposal for Christian Unity* (Grand Rapids, Mich.: Eerdmans, 2003), 28.

we call *typikon* (τυπικό). The locality, or else the contextuality, plays a very important role in the development of the Christian ethos and of liturgical praxis. In other words, unity is not something which either should be taken for granted, nor as something that someone could possesses for his/her own benefit. Unity is a prerequisite for catholicity and diversity is a precondition of unity. Catholicity on the other hand expresses the inner being of the church, the internal unity addressed outwards.

2 Catholicity

The ancient church understood *catholicity* to mean *wholeness, fullness, integrity* and *totality* regarding the truth, and not describing the geographical dimension or expansion of the church as an institution. It is the possession of truth which makes the church catholic and not its existence in a world-wide structure. The criterion of catholicity is not to be part of a number of local churches, but to bear witness to the true message of Christ. Catholicity never implied the total of all individual local churches, but rather it was a reference to the church's inner being. This means that the church from its very beginning was catholic, even if the borders of the Christian community were limited just to Jerusalem. This is the primary meaning of the Greek word καθόλον – catholic.

The local church is a true representation and manifestation of the *one* church which exists in *many* places, because each local church is catholic in its full expression of the faith, teaching, life and communion. The body of Christ is *in*, *with*, and *among* each local assembly. This truth creates no tension between local and universal in the church's catholicity. The church exists universally only because it exists locally. The »universal« church can only be manifest in the *local* church, because the Eucharist can only be celebrated locally. And it is the Eucharistic assembly, as the body of Christ, which makes the local church, transcends its geographical limitations. Alexander Schmemann sums up the catholicity of the church:

> [T]he Church manifests itself as a plurality of churches, each one of which is a part and a whole. It is because only in unity with all churches and in obedience to the universal Truth can it be the Church; yet it is also a whole because in each church by virtue of her unity with the One, Holy, Catholic, and Apostolic Church [i.e. catholicity], the whole Christ is present.

Finally, the local church is one and the same with every other local worshipping community, because of the common relationship each shares in Christ's body. The local church must recognize in each other the *same* faith, the *same* fullness and the *same* life.

Let me quote from the report of the WCC's assembly at Uppsala in 1968:

> Catholicity is a constant possession and pursuit of the mystery of faith, the sacramental experience of that incorporation into Christ and involvement with human kind of which the Church is the form and the Eucharist the substantial focus. In its deepest sense, liturgy is the hollowing of all we are for the sake of all that is, that God may be all in all...Only in the fullness of redeemed humanity shall we experience the fullness of the Spirit's gifts.[2]

3 Unity

These are the three pillars of unity: faith, life and witness. Koinonia is central in articulating the visible unity of the Church and the proving ground of unity is the local church.[3] From there follows that the unity of the church is realized in a shared faith and a shared life, not just in a shared administration. It is not a person, or just a historical ecclesial *locus* which guarantee the catholicity or the unity of the church, but the shared faith in one truth in Christ. The greatest heretics were prominent figures of their time coming from ancient and glorious cities. Unity is the experience and reality of the triune God drawing Christians from diverse ecclesial bodies towards one body, the body of the incarnated Christ. In other terms unity is the fellowship of the humankind in Christ and as such it expresses the richness of God's gift. It is a gift but at the same time it is a calling to all of us in order to leave ourselves free to the impulse and to the inspiration of the Spirit. Worship of the triune God, confession of the apostolic faith, sharing the bread and wine of life and witnessing the Gospel are the main elements of unity.

The local church is a fully catholic church in a given place, and not a fragment or division of some universal church. The local church has full catholicity in dogma and in liturgy, but has no power or authority to change decisions taken in the Ecumenical synods. The unity of the local

---

[2] Norman Goodall, *The Uppsala Report 1968* (Geneva: WCC, 1968), 5.
[3] P. Rodger and L. Vischer, *The Fourth World Conference on Faith and Order – Montreal 1963*, Faith and Order Paper No.42 (London: SCM Press, 1964), 81.

churches must be based on the body of Christ and not on rigid uniformity, or confessionalism or centralization.[4]

Unity by definition means recognition of complementarity of entities and it comes in opposition to the notion of absoluteness. Who has the authority to be absolute regarding the salvation? On the other hand recognition of complementarity means recognition of integrity of every person, who is made according to the image of God. Therefore the ecumenical vision of unity is profoundly biblical as it is expressed in John's gospel. Besides it is a missiological vision. John places the question of unity too simple and too honest: if the church is united, it becomes true to Jesus and to itself; if the church is disunited, it becomes untrue to Jesus and to itself. Anything more, anything less does not make any difference to this fact. Catholicity means that I perceive a person who is different, not as a threat, but as a gift and as a chance for my salvation. Unity consequently requires respect for the other and mostly demands willingness to listen to the different one, even if I do not agree with him/her. This means as a matter of fact *dialogue*. The process of dialoguing is to be open to every result, since dialogue does not mean confrontation, neither does it mean total agreement. Dialogue with the different might leads us to the status of accepting the diversity through the conception of *consensus,* which has as a result a *convergence* process. Consensus does not mean uniformity, since it leaves space for diversity. That means, that we must not be satisfied with mutual tolerance, but we have to move one step further to mutual recognition; otherwise tolerance becomes synonymous to offense.

But how close are we as churches in that perspective? I think we are not yet mature as Christian communities to accept fully in our lives the consequences of *convergence*. Still we are not aware as Christians of the pain of brokenness. And I say so because we do not recognize mutually the ministry and members of all churches; we even sometimes re-baptize former members of other communities who wish to come into our denominational flock; we exclude the members of other ecclesial traditions from the Lord's Table and we are still in some regions proselytising. All these negative features manifest that we are not ready to sacrifice our comfort in order to live in unity, because unity is costly and I believe that nobody desires to let his/her privileges and authorities for that purpose. All these describe the imperfection of our fellowship.

---

[4] Ion Bria, *The Sense of Ecumenical Tradition* (Geneva: WCC, 1991), 52f.

How then do we expect the world to believe in us, if we present ourselves in disunity and in brokenness? How are churches supposed to support the helpless and to listen to the cry of the poor [5] and oppressed [6] and also of the earth when the gifts of the earth are not shared equally for all people? The answer could come from the openness and from the act of embracing the other, the different, the neighbor and the marginalized.[7] The church is ready even to be abused or abolished for the sake of those whom she serves.[8] Unity without justice and caring for humanity and creation is not a true unity. God's will, revealed in Jesus Christ, calls the churches both to visible unity among themselves and to common witness and service of the renewal of human community.[9] Unity therefore must have a catholic perception of life and in order to be catholic it has to be based on the ministry of *kenosis* – I empty myself in order to be fulfilled by the other.

All Christians belong to Christ, but we are not all the same. There are differences in race, language, culture, gender, social and economic status, physical abilities, but all these reasons can not work against unity. The unity of the church is manifested locally, but at the same time it is catholic, universal, ecumenical. There is a dynamic relation between the one and the many. As Christ is one with the Father and the Holy Spirit, and as just the unity of the triune God cannot be broken, so the unity of the local churches cannot be broken, since they base their unity on the doctrine of the Trinity. The mystery of the inter-relationship of the unity of the three persons of the Trinity reveals the existing inter-relationship of unity of the local churches. In other words, as God is one and unique, so is his church one and unique. As the

---

[5] Julio de Santa Ana, *Good News to the Poor: The Challenge of the Poor in the History of the Church*, Commission on the Churches' Participation in Development (Geneva: WCC, 1977), 19–22.

[6] R. Dickinson, *To Set at Liberty the Oppressed: Towards an Understanding of Christian Responsibilities for Development/Liberation* (Geneva: WCC Commission on the Churches' Participation in Development, 1975), 95.

[7] T. Best, *Vancouver to Canberra 1983–1990: Report of the Central Committee to the Seventh Assembly of the World Council of Churches* (Geneva: WCC, 1990), 141–144.

[8] Ans van der Bent, *Commitment to God's Word: A Concise Critical Survey of Ecumenical Social Thought* (Geneva: WCC, 1995), 133.

[9] *Church and World – The Unity of the Church and the Renewal of Human Community: A Faith and Order Study Document*, Faith and Order Paper 151 (Geneva: WCC, 1990), 5. See also, T. Best, *Faith and Renewal: Reports and Documents of the Commission on Faith and Order in Stavanger 1985*, Faith and Order Paper 131 (Geneva: WCC, 1986), 169–177.

Father, Son and Holy Spirit are without inner division or even contradiction, so is the church to be. The pattern of the churches' unity is God's unity between the divine persons.

How does this work? Who can really tell? We have to keep in our mind that it is not everything accessible and understandable to our human mind's capacity. Who can claim that he is able to express in human words God's essence? Who can claim that he is able to describe in human terms the way the incarnation happened, or the resurrection, the assumption, and the miracles of Jesus? Jesus on the cross is the prototype not only for the churches, but also for the society.[10] The agenda of the society has become the agenda of the church. We as Christians must not sacrifice the truth for the benefit of unity, but we must sacrifice everything for the benefit of truth. In that perspective we have to sacrifice our arrogance, our hypocrisy, our intolerance and our intransigence. »As we come closer to Jesus, we come closer to each other« – the third World Conference on Faith and Order in Lund in 1952 declared. In other words: as we isolate ourselves from each other, we set Jesus outside of our lives, as we experience in 2014.

4 Conciliarity

Conciliarity touches the very core of ecclesial unity. The basic structure of conciliarity is twofold: (a) to safeguard and strengthen the existing unity between churches and (b) to restore and heal the broken unity between churches.[11]

In 1961 at the WCC Assembly in New Delhi unity was described as »all in each place«, while in 1968 at the Uppsala Assembly the universal dimension of unity »all in all places« was added. At a consultation of the Faith and Order Commission in Salamanca (1973) it was stated that »conciliar fellowship is the vision of a united Church«. Two years later the Nairobi Assembly (1975) of WCC noted that »the One Church is a

---

[10] *Your Kingdom Come – Mission Perspectives, Report on the World Conference on Mission and Evangelism, Melbourne, Australia 12–25 May 1980* (Geneva: WCC Commission on World Mission and Evangelism, 1980), 37–51.

[11] John Zizioulas, »Conciliarity and the Way to Unity: An Orthodox Point of View,« in *Churches in Conciliar Fellowship? Report of a Consultation at Sofia, Bulgaria, October 1977* (Geneva, Confenrence of European Churches, 1978), 20: »[C]onciliarity comprises the form and the structure of Church unity and it points at the same time to the final goal of unity as well as to the way to this goal.«

conciliar fellowship of local Churches«. It becomes clear here that the one church is not a single ecclesial entity. The one church is the communion of local churches. Thus, we see a strong relation between the local and the catholic dimension of unity. In other terms the visible unity of the church is a local reality which crosses national, ethnic and cultural boundaries.[12] The Orthodox Church gives importance to the local church as a eucharistic community, while the Protestant churches stress the vital importance of conciliar gatherings at local and international level concerning the demands and the concerns that Christianity faces today. And the Roman Catholic Church emphasizes the communion of the local churches both among themselves and with the bishop of Rome.

5 Diversity

Diversity comes as a result of our human existence, since we are growing and since we are members of certain local churches. So there is a certain tension between the »church« as a singular notion and its use in plural. The plural can be used only when it is used geographically. Otherwise all Christian churches have in one or another way their own historical roots in the same community of Jerusalem. The problem is how we understand unity and how do we receive diversity. How are we united, if we are different? Is difference the same thing as diversity? The answer is: no. Unfortunately, until now each Christian denomination was growing emphasising the differences between them and the other Christian traditions, instead of promoting the common elements. Unfortunately, until a few decades ago Christians preferred to destroy bridges of communication, instead of building roads of reconciliation. Selfish denominationalism gives the impression that the church could be divided encouraging neither unity, nor diversity.

As the disciples of Jesus were not the same character, but they were enriched by their diversity, so do we today feel enriched by our diversity. It is clear after all that there is an interdependence of unity and diversity. One cannot speak of the one, without referring to the other. Our life is a relational one, that is why unity is a giving and a receiving, it is a cross of martyrdom and a joy of resurrection, it is a personal

---

[12] Aram Keshishian, *Conciliar Fellowship: A Common Goal* (Geneva: WCC, 1992), 54f.

calling for each Christian and a communal mission for each church in order to proclaim the same Gospel in diverse ways respectfully to the local peoples' needs. Truth can be expressed in a diversity of cultures, styles of worship, or even theological systems. But this does not mean that truth is relative to culture or anything else, only that various cultures can be used by God to communicate the one and the same truth to peoples.[13] The catholicity of the church encourages both the unity of faith, and at the same time, the Spirit-inspired diversity. Diversity, however, neither contradicts the one truth, nor divides the one church.

It is at this point where the World Council of Churches took the initiative of bringing together the disunited parts of Christianity. This is where all Christian churches started a sincere self-critical attitude putting some question marks on issues granted until then. Repentance is the key element for the unity of the churches. Without this calling to repentance (metanoia) we might live a permanent death. Metanoia is built up step by step on critical approach and on spiritual renewal.

The church's tradition and doctrinal teaching through the sacramental life undoubtedly offers to humanity an orientation, but this orientation in no way can be imposed by force or by law to the modern society. Today, the world questions the church all the time, and it challenges churches' faithfulness to Christ and to the truth. Unity in our times as well as mission must be rediscovered from within and cannot be imposed by a detached alien and superior perspective, as was done in imperial and colonial times, when the churches' missionary enterprise was used to further the foreign policies of states and the imperialistic designs of the powers of the West and of the North.[14] Only the freedom of choice and the will of God can achieve this issue. Churches exist to bring the message of reconciliation and salvation in Christ to the world, but on the other hand the society demands the churches to live up to their own message. How can we proclaim the truth to the society, if we remain divided, separated with a desire to dominate each other? Unfortunately we, as Christians remaining in the field of disunity,

---

[13] M. Kinnamon, *Signs of the Spirit: Official Report Seventh Assembly Canberra, Australia, 7–20 February 1991* (Geneva: WCC, 1991), 280.

[14] G. Lemopoulos, *Your Will be Done: Orthodoxy in Mission* (Katerini/Geneva: Tertios/WCC, 1989), 157.

loose our credibility and our witness in the eyes of the world.[15] That is why it is important to proclaim the common Gospel to the people in order that they believe.

6   Christ's Unity as the Prototype of the Church's Unity

What we can do in order to change the situation? First an answer needs to be given to the question: What is the church?

There are many answers. One of them is to say that the church is a faithful community created to the image of Christ by the power of the Holy Spirit living united through the Eucharist.[16] The church, visible and invisible, is a sacramental reality existing between the divine and the human nature of Jesus. We experience Christ within the church, but also outside of the church.

According to the late Professor Nikos Nissiotis there are two different ecclesiological trends in contemporary ecumenical theology: (a) The *pro– catholicizing* and (b) the *pro-congregationalist*.[17] The first one is conceived on the basis of incorporation of all in Christ and sharing the experience in the sacramental body and the second one starts with the gathering of the people of God around the Gospel and following the word of the Gospel. The community listens to and shares the supremacy of the evangelical message trying to transmit it to the world. These two different approaches are not by definition in confrontation; on the contrary, they could work in complementarity.

In any case, the church is a sacrament but at the same it is time a mystery; a mystery which is called to be lived, and not a problem which must be solved. We are not mathematicians, but theologians, and as such we have to let the Spirit operate in our lives. The Spirit operates where it feels humans' hearts opened and humbled. There is a great need of giving emphasis to the charismatic limits of the church and not to the canonical limits. Church is not a court, but a spiritual hospital. We are confronted in other words with the issue of the christological and

---

[15] M. Kinnamon, *Towards Visible Unity: Commission on Faith and Order Lima 1982*, vol. 2: *Study Papers and Reports*, Faith and Order Paper 113 (Geneva: WCC, 1982), 125.

[16] N. Ehrenström and G. Gassmann, *Confessions in Dialogue* (Geneva: WCC, 1975), 171.

[17] N. Nissiotis, »Some Thoughts on Orthodoxy,« in *Preparatory Essays for the Lambeth Conference 1968* (London: SPCK, 1968), 388.

pneumatological basis of ecclesiology. In that way we move from the periphery to the centre, and that way to the centre is crossing unity in Christ through the Holy Spirit. Our primary task therefore is to acknowledge the existing church's unity, which is a gift, and draw some results from this fact for the present life of our communities.

If in the work for unity of our churches we start with the differences seeking possible ways of reaching agreements, it is more than certain that we will not be able to avoid new obstacles to a genuine unity, because the method based on »agreement – disagreement« increases more disunity, since every community stresses its own historic and ecclesiastical features. At best this method could lead to a compromise for the sake of unity. But is this what we really want? In the conception of diversity the autonomy that every Christian tradition has, can only remain. Thus it is necessary to start our dialogue from the unity given by Christ to his church and not to try to fabricate some sort of unity, or to find an average Christian view, or to place a minimum of agreement. The more attention is given to the denominational character of the unity and of the church, the more we move away from Christ and from unity, because only in Christ there is true unity. For these reasons we should start thinking that we do not belong primarily to the church, but to Christ, which comes closer to the message of the Gospel. Churches should search for their unity and catholicity not only on the doctrinal level, but mainly in the sharing of Christ in faith, life and witness, something which includes the doctrines. The resurrected body of Christ connects the members of the church through the Eucharist, where the Holy Spirit builds bonds of unity in the name of love.

7 Baptism – the Path to Unity [18]

The subject of baptism is closely related to the broader question of unity among Christians. Of course there is a great danger in case that we fix baptism solely as an external sign and guarantee of the church's unity. In order to avoid that danger there is a great need to link the sacrament of baptism with the person and the work of Christ himself and not with the one who performs it, nor in which church is performed. One could ask: do the differences on practicing baptism point

---

[18] See on that issue the very helpful book of Dagmar Heller, *Baptized into Christ: A Guide to the Ecumenical Discussion on Baptism* (Geneva: WCC, 2012), 288.

to disunity? Or do these differences on baptismal praxis just imply a legitimate diversity? Can we find a common ground centered on baptism in spite of our differences?[19] Some hold that the different practices of baptism have arisen from different understandings of the church, something which calls for a further study on ecclesiology.[20] Therefore, different understandings of baptism, faith, unity, and church reveal the lack of an adequate ecumenical hermeneutics, for which deeper exploration is needed.[21]

The late Professor Thomas Torrance writes somewhere:

> To refuse the Eucharist to those baptized into Christ Jesus and incorporated into his resurrection body amounts either to a denial of the transcendent reality of baptism or to attempted schism within the Body of Christ.[22]

I strongly believe that little attention has been given to the baptismal implications for the fellowship of the church. Many ecclesiological voices and various traditions claim that we are baptized into and with Christ, but what do we do after? Even in 1957 in the meeting of the Faith and Order Commission in New Haven it was clearly declared that: »within the disunity of the Churches, the unity of baptism has remained«,[23] but how do we proceed with the issue of unity? I think that the climax of that discussion was in Lima in 1982 through the Faith and Order Commission's study on »Baptism Eucharist and Ministry« (*BEM*). As I said in the beginning of my paper it is a common realization that unity is a gift, it is given to us in Christ. Thus, to what extent is baptism connected to unity?[24] If in baptism, as it is our faith, we die to sin, how then is it possible to live still in sin, where sin means also disunity?

---

[19] Thomas Best and Dagmar Heller, *Becoming a Christian: The Ecumenical Implications of Our Common Baptism* (Geneva: WCC, 1999), 11f.
[20] *One Lord, One Baptism* (London: SCM Press Ltd, 1960), 45–71.
[21] *New Directions in Faith and Order Bristol 1967: Reports, Minutes, Documents*, Faith and Order Paper 50 (Geneva: WCC, 1968), 32–38.
[22] L. Vischer, *A Documentary History of the Faith and Order Movement, 1927–1963* (Missouri :The Bethany Press, 1963), 135.
[23] S. Tsompanidis, *The Contribution of the Orthodox Church and Theology in the World Council of Churches* [in Greek] (Thessaloniki: Pournaras, 2008), 108.
[24] *Baptism, Eucharist and Ministry 1982–1990: Report on the Process and Responses*, Faith and Order Paper 149 (Geneva: WCC, 1992), 51.

8 Concluding Observations

Unity, diversity and koinonia find us to be brothers in Christ, despite of the existence of differences. The concept of baptismal unity can help us to overcome traditional dichotomies such as institutional and charismatic, local and universal, conciliarity and primacy etc.[25] If we want to have some positive results in the ecumenical, inter-Christian, dialogue we must be realists. In that framework there are differences which could be received as parts of spiritual richness. But, at the same time there are differences which are real points of controversy and division, and as such they have to be tackled through sincere dialogue and mutual comprehension.

It must be accepted by all parts that baptism, infant or individual one, since in any case it is the faith of the community which guarantees the incorporation into the body of Christ, is something which is done to us, and not something that we ourselves do.[26] Baptism is not merely a human act, but rather a divine one, for Christ himself in reality baptizes us. Apostle Paul in his first letter to the Corinthians says that »by one Spirit we are baptized into one body« (1 Cor 12:13). So, Christian baptism is performed into, within and by Christ and therefore has a catholic and eschatological meaning. If we as Christians respond to his calling by our participation in his death and in his resurrection, what then it is stronger than that which still divides us? Either we do not believe in the meaning and power of baptism, or we do not believe in Christ, and we believe mainly in our denomination. Once more Paul notes significantly:

> For all of you who were baptized into Christ have clothed yourselves with Christ. There is neither Jew nor Greek, there is neither slave nor free man, there is neither male nor female; for you are all one in Christ Jesus. And if you belong to Christ, then you are Abraham's descendants, heirs according to promise (Gal 3:27–29).

Finally, as it is manifested, baptism stands guard against all ecclesiastical isolationism and introversion showing its catholic and unifying role.

---

[25] T. Best and G. Gassman, *On the Way to Fuller Koinonia: Official Report of the Fifth World Conference on Faith and Order, Santiago de Compostela 1993*, Faith and Order Paper 166 (Geneva: WCC, 1993), 236. See also M. Thurian, *Churches respond to BEM*, vol. 5, Faith and Order Paper 143 (Geneva: WCC, 1988), 33.

[26] *Baptism, Eucharist and Ministrys* (Geneva: WCC, 1982), 2–7.

Unity and Diversity in the Church
Vladimir Lossky's Reflection on the Roles of Christ and the Spirit in the Church and Its Critical Reception in Dumitru Stăniloae's Theology

Viorel Coman

20th century Orthodox theological inquiries into the field of ecclesiology have come to the conclusion that the church should reflect in itself the way God exists. i.e, the church has to be modelled according to the pattern of the Trinity. Aiming at harmonizing Ignatius's statement, »wherever Jesus Christ is, there is the Catholic Church,«[1] with Irenaeus' assertion, »wherever the Spirit of God is, there is the church, and all grace,«[2] Orthodox theologians have embarked themselves on one of the most fascinating and demanding theological projects: the proper synthesis between christology and pneumatology in ecclesiology. Given the fact that the ecclesiological synthesis elaborated – with varying degrees of success – by two of the most important Orthodox theologians, i.e., Vladimir Lossky (1903–1958) and and Dumitru Stăniloae (1903–1993), who subsumed and structured their reflections on unity and diversity, the present article argues that two slightly different ways of picturing the relationship between christology and pneumatology resulted in two different ways of conceiving unity and diversity in the church. In doing so, the two parts of the article point out that, while Lossky's

---

[1] Ignatius of Antioch, *Ad Smyrnaeos* VIII, in PG V, 852 [*Epistle of Ignatius to the Smyrnaeans*, in Ante-Nicene Fathers, vol. I (Edinburgh: T&T Clark, 1996), 90].
[2] Irenaeus of Lyon, *Adversus haereses* III, in PG VII, 966 [*Against Heresies* III, 24, 1, in Ante-Nicene Fathers, vol. I, 458].

overemphasis on the Spirit's hypostatic independence in relation to the Son has led to a narrow association between christology (the principle of unity) and pneumatology (the principle of diversity) in the church, Stăniloae's understanding of the Spirit's eternal resting in/shining forth from the Son as the basis of their relationship in the church has eventuated in a much more balanced approach of the issue at stake: the eternal inseparability, interiority and mutual interpenetration between the Son and the Spirit are revealed in the life of the church; therefore, in the church Christ and the Spirit have to be equally seen as unifying and diversifying factors. This leads to several conclusions.

1   Vladimir Lossky on Unity and Diversity in the Church

1.1 The Mystical Theology of the Eastern Church (1944)

A leading representative of Florovsky's seminal programme of a »Neo-Patristic Synthesis«[3], Vladimir Lossky is generally recognized as a towering figure in the Orthodox theology of the past century. His dense, systematic, and vastly influential *Essai sur la théologie mystique de l'église d'Orient*,[4] is generally considered »the single most important book of Orthodox theology in modern times.«[5] As Rowan Williams

---

[3]   Paul Gavrilyuk, *Georges Florovsky and the Russian Religious Renaissance: Changing Paradigms in Historical and Systematic Theology* (Oxford: Oxford University Press, 2013); Andrew Louth, »French Ressourcement Theology and Orthodoxy: A Living Mutual Relationship?« in *Ressourcement: A Movement for Renewal in Twentieth Century Roman-Catholic Theology*, eds. Gabriel Flynn and Paul D. Murray (Oxford: Oxford University Press, 2012), 495–507; ibid., »The Patristic Revival and Its Protagonists,« in *The Cambridge Companion to Orthodox Christian Theology*, eds. Mary B. Cunninghma and Elizabeth Tkeokritoff (Cambridge: Cambridge University Press, 2008), 188–203; Paul Ladouceur, »Treasures New and Old: Landmarks of Orthodox Neopatristic Theology,« *St. Vladimir's Theological Quarterly* 56, no. 2 (2012): 191–227; Pantelis Kalaitzidis, »From the ›Return to the Fathers‹ to the Need for a Modern Orthodox Theology,« *St. Vladimir's Theological Quarterly* 54, no. 1 (2010): 5–36.

[4]   Vladimir Lossky, *Essai sur la théologie mystique de l'église d'Orient* (Paris: Aubier Montaigne, 1944). English translation: *The Mystical Theology of the Eastern Church* (London: James Clarke, 1957).

[5]   P. Ladouceur, »Treasures New and Old,« 201–202; Christos Yannaras described the English translation of this book as »the most influential Orthodox book of the twentieth century.« See: Ch. Yannaras, *Orthodoxy and the West: Hellenic Self-Identity in the Modern Age* (Brookline, MA: Holy Cross Orthodox Press, 2006), 292.

pointed out, the *Essai* grew out of Lossky's participation at the meetings at the house of Marcel Moré in Paris attended by theologians and philosophers from different Christian traditions in 1941-1942.[6] Capturing the basic tenets of Orthodox doctrine and spirituality for a Western audience, Lossky's masterpiece aimed at detecting the root of all theological tensions that divide East and West. In doing so, Lossky assumed that the *filioque* is the key to practically all Western ecclesiological »distortions«, i.e., the subordination of charisma to the institution, of the laity to the clergy, of the person to the institution, of freedom to power.[7] According to Lossky, the Latin doctrine of the Trinity compromises the full equality of the Holy Spirit with the Father and the Son, and subordinates the Sprit to the Son; at the level of ecclesiology, Christology overshadows pneumatology. While Roman Catholic ecclesiology tends to neglect ecclesial diversity (the work of the Holy Spirit) in favour of church unity (the work of Christ), Protestant ecclesiology overemphasizes ecclesial diversity, and loses the factor of unity. Lossky's inaccurate assessment of Western ecclesiology has been severely called into question over the past decades. Yves Congar,[8] André de Halleux,[9] Rowan Williams,[10] Theodore G. Stylianopoulos,[11] and many other theologians, have persuasively rejected Lossky's claim that the *filioque* has to be regarded as the »root« of all subsequent Western ecclesiological »deviations.« Since it is not the aim of this paper to assess the validity of the Russian theologian's treatment of the Western doctrine of the church, this brief introduction into Lossky's critique of both Roman Catholic ecclesial »christomonism« and Protestant »pneumatomonism« serves only to explaining his attempt at presenting Orthodox ecclesiology

---

[6] Rowan Williams, »The Theology of Vladimir Nikolaievitch Lossky: An Exposition and Critique« (doctoral dissertation, Oxford University, 1975), 21.

[7] Lossky's criticism of the ecclesiological implications of the *filioque* is scarcely developed in his *Essai sur la théologie mystique*, but his disciple Olivier Clément, publishing Lossky's course notes, unpacked and amplified his ideas. See: O. Clément, »Vladimir Lossky, un théologien de la personne et du Saint Esprit,« *Messager de l'exarchat du Patriarche russe en Europe occidentale* 8 (1959): 137-206. The article has been republished in *Orient-Occident. Deux passeurs: Vladimir Lossky and Paul Evdokimov* (Geneva: Labor et Fides, 1985), 17-103.

[8] Y. Congar, *Je crois en l'Esprit Saint*, vol. 3 (Paris: Cerf, 1980), 271-276 [*I Believe in the Holy Spirit*, vol. 3 (New York: The Seabury Press, 1983), 208-212].

[9] A. de Halleux, »Orthodoxie et Catholicisme: Du personnalisme en pneumatologie,« *Revue théologique de Louvain* 6 (1975): 3-30.

[10] Williams, »The Theology of Vladimir Nikolaievitch Lossky,« 156.

[11] T. G. Stylianopoulos, »The Filioque: Dogma, Theologoumenon or Error?,« *The Greek Orthodox Theological Review* 31:3-4 (1986): 285.

as effecting a reconciling harmony between unity and diversity, according to the pattern of the Trinity.[12] However, reacting against the Roman Catholic »pneumatological deficit« in ecclesiology, Lossky overemphasized the independence of the Holy Spirit in the life of the church to the extent of disconnecting pneumatology from christology.

1.2 Christ and the Spirit in the Church

Lossky notices that St. Paul's depiction of the church as »the body of Christ« (Ephesians 1:22-23; I Corinthians 12:12-13) whose »fullness« is guaranteed by the Holy Spirit (Ephesians 1:23) points to the fact that the church is »founded on a twofold divine economy: the work of Christ and the work of the Holy Spirit.«[13] Even though the Spirit and the Son are intimately linked in the economy of salvation, they »remain nevertheless in this same work two Persons independent the one of the other as to their hypostatic being.«[14] The Russian theologian is of the opinion that only a trinitarian theology that rejects the *filioque* in line with East can provide the foundation for a pneumatology that retains its inde-

---

[12] Lossky's doctrine of the church was equally intended to serve as a corrective to the Orthodox ecclesiology of *sobornost* advanced by Aleksei Stephanovici Khomiakov, a leader of the 19th century Slavophile movement. Largely influenced by the philosophy of German idealism, Khomiakov's ecclesiology intended to reconcile (a) human personal identity with the communion that subsists among human beings, (b) unity with multiplicity, and (c) freedom with unanimity. Depicting the church primarily not as an institution but as a live organism, or as a community the decisive ruling factor of which is not power but love, Khomiakov found in the traditional peasant Russian community a real model of interpersonal unity that promotes unanimity (common mind, *sobornost*, or conciliarity) without sacrificing the particular. According to Kallistos Ware Khomiakov's ecclesiology is (1) insufficiently patristic; (2) too nationalistic; (3) a »monophysite« ecclesiology, i.e., the historical aspect is not taken into account; (4) reduced too much to the social dimension; and (5) the Eucharist plays no significant role in her ecclesiology. See Kallistos Ware, »Sobornost and Eucharistic Ecclesiology: Aleksei Khomiakov and his Successors,« *International Journal for the Study of the Christian Church* 11:2-3 (2011): 224-225. A. Khomiakov's major ideas have been expounded in his book entitled *L'Église latine et le Protestantisme au point de vue de l'Église d'Orient* (Lausanne/Vevey: B. Benda, 1872).

[13] Lossky, *Essai sur la théologie mystique*, 153 [*The Mystical Theology*, 156]. At the beginning of chapter 9, Lossky points out again: »Since the Church is the work of Christ and of the Holy Spirit, the doctrine of the Church has a double foundation – it is rooted both in Christology and in pneumatology.« Ibid., 171 [174].

[14] Ibid., 156 [159].

pendence in relation to christology in the life of the church. Otherwise, pneumatology becomes solely an appendix of christology.[15] As a matter of fact, striving to put the pneumatological component of the ecclesiological construct on an equal footing with the christological one, Lossky detects two communications of the Spirit to the church:

> One was effected by the breath of Christ when He appeared to His apostles on the evening of the day of His resurrection (John XX, 19–23); the other by the personal coming of the Holy Spirit on the day of Pentecost (Acts II, 1–5).[16]

The »first« communication of the Spirit to the church, i.e., the Johannine Pentecost, has a functional character in relation to Christ. Under the outward form of breath, the Spirit was given by Christ to the church as a whole, or as a body, and, moreover, it appears as a »bond of unity« and a »sacerdotal power.«[17] Being rather an impersonal communication of the Spirit, the Johannine Pentecost guarantees the objective sanctity of the church as a corporate entity.

The »second« outpouring of the Spirit, i.e., the Lukan Pentecost, is no longer a communication to the church as a whole, but has a personal character and, moreover, is an independent work of the Spirit in relation to Christ so that

> Pentecost is not a »continuation« of the Incarnation. It is its sequel. Its result ... One can say that in a certain sense the work of Christ was a

---

[15] »The personal coming of the Holy Spirit – ›sovereignly free‹, to use an expression from a hymn for Pentecost – could not be conceived as a plenitude, as an infinite treasure suddenly disclosed within each person, did not the Eastern Church acknowledge the independence (as to His eternal origin) of the hypostasis of the Holy Spirit in relation to the Son.« (Lossky, *Essai sur la théologie mystique*, 166 [*Mystical Theology*, 169]).

[16] Ibid., 164 [167]. While Patristic Tradition and Contemporary Orthodox theologians have always distinguished the event reported in John 20:19-23 from the event described in Acts 2, modern Roman Catholic and Protestant biblical exegesis hold that both scriptural passages describe the same event. See Raymond E. Brown, *The Gospel According to John* [XIII–XXI] (NY: Doubleday, 1970), 1038; J. van Rossum, »The ›Johannine Pentecost‹: John 20:22 in Modern Exegesis and in Orthodox Theology,« *St. Vladimir's Theological Quarterly* 35: 2-3 (1991): 149-167.

[17] Lossky, *Essai sur la théologie mystique*, 164 [*The Mystical Theology*, 167].

preparation for that of the Holy Spirit ... Pentecost is thus the object, the final goal, of the divine economy upon earth.[18]

While at the Johannine Pentecost the Holy Spirit remains »unknown to persons and imparts to them no personal holiness,«[19] at the Lukan Pentecost, the Spirit »communicates Himself to persons, marking each member of the church with a seal of personal and unique relationship to the Trinity, becoming present in each person.«[20] However, Lossky's major but very often criticized contribution to the relationship between christology and pneumatology in ecclesiology concerns the identification of the distinct roles that Christ and the Holy Spirit perform in building up the church. His crucial axiom is captured in the following lines:

> The work of Christ concerns human nature which He recapitulates in His hypostasis. The work of the Holy Spirit ... concerns persons, being applied to each one singly ... Christ becomes the sole image appropriate to the common nature of humanity. The Holy Spirit grants to each person created in the image of God the possibility of fulfilling the likeness in the common nature. The one lends His hypostasis to the nature, the other gives His divinity to the persons. Thus, the work of Christ unifies, the work of the Holy Spirit diversifies. Yet, the one is impossible without the other.[21]

Lossky claims that, through Incarnation the divine Logos took on human nature and deified it; therefore, Christ is the principle or the head of the renewed humanity he assumed. Through Baptism, each person becomes member of Christ's body and has access to the unity of the

---

[18] Ibid., 156 [159]. Michel Stavrou is of the opinion that Lossky's depiction of Pentecost not as the continuation of the incarnation was a response to different Roman Catholic theologians who understood Pentecost as an instrument of incarnation: Stavrou, »Quelques réflexions sur l'ecclésiologie de Vladimir Lossky,« *Contacts* 62, no. 229 (2010): 64–65.

[19] Lossky, *Essai sur la théologie mystique*, 164 [*The Mystical Theology*, 167]

[20] Ibid., 165 [168].

[21] Ibid., 162–163 [166–167]. M. Stavrou highlights the fact that: »L'ecclésiologie ainsi développée par V. Lossky est la vision d'un rapport ›dialectique‹ entre les fonctions du Christ et de l'Esprit Saint. Face à la polarité nature – personnes, il voit dans l'Économie du salut une sorte de répartition des rôles entre les deux ›Main du Père‹ (saint Irénée): la restauration de la nature humaine est assurée par l'action du Christ, et celle des personnes humaines est fait par l'action de l'Esprit.« Stavrou, »Quelques réflexions sur l'ecclésiologie de Vladimir Lossky,« 62.

»new man« in whom all divisions are overcome. As members of the body of Christ – adds Lossky – human persons are not annihilated in the unique Christ, each of them preserving their own identity. In this regard, the Holy Spirit becomes the principle of diversity in the church, the One who »imparts to human hypostases the fullness of deity after a manner which is unique, ›personal‹, appropriate to every man as person created in the image of God.«[22] While christology is the foundation of the unity of nature, pneumatology is the affirmation of multiplicity and diversity in the church. Moreover, Lossky goes on to say that while the christological aspect of the church – grounded upon the incarnation of the Word – concerns its objective, unchangeable, perfectly stable, and immovable dimension, the pneumatological aspect – rooted in the Pentecost event – refers to its dynamic, continuous, and progressive dimension. However, the Russian theologian is of the opinion that both aspects of the church are inseparable and intimately connected so that if one of them is undermined the church becomes either a purely juridical and oppressive institution, or a purely charismatic one.[23]

---

[22] Lossky, *Essai sur la théologie mystique,* 163 [*The Mystical Theology,* 166]. Lossky quotes St. Basil who says that the Holy Spirit is »the source of sanctification which never fails by reason of the multitude of those who share in it ... who is wholly present to every being, and wholly everywhere; impassibly divided, and shared without division, like a sunbeam, whose gracious influence is as much his who enjoys it as though he were alone in the world, but which also blends with the air, and shines over land and sea. Thus, too, the Spirit is present with everyone who receives Him as if there were but one receiver, but bestows sufficient and complete grace on all; whom all things that partake of Him enjoy according to the capacity of their nature, not according to the extent of His power« – St. Basil, *De Spiritu Sancto* IX, 22, in PG XXXII, 108–109, quoted by Lossky, *Essai sur la théologie mystique,* 163 [*The Mystical Theology,* 166].

[23] »When, as often happens in the treatment of catholicity, the emphasis is placed on unity, when catholicity is above all other consideration based upon the dogma of the Body of Christ, the result is Christocentrism in ecclesiology. The catholicity of the Church becomes a function of her unity, becomes a universal doctrine that absorbs in imposing itself, instead of being a tradition evident to everyone, affirmed by all, at all times an in all places, in an infinite richness of living witness. On the other hand, when the emphasis is placed on the diversity at the expense of unity, there is a tendency to base catholicity exclusively on Pentecost, forgetting that the Holy Spirit was communicated in the unity of the Body of Christ. The result is the disaggregation of the Church: the truth that is attributed to individual inspirations becomes multiple and therefore relative.« Vladimir Lossky, *À l'image et à la ressemblance de Dieu* (Paris: Aubier-Montaigne, 1967), 177 [*In the Image and Likeness of God* (Crestwood, NY: St. Vladimir's Seminary Press, 1974), 179].

The Losskian understanding of the mystery of the church as »one in Christ, multiple through the Holy Spirit«[24] reveals his concern to express the catholicity of the church as completely modelled according to the pattern of the Holy Trinity, i.e. as unity in diversity, or as diversity in unity. Unity and diversity can coexist in the church, Lossky says, as long as the work of the Holy Spirit preserves its independent and personal character in relation to the work of Christ. It is only when the Holy Spirit originates solely from the Father that the Spirit preserves its independence from Christ in the economy of salvation. Otherwise,

> Pentecost – the source of sanctification – would not be distinct from the breath which Christ communicated to His apostles, the Holy Spirit acting as a helper in the work of Christ, creating the unity of His mystical body. If the Holy Spirit, as a divine Person, were to be considered dependent upon the Son, He would appear – even in His personal advent – as a bond which connects us with the Son. The mystical life would then unfold as a way towards the union of the soul with Christ through the medium of the Holy Spirit. This raises again the question of the place of human persons in this union: either they would be annihilated in being united with the Person of Christ, or else the Person of Christ would be imposed upon them from without.[25]

Lossky's essay on the church has prompted critical reactions among Orthodox theologians. In 1955, Georges Florovsky becomes the first

---

[24] Lossky, *Essai sur la théologie mystique*, 180 [*The Mystical Theology* 183]. For Lossky, catholicity involves a perfect harmony between unity and diversity, i.e., the mysterious identity of the whole (nature) and of the pars (persons). Consequently, the catholicity of the church requires the twofold foundation of the church: the work of Christ (nature/whole/unity) and the work of the Spirit (persons/ pars/ diversity). Therefore, at the root of catholicity there is not only the christological element but also the pneumatological one. Lossky adds: »The Christological element of catholicity has a negative character: The Church redeemed by the blood of Christ, is pure of all spot, separated from the principles of this world, free of sin, of all exterior necessity, of all natural determinism. The unity of the Body of Christ is a sphere in which the truth can manifest itself fully, without any restriction, without any mixture with that which is foreign to it, with that which is not the truth. For the Church this Christological element – the unity of human nature recapitulated by Christ – cannot suffice. Another element, and that a positive one, is necessary in order for the Church to become not only ›the body of Christ‹, but also (as the same text of St Paul has it) ›the fullness of Him who fills all in all (Eph. 1:23).« See Lossky, *À l'image et à la ressemblance*, 174–175 [*In the Image and Likeness*, 176–177].

[25] Lossky, *Essai sur la théologie mystique*, 166 [*The Mystical Theology*, 169–170].

Orthodox theologian who vocalized publically his criticism of Lossky's ecclesiological synthesis. Florovsky's basic argument against Lossky's depiction of the church as »one in Christ, multiple by the Spirit« runs as follows: if Christ's redemptive work concerns human nature, and if the Spirit imparts the fullness of deity to human persons, then *only* in the Holy Spirit, and *not* in Christ, is human personality fully and ontologically (re-)established. Lossky's synthesis, argues Florovsky, does not leave enough room for the *personal relationship* of individuals *with Christ*.[26] As the second part of this article will present, almost ten years later, Dumitru Stăniloae offered an extended critique of Lossky's ecclesiology.

Lossky's ecclesiology played an important role in highlighting the relevance of pneumatology in the life of the church, along with christology. However, since Lossky's attempt to construct a synthesis between pneumatology and christology in ecclesiology is grounded on a trinitarian theology that does not speak of any eternal relationship between the Son and the Spirit, it failed to show how christology and pneumatology relate in the life of the church. Consequently, Lossky's ecclesiology perpetuates a certain tension between christology and pneumatology, unity and diversity, institution and charism. The representation of Christ as the exclusive factor of ecclesial unity »recalls rather the image of Uranus devouring his children,«[27] whereas pneumatology becomes the liberating principle, or the source of freedom and escape.

1.3 The Root of the Problem

Two main reasons lie behind Lossky's reluctance to address the issue of any eternal relationship between the Son and the Spirit:

a) In terms of the controversy over the filioque, Lossky's theology is rather indebted to Photius' polemical and rigid approach

---

[26] »Is not the relationship with Christ, established and wrought ›by sacraments,‹ precisely personal – *a personal encounter* – and is it not effected by the Spirit? And, on the other hand, are not all personal encounters of Christians with Christ possible only in the ›fellowship of the Holy Ghost,‹ and by the ›grace of the Our Lord Jesus Christ‹?« See »Christ and His Church: Suggestions and Comments,« in *1054–1954: L'Église et les églises: Neuf siècles de douloureuse séparation entre l'orient et l'occident*, vol. 2 (Chevetogne: Ed. De Chevetogne, 1955), 169.

[27] Lossky, *À l'image et à la ressemblance*, 185 [*In the Image and Likeness of God*, 188].

In the dispute over the *filioque*, there is no other patristic figure in Eastern tradition who occupies such an important place as Photius of Constantinople (c. 820–895). *The Mystagogy of the Holy Spirit*,[28] written by Photius after his second deposition, represents a milestone in the history of the *filioque* dispute, being the first consistent Eastern critique of the Western Trinitarian doctrine, and an authoritative work for all subsequent generations of Orthodox theologians who aim at defending the doctrine of the procession of the Holy Spirit from the Father alone. Owing to his strong polemical manner of approaching the issue, as Markos Orphanos remarked, Photius did not explore the topic of a certain eternal non-causal relationship between the Son and the Spirit, even though the procession of the Spirit from the Father through the Son (διὰ τοῦ Υἱοῦ) »was a traditional teaching of the previous Greek Father.«[29] Attempting at defending the procession of the Spirit from the Father alone, Photius claimed that the sending of the Spirit through the Son takes place only in His temporary mission. It was not until the end of the thirteenth century that the principle of an »eternal manifestation« of the Spirit through the Son was largely advocated by Gregory II of Cyprus. Although Lossky's critique of the *filioque* relied heavily on Photius' methods of reasoning, he did not lose sight of the thirteenth-century Byzantine pneumatology. In his well-known article on the procession of the Holy Spirit Lossky pointed out that »it would not be exact to say ... that the procession διὰ τοῦ Υἱοῦ signifies solely the temporal mission of the Holy Spirit.«[30] However, as in the case of Photius, Lossky's fiercely anti-Western and anti-ecumenical attitude led him to rather focus on rejecting the *filioque* doctrine than on developing a solid trinitarian theology that explores properly the Greek patristic intuitions about the eternal relationship between the Son and the Spirit.

b) Lossky's plea for »radical apophaticism«

Lossky's commitment to »radical apophaticism« should be regarded as the guiding principle of his entire theological construct, including

---

[28] Περὶ τῆς τοῦ ἁγίου Πνεύματος μυσταγωγίας, P.G. 102, 263–393 [English translation by Joseph P. Farell, Saint Photios, *The Mystagogy of the Holy Spirit* (Brookline, MA: Holy Cross Orthodox Press, 1987), 57–111.

[29] Markos Orphanos, »The Procession of the Holy Spirit according to Certain Later Greek Fathers,« in, *Spirit of God, Spirit of Christ: Ecumenical Reflections on the Filioque Controversy*, ed. Lukas Vischer, Faith and Order Paper 103 (Geneva: World Council of Churches, 1981), 25.

[30] Lossky, »La procession du Saint-Esprit dans la doctrine trinitaire orthodoxe,« *À l'image et à la ressemblance*, 91; [»The Procession of the Holy Spirit in Orthodox Trinitarian Tradition,« *In the Image and Likeness of God*, 94].

therefore the doctrine of the Trinity. Challenging the Western intellectualist approach to theology adopted by scholasticism, Lossky considered apophaticism as »the fundamental characteristic of the whole theological tradition of the Eastern Church.«[31] Referring to Pseudo-Dyonisios' two ways of knowing God, he points out that while cataphatic theology proceeds by affirmation and implies rational observation, apophatic theology proceeds by negations and becomes knowledge / union which knows nothing at all of concepts. Even though cataphatic theology leads to some knowledge of God, it is an imperfect way. Lossky states that »the perfect way, the only way which is fitting in regard to God, who is of His very nature unknowable, is the second – which leads us finally to total ignorance.«[32] Undermining the importance of cataphatic theology that does not get beyond the intellect, Lossky concludes by saying that »radical apophaticism« does not serve as a corrective to the rational or intellectual forms of divine knowledge, but is mystical union with God in which all positive forms of knowledge have to be transcended as totally inadequate to express the One who is incomprehensible and antinomic.[33] Lossky's plea for »radical apophaticism« does not allow him to inquire any further into the immanent mystery of God than pointing out that the Trinity is an antinomy.[34] Accordingly, the

---

[31] Lossky, *Essai sur la théologie mystique*, 24 [*The Mystical Theology*, 26]. Lossky's understanding of apophatic theology has been largely assessed by Aristotle Papanikolaou and Silviu Eugen Rogobete.

[32] Ibid., 23 [25]. Rowan Williams emphasizes that in Lossky's understanding apophaticism is not »›a branch of theology‹, but an attitude which should undergird all theological discourses, and lead it towards the silence of contemplation and communion.« Williams, »The Theology of Vladimir Nikolaievitch Lossky,« 65. However, as S. E. Rogobete remarks, Lossky's depiction of the apophatic way »operates from a categorical mistake, namely he took superiority to mean uniqueness«; see Rogobete, »Mystical Existentialism or Communitarian Participation? Vladimir Lossky and Dumitru Stăniloae,« in *Dumitru Staniloae. Tradition and Modernity in Theology*, ed. L. Turcescu (Oxford: The Center for Romanian Studies, 2002), 170.

[33] »It is above all, an attitude of mind which refuses to form concepts about God. Such an attitude utterly excludes all abstract and purely intellectual theology which would adapt the mysteries of the wisdom of God to human ways of thoughts. It is an existential attitude which involves the whole man: there is no theology apart from experience; it is necessary to change, to become a new man … Apophaticism is, therefore, a criterion: the sure sign of an attitude of mind conformed to truth. In this sense all true theology is fundamentally apophatic.« Lossky, *Essai sur la théologie mystique*, 36–37 [*The Mystical Theology*, 38–39].

[34] »The highest point of revelation, the dogma of the Holy Trinity, is pre-eminently an antinomy.« – Ibid. 41 [43].

doctrine of the Trinity as it has been developed by the Cappadocian Fathers, i.e., the Father, the Son, and the Holy Spirit are of the same nature, but distinct according to their hypostases, intended rather at preserving the antinomy of the transcendent-God who is neither one nor three, but unitrinity,[35] than at providing rational or positive knowledge of God.

In Lossky's perception, in trying to explain rationally the mystery of the Holy Trinity, Western scholastic theology transformed God into an object of human speculation which did not remain faithful to the regulating apophatic principle. As a matter of fact, given the early 20th-century debates on the *filioque*, and taking into consideration the Russian theologian's strong emphasis on »radical apophaticism«, Lossky's trinitarian theology remains dependent on Photius' rigid reasoning, i.e, the Father is the sole cause both of the Son and of the Spirit. It is therefore reasonable to think that – for Lossky – any other inquiry into the mystery of the Trinity, including Gregory II of Cyprus's reflections on the Spirit's eternal resting in/shining forth from the Son, would most probably forsake what he calls the »apophatic attitude.«

2 Dumitru Stăniloae on Unity and Diversity in the Church

The Romanian theologian Dumitru Stăniloae – says Kallistos Ware – »occupies a position in present-day Orthodoxy comparable to that of Karl Barth in Protestantism and Karl Rahner in Roman Catholicism.«[36] However, unlike Lossky, Stăniloae's theological influence has not extended largely outside the borders of Orthodoxy. Although over the past few decades, many of his books and articles have been translated into languages of international circulation,[37] Stăniloae's theology still

---

[35] Lossky, *À l'image et à la ressemblance*, 23 [*In the Image and Likeness of God*, 29].
[36] K. Ware, »Foreword,« in Dumitru Stăniloae, *Orthodox Dogmatic Theology: The Experience of God*, vol. 1: *Revelation and Knowledge of the Triune God*, transl. Ioan Ioniță and Robert Barringer (Brookline, MA: Holy Cross Orthodox Press, 1998), xxiv.
[37] In 1980, Robert Barringer translated into English several major articles of Stăniloae, and published them in a volume entitled *Theology and the Church* (New York: St. Vladimir's Seminary Press, 1980). Five years later, Dan Ilie Ciubotea, currently the Patriarch of Romania, translated into French a small part of the first volume of Stăniloae's *Orthodox Dogmatic Theology*. Over the last decades, Stăniloae's *Orthodox Dogmatic Theology* was entirely translated into German and English. While the German edition follows the original Romanian edi-

remains insufficiently known to Western scholars.[38] Perhaps, this anonymity of Stăniloae's theology explains why Jaroslav Z. Skira's article on the synthesis between christology and pneumatology in modern Orthodox theology[39] does not take into account his original contribution to this topic.

> tion that was published in three volumes, the English translation was published in six volumes, subdividing each volume of the original edition. See Dumitru Stăniloae, *Orthodoxe Dogmatik*, transl. Hermann Pitters, 3 vols., Ökumenische Theologie 12, 15, 16 (Zürich: Benziger, 1984–1995); idem, *Orthodox Dogmatic Theology: The Experience of God*, 6 vols., transl. Ioan Ioniță and Robert Barringer (Brookline, MA: Holy Cross Orthodox Press, 1998–2013). Furthermore, Stăniloae's treatise on Orthodox spirituality has been recently translated into both English and French. See Stăniloae, *Orthodox Spirituality: A Practical Guide for the Faithful and a Definitive Manual for the Scholar*, transl. Archimandrite Jerome and Otilia Kloos (South Canaan, PA.: St. Tikhon's Seminary Press, 2003); idem, *Théologie ascétique et mystique de l'église orthodoxe*, transl. Jean Boboc and Romain Otal (Paris: Cerf, 2011). Nevertheless, one of the last books published by Stăniloae was translated into English in 2012: *The Holy Trinity: In the Beginning There Was Love*, translated by Roland Clark (Brookline, MA: Holy Cross Orthodox Press, 2012). Several other articles of Stăniloae have been translated into English or French: »The Orthodox Conception of Tradition and the Development of Doctrine,« *Sobornost* 5, no. (1969): 625–662; »La catholicité de l'église et les prières pour autrui,« *Contacts* 77 (1972): 9–28; »Unity and diversity in Orthodox Tradition,« *The Orthodox Greek Theological Review* 17 (1972): 19–37; »Jesus Christ Incarnate Logos of God, Source of Freedom and Unity,« *The Ecumenical Review* 26:3 (1974): 403–412; »The Role of the Holy Spirit in the Theology and Life of the Orthodox Church,« *Diakonia* 9, no. (1974): 343–366; »La centralité du Christ dans la théologie, dans la spiritualité et dans la mission orthodoxe,« *Contacts* 92 (1975): 447–457.
>
> [38] For example, as Radu Bordeianu noticed that »despite the importance of Stăniloae's theology, its study is barely in its infancy. It is impossible here to look at Western perceptions of the East, but a quick glance at five major journals offers a significant insight about what constitutes Orthodox theology in the West. Until recently, Stăniloae was mentioned episodically together with Zizioulas and Lossky, and sometimes Florovsky and Schmemann appeared as other representatives of Orthodoxy. Around 2005, Stăniloae began to be regarded as an alternative to Zizioulas and Lossky, but mention of him remains drastically minimal. Overall, Stăniloae is quoted 3.5 times less than Zizioulas and almost four times less than Lossky. The ratio is even more unfavourable to Stăniloae when counting only Catholic and Protestant journals.« R. Bordeianu, *Dumitru Staniloae: An Ecumenical Ecclesiology* (New York: T&T Clark, 2011), 4.
>
> [39] J. Skira, »The Synthesis between Christology and Pneumatology in Modern Orthodox Theology,« *Orientalia Christiana Periodica* 68, no. 2 (2002): 435–465. The article is a summary of the author's doctoral dissertation: »Christ, the Spirit and the Church in Modern Orthodox Theology: A Comparison of Georges Florovsky, Vladimir Lossky, Nikos Nissiotis and John Zizioulas« (Ph.D. Dissertation, University of St. Michael's College, 1998). Stăniloae's ecclesiological synthesis

Walking on the path of Lossky, Stăniloae emphasized that the doctrine of the Trinity has to be regarded as the essential and crucial principle of an appropriate understanding of the way in which ecclesial unity and diversity coexist. However, Stăniloae's slightly different treatment of the eternal relationship between the Son and the Spirit eventuated in a distinct way of understanding the relationship between christology and pneumatology in ecclesiology, and, consequently, between unity and diversity. While Lossky's lack of clarity on the eternal relationship between the Son and the Spirit led to a narrow association between christology and pneumatology in ecclesiology, Stăniloae shows that the Spirit's eternal »resting upon/shining forth the Son« has to be seen as the basis of their relationship in the life of the church. In so doing, Stăniloae offers a unique and balanced contribution on the topic of the relationship between Christ and the Spirit in the life of the church, which provides a corrective to Lossky's ecclesiology. In my conviction, Stăniloae's contribution stems from his nuanced approach of the relationship between cataphatic and apophatic theology, along with his preference for the doctrine of the Trinity as it has been developed by the Byzantine theologians throughout the 13th, 14th, and 15th centuries.

2.1 Apophatism and Trinitarian Theology in Stăniloae

As Kevin M. Berger remarks, »Stăniloae credits Lossky for bringing the centrality of apophaticism in Orthodox spirituality to the consciousness of contemporary Orthodox thought.«[40] However, even though Stăniloae

> has been made known to the English-speaking world by: Radu Bordeianu, *Dumitru Staniloae: An Ecumenical Ecclesiology,* 41–144; Viorel Coman, »Dumitru Stăniloae on the *Filioque*: The Trinitarian Relationship between the Son and the Spirit, and Its Relevance for the Ecclesiological Synthesis between Christology and Pneumatology,« *Journal of Ecumenical Studies* (forthcoming); Calinic (Kevin M.) Berger, »Does the Eucharist Make the Church? An Ecclesiological Comparison between Stăniloae and Zizioulas,« *St. Vladimir's Theological Quarterly* 51, no. 1 (2007): 23–70.
>
> [40] Kevin M. Berger, »An Integral Approach to Spirituality: The *Orthodox Spirituality* of Dumitru Stăniloae,« *St. Vladimir's Theological Quarterly* 48, no. 1 (2004): 139. For a detailed presentation of Stăniloae's gnoseology, see Natalia Tserklevych, »The Knowledge of God and Participation in the Trinitarian Community: The Balanced Approach of Dumitru Stăniloae« (doctoral disseration, KU Leuven, 2007); Kevin M. Berger, »Towards a Theological Gnoseology: The Synthesis of Fr. Dumitru Stăniloae« (doctoral dissertation, Catholic University

considers Lossky's insights on apophaticism to be accurate, he supplements it »with certain nuances and additions.«[41] Stăniloae starts from the same patristic distinction between cataphatic and apophatic theology. In so doing, he acknowledges that »the latter is superior to the first because it completes it.«[42] But, unlike Lossky who held exclusively to a knowledge of God which is apophatic, Stăniloae points out that cataphatism and apophatism »are neither contradictory nor mutually exclusive, rather they complete each other.«[43] Thus, Stăniloae adds, »one who has a rational knowledge of God often completes this with apophatic knowledge, while the one whose apophatic experience is more pronounced will have recourse to the terms of rational knowledge when giving expression to this experience.«[44] While Lossky emphasized that the highest stage of union with God leads to the fundamental impossibility of the knowledge of God, Stăniloae, on the contrary, affirms that union with God implies infinite progress in knowledge. Since apophaticism throws light on everything, it does not prevent Stăniloae to remain silent about the eternal non-causal relationship between the Son and the Spirit, and to describe the trinitarian mystery in terms of interpersonal love and communion.

Relying heavily on the later Byzantine theologians, e.g., Gregory II of Cyprus, Gregory Palamas, and Joseph Bryennios, who interpreted the Greek patristic formula »through the Son« as referring to the eternal manifestation of the Spirit through the Son, Stăniloae conceives the

---

of America, 2003); Emil Bartoş, *Deification in Eastern Orthodox Theology: An Evaluation and Critique of the Theology of Dumitru Stăniloae* (Carlisle: Paternoster periodicals, 2002); Silviu Eugen Rogobete, »Subject and Supreme Personal Reality in the Theological Thought of Fr. Dumitru Stăniloae: An Ontology of Love« (doctoral dissertation, London Bible College, Brunel University, 1998); Peter de Mey, »Apophatic and Kataphatic Theology in Dumitru Stăniloae (1903-1993),« *Orizonturi Teologice* 12, no. (2011): 9–22.

41   Dumitru Stăniloae, *Ascetica si mistica Bisericii Ortodoxe*, ediţia a III-a (Bucureşti: Editura Institutului Biblic şi de Misiune al Bisericii Ortodoxe Române, 2002), 266 [Dumitru Stăniloae, *Orthodox Spirituality: A Practical Guide for the Faithful and a Definitive Manual for the Scholar*, translated by Jerome Newville and Otilia Kloos (South Canaan: St. Tikhon's Seminary Press, 2002), 235].
42   Dumitru Stăniloae, *Teologia Dogmatică Ortodoxă*, vol. 1, 3rd ed. (Bucureşti: Editura Institutului Biblic şi de Misiune al Bisericii Ortodoxe Române, 2003), 115 [*The Experience of God* I, 95].
43   Ibid., 117 [96].
44   Ibid.

intra-trinitarian relationship between the Son and the Spirit as the basis of their relationship in the church.

According to Stăniloae:

1. The Holy Spirit proceeds eternally from the Father and rests in the Son. The Son is therefore the eternal resting place of the Son. In proceeding from the Father in order to rest in the Son, the Spirit communicates the Father's love to the Son, which is the goal of procession;[45]
2. The Holy Spirit is equally manifested or shines out from the Son towards the Father, as the Son's loving answer to the paternal love, which is the goal of manifestation;[46]
3. The procession of the Holy Spirit from the Father and the generation of the Son from the Father happen simultaneously and inseparably;[47]
4. The Spirit – the third Person of the Trinity – not only »keeps the other two Persons from immersing themselves in each other,«[48] but is the »loving tie formed between the Father and the Son.«[49]

---

[45] Dumitru Stăniloae, »Purcederea Duhului Sfânt de la Tatăl și relația lui cu Fiul, ca temei al îndumnezeirii și înfierii noastre,« *Ortodoxia* 31, no. 3-4 (1979): 588-589 [»The Procession of the Holy Spirit from the Father and His Relation to the Son, as the Basis of Our Deification and Adoption,« in *Spirit of God, Spirit of Christ*, ed. Lukas Vischer, 181]; idem, »Relațiile treimice și viața bisericii,« *Ortodoxia* 16:4 (1964): 515-516 [»Trinitarian Relations and The Life of The Church,« *Theology and The Church*, 29].

[46] Ibid., 516-517 [30-31].

[47] Ibid., 516 [30].

[48] »The third fulfils the role of ›object‹ or horizon, assuring the sense of objectivity for the two by the fact that he keeps the two from becoming confused within an indistinct unity because of the exclusiveness of their love, an exclusiveness which can flow from the conviction of each that nothing worthy of love exists outside the other. With a third of the same worth exists, neither of the two who love each other loses sight of the merit of loving that belongs to the third, and both are thereby kept from becoming confused, the one in the other« – Stăniloae, *Teologia dogmatică ortodoxă*, vol. 1, 323 [*The Experience of God*, vol. 1, 268-269].

[49] »The Spirit is sent by the Father to rest in the Son as a demonstration of the Father's love for the Son. For the Father Himself is pleased to rest in the Son through the Spirit who proceeds from Him. But the Son does no remain passive and uncaring in the face of the Father's loving attention. He is pleased that the Father sends His Spirit to Him, and by accepting the Spirit He shows the Father His joy … The Spirit does not proceed from the Father as an end in Himself, but the Spirit constitutes a loving tie formed between the Father and the Son … The Father and the Son unite as Father and Son even more through the Spirit. They are three Persons, but the third does not stand to the side of the other two; He

Consequently, since the Spirit is both the hypostatic principle of unity in the Trinity and the One who keeps the Father and the Son distinct, pneumatology cannot be depicted as a mere factor of ecclesial diversity.

The same inseparability, simultaneity, interiority, reciprocity, and mutual interpenetration that characterize the eternal relationship between the Son and the Spirit are reflected in the life of the Church, where the »union with Christ can be lived only in the Holy Spirit, and ... the experience of being in the Holy Spirit is nothing other than union with Christ.«[50] Stăniloae concludes by saying that the institutional aspect of the church is not therefore devoid of spirituality just as spirituality does not imply a lack of structure and institutional order.[51] Nonetheless, »it is inadmissible to say ... that the institutional priesthood is Christological while the non-institutional priesthood is pneumatological. Nor it can be said that Christ unifies us within a unity of nature while the Spirit distinguishes us within this institutional or pantheist unity (Lossky).«[52] In each and every ecclesial event, aspect, component or structure, the church is both christological and pneumatological at the same time.

2.2 Unity and Diversity

In 1967, Stăniloae wrote an article entitled »The Holy Spirit and the Sobornicity of the Church: Extracts from the Report of an Orthodox Observer at the Second Vatican Council.«[53] Aiming at deepening the reflections of Nikos Nissiotis on the role of the Holy Spirit in the life of the church, the article provides the reader with an extensive critique of Lossky's depiction of the church as »One in Christ, multiple in the Spir-

---

unites Them. He is in each, uniting Them and reinforcing Them in Their distinct qualities even when They speak to us« – Dumitru Stăniloae, *Sfânta Treime sau la început a fost iubirea* (București: Editura Institutului Biblic și de Misiune al Bisericii Ortodoxe Române, 1993), 70, 71, 73 [*The Holy Trinity: In the Beginning There Was Love*, 62, 63, 65].

50   Stăniloae, Relațiile treimice și viața bisericii,« 505–506 [»Trinitarian Relations and the Life of the Church,« 14].
51   Ibid., 522 [40].
52   Ibid. 522 [39].
53   Dumitru Stăniloae, »Duhul Sfânt și sobornicitatea bisericii. Extrase din raportul unui observator la conciliul al II-lea de la Vatican,« *Ortodoxia* 19, no. (1967): 32–48 [»The Holy Spirit and the Sobornicity of the Chruch. Extracts from the Report of an Orthodox Observer at the Second Vatican Council,« *Theology and the Church*, 45–71].

it.« Later on, different articles[54] and books[55] written by the Romanian theologian have brought back into question Lossky's ecclesiological synthesis.

According to Staniloae, since the Holy Spirit is both the hypostatic principle of unity and the One who keeps the Father and the Son distinct,

> both in its unity and in its diversity the Church comes into being as much through the Holy Spirit as through Christ. And the Son and the Spirit do not work separately but in perfect unity, bound together as they are both by their essential unity and also by their personal relations.[56]

Drawing on patristic thinkers, such as Gregory of Nazianzus, Gregory of Nyssa, Basil of Caesarea and John Chrysostom, Stăniloae points out that the role of the Holy Spirit in the church is both to make the church a well-ordered whole through the unifying force of His spiritual gift, and to maintain diversity in unity. Moreover, since the Holy Spirit »is communicated within the unity of the Body of Christ,« and since the Holy Spirit »does not come into a pre-existing unity in the Body of Christ, but is himself the power of unification, the gift of unity in communion, and hence the factor which constitutes ... the Church,«[57] it would be completely wrong to conceive the Spirit as a cause of disintegration or as a mere factor of diversification in the church. Commenting both upon the unifying and the diversifying role of the Spirit in the church, Stăniloae emphasizes that

> the one who makes a single Body of all the faithful, each endowed with his own different gift, is the Holy Spirit. He binds men to one another and creates in each an awareness of belonging to all the rest. He impresses on

---

54 Dumitru Stăniloae, »Le Saint Esprit dans la théologie byzantine et dans la réflexion orthodoxe contemporaine,« in *Credo in Spiritum Sanctum. Atti del congress teologico internazionale di pneumatologia. Roma, 22–26 marzo 1982*, vol. 1 (Vatican: Libreria Editrice Vaticana, 1983), 661–679.

55 Stăniloae, *Teologia Dogmatică Ortodoxă*, vol. 2, 3rd ed. (București: Editura Institutului Biblic și de Misiune al Bisericii Ortodoxe Române, 2003), 311–340 [*The Experience of God: The Church – Communion in the Holy Spirit*, vol. 4, translated by Ioan Ioniță (Brookline, MA: Holy Cross Orthodox Press, 2012), 95–118].

56 Stăniloae, »Duhul Sfânt și sobornicitatea bisericii,« 45 [English translation »The Holy Spirit and the Sobornicity of the Church,« 66].

57 Ibid.

the faithful the conviction that the gift of each exist for the sake of the others; the Spirit is the spiritual bond between men, the integrating force which unites the whole, the power of cohesion in the community. Just as the organs of the body have within themselves a force which keeps them all together, so the Holy Spirit, present within faithful, is the force holding them together in one whole and making them aware of the fact that integration is possible only through the others ... But the Spirit is wholly present in every member by a different gift, or by way of mutually interdependent gift which neither make all member the same nor allow them to work in isolation from one another, for no single member remains unconditioned by others.[58]

Similarly, Christ is factor of both unity and diversity in the church. Referring to Maximus the Confessor's theory of »the divine logoi,« Stăniloae states explicitly that the Son »is not an indistinct whole; his unity is at the same time a plenitude of meanings and as such the structures which he creates in his image is also a unity filled with meanings«[59] whose constitutive elements maintains their diversity without being swallowed up by the whole. Additionally, Stăniloae brings up another argument to reinforce even more the idea that the Son is equally a factor of unity and diversity. Since Christ – Stăniloae says – is not just a human nature, but a divine person in whom human nature and divine nature are fully united, he represents a »distinct principle and as such he enters into personal relations with those who form His Mystical Body, affirming their personal identity.«[60] Lossky's theory that associates Christ's work with nature and unity, while the work of the Spirit is directed towards the persons and diversity, »encourages the conclusion that within Trinity the Son is not a Person but Nature while the Holy Spirit does not himself possess the one divine nature but exclusively represents the personal principle.«[61]

---

[58] Ibid., 37, 38 [54, 55]. Stăniloae's intuitions on the unifying and diversifying role of the Spirit relies heavily on patristic theology. Different Fathers of the Church remarked that every gift received by a member of the church has both a diversifying role and a unifying force, serving the church as a whole and each member that possesses that gift.
[59] Ibid., 46 [68].
[60] Ibid., 45 [66].
[61] Ibid. Stăniloae goes on to say that Lossky's theory approximates to a certain extent the *filioque*. According to Stăniloae, by causing the procession of the Holy Spirit as from a single unity, the Father and the Son are conceived as one being.

3 Conclusions

The present article has strived to demonstrate that Vladimir Lossky's and Dumitru Stăniloae's reflections on unity and diversity in the church have been guided by their understandings of the relationship between christology and pneumatology in ecclesiology. Although no one can deny Lossky's valuable attempt to highlight that pneumatology is an essential component of the ecclesiological construct, his overemphasis on the hypostatic independence of the Spirit in relation with Christ, along with the unwillingness to explore the intra-trinitarian relationship between the Son and the Spirit, led to a split between the work of Christ and the work of the Spirit in the life of the church: while Christology refers to the unifying/objective/ institutional aspect of the church, pneumatology refers to the diversifying/subjective/charismatic one.

Lossky's axiom, »Christ unifies while the Spirit diversifies,« encourages the idea that the Christological aspect of the church goes against the pneumatological one, just as the unifying/institutional principle goes against the diversifying/charismatic one. Stăniloae's efforts to revise Lossky's simplistic solution to a complicated problem have come out of his attempt to integrate the doctrine of the church into a solid trinitarian theology. Accordingly, the intra-trinitarian relationship between the Son and the Spirit is revealed in the life of the church, where Christ and the Spirit are so intimately and perichoretically linked that in both its unifying/objective/institutional aspect and diversifying/subjective/charismatic aspect the church is Christological and pneumatological.

The Church and Its Characteristics in the Document *The Church* (2013) of the WCC's Commission on Faith and Order

A Constructive Critique from an Evangelical Free Church Perspective

Jelle Creemers

This article aims at a constructive critique of the understanding of the church and its characteristics in the second Faith and Order (F&O) convergence document, *The Church: Towards a Common Vision* (TCV), from an Evangelical free church perspective. After a short description of the perspective from which I speak, the said document is reflected on, particularly its understanding of the church and the *notae ecclesiae*, and elements that are deemed problematic are pinpointed. Focus is on an underlying tension between essentialist and historical perspectives on the church and its attributes. Considerations from the ecumenical free church ecclesiology written by Miroslav Volf are brought in to help alleviate the tension. In conclusion, it is highlighted how from a free church perspective helpful elements can be afforded in the construction of a broadly ecumenical ecclesiology.

1 An Evangelical Free Church Perspective: Typological Description

The terms »evangelical« and »free churches« can refer to a wide variety of ecclesial traditions with very different structures and outlooks. Therefore, a short typological description is afforded in this first section, with the explicit acknowledgement that both signifiers can also have other referents.

Free churches in Europe have usually originated in Protestant contexts through individuals and groups which felt the need to break away from an existing visible ecclesial community, when in their eyes its pastors and members no longer exhibited holiness in their lives. Free churches are characterised by a conversionist soteriology, which connects personal salvation and church membership to an individual's conscious conversion to Christ.[1] As such, free church ecclesiology is very compatible with a so-called »evangelical« mind-set. »Evangelical« is used here in accordance with the famous definition of British historian, David Bebbington, in his classic, *Evangelicalism in Britain*. In the introductory chapter Bebbington describes »evangelical religion« with the four characteristics of *conversionism, activism, biblicism*, and »what may be called *crucicentrism*, a stress on the sacrifice of Christ on the cross.«[2]

As a direct consequence of the conversionist soteriology free church ecclesiology starts from below. The church is primarily considered as a local gathering of believers. Each group of believers which assembles around Christ is considered a church, independent of any supra-local structures or the presence of a particular ecclesial officer. As a consequence, free churches usually easily recognize the ecclesiality of other Christian communities. On the basis of their conversionist perspective, free churches also acknowledge that the church can be considered as the wide existence as the communion of all believers. Consequently, while free churches start from the full ecclesiality of the local congregation, they seldom consider their independence absolute. Free churches tend to cluster in denominations based on shared origin or form alliances for pragmatic purposes.

---

[1] See, e.g., art. 2 of the constitution of the International Fellowship of Free Evangelical Churches: »The IFFEC is a spiritual and organizational fellowship of federations of churches in which personal faith in Jesus Christ ..., according to the Bible ..., is the only condition of membership in the local church.« http://www.iffec.org/constitution (accessed September 1, 2014).

[2] Recognizing the theological diversity within »Evangelicalism,« this typological definition has proven very helpful and is widely used. See D. W. Bebbington, *Evangelicalism in Modern Britain: A History from the 1730s to the 1980s* (London: Routledge, 1988), 3. A critical appraisal was published two decades years later: Michael A. G. Haykin and Kenneth J. Stewart (eds.), *The Emergence of Evangelicalism: Exploring Historical Continuities* (Leicester, UK: Apollos, 2008).

Theology in Evangelical free churches usually is constructed in very close connection to the teaching and praxis of the New Testament church and in constant dialogue with the own ecclesial life. As such, its theological starting point differs from most churches since long active in the ecumenical movement, which often argue primarily from »the teaching of the church« rather than from »what the church members believe or practice.« This seriously affects the way Evangelical free churches (including Pentecostal churches) can and do participate in ecumenical dialogues.[3] While the opposition of »evangelical« and »ecumenical« is an incorrect and unhelpful cliché, it cannot be denied that in the history of the ecumenical movement, and particularly in the history of the Faith and Order Commission of the World Council of Churches, Evangelical free church involvement has long been quasi absent and still is of limited influence today.

The absence of Evangelical free churches logically implies that they had virtually no input in the selection of themes and the development of theological discourses in the course of over eighty years of multilateral ecumenical dialogue in Faith and Order context. By consequence, the themes, discourses and emphases of Faith and Order texts often resonate poorly with Evangelical free church perspectives.[4] This seems to be an impasse and many reasons can be given why a stronger integration of theological perspectives of free churches in ecumenical theology is difficult to achieve. Still, growing involvement of Evangelical free churches in ecumenical dialogue can be demonstrated.[5] Taking up the consequent challenges is essential if ecumenical theology wants to remain relevant to the majority church in the 21st century. The very topic of »catholicity,« the characteristic attributed to the church to indicate its capacity and limits of unity in diversity, is very fit as an exemplary case study of how an Evangelical free church perspective can interact with and contribute to ecumenical theology today.

---

[3] This is argued in detail in Jelle Creemers, *Theological Dialogue with Classical Pentecostals: Challenges and Opportunities* (London: Bloomsbury, 2015).

[4] See Jelle Creemers, »Dance to the Beat of Your Own Drum: Classical Pentecostals in Ecumenical Dialogue,« *Journal of the European Pentecostal Theological Association* 35, no. 1 (2015): 58–68.

[5] One can point to initiatives that have grown strong in the past two decades, such as official bilateral dialogues with the *World Evangelical Alliance* and with Classical Pentecostals, targeted conversations with Pentecostals and Evangelicals in the Faith & Order context, the *Global Christian Forum, Evangelicals and Catholics Together*, etc.

2 Church and Catholicity in the Church: Towards a Common Vision

In its introduction and historical note, the Faith and Order document *The Church: Towards a Common Vision* is consciously placed in line with earlier Faith and Order work on the essence and characteristics of the church. In what follows here, I seek to capture the main relevant perspectives of the document on the church *in se* and add valuations from an Evangelical free church perspective.

The descriptions of the church *in via* and the church as it should be are very recognizable in general, but some elements can be considered improper, unusual, or unhelpful when looking from this particular angle.

In chapter I, the church is introduced as communion with God and with one another (§1), dedicated »to proclaiming in word and deed the good news of salvation in Christ, celebrating the sacraments ... , and forming Christian communities« (§5). The emphasis on the expansive mission of the church in service of the Gospel in this chapter is certainly appreciated in Evangelical free churches, which are often known for their activism and evangelistic fervour. The Christological foundation given in §4 would however probably be considered improper by many. It states that »[t]he mission of the Church ensues from the nature of the Church as the body of Christ, sharing in the ministry of Christ as Mediator between God and his creation.« Particularly the church being seen as partaking in the ministry of Christ as mediator can be considered troubling, as Evangelical free church theology focuses on the unicity of Jesus Christ as sole Mediator between God and creation and eschews direct explications of mediatory functions of the church.

Chapter two, describing the »Church of the Triune God,« calls the church »a divinely established communion« which »belongs to God and does not exist for itself« (§13). With a focus on the variety within the church, §19 states that »the whole people of God is called to be a prophetic people ... , a priestly people ... , and a royal people,« a statement certainly appreciated in Evangelical free churches due to their focus on the responsibility of all believers in the life of the church. The addition that some in the church are given a specific authority to help the community to fulfil its calling, i.e., ordained ministers chosen under the guidance of the Spirit, is food for thought in not a few free churches. Participation and the responsibility of all in the church can in free churches be stressed at the expense of a balanced theology of ministry, which includes a deliberation of the desirability and/or particular status and role of ordained ministry.

When speaking about »Communion in Unity and Diversity,« the chapter stresses that diversity is a gift from the Lord and that the faithful receive from the Spirit a variety of complementary gifts (§28). This charismatic principle, which is fundamental for a participatory church, is very dear to Evangelical free churches.

The counterbalance in the next paragraph, that unity must not be surrendered and that all are »mutually accountable to each other« (§29) requires careful consideration in our circles as well. The chapter further asks questions regarding the limits of legitimate and divisive diversity and the relation between the local and universal church. Due to their focus on the local congregation, for Evangelical free churches these are certainly important questions to ponder.

The third chapter stresses the need for the church to grow towards the full realization of its calling. It contains helpful reminders and probing questions regarding the current divisive state of Christian communities and calls for a continuing quest for growing agreement on faith, sacraments and ministry. In this quest, Evangelical free churches should take up their responsibility as well, even if they may consider the current provisory answers quite far removed from their own ecclesiological sensing. In the paragraphs on »faith,« a clear distinction between and separate discussions of *fides qua* and *fides quae* are certainly missed, and the limited place attributed to discussing the church's faith (two paragraphs) in comparison to the attention for its sacraments (five paragraphs) and to the understanding of ordained ministry and authority in the church (thirteen paragraphs!) is hard to grasp. Particularly the extensive attention given to the inner organisation of the church can be considered unnecessary and counterproductive, as Evangelical free churches tend to consider this adiaphoric rather than essential for the ecclesiality of a Christian community. As said earlier, this different perspective and the subsequent sense of imbalance is arguably to be attributed to the limited participation of Evangelical free church theologians in 20th century F&O constructive ecclesiology. While newcomers should certainly be open to learn why certain elements are valuable to the experienced dialogue partners, the latter can also learn why and how these questions, which seem to have come to a deadlock in a number of ways, may be put in perspective.

The fourth chapter, finally, calls the church to take up its role in society on the basis of the challenging gospel, in defence of the needy and marginalized and in order to »participat[e] in God's healing of broken relationships between creation and humanity.« This chapter is definitely a worthy read for Evangelical free church theologians as in this mission, churches of very different outlooks should be able to stand together firmly, mastering the service in serving the Master.

Those familiar with the document will have noted that, in this short overview, a few key paragraphs of TCV in view of ecclesiology proper and the attributes of the church have been passed over, i.e. paragraphs 22 and 23. I did so deliberately, as these paragraphs in my feeling differ markedly from the ecclesiological approach of the rest of the document. With the exception of the said paragraphs, the whole document can be understood well from a viewpoint which considers the church essentially as a communion *in via*, as I have done until now. In paragraphs 22 and 23, however, a perspective on the church surfaces which seems non-essential elsewhere. This perspective posits the church (1) as a monistic entity with essential characteristics rather than a communion in history, and (2) as in its essence so strongly related to God that it is divinized and virtually stripped of historicity and earthliness. To be clear, this is not the *only* perspective on the church present in these paragraphs. The paragraphs purposely mix this essentialist perspective on the church with the historical perspective on the church which is predominant in the rest of the document. The sections on the *notae ecclesiae* seek to balance an understanding of the church as a communion on its way with an understanding of the church as an essentialized and divinized entity, in a way I consider strange and ambiguous.

A short overview of the subparagraphs on the *notae ecclesiae* may clarify what I intend to say. The first attribute is introduced as follows: »The Church is one because God is one.« This statement is beautiful as a one-liner, but it is not entirely clear what it means to communicate. For, what warrants the causative relation? The text continues with a reference to John 17, but in this prayer of Jesus, the unity of his disciples mirroring the unity of God is not a given, as the opening sentence seems to suggest. It is, rather, a prayer, a desire of the Lord for the church which starts its journey through the centuries. The section on the second attribute opens with a similar statement: »The Church is holy because God is holy.« In what follows, human sin is explicitly contrasted with the »essential holiness of the Church.« Again, it must be asked what these phrases intend to say precisely. If the church is a communion of believers and if »sin ... has again and again disfigured the lives of believers,« how then can the church simultaneously be called »without blemish« on this side of the *eschaton*? This is only possible, it seems to me, if the church is essentialized and divinized. Third, the text states that »[t]he Church is catholic because of the abundant goodness of God.« On the one hand, this section on catholicity acknowledges that the transcending of all barriers is part of the church's *mission* (and thus not yet realized). On the other hand, however, the text speaks of an »*essential* catholicity of the church,«[6] which can be found »where the whole mystery of Christ is present.« The celebration of the eucharist is given as an example. It is beyond comprehension for me as an Evangelical free church theologian what this actually entails. It can of course be considered a mystery, but that does not suffice as a warrant for simply posing this perspective. In addition, I wonder in which other instances in the church it can be said that the whole mystery of Christ is present. Finally, the Church is called »apostolic because the Father sent the Son to establish it.« In itself, this sentence is, in my humble opinion, without clear meaning as well.

To be sure, the direct predecessor of this document, *The Nature and Mission of the Church* (NMC – 2006), has comparable introductions to the *notae ecclesiae*. The structure of NMC, however, makes much more clear the dual perspective on the church which I criticize here. The document distinguishes clearly in different chapters »The Church of the Triune God« (chapter I) and »The Church in History« (chapter II), as does *The Nature and Purpose of the Church* (1998). The *notae ecclesiae* are discussed first in chapter I under »A. The nature of the Church« in a section »(I) The Church as a Gift of God …« which, notably, *precedes* section (II) offering »Biblical Insights« (§12). A second time, they are discussed in chapter II under the heading »The Church in via« (§52–56), where the *contrast* between the essential and historical presence of these characteristics are explicated time and again. A proponent of both perspectives could certainly argue that it is counterproductive to tear apart what in reality belongs together. From my perspective as a reader critical of the essentialist understanding of the church, however, the bringing together of both perspectives comes across as artificial and confusing, and the downgrading of the contrasts, even if in a careful way by circumscription, as biased.

More than other paragraphs in TCV, the said section contains statements which can be interpreted in a variety of ways. This ambiguity allows my questions for clarification. What is very clear, however, is that the characteristics of the church are considered a consequence of, a reflection of, the characteristics of God. In short, the *notae ecclesiae* are in this section primarily considered as *notae divinae*, in which the church shares. This should make one wonder then: how and why does

---

[6] Italics mine.

the church share in these divine characteristics? Is it simply a gift of God to the church, or does it imply an essential unity of God and Church? I already suggested a certain divinization of the church may hold the answer, and this is explicitly stated in paragraph 23:

> In the light of the previous paragraphs (13–22),[7] it is clear that the Church is not merely the sum of individual believers among themselves. The Church is fundamentally a communion in the Triune God and, at the same time, a communion whose members partake together in the life and mission of God (cf. 2 Pet. 1:4), who, as Trinity, is the source and focus of all communion. Thus the Church is both a divine and a human reality.

This paragraph contains a number of hard nuts to crack for an Evangelical free church theologian. Particularly, the expressions of the church as »a communion in the Triune God« and the Church as »both a divine and a human reality« are not common in our ecclesiological thinking. While I can imagine interpretations of both expressions with which I could agree, the text does not give hints for interpretation and thus I am not much inclined to invent them. From an Evangelical free church perspective, the church as community of believers is an answer to and result of divine initiative rather than divine itself, communion *with* rather than communion *in* the Triune God. In short, the church always has God as a partner, as *Gegenüber*. Interestingly, the text unanimously approved by the F&O Standing Commission in Penang, Malaysia, 21 June 2012, speaks of the church as communion *with* the Triune God. In the intervening two months before the »reception« of this document by the WCC Central Committee at its meeting in Crete, Greece, in early September 2012, this change to »communion *in* the Triune God« was made, thus strengthening the identification of God and Church in a more radical way.[8]

As I indicated earlier, the paragraphs that follow have a quite different sense again. Paragraph 24 indicates more clearly the distance between the divine and the church, speaking of the Church as »a meet-

---

[7] As said earlier, it appears to me that paragraphs 22–23 rather »suddenly« speaks of the Church in an monistic way and connects the Church essentially to God, while this was barely present for in the preceding paragraphs. Notably, paragraph 23 disagrees.

[8] The divinisation language is also stronger than in the preceding document, NMC, which reads: »[The Church] is [the believers'] common partaking in the life of God (2 Pet 1:4)« (§12).

ing place between the divine and the human.« Paragraph 25 posits an *imago dei* correlation, describing it as »a *reflection* of the communion of the Triune God.«[9] Paragraph 26 again speaks of an »intimate relation between Christ and the Church,« but is much more careful, stating only that it »enjoys a spiritual, transcendent quality which cannot be grasped simply by looking at its visible appearance.« When paragraph 27 discusses the sensitivities concerning the expression of the »Church as sacrament«, the focus is on the church as »the communion of human beings with one another through their communion in the Triune God«. While the expression of paragraph 23 returns here, the meaning is different: it does not state that the church is a communion in the Triune God but that individual Christians are chained together through the relationship they each have with the Triune God (cf. NMC §12).

In summary, a dual perspective on the church, i.e., both as a communion of believers on the way and as an essentialized and divinized entity, is clearly present in paragraphs 22–23. Depending on one's perspective, it can also be found implicitly in the rest of the document. The tension can be considered a confusion between the calling of the church and its being. Consequent to this tension is a struggle with the notions of sin and change in the life of the church, as is most clear in paragraphs 34–36. TCV is careful not to attribute »change« or »sin« to the church directly. Change is considered »a condition of the world« to which human beings, of which the church is admittedly made of, are subject (§34).[10] Paragraph 35 readily acknowledges that ecclesial traditions differ in their articulations of the church's relation to sin and that these »have sometimes been seen as conflicting views … For some, their tradition affirms that the Church is sinless since, as the body of the sinless Christ, it cannot sin. Others consider that it is appropriate to refer to the Church as sinning.« While TCV is to be commended for explicating the diverging perspectives on the sinfulness of the church, it is rather surprising that no mention is made of diverging perspectives on the church's relation to the Triune God, which is underlying this tension. Both tensions, I would argue, can be relaxed with the help of Miroslav Volf's ecclesiology.

---

[9] Italics mine.
[10] After paragraph 24, a paragraph in italics also indicates that churches have different sensitivities and convictions regarding continuity and change in the church. The focus is, however, on the relative priorities regarding the ordering of the church.

3 Church and Catholicity in Miroslav Volf's Free Church Ecclesiology

In his 1998 publication *After Our Likeness*, Miroslav Volf has afforded a very helpful description and theological defence of ecclesiality and catholicity in Evangelical/Pentecostal free church perspective.[11] The church, so Volf explains, is essentially understood in free church perspective as the concrete assembly of believers in the name of Christ, the Lord. Volf states that every local congregation is considered wholly church because of the presence of the one and whole Christ through his Spirit.[12] TCV argues along similar lines and consequently sets the local church in dynamic relation with the universal church as »the communion of all local churches united in faith and worship around the world« (§31). Volf argues, however, that »the local church is to be defined not from the perspective of its relation to the existing *communio sanctorum*, but from the perspective of its relation to the perfected church in the new creation of God. The category of anticipation expresses this situation.«[13] As Volf explains, the local church, or a certain community of churches, or even the universal church always stands in relative and proleptic relation to »the eschatological gathering of the entire people of God.«

Volf devotes a whole chapter to discuss the church as a correspondence to the Trinity.[14] He fully agrees, as TCV would say in paragraph 25, that the church is »a reflection of the communion of the Triune God.« But as the church is in history, it is not yet a *full* reflection of this communion. It is growing in this direction, it is on its way. Only a dynamic understanding of the church's correspondence to the Trinity, moving in history between a minimum and the eschatological maximum, is considered meaningful by Volf.[15] In other words, the local church, a community of churches and even the current universal church is always and only a partial reflection of the Triune God. This has a bearing on the *notae ecclesiae* as well. In discussing catholicity, Volf follows the ecumenical consensus that the church is primarily catholic because the fullness of salvation is realized within it.[16] This will be,

---

[11] Miroslav Volf, *After Our Likeness: The Church as the Image of the Trinity*, Sacra Doctrina (Grand Rapids, MI: Eerdmans, 1998).
[12] Ibid., 129. Volf even states later that each local church is the whole church, but that requires a specific interpretation, which I will pass over now.
[13] Ibid., 140.
[14] Ibid., 191–220.
[15] Ibid., 206–208.
[16] Ibid., 266.

however, only fully the case for the eschatological gathering of the entire people of God. Historical catholicity, i.e. the presence of catholicity in the church *in via*, must be seen as a relative category in line with the above. Each church, church community or even the current universal church can only be partially catholic, one must speak of a (historical) *minimum* of catholicity and its (eschatological) *maximum*, to which the church constantly strives. On the meaning of the latter, the eschatological maximum of catholicity, there is a relative ecumenical consensus. In Volf's line of argumentation, this maximal catholicity is however often incorrectly attributed to the wrong referent: the church *in via* rather than the eschatological gathering. Second, according to Volf, not only maximal but also minimal catholicity need to be considered and theologically »defined«. And for him, the minimum for the catholicity of a church and an indispensable condition for its ecclesiality is »openness to all other churches of God.«[17] It is realized that this understanding of catholicity as »openness to all other churches of God« is very minimal. Volf adds that a church without any other sign of catholicity is, albeit a catholic church, certainly a *poor* catholic church.[18] It is, however, truly a catholic church. Having laid down the principles of minimal and maximal or full catholicity, Volf leaves it to the reader to consider the outlook of the *optimal* form of catholicity in their church in their context today.

4 Catholicity: A Way Forward in Free Church Perspective

In contrast to the said sections in TCV, the free church ecclesiology of Miroslav Volf stresses that the church is currently *in via*, is developing towards fullness, and is therefore not without weakness and sin. In his ecclesiological construct, Volf has no problem to admit that free churches struggle with their catholicity. They are weak in catholicity, in many ways. Some close themselves off from other churches, and are more sectarian than catholic. Some refuse to give space to certain gifts and ministries of the Spirit because of a fixed interpretation of Scripture and are legalistic rather than catholic. Some proclaim a minimal rather than a holistic gospel and are reductionistic rather than catholic. Yes, evangelical free churches are struggling with their catholicity, often

---

[17] Ibid., 156, 274.
[18] Ibid., 275.

and in diverse ways. As long as they have a certain minimal catholicity based on the presence of Christ's Spirit in the believing community, they are, however, to be seen as catholic Christian communities on the way. And, by the way, the free churches are not the only ones struggling. All churches have strengths and weaknesses, also in view of their catholicity by allowing either too much or too little unity and/or diversity. This acknowledgement of the inherent weakness of churches and their dependence on Christ opens up a space for ecumenical theologians to discuss constructively what growth in catholicity should mean today for the diverse communities. It involves, first, a joint reconsideration of the limits and riches of the relations of correspondence of the church as community of believers to its Triune God. Second, it implies that the historicity and earthliness of the Church as communion of believers, including the possibility of weakness and sin of the church in all of its elements, are taken more seriously than TCV currently allows for. Third, it involves a shared consideration of what can be considered minimal and maximal catholicity, taking into account hierarchies of Christian truths. This does not imply a negation of God's grace and generosity nor a negation of the church's high calling. But in acknowledging its own weakness and the limits of its correspondence to the divine life, the church is constantly reminded of its need for conversion, challenged to continual growth in holiness, and given compassion for its mission in and for the world.

Catholicity and the Way of Just Peace

Sara Gehlin

1 Queries at the Outset of a Peace-making Journey

The 8th of November 2013 was the day on which the Tenth Assembly of the World Council of Churches concluded. Thousands of participants had come to Busan, South Korea, from all over the world, from member churches and beyond, to take part in the Assembly. Now they were about to leave for their home countries. For the participants the close of the Assembly was not only the finale of this big meeting, but also the beginning of something new. It marked the outset of a pilgrimage. Before leaving South Korea the Assembly formulated in its message an invitation: *Join the Pilgrimage of Justice and Peace*. This invitation is inclusive. It is calling all people of good will to join the pilgrimage and engage their God-given gifts in transforming actions. The Assembly declares in the message that »we intend to move together« on the way of peace and it prays: »May the illuminating Word of God guide us on our journey.«[1]

The metaphor of pilgrimage and of people journeying together on a common way raises interesting questions about the fellow-travellers

---

[1] »Message of the 10th Assembly of the WCC: Join the Pilgrimage of Justice and Peace.« Document No. MC 01, http://www.oikoumene.org/en/resources/documents/assembly/2013-busan/adopted-documents-statements/message-of-the-wcc-10th-assembly (accessed July 7, 2014); printed in Erlinda Senturias and Theodore A. Gill, Jr. (eds.), *Encountering the God of Life: Report of the 10th Assembly of the World Council of Churches* (Geneva: WCC Publications, 2014), 35f.

and thus also about the visions of community that guide the ecumenical movement. The metaphors are settled in the ecumenical vocabulary. Nevertheless, I think that the way they are related to the issue of peace today raises some critical questions. While the invitation to the pilgrimage is inclusive, peace and its actual meaning is a disputed issue in the Christian world community. The issue of peace has not fostered a common mind or a common will, but generated a conspicuous ambiguity. Whereas multiple Christian communities in different ways commit to the pursuit of peace, there are also Christian groups and factions that tend towards religiously motivated violence. The ecumenical way of peace, opening up for all people of good will, seems to be sided with another path that takes a different course of direction. Still, it is a course that is taken by members of the faith community. Does the ecumenical invitation appeal to them? If so, would their company make the peace-making journey imply two steps back and one step forward? If not, would not the ecumenical pilgrimage miss an indispensable group of fellow-travellers for the eventual fulfilment of its goal of faith-based peace-making?

Religiously motivated violence is not only a critical issue in the field of international conflict resolution, but it is also a critical ecumenical issue. Religiously motivated violence and religiously motivated peace-making are opposite forms of commitment that split the Christian world community. To which aim its members commit themselves may have considerable consequences in situations of conflict. There is need for a faith-based dialogue which serves the aim of peace-making and which engages a broad group of Christians, also those reluctant and adverse. Which resources are existing within ecumenical thought and practice to open up such ways of communication within the miscellaneous community of Christians?

We will approach this question from the starting point of catholicity and the way it embraces the tension between unity and diversity within Christianity. The vision of making this tension a fruitful exchange is certainly challenged by the divisive effect of religiously motivated violence. Violent expressions of Christianity pose a challenge which at first sight may seem dissociated from those factors that put ecumenical work under pressure. The discussions on whether we agree on doctrine or not, on whether we celebrate Eucharist together or not and on whether we envision Christian unity in the same way or not, are discussions that may appear detached from the battle-grounds of religiously motivated violence. But are they?

Violent expressions of Christianity may on the one hand evoke the urge for clearer lines of demarcation around what catholicity allows within its frameworks. Where are we to find the threshold that separates fruitful diversity from destructive division? On the other hand, religiously motivated violence can challenge us to go even deeper into the reflection on the ways our common discourse on the meaning of catholicity may facilitate the communication across divisions. Can the contemporary elaboration of the concept of catholicity bring about a framework for a dialogue, which constructs bridges that bring divided groups together in faith-based peace endeavours? Violent expressions of Christianity may put pressure on our frames of imagination for the meaning of catholicity. What if we imagined these frames anew and asked ourselves whether our discourse on the meaning of catholicity possibly can generate theological tools that press for further Christian peace-making efforts.

2   An Ecumenical Conversation on Just Peace

We will embark upon such a way of reasoning by discussing catholicity with regard to its dimensions of unity and diversity and weave into our discussion the aspect of Christian peace-making. We will do so by attending to a conversation that preceded the World Council of Churches' Assembly and its invitation to a *Pilgrimage of Justice and Peace*. This is the conversation that took shape through the WCC process towards an ecumenical declaration on just peace; a process which eventually resulted in the publication of the two documents *An Ecumenical Call to Just Peace* and *Just Peace Companion* in 2011.[2]

The conversation unfolding through this process of composition does not handle the issues of Christian unity, diversity and peace-making in terms of catholicity. And when it comes to the issue of unity, the authors are strikingly taciturn. Unity and catholicity appear to be concepts which are not self-evident in a contemporary ecumenical

---

[2]   The process towards an ecumenical declaration on just peace (2008–2011) involved the composition of two drafts (»An Initial Statement towards an Ecumenical Declaration on Just Peace and Second Draft: Ecumenical Declaration on Just Peace«), response to both drafts and eventually the publication of *An Ecumenical Call to Just Peace* and its resource document *Just Peace Companion*. In this article, the scope of references is confined to the two drafts and the two publications. (Hereafter the abbreviation WCC will be used for the World Council of Churches.)

peace discourse. The central position of the concepts of unity and catholicity in ecumenical theology stands in sharp contrast to their peripheral location in the conversation on ecumenical peace-making. The contrast provokes the question: Are unity and catholicity outdated concepts in the ecumenical peace-making arena? Or do they still make sense? In the following we will make the experiment of making catholicity our framework of reasoning around Christian peace-making, as well as around diversity and unity.

In spite of the scarce references to unity, classic ecumenical theological models of Christian unity are frequently used throughout the process towards an ecumenical declaration on just peace. But here, the ecumenical models are primarily used for the purpose of building community in the service of peace. Several models are referred to, but three of them are particularly salient. These are the notion of *oikoumene*, the doctrine of the *Trinity* and a metaphor which is already at the centre of our attention: the metaphor of the people journeying together on a common *way*.[3]

The way of just peace emerges as a central image through the process towards an ecumenical peace declaration.[4] The second draft of the declaration underscores that the way of just peace requires both movement towards the goal and commitment to the journey.[5] What is then implied in the commitment and what is the shape of the goal? By following the process of composition, I discern the way community building stands out as a key commitment on the journey towards a just peace; a commitment which also shapes the goal. *An Ecumenical Call to Just Peace* defines the concept of just peace in terms of a process. It states that just peace may be understood as:

> a collective and dynamic yet grounded process of freeing human beings from fear and want, of overcoming enmity, discrimination and oppression,

---

[3] »Initial Statement towards an Ecumenical Declaration on Just Peace,« Geneva, WCC Archives, 2008, to be filed, 6–7; 11–12; 16–22; »Second Draft: Ecumenical Declaration on Just Peace,« Geneva: WCC Archives, 2010, to be filed, 2–5; *An Ecumenical Call to Just Peace* (Geneva: World Council of Churches, 2011), 1 and 4–10; *Just Peace Companion* (Geneva: WCC Publications, 2011), 19–23, 29, 34, 37–47, 53, 84–85.

[4] »Initial Statement,« 18–22; »Second Draft,« 2–5; *An Ecumenical Call*, 4–10; *Just Peace Companion*, 18–20, 34–47, 53, 85, 136.

[5] »Second Draft,« 2.

and of establishing conditions for just relationships that privilege the experience of the most vulnerable and respect the integrity of creation.[6]

The composition of an ecumenical peace declaration indeed furthers an understanding of just peace as implying community building at every level of human life; as a process that concerns the closest relationships of every individual as much as the shape of international relations. It is understood in terms of human mutuality and sharing as well as harmonious coexistence with all of God's creation.[7] Yet, the very fact that the call to just peace stems from an ecumenical worldwide community arouses my curiosity about the way this expansive vision of a just peace is related to the principal ecumenical vision of Christian unity. The coincidence in the use of ecumenical models, today serving both visions, indicates a relationship between the two visions that is not simply superficial.

The scarce references to unity made throughout the process towards an ecumenical peace declaration mainly concern the issue of credibility. The second draft of the peace declaration states that, if groups of Christians walk their own way, the journey of just peace slows down and stops. A church that is divided on the issue of peace and torn by interior conflicts is hardly a trustworthy worker for peace.[8] The references however leave out an explanation of the intimate relationship between unity and peace that somehow appears fundamental to ecumenical thought and practice. In order to find out more about this relationship, we will turn to the idea of catholicity and relate it to the three mentioned ecumenical models of unity that serve the ecumenical vision of just peace today.

3 Catholicity, the Unity of the Church and the Unity of Humankind

That catholicity is a wide, almost elusive, concept is a notion that many ecumenical theologians subscribe to. Still, I contend that it may infuse

---

[6] *An Ecumenical Call*, 5.
[7] A comprehensive understanding of just peace is furthered throughout the process of composition and eventually developed with regard to four perspectives: peace in the community, peace with the earth, peace in the marketplace and peace among the peoples (see: *An Ecumenical Call*, 10–15).
[8] »Second Draft,« 4; Cf. »Initial Statement,« 13; *An Ecumenical Call*, 3, 6, 10–11; *Just Peace Companion*, 23–24, 115–116.

energy and dynamics to the contemporary ecumenical debate on just peace. By following the historical discussion of the WCC Commission on Faith and Order the theologian John St-Helier Gibaut gives heed to the way the ecumenical dialogue on catholicity has gained breadth and depth through the last decades. He notes that the concept of catholicity has been likened with a Russian doll, keeping ever new significations behind its covers. Whereas history has proven the tendency of claiming the word catholicity for one's own ecclesiological possession, the Faith and Order discussion has nurtured an understanding of catholicity as being neither a possession, nor an achievement to be maintained. Rather, it is understood as a gift of the Holy Spirit as well as a task, a calling and an engagement. This vision of catholicity is not fundamentally about doctrinal truth or formulation, but it is manifested more in praxis around right relationships between the churches, between the churches and the wider human family and with creation.[9] Gibaut points to the words of the Faith and Order report applied by the WCC Fourth Assembly in 1968:

> The purpose of Christ is to bring people of all times, all races, of all places, of all conditions, into an organic and living unity in Christ by the Holy Spirit under the universal fatherhood of God. This unity is not solely external; it has a deeper, internal dimension which is also expressed by the term catholicity.[10]

What does this bring to the understanding of catholicity as a possible vital infusion into the ecumenical debate on just peace-making? Theologian John D'Arcy May, analysing the statement of the same Assembly in tandem with the opening paragraphs of the Second Vatican Council document *Lumen Gentium*, establishes that the unity of the church is to be seen as the sign of the unity of humankind. Catholicity, he states, is the form in which the unity of the church and the unity of humankind are realised in local and global contexts. According to D'Arcy May, there is an urgent need for re-visioning the *oikoumene* of faith in order to

---

[9] John St-Helier Gibaut, »Catholicity, Faith and Order, and the Unity of the Church,« *The Ecumenical Review*, vol. 63, no. 2 (2011): 177–185.

[10] Gibaut, »Catholicity,« 180–181; cf. Norman Goodall (ed.), *The Uppsala Report 1968: Official Report of the Fourth Assembly of the World Council of Churches, Uppsala, July 4–20, 1968* (Geneva: World Council of Churches, 1968), 13.

build a moral communion which can stand up to the twin tests of the unity of the church and the unity of humankind.[11]

The process towards an ecumenical peace declaration, though bringing the notion of community rather than of unity into the centre of attention, exemplifies such a re-visioning. The first draft of the peace declaration uses the image of *oikoumene* in the double sense of the community of Christians as well as the earth with all its inhabitants; a double sense that fosters an understanding of the church as inevitably intertwined with the world. The first draft makes this understanding the very basis of the call to peace-making for the sake of strengthening the whole *oikoumene* and for making the community of faith a sign of healing and justice in the world.[12] According to *Just Peace Companion* the community of Christ's followers are called to live as that force within humanity, which witnesses to God's purpose of salvation through justice and peace.[13]

The *Just Peace Companion* moreover claims that the *oikoumene* of the church and the world finds its very meaning in the community of love, justice and peace between the three persons of the Trinity. The *Companion* elucidates the way Christians are enabled to build justice and peace through their belief that in Christ they participate in this divine community. Nevertheless, it is stressed that Christian peace-making ultimately is about making the *oikoumene* a mirror of the community between the Trinitarian persons; a community which in the first draft is described as a divine unity in diversity.[14] The theologian Avery Dulles acknowledges that in speaking of the Trinity, unity is not only compatible with, but demands multiplicity. In speaking of the church Dulles stresses that Christ, as its living centre, draws its members together but at the same time impels them to actualise their individuality to the utmost. Catholicity, he underscores, implies diversified unity.[15]

---

[11] John D'Arcy May, »Visible Unity as Realised Catholicity,« *Swedish Missiological Themes*, vol. 92, no. 1 (2004): 58-60.
[12] »Initial Statement,« 6.
[13] *Just Peace Companion*, 20.
[14] »Initial Statement,« 6-7; *Just Peace Companion*, 21-22.
[15] Avery Dulles, *The Catholicity of the Church* (Oxford: Clarendon Press, 1985), 42.

4 Theological Outreach for a Peaceful Future?

In a time when religiously motivated violence brings communities of faith far away from the fruitful diversified unity that Dulles envisions, it is easy to reject the idea of theological dialogue as an effective means of peace-making. However, I mean that catholicity gives us an illuminative example of a theological concept that comprehends profound resources for a faith-based dialogue dedicated to the pursuit of peace. While bringing the visions of unity and peace together, it simultaneously requires the serious consideration and appreciation of differences. In face of divisions threatening peace, the praxis of such consideration and appreciation might be difficult, but still of vital importance.

The researcher of Religion and Conflict Resolution Marc Gopin is of the opinion that a peaceful future cannot be constructed without inviting even the most adverse and reluctant religious groups on the peace-making journey. This however presupposes an in-depth understanding of what they hold dear. Moreover, it might presuppose that peace and coexistence emerge as defensible metaphysical and legal possibilities within the actual system of belief and that methods of conflict resolution derive from religious moral guidelines. Gopin emphasises that peacefully minded believers, rather than retreating into safe enclaves, need to form bridges between the more angry expressions of each religion and the rest of the world. They need to engage religious groups on their own terms and interact with their categories of thinking in order to encourage a greater commitment to peaceful coexistence.[16]

Gopin's way of reasoning gets resonance in the ecumenical discussion within Faith and Order, which brings light to the fact that the catholicity of the church is confronted with divisions between and within Christian communities. Nevertheless, the discussion also conveys the idea that the catholicity of the church transcends all human barriers, whether they are set up by nationalism or particular traditions.[17]

---

[16] Marc Gopin, *Between Eden and Armageddon: The Future of World Religions, Violence, and Peacemaking* (Oxford: Oxford University Press, 2000), 28–31, 223–224.

[17] Gibaut, »Catholicity,« 181–183; cf. *Confessing the One Faith. An Ecumenical Explication of the Apostolic Faith as it is Confessed in the Nicene-Constantinopolitan Creed (381)*, Faith and Order Paper 153 (Geneva: WCC Publications, 1991), § 240; *The Nature and Mission of the Church*, Faith and Order Paper 198 (Geneva: World Council of Churches, 2005), § 55. See also: *The Church: Towards a Common Vision*, Faith and Order Paper 214 (Geneva: WCC Publications, 2013), § 22.

I conclude that if we consider the way of just peace in the light of catholicity, the way is not only about a journey but as much about bridge-building. But how far do our bridges reach and towards which shores do we stretch out? The invitation to join the *Pilgrimage of Justice and Peace* is directed to all people of good will. What if the invitation also reached out to those communities of faith who still do not make the will to peace their characteristic? If such an outreach, as Gopin suggests, is an indispensable condition for reaching a peaceful future, what will come out of the Russian doll next? By involving a discussion that takes opposed positions seriously and simultaneously brings together the visions of peace and Christian unity, catholicity makes a relevant theological tool for furthering faith-based dialogues dedicated to the goal of peace. In this sense, I think, the concept of catholicity does not belong to the periphery, but to the centre of the ecumenical peace-making arena.

To be Male is Less Important than It Seems to Be

Catholicity and Gender Focussing on: the Ordination of Women

Margriet Gosker

> Catholicity is no uniformity.
> Catholicity creates free space
> for all Christian believers worldwide
> and asks respect for all denominations.
> Catholicity is binding all Christians together
> and is accepting them all in their otherness.
> To be male is less important
> than it seems to be.

In this article I would like to discuss why catholicity should not exclude women from the altar. All I will say in the following pages is also valid for other gender issues (like homosexuality), but I choose to focus on the ordination of women. Catholicity is a comprehensive notion in such a way that all basic ecumenical problems and differences are somehow connected to it.[1] Ordination of women is certainly not only a question related to catholicity, but it is one of the issues to be discussed on this occasion of Societas Oecumenica's gathering in Budapest 2014.

Since nearly everything has already been said on the ordination of women and all the arguments have been shared over and over again, I do not want to flog a dead horse. Therefore I decided to speak from the point of view of my own biography. I have been ordained in 1972, nearly 42 years ago, and I was one of the first women ordained in my church, which was one of the Reformed churches in the Netherlands. I served as a minister in several congregations and I am also involved in many ecumenical bodies. If my church had not recognised my vocation in 1972, my life would have been totally different. So I am grateful to God for all the possibilities given to me to serve as a minister in the church. I also speak here as a theologian, specialized in theology of the ministry. I wrote my dissertation on the part on »Ministry« in the text

---

[1] H. Berkhof, *De katholiciteit der kerk* (Nijkerk: Callenbach, 1962), 7.

»Baptism, Eucharist and Ministry«[2] of the Faith and Order Commission of the World Council of Churches and I have been advocating my whole adult life in many ways for the ordination of women.

I would like to begin with two short personal stories. The first one happened in Romania in 2011. I was defending the ordination of women for an audience of – to a large extent – Romanian Orthodox theologians in Oradea. I was then invited by Nicu Dumitrascu, one of the members of the Standing Committee of the Societas Oecumenica. Afterwards I asked Nicu: »Wasn't I too passionate in defending my point of view?« He answered: »Not at all, that's why I asked you to come over to Oradea«. The second story took place in the spring of 2014. I tried to put the ordination of women on the agenda of our own Dutch Council of Churches in the Netherlands. I finally succeeded, but I had to choose my words very carefully. The meeting was friendly and respectful and I was happy we finally could get the subject on the agenda.[3] But at the same time it was a rather disappointing experience and it showed clearly how difficult it is to handle these issues in a proper way, especially in your own context.

Every decision has a cost. My first article on the ordination of women appeared in 1978 under the title: Resistance against women's ordination, how to handle it? If Canterbury admits women to the altar, the flirtation with Rome is over.[4] Anglican women have been ordained since 1970. The Church of England finally allowed women to be priests in the year 1993 and while writing this contribution in July 2014 I receive the historic news, that the Church of England on 14th of July surprisingly said »yes« also to female bishops.[5] But as we all know: every decision has a cost. Obviously we hear voices from the Orthodox and the Roman Catholic side saying the same thing: »Canterbury admits women to the altar and the flirtation with Rome is over«. So we hear

---

[2] M. Gosker, *Het ambt in de oecumenische discussie, de betekenis van de Lima-Ambtstekst voor de voortgang van de oecumene en de doorwerking in de Nederlandse SoW-Kerken* (Delft: Eburon, 2000).

[3] http://www.raadvankerken.nl/pagina/2962/dilemma_rond_vrouw&highlight =vrouw (accessed July 20, 2014).

[4] M. Gosker, »Weerstanden tegen de vrouw in het ambt. Hoe pak je dat aan? Als Canterbury vrouw toelaat is flirt met Rome voorbij,« *Ouderlingenblad* 56 (1978): 655, quoted in the daily newspaper *Trouw*, October 16, 1978.

[5] http://www.anglicannews.org/news/2014/07/church-of-england-says-yes-to-women-bishops.aspx (accessed July 20, 2014).

Metropolitan Hilarion of Volokolamsk[6] and – among others – Mgr Keith Newton, Ordinary of the Personal Ordinariate of Our Lady of Walsingham, saying:

> Having agreed to permit women priests in 1992, the Church of England's decision to allow women bishops is the next logical step. What is undeniable is that both developments make harder the position of those within the Church of England who still long for corporate unity with the Catholic and Orthodox Churches.[7]

Here we see clearly the problem of catholicity, church communion and the ordination of women. I wrote several articles on the subject[8] and I was also part of the drafting group of the document of the Community of Protestant Churches in Europe (CPCE) on Ministry, Ordination and Episkopé, accepted by the CPCE Assembly in 2012. I would like to draw your kind attention now to the following ten points of reflection.

(1) Catholicity is not restricted to one of the churches, neither is it restricted to one gender. Also the ministry of the church cannot be restricted to one gender. The question is not why some churches ordain women, the real question is for what reasons some churches are refusing it. In my view it is not the ordination of women which is the problem, the problem is the non-ordination of women. But why then in many churches ordination is a matter of gender and restricted to male persons? It is not because women are not good enough. They are good enough. It is not because women are not capable. They are capable. It is not because women miss the needed spiritual gifts. They are very much spiritually gifted. It is not because a woman cannot be called by God. A woman can be called by God indeed and many of them have received a

---

[6] http://www.virtueonline.org/villanova-pa-metropolitan-hilarion-blasts-anglicans-renouncing-faith (accessed July 20, 2014).

[7] Cf. M.J. Van Dyck, *Worden Rome en Canterbury één* (Tielt: Lannoo, 1990), 223–227. http://www.catholicherald.co.uk/news/2014/07/15/ordinariate-reaches-out-to-anglicans-after-women-bishops-vote (accessed July 20, 2014).

[8] M. Gosker, »Gods ›ja‹ en het ›nee‹ van de kerk: Ambtstheologische notities bij de vrouw in het ambt,« in *Honderd jaar vrouwen op de kansel, 1911–2011*, eds. M. de Baar, F. Cossee, M. van Veen and A. Voolstra (Hilversum: Verloren, 2011), 53–65; M. Gosker, »Mogen het ook pumps zijn? In de schoenen van de apostelen. Over apostoliciteit van vrouwen in de kerk,« lecture given for a Study Day of the Dutch Council of Churches, March 5, 2012 Amersfoort, published on their website (link of 14–07–2014): http://www.raadvankerken.nl/pagina/1850/apostel_naar_letter_en_geest&highlight=apostoliciteit (accessed July 20, 2014).

true vocation. So why are not all churches ordaining women? One of the answers is that women cannot be ordained because of a long tradition. Here we have to deal with the question of traditionalism. Another answer is, that women cannot be ordained because of a certain interpretation of Scripture, silencing the voices of women in the church. If that was true, I would not be here. Another answer is that women cannot be ordained because of the idea that Jesus chose only men as his apostles. By the way – Jesus never chose Germans, Italians or men from Argentina. He chose just Jews as his disciples. There is a refusal to ordain women because the ordination of women is understood as being against the will of God. My question: who knows that for sure? Women are refused to be ordained because a woman cannot represent Christ. My question is: why is it necessary to have male sex in order to gain the possibility to represent Christ?

(2) Protestants are also catholics. And sometimes some Protestants are more catholic than some Roman-Catholics are catholic. In the Netherlands we have now a *Protestant Forum for Catholicity*.[9] Catholicity can cover a wide range of meanings. Catholicity means the whole world geographically, from the one end to the other. It also means the totality of all Christian orthodox teaching. It covers the totality of all humankind (young and old, rulers and citizens, erudite and simply-hearted)[10] and more. So catholicity cannot be restricted to one of the churches, neither can it be restricted to one gender. Churches who ordain both women and men are more catholic, because they are not exclusive.

(3) Cyril of Jerusalem (315–386) said: »The church is catholic because it has spread throughout the entire world, because it teaches fully and unfailingly the content of Christian belief (the doctrines) and because it brings under obedience all classes and races of men. Finally, it deserves the title ›catholic‹ because it heals and cures every sin that can be committed in soul or body and because it possesses and spreads various spiritual charisms.«[11] Vincentius of Lerinum said: »The true faith is what everywhere, always and by everybody has been believed.«[12] This does not mean however, that we can never change a custom or a ritual. Many use the term »catholic« meaning »Roman-Catholic« without realising that this exclusive language in fact robs

---

[9] http://forumkatholiciteit.nl/#.UJvJgnDiYuc (accessed July 20, 2014).
[10] *Catecheses* XVIII, 23.
[11] *Catecheses* XVIII, 23.
[12] http://www.ccel.org/ccel/schaff/npnf211.iii.iii.html (accessed July 20, 2014).

many Christians of their catholicity. No one is allowed to claim the term »catholic« exclusively for one's own church or gender.

(4) Now I draw your special attention to the female aspect of catholicity. As baptised and confessing members of the one holy catholic and apostolic church, women are not to be excluded from unity, holiness, apostolicity or catholicity. It has been said that in times of heathen antiquity women were not accepted in structures of teaching and preaching[13] and for this reason they were also not accepted in early Christian church ministry. But there were still women priests in antiquity, and in the area of priesthood, women were equal to men.[14]

(5) Many churches do not ordain women. Despite encouraging words of Pope Francis concerning the role of women in the decision making processes of the Roman-Catholic Church and the decision for sister Mary Melone as the first ever female Rector Major of a pontifical university,[15] in too many churches women are still kept outside of apostolicity and catholicity, because they are still excluded from the ministry of word and sacraments. Beginning in the 19th century most Reformed, Lutheran, and Methodist churches step by step opened their ministries for women and finally established equal rights for everyone concerning all levels of ministry without regard to gender. Most Anglican, Baptist and Old Catholic churches did the same. I know very well, that this raises ecumenical problems. The World Communion of Reformed Churches officially stated: »Some churches still do not ordain women although this is not supported biblically or theologically. Often the reason for not ordaining women is founded in the prevailing patriarchal social, cultural and religious environment of the nation in which a church exists. We need to help each other restore the supremacy of relevant theological insight over domination by non-theological factors. A full understanding of the Christian ministry is inclusive and supports

---

[13] J. Müller, *In der Kirche Priester sein: Das Priesterbild in der deutschsprachigen katholischen Dogmatik des 20. Jahrhunderts* (Würzburg: Echter, 2001), 198, footnote 57: »So war beispielsweise für den sukzessiven Ausschluss von Frauen aus Lehr- und Verkündigungsfunktionen die fehlende Akzeptanz in der heidnisch-antiken Gesellschaft ausschlaggebend, wie Rosemarie Nürnberg nachweist: »›Non decet neque necessarium est, ut mulieres doceant‹: Überlegungen zum altkirchlichen Lehrverbot für Frauen,« *Jahrbuch für Antike und Christentum* 31 (1988): 57–73).

[14] J.B. Connelly, *Portrait of a Priestess: Women and Ritual in Ancient Greece* (Princeton: Princeton University Press, 2007).

[15] http://saltandlighttv.org/blog/vatican-connections/vatican-connections-woman-named-president-of-pontifical-university (accessed July 20, 2014).

the ordination of women.«[16] But it is also clear that not all Reformed Churches agree with this. Also the Lutheran World Federation took a stance. Their statement on the episcopal ministry (2007) says:

> Today the great majority of Lutherans belong to churches that ordain both women and men. This practice reflects a renewed understanding of the biblical witness. Ordination of women expresses the conviction that the mission of the church requires the gifts of both men and women in the public ministry of word and sacraments, and that limiting the ordained ministry to men obscures the nature of the church as a sign of our reconciliation and unity in Christ through baptism across the divides of ethnicity, social status and gender (cf. Gal. 3:27–28).[17]

Also the Methodist churches opened all levels of ministry to women and men: »Methodists ordain women because they believe that women also receive the call, evidenced by inward conviction and outward manifestation of the gifts and graces, and confirmed by the gathering of the faithful.«[18]

(6) In the Roman Catholic Church and in the Eastern Orthodox Churches this is totally different. Of course the discussion are going on there too. *Inter Insigniores* (1976)[19] said »no« and *Ordinatio Sacerdotalis* (1994)[20] declared the discussion closed. Roma locuta causa finita? What if we could restore catholicity for all churches and both genders? Take for example Olympias, a female deacon (±400 in Constantinople). According to John Wijngaards she was ordained in a sacramental way.[21]

---

[16] »A New Community: Affirmations of The Ordination of Women,« in *Walk, My Sister: The Ordination of Women: Reformed Perspectives*, eds. Ursel Rosenhäger and Sarah Stephens, Studies from the World Alliance of Reformed Churches 18 ([Geneva]: [World Alliance of Reformed Churches], 1993), 5.
[17] The Lund Statement, no. 20.
[18] »The Apostolic Tradition« (Methodist–Roman Catholic Dialogue 1991), no. 96 (in *Growth in Agreement II*, 616). Cf. also the Anglican-Methodist document »Sharing in the Apostolic Communion« (1996), no. 55: »God's calling of women to serve the ministry in all its forms is accepted throughout Methodism.« (Ibid., 67).
[19] http://www.newadvent.org/library/docs_df76ii.htm (accessed July 20, 2014).
[20] *Ordinatio Sacerdotalis* came out on Pentecost 1993: http://www.vatican.va/holy_father/john_paul_ii/apost_letters/1994/documents/hf_jp-ii_apl_19940522_ordinatio-sacerdotalis_en.html (accessed July 20, 2014).
[21] J. Wijngaards, *The Ordained Women Deacons of the Church's First Millennium* (Norwich: The Canterbury Press, 2002).

So in his view this can become also a reality in our times: *E facto sequitur posse*.

(7) In my view there are no valid biblical arguments to keep women out of the ordained ministry. All the arguments circulate already for ages and this will not lead any further. There is no need for new reflection on the old theological issues, like the concepts of *representation* or *the Twelve*, which have also been discussed many times. Recently (in May 2014) there was a new theological Lutheran-Orthodox dialogue in Tallinn (Estonia)[22] again focusing on the ordination of women. Like the discussion in the Dutch Council of Churches in June 2014 there was also a warm and good atmosphere[23] also in Tallinn, but we still seem to be in dead end. Churches are really in need of reformation these days and guided by the Holy Spirit, they cannot remain captured by old traditions of earlier times.

(8) In our modern society women are active in the whole alphabet, working as artists, bibliographers, curators, drivers, economists, flute players, generals, housekeepers, industrials, judges, kings (!), lawyers, ministers, notaries, opticians, professors, queens, radiologists, soldiers, teachers, usurpers, volunteers, wardresses, yachters and zappers. Sometimes the Protestant churches are accused of only following changes in social structures, led by feminist ideas. Certainly such modern social developments are important and influential, but they are not the only reason and they do not automatically lead to the ordination of women.[24] Protestant churches that ordain women do so as a result of their biblical interpretation and their theological insights. As it was already stated in the BEM document:

---

[22] http://www.lutheranworld.org/news/spiritual-community#sthash.MFuyjSqr.dpuf (accessed July 20, 2014).

[23] This was also the experience of Rev. van Reijendam-Beek. L. W. van Reijendam-Beek, »Vrouwen in het Vaticaan, gewenst?« in *In gesprek met het Vaticaan*, eds. C. P. van Andel and R. van den Beld (Kampen: Kok, 1986), 60–75, here 65.

[24] We read in a study of the World Alliance of Reformed Churches the following: »As a part of the human community, the Christian community is bound to be shaped by the changes that take place in that larger community. A glance at the history of Christianity gives us enough evidence to show that the Christian community does not slavishly follow whatever changes take place in the human community. It applies its own judgment based on its interpretations of the Bible, traditions, dogmas, doctrines, ecclesiastical practices and so on. Such encounters also vary since the practice of Christian communities is not homogenous throughout the world or even within regional and national situations.« H. S. Wilson, »Towards a New Understanding of Ministry: Some Theological Considerations,« in *Walk, My Sister*, eds. Rosenhäger and Stephens, 75.

Those churches which practice the ordination of women do so because of their understanding of the Gospel and of the ministry. It rests for them on the deeply held theological conviction that the ordained ministry of the Church lacks fullness when it is limited to one sex. This theological conviction has been reinforced by their experience during the years in which they have included women in their ordained ministries. They have found that woman's gifts are as wide and varied as men's and that their ministry is as fully blessed by the Holy Spirit as the ministry of men.[25]

(9) So my question is again: how can churches be fruitful and recognizable in our modern society while the ordination of women is still rejected? And how is it possible, that in the new document of Faith and Order, *The Church: Towards a Common Vision* (2013),[26] the whole question of women's ordination is hardly mentioned?[27]

(10) It is well known, that the Vatican states that Protestant churches lack the fullness of sacramental ordination. They suffer from a »defectus ordinis«. I dare say today that all churches that still refuse to ordain women in my view have also a »defectus ordinis«. Is this an accusation? Not at all. But we shall have to continue our ecumenical talks in friendship and mutual respect in order to overcome our differences. But it is true: In stating the non-negotiability of female ministry, I can understand, but I cannot accept that other churches make a gender difference for their (ordained) ministries.

---

[25] BEM, Ministry, no. 18, commentary.
[26] http://www.oikoumene.org/en/resources/documents/commissions/faith-and-order/i-unity-the-church-and-its-mission/the-church-towards-a-common-vision (accessed July 20, 2014).
[27] »Christians disagree as well over the traditional restriction of ordination to the ministry of word and sacrament to men only,« *The Church: Towards a Common Vision*, Faith and Order Paper 214 (Geneva: WCC, 2013), 26 (§ 45).

Orthodox Understanding of Catholicity as the Wholeness of the Church

Mihai Iordache

1 Introduction

The concept of »catholicity« in the Orthodox Church has an old, deep and profound meaning. As one of the four attributes of the church, catholicity has developed during the history a strong connection with the other three: unity, holiness and apostolicity.

According to Orthodox understanding, the significance of the word »catholicity« can be expressed by the terms »wholeness« (ὅλον), »plenitude« and »fullness«.[1] The words of Metropolitan John Zizioulas describe the meaning of the concept of »catholicity« in the first centuries:

> It is not an accident that in adopting the term »catholic« from Aristotelian language the early Christians did not conceptualize it, but instead of speaking of »catholicity«, as we do today, they spoke of a »catholic Church« or even – and this is more significant – of »catholic Churches« in the plural. This means that we cannot speak of »catholicity« and ignore the concrete local Church.[2]

---

[1] Fr Dumitru Stăniloae, *The Experience of God: Orthodox Dogmatic Theology*, vol. 4: *The Church: Communion in the Holy Spirit* (Brookline, Mass.: Holy Cross Orthodox Press, 2012), 80.

[2] John D. Zizioulas, *Being as Communion: Studies in Personhood and the Church* (Crestwood, New York: St Vladimir's Seminary Press, 1985), 143.

Hence in the beginning the word »catholic« church had the significance of the whole church or the plenitude and fullness of the body of Christ, as »the accommodation of unity of purpose.«[3] By extension we can apply this to the concrete persons as well, as members of the church of Christ.

In order to keep close to this original meaning of the church's wholeness, I will only seldom use the word »catholicity«, in order to avoid its understanding as universality, geographical expansion and horizontal comprehension, significations which appeared later. Wholeness expresses something different: the sign of the church's life in Christ, of the experience of God and the reality of a living church. Through wholeness every believer feels him/herself as member of a living *whole* which is the church of Jesus Christ. »Khomiakov neatly defines the Church as ›the life of God in human beings‹.«[4] In this respect, the church through *wholeness* has a *meaning* in all places and in each of its believers.

Therefore I will try to show how the Word of God, our Saviour, can become »*the life of our life*«[5] through the wholeness of His Church.

2 Wholeness in the Creed

In the Nicene-Constantinopolitan Creed we confess to believe in one, holy, catholic and apostolic Church. In the Orthodox Church, the word »catholic« was either kept, – as in Greece today –, or it was translated, – as in the case of non-Greek Orthodox churches.

> The Slavic translators of the Nicene-Constantinopolitan Creed have rendered the Greek term »catholiki« as »sobornuiu« out of resentment toward the Church in the West and probably also because the sense of »universal« given by the Church to the term »catholiki« does not faithfully

---

[3] St Cyprian of Carthage, De Catholicae Ecclesiae Unitate [The Unity of the Catholic Church], in *On the Church: Select Treatises*, translation, introduction and commentary by Allen Brent (Crestwood, New York: St Vladimir's Seminary Press, 2006), 160.
[4] Paul Evdokimov, *Orthodoxy* (Hyde Park, New York: New City Press, 2011), 165.
[5] † Daniel, Patriarch of the Romanian Orthodox Church, *Teologie si Spiritualitate* [Theology and Spirituality] (Bucharest: Editura Basilica a Patriarhiei Romane, 2010), 203 (translation MI).

transmit its meaning. For the same reasons, the Romanian translation adopted the Slavic term, naming the Church »sobornicească« (synodal).[6]

The sobornicity expresses not only the synodal preserving of the church's teaching at the episcopal level, but especially the communion and the permanent cooperation of all her members, hierarchy and believers. This communion is a dynamic one through the living participation and personal contribution of each member of the church which implies complementarity.

For the Eastern tradition catholicity or the wholeness of the church has not been embodied into one visible person or place, nor into the entire universal church. On the contrary it is achieved through a living *communion (symphony)* of all the persons and places, starting from the local churches to the whole church.

> The episcopate is one, an individual share in which individual bishops hold as owners of a common property. The Church is a unity, which extends into a plurality by the widespread increase of her fruitfulness. The rays of the sun are many but its light one, and the boughs of a tree many but its trunk is one, established in a root that holds it firm. When from one fountain many streams flow forth, their multiplicity may be seen to be poured forth from the abundance of their overflowing supply. Granted these are examples of a multiplicity, nevertheless their unity is preserved in their source.[7]

Vladimir Lossky affirmed in this respect:

> Orthodoxy recognizes no visible head of the Church. The unity of the Church expresses itself through the communion of the heads of local churches among themselves, by the agreement of all the churches in regard to a local council – which thus acquires a universal import. The catholicity of the Church, far from being the privilege of any one see or specific centre, is realized rather in the richness and multiplicity of the local traditions which bear witness unanimously to a single truth: to that which is preserved always, everywhere and by all. Since the Church is catholic in all her parts, each one of her members – not only the clergy but also each

---

[6] Stăniloae, *The Church*, 79f.
[7] St Cyprian of Carthage, De Catholicae Ecclesiae Unitate, 154f.

layman – is called to confess and to defend the truth of tradition; opposing even the bishops should they fall into heresy.[8]

Concerning the catholicity of the church, St Cyril of Jerusalem (315–386) affirmed in the 4th century:

> The Church is called catholic because she exists within the world, from one end of the earth to the other; and because she teaches universally and completely one and all the doctrines which ought to come to men's knowledge, concerning things both visible and invisible, heavenly and earthly; and because she brings into subjection to godliness the whole race of mankind, governors and governed, learned and unlearned; and because she universally treats and heals the whole class of sins, which are committed by soul or body, and possesses in herself every form of virtue which is named, both in deeds and words, and in every kind of spiritual gifts.[9]

From this old text we can perceive that catholicity did not mean a geographical extension of a *corpus universalis* or a territorial covering under one bishop, but something totally different. The church is catholic because »she teaches... one and all the doctrines«, she »brings into subjection to godliness the whole race of mankind«, she »treats and heals the whole class of sins« and because she »possesses in herself every form of virtue.«

In this respect, Paul Evdokimov asserted: »Καθολική derived from ›καθ'όλου‹ – *secundum totum*, according to the whole, *quia per totum est*, conveys an entirety which is not geographical, horizontal and quantitative, but vertical and qualitative, resistant to any fragmentation of doctrine.«[10]

Thereby we can assert that the wholeness represents the *modality* in which the church's unity exists, and how this unity is put into practice. Although »the unity of the Church constitutes an actual problem of the human beings' life in its ensemble,«[11] we can perceive through the

---

[8] Vladimir Lossky, *The Mystical Theology of the Eastern Church* (Crestwood, New York: St Vladimir's Seminary Press, 1997), 15f.
[9] St Cyril of Jerusalem, Catechesis 18, 23, PG 33: 1044B, in Archbishop Anastasios (Yannoulatos), *Mission in Christ's Way: An Orthodox Understanding of Mission* (Brookline, Massachusetts: Holy Cross Orthodox Press, 2010), 241.
[10] Evdokimov, *Orthodoxy*, 164.
[11] Christos Yannaras, *Truth and Unity of the Church* [in Romanian] (Bucharest: Sofia Press, 2009), 15.

wholeness what the nature of this unity is. The church, as the mystical body of the Word of God, Jesus Christ, the true God and Human, is an organic whole, a spiritual body that has everything *through* and *in* the Holy Spirit.[12]

3 Wholeness in the Church Fathers' Thinking

In the New Testament, St Apostle Paul refers to the wholeness of the church members, talking about the various gifts given to the human beings in the body of Christ, gifts that come from and are sustained by the Holy Spirit:

> There are different kinds of spiritual gifts, but the same Spirit gives them. There are different ways of serving, but the same Lord is served. There are different abilities to perform service, but the same God gives ability to all for their particular service. The Spirit's presence is shown in some way in each person for the good of all. The Spirit gives one person a message full of wisdom, while to another person the same Spirit gives a message full of knowledge. One and the same Spirit gives faith to one person, while to another person he gives the power to heal. The Spirit gives one person the power to work miracles; to another, the gift of speaking God's message; and to yet another, the ability to tell the difference between gifts that come from the Spirit and those that do not. To one person he gives the ability to speak in strange tongues, and to another he gives the ability to explain what is said. But it is one and the same Spirit who does all this; as he wishes, he gives a different gift to each person. (1 Cor 12:4–11).

The Holy Fathers spoke of an organic-spiritual interpretation of the church, this »pledge of unity, this bond of a concord that is held together in a way that cannot be split into individual links«[13] having a theandric constitution and being the extended body of Christ. Starting from the idea of St Apostle Paul, they see the plenitude of the church being present in every member on different manners. Just as in every cell of a body there is the entire body through its activity and specificity (»in micro«), so is the whole church found in each of her members.

---

[12] † Daniel, Patriarch of the Romanian Orthodox Church, *Confessing the Truth in Love: Orthodox Perceptions of Life, Mission and Unity* (Bucharest: Basilica Press, 2008), 147–149.

[13] St Cyprian of Carthage, De Catholicae Ecclesiae Unitate, 158.

St John Chrysostom (347–407) affirms the diversity of the members of the church and the realizing of her unity through the fulfilling of a *common task* of the members, through solidarity and complementarity, based on 1 Cor 12:19f.:

> If there were not among you great diversity, you could not be a body. And not being a body, you could not be one. As it is, however, because you are not all endowed with the same one gift, therefore are you a body; and being a body, you are all one, and differ nothing from one another in this that you are a body.[14]

The unity is due to the fact that all the members of the church fulfil a common task: »Every one of our members – continued St Chrysostom – has both a working of its own and one which is common. And likewise there is in us a beauty which is peculiar and another which is common.«[15]

One should observe the paradox: being diverse, you are one body; and being one body, or a unity, you differ in nothing from one another. In commenting the words of St John Chrysostom, the Romanian Orthodox theologian Dumitru Stăniloae (1903–1993), remarks:

> In reality, the entire body effectuates every working proper to every member, and every member fulfils the function of the entire body through his own function. Thus every one is open to the working of the entire body and rejoices in it. But no member is confused with the others, because each member assumes the whole body's working and powers in his own form. Even through this, the working of each member is useful to the whole and enriches it. Similarly, the same integral Spirit of Christ, or the same integral Church, is effective in the gift and working of each member.[16]

St Basil the Great (330–379) speaks about the *presence of the Holy Spirit* in every believer, in every member of the church through a *gift* or through various gifts. Therefore the members are not thereby made uniform, but they cooperate among themselves in a deep complementarity for keeping the whole body in its integrity. Continuing Apostle Paul's assertions, St Basil affirmed that

---

[14] St John Chrysostom, Homily 30 on First Corinthians, PG 47: 258, in Stăniloae, *The Church*, 83.
[15] St John Chrysostom, Homily 30 on First Corinthians, PG 47: 258.
[16] Stăniloae, *The Church*, 83.

the members of the body have the same care for one another, according to the inborn spiritual communion of their sympathy. Whether one member suffers, all the members suffer with it; or if one member be honoured, all the members rejoice with it.[17]

The complementarity represents the proceeding of realising the unity of Church and of the whole creation through the activity of the Holy Spirit.

In the church, every person (priest or believer) is a true member of Christ's body and in this respect everybody has Jesus Christ through the Holy Spirit, because the church has Christ, with all His saving and deifying gifts.[18] In the Eucharist a believer receives Christ and not just a part of Him, nor simply a symbol of His presence.[19] Being a member of the body of Christ, on the one hand, the person receives the power from the body's fullness and from its Head and, on the other hand, he contributes through his work and specificity to the whole body's richness and life. »Catholicity, therefore, in this context, does not mean anything else but the *wholeness* and *fullness* and *totality* of the body of Christ.«[20]

In the church no one is alone, but all the members are in communion, in convergence and in complementarity loving each other and loving God in the same time because

> love is the essence of the *holiness* of the Church, for it »has been poured into our hearts through the Holy Spirit' the essence of the *unity* of the Church, who works for itself the increase of the body to its self-building up in love (Eph 4:16) and it is the essence of the apostolicity and sobornicity because the Church is all the time and everywhere the same unique apostolic unity.[21]

Every person has his/her own place in the church and through his/her life and participation he/she contributes to the life of the church. »An Orthodox believer, says Metropolitan Kallistos Ware, is all the time very

---

[17] St Basil the Great, On the Holy Spirit, 26. 61, PG 32: 181, in Stăniloae, *The Church*, 81f.
[18] Stăniloae, *The Church*, 80.
[19] Cardinal Christoph Schönborn, *Les sources de notre foi* (Paris: Edition Parole et Silence, 2012), 136.
[20] Zizioulas, *Being as Communion*, 149.
[21] Alexander Schmemann, *The Eucharist: Sacrament of the Kingdom* (Crestwood, New York: St Vladimir's Seminary Press, 1988), 137.

aware that he belongs to a community or parish.«[22] His/her position could not be replaced by another person because each one has his/her own specificity and uniqueness.

In the church, everyone receives all the gifts and talents from God (Mt 25:14–30) within the framework of the wholeness through the Holy Spirit, and so everyone enjoys the fullness only in communion with the others and with the persons of the Holy Trinity, not in isolation. »The Church is the creation of communion, the creation of a concrete mode of human communion.«[23]

4 Wholeness and Christ's Presence in the Church

The church is whole because she has Jesus Christ as her head. She possesses all the healing graces that bring all creation to deification. The church has all the teaching that potentially includes all the knowledge necessary for the salvation of the people.

> Because the Church has the plenitude of teaching and grace as the expression of Christ's full presence within her, nothing can be added to this teaching. No heresy has ever added anything to it. On the contrary, the heresies limited it, and thus they made it to a great extent sterile. The heresies distanced themselves from this whole – from the plenitude of Christ's presence and gifts, and of the Church's teaching as the expression of that plenitude – because they no longer expressed the belief that Christ is found wholly in the intimacy of believing humanity.[24]

It is Christ's presence only that gives to the church the power and the wholeness of her teaching and existence. And this is due to the fact that Jesus not only speaks about the unity of the church, but also prays for it (Jn 17:20–21).

> Very often, these words of Jesus are quoted: *omnes sint unum* (that they may be all one) but no notice is taken of the fact, that he talks also about the »how«, which is the model of Trinitarian life: »As Thou, Father, art in Me, and I in Thee«. Jesus' prayer for the unity of the Church shows that the

---

[22] Metropolitan Kallistos Ware, *L'Orthodoxie, l'Église des sept conciles* (Paris: Desclée de Brouwer, 1997), 309.
[23] Yannaras, *Truth and Unity of the Church*, 22.
[24] Stăniloae, *The Church*, 86.

Trinity is not only a model for the life of the Church, but also its source and aim: »that they also may be one in Us«.[25]

The presence of Christ in the church gives her a theandric aspect and character. In this respect the church is not just an institution which struggles for the salvation of people and the eternal life, but a holy place or gathering where heaven meets earth and the uncreated encounters the created. The Orthodox conception concerning the church is spiritually and mystic, in the sense that theology does not treat at any time any of the church's temporal aspects in isolation, but it considers it always in connection with Jesus Christ and the Holy Spirit. The whole Orthodox thinking about the church starts from the special relationship which exists between God and the church. Hence the church can be illustrated in three aspects: the image of the Holy Trinity, the body of Christ and a continuous Pentecost. Therefore the Orthodox doctrine of the church is trinitarian, christological and pneumatological.[26] We could not look to Christ without looking also to the Father and to the Holy Spirit. Moreover all the important events in the earthly Christ's life for our salvation, namely incarnation, crucifixion, resurrection and ascension, were done also by God the Father and God the Holy Spirit.

The wholeness of the church is preserved from above to below, from the model of the Holy Trinity to the seeking communion and plenitude of human beings.

> For the Orthodox Christian, the Holy Trinity is the source, the starting point and the ultimate goal of the entire theology and spirituality, of the entire anthropology and ecclesiology, of the entire understanding of the world and of existence.[27]

All of us are members of the same whole body and we »are under the foremost obligation to grasp tightly this unity«[28] because the Word of God Himself became a true body, through His »kenosis« and »incarnation«.

> This kenosis is best described as consisting in the fact that, through the humanity He assumed, through the body which occupied a place in space,

---

[25] † Daniel, *Confessing the Truth in Love,* 70.
[26] Ware, *L'Orthodoxie, l'Église des sept conciles,* 310.
[27] † Daniel, *Confessing the Truth in Love,* 67.
[28] St Cyprian of Carthage, De Catholicae Ecclesiae Unitate, 153.

He made Himself accessible and able to be grasped as God in the highest degree.[29]

5   Eucharist as the Central Part of the Church's Wholeness

Above all, in the Eucharist we partake of Christ's body according to His words: »Take and eat it; this is my body. Drink it, all of you; this is my blood, which seals God's covenant, my blood poured out for many for the forgiveness of sins« (Mt 26:26–28). For »he who eats my flesh and drinks my blood abides in me, and I in him« (Jn 6:56). Jesus Christ is present in His church in various manners but He is present in the highest form in the Eucharist.[30] Only in communion with the Word of God we can partake of His wholeness and inherit the eternal life: »Whoever eats my flesh and drinks my blood has eternal life, and I will raise him up at the last day« (Jn 6:54).

Through the Eucharist, all the members receive the whole Christ through the Holy Spirit. »The Lamb of God is broken and shared, broken but not divided, ever eaten but not consumed, sanctifying those who partake,«[31] are the words of a prayer before the Communion during the Divine Liturgy. The Eucharist becomes in this respect the mystery of the church's unity. We can understand the nature of the church's wholeness through the real and different *meanings* of Eucharist for every believer as individual and for the whole church.

> It was a clear indication that – affirms Zizioulas – although the catholicity of the Church is ultimately an eschatological reality, its nature is revealed and realistically apprehended *here* and *now* in the Eucharist. The Eucharist understood primarily not as a *thing* and an objectified means of grace but as an *act* and a *synaxis* of the local Church, *a »catholic« act of a »catholic« Church*, can, therefore, be of importance in any attempt to understand the catholicity of the Church.[32]

---

[29] Fr Dumitru Stăniloae, *The Experience of God: Orthodox Dogmatic Theology*, Vol. 1: *Revelation and Knowledge of the Triune God* (Brookline, Massachusetts: Holy Cross Orthodox Press, 1998), 181.
[30] Schönborn, *Les sources de notre foi*, 135.
[31] Liturgikon, 186.
[32] Zizioulas, *Being as Communion*, 144f.

The partaking of Christ's body and blood strengthens the communion among all persons, although in the Orthodox Church each one is called personally by his/her name while receiving the Eucharist.[33] This is possible because

> the whole Christ, the catholic Church, was present and incarnate in each eucharistic community. Each eucharistic community was, therefore, in full unity with the rest by virtue not of an *external superimposed structure* but of the whole Christ represented in each of them.[34]

For this reason a common prayer implores God the Father at the end of the Divine Liturgy – being the last prayer of the priest in the middle of the whole people – with these words:

> Lord, who blesses those who bless You and sanctify those who put their trust in You, save your people and bless your heritage. Guard the *wholeness* of your Church. Sanctify those who love the beauty of your house. Glorify them by your divine power. And do not abandon us who put our hope in you. Grant peace to your world, to *your Churches*, to your clergy, to civil authorities and to all your people.[35]

6 Wholeness and Sanctification of Persons

According to the Orthodox thinking there is an intimate relationship between the wholeness and the holiness of the church. This interior relation is possible due to the activity of the person of the Holy Spirit in the church. Through the Holy Spirit, Jesus Christ is present within His church until the end of the days. »And I will be with you always, to the end of the age« (Mt 28:20). Nevertheless, St Apostle Paul affirmed that »no one can confess ›Jesus is Lord‹, unless he is guided by the Holy Spirit« (1 Cor 12:3). Through the Holy Spirit the church is preserved as the mystical body of Jesus Christ, as a divine-human foundation leading the believers to the salvation.

> The life of Christ, – affirmed Patriarch Daniel –, is communicated to the Church through the Holy Spirit. The church is the mystical body of Jesus

---

[33] Liturgikon, 195.
[34] Zizioulas, *Being as Communion*, 157.
[35] Liturgikon, 198.

> Christ, and the Holy Spirit is the »soul« of the Church. The human nature is being sanctified through the Holy Spirit and it is being moulded in the configuration of Christ's humanity. Hence the Holy Spirit was called »the architect of the Church« (St Basil the Great).[36]

Through the Holy Spirit the church is holy and can sanctify her members and the whole creation.[37] The sanctified persons, saints, can overcome the material *duality* between the soul (reason) that tends towards the union with the three persons of the Holy Trinity and sensations (passions) that strive toward the material pleasure. In this respect they reach not only the true and blessed union with the Holy Trinity but they can even perceive the *meaning* of unity *in* the Holy Trinity[38] obtaining at the same time an upper enjoyment.

The church is sanctifying the believers through the Holy Spirit but the sanctified believers preserve the wholeness of the body of Christ through their own personal contribution making possible the unity of all.

> The Trinitarian prototype of the human being's true, the manner of Christ's existence, namely the unity of the Church, is realised on a dynamic course in the mysterious fullness of life and of personal perfection, which is embodied into the images of saints. However it may seem discrepant, the Church's unity may be realised in every moment even into a single human existence, and it can be incarnated into a single person. When you are approaching a saint of the Church ... you are living truly the unity as universal presence of all the people.[39]

Through wholeness we are all real and diverse members of the body of Christ, and in this way, we are in a permanent inner connection with the holiness's source, the Word of God that sanctifies us in the church. The church is holy because »one is her head and source, and the one

---

[36] † Daniel, *Theology and Spirituality*, 188.
[37] See Lars Thunberg, *Man and the Cosmos: The Vision of St Maximus the Confessor* (New York: St Vladimir's Seminary Press, 1997).
[38] St Maximus the Confessor, The Ambigua: On Difficulties in the Church Fathers, PG 91, 1193 C–1196 C, ed. and trans. Nicholas Constas, vol. I, Dumbarton Oaks Medieval Library (Cambridge, Mass.: Harvard University Press, 2014), 321-323.
[39] Yannaras, *Truth and Unity of the Church*, 33-34.

Mother is rich with the offspring of her fertility.«[40] In this sense, Fr. Dumitru Stăniloae affirmed:

> The Church's main concern is the sanctification of her members, because only in this way are they saved. The Holy Spirit works toward the sanctification of the faithful within the Church, whose intimate life is imprinted with Christ's sanctified body – a body that the Church bears in her bosom and from which the Holy Spirit shines forth. The Church works toward this sanctification of her members as she maintains them in the movement of love and of their communion with each other.[41]

The sanctification gives an orientation and an aim to the wholeness of the church. The person who is a member of the mystical body does not live any more for the past; he who believes in Christ is dead to the past. He lives in the present and for the future. The past, the present and the future are merging into a continuous »presence of movement« to Christ. In this way, Son of God is the *aim* but also the actualized *path* through His real and luminous presence in the interior of each believer. The important historical »events« of salvation (incarnation, crucifixion, resurrection and Pentecost) are becoming present and actual either through the great feasts during the year, or through their actualization in every Divine Liturgy. The past is becoming present. In the Orthodox Church, one of the songs during the Easter is saying: »Yesterday I was buried together with You, O Christ, *today* I am rising together with You, when You are rising from the dead.«[42] During the Divine Liturgy, before the Eucharist, the priests and believers are praying:

> O Son of God, accept me *today* as a communicant of your Mystic Supper for I will not speak to your enemies of your mystery, nor will I give you a kiss as Judas did. But I will confess you as did the thief: Remember me, O Lord, in your kingdom.[43]

Sören Kierkegaard (1813–1855) affirms that the life has to be understood as we are looking backwards, but it has to be lived as we are look-

---

[40] St Cyprian of Carthage, De Catholicae Ecclesiae Unitate, 155.
[41] Stăniloae, *The Church*, 73.
[42] *Pentecostarion* [in Romanian] (Bucharest: EIBM BOR Press, 2012), 16.
[43] Liturgikon, 189.

ing forward.[44] He sustains that the true Christian must be »contemporaneous« with Jesus Christ.

> For with regard to the absolute there is but one time, namely the present. He who is not contemporaneous with the absolute, for him it does not exist at all. And since Christ is the absolute, it is evident that in respect of him there is but one situation: contemporaneousness.[45]

The tendency of the wholeness of the church is the ceasing of time and the overwhelming of space on a progressive manner through our increasing communion with the persons of the Holy Trinity. In part, this can be realized on our time in the church, but the fullness of this communion is to be achieved afterwards, because »we see now through a dim window obscurely, but then face to face; now I know partially, but then I shall know complete« (1 Cor 13:12). Fr Dumitru Stăniloae wrote in his first volume of *Orthodox Dogmatic Theology*:

> When we have reached the goal of perfect communion with him and among ourselves, there will no longer be a variety of distances, but God will be close and intimate to everyone in the same way, in every place and time, so that there will no longer be a distinction, properly speaking, between here and there, between now and then. We will find ourselves purely and simply within the divine eternity and infinity having neither past nor future, neither here not there.[46]

The wholeness of the church includes also the sinners, because they are also in the church and somehow they remain in connection with the body of Christ. No one knows when a sinner renounces to his immoral life and begins to repent, to believe or even to witness the faith of the church. Paul Evdokimov (1901–1970) affirmed:

> The Church presents the precise and clear understanding that she is not a society of perfected saints, of only the elect and the pure. Her mystery consists in being at one and the same time »the Church of the repentant, of those perishing« (St Ephrem the Syrian) and the communion of sinners

---

[44] http://www.ardmediathek.de/Bayern-2/Radiowissen/Soren-Kierkegaard-Freiheit-ohne-Grenzen (accessed July 30, 2014).
[45] Sören Kierkegaard, *Preparation for a Christian Life* [in Romanian] (Bucharest: Adonai Press, 1995), 87.
[46] Stăniloae, *Revelation and Knowledge of the Triune God*, 178.

with the holy things (the sacraments), of their deifying sharing in the one and only holy One.[47]

And St Cyril of Jerusalem declared: »The Church is given the name *ecclesia*, because she calls all people to gather in the same place for a common cause.«[48]

Everything that is good in the world represents an enclosure which is opening up, as for example the life, the language, the number, the mystery etc. Life is the enclosure into a genetic code and the opening through it.[49] In this sense the wholeness of the church can be perceived also as an enclosure which is opening up. The church encloses into the life of a local church in order to open up to the whole church of Christ. The grace of the Holy Spirit encloses into a person in order to open up towards all the other persons in their community and in the entire church.

7 Instead of Conclusions

In this sense, we can conclude that the wholeness represents the life of each believer of the church, lived consciously as part of the life of Jesus Christ in His mystical body (Col. 1:18). This life is a dynamic one and it tends continuously on a *progressive* mode to pneumatization and deification.

Wholeness could help us to understand the inner relationship between the *whole* and the *part*, between universal and particular, between infinite and finite, between God and human being, between the Lord Jesus Christ and His church, between the church and the believers. Inspired by the thinking of St Maximus the Confessor in his work *The Ambigua*, by St Basil the Great in his *Homilies on the Hexaemeron*, by the ideas of St Gregory of Nyssa in his works *The Making of Man* and *The Life of Moses*, as well as inspired by the *unfolding* thought of vision concerning the relationship between *whole* and *part* from Hegel's

---

[47] Paul Evdokimov, »Holiness in the Tradition of the Orthodox Church,« in *In the World, of the Church: A Paul Evdokimov Reader*, ed. and trans. Michael Plekon and Alexis Vinogradov (New York: St. Vladimir's Seminary Press, 2001), 103.
[48] St Cyril of Jerusalem, Catechesis 18, 23, in Archbishop Anastasios (Yannoulatos), *Mission in Christ's Way*, 240.
[49] Constantin Noica, *Simple Introductions to the Goodness of Our Time* [in Romanian] (Bucharest: Humanitas Press, 1992), 11.

(1770–1831) philosophy⁵⁰ we can conclude that *the part* does not have its veritable reality and its truth in itself, namely in its immediate given existence, but *only in the whole* the part of which it is.

---

[50] See Hegel's works: *Phenomenology of Spirit* (1807), *Science of Logic* (1812) and *Encyclopedia of the Philosophical Sciences* (1817).

The Creed as Basis for the Unity of the Church

Jutta Koslowski

1 The Symbol of Nicaea-Constantinople as an Ecumenical Confession of the Church

»Catholicity under pressure« – the topic of the 18th Academic Consultation of *Societas Oecumenica* in Budapest relates to one of the most important subjects of systematic and ecumenical theology. The catholicity of the Church is indeed a point of controversy in the interconfessional dialogue; at the same time it is one of the fundamental dogmatic teachings of various ecclesiological traditions – and it has a long history: the catholicity of the church is one of the four *notae ecclesiae* stipulated in the Creed of Nicaea-Constantinople of AD 381. The third article of this Creed says: »[We believe] in the one holy catholic and apostolic Church.«[1] In the Eastern churches, this credo is normative to this day; it is the only creed used in the Orthodox liturgy. And also in the Western churches it remains significant: it is used in the Anglican Church,[2] where it is a regular part of *Sunday Worship*, and in the Roman Catholic tradition the so called »Great Creed« is used on high-ranking feast days.

---

[1] See Heinrich Denzinger, *Kompendium der Glaubensbekenntnisse und kirchlichen Lehrentscheidungen*, ed. Peter Hünermann, 38th ed. (Freiburg: Herder, 1999), 85.

[2] In the Anglican »Book of Common Prayer« of 1662 it is stressed that this creed »must be accepted and confessed under all circumstances«; cf. Cajus Fabricius (ed.), *Die Kirche von England: Ihr Gebetbuch, Bekenntnis und kanonisches Recht*, Corpus Confessionum – Die Bekenntnisse der Christenheit 17/1 (Berlin: Walter de Gruyter, 1937), 381.

It appears in the »Book of Concord«, the historic doctrinal standard of the Lutheran Church of 1580, and it is confirmed right at the beginning of Article I of the *Confessio Augustana*, the key confessional document of the Lutheran churches.[3]

Thus, the Nicene-Constantinopolitan Creed is of fundamental importance for the ecumenical movement since, in its original version, it is the only »ecumenical creed« that is common to the Western and Eastern Churches.[4] It is important for various reasons: because of its universal character, its old age and its canonical status (since it was defined at the first two Christian councils which both, Eastern and Western churches recognize as »ecumenical«). Moreover, its special importance in the ecumenical dialogue has been confirmed on several occasions (for example, in the context of the study project »On the Path to a Common Expression of Apostolic Faith Today« of the WCC Commission on Faith and Order).[5] Because this creed dates back to the time of the Early Church, before the schisms of today emerged, it offers a common basis of the faith, which may serve to re-establish the unity of the Church.[6]

---

[3] CA I. See Horst Georg Pöhlmann (ed.), *Unser Glaube: Die Bekenntnisschriften der evangelisch-lutherischen Kirche*, 3rd ed. (Gütersloh: Gütersloher, 1991), 58.

[4] About the confession of faith and its ecumenical relevance cf. Hans-Georg Link, *Bekennen und Bekenntnis*, Bensheimer Hefte 86 / Ökumenische Studienhefte 7 (Göttingen: Vandenhoeck & Ruprecht, 1998); idem (ed.), *Gemeinsam glauben und bekennen: Handbuch zum Apostolischen Glauben* (Neukirchen-Vluyn: Neukirchener, 1987).

[5] Cf. Gemeinsame Arbeitsgruppe der römisch-katholischen Kirche und des Ökumenischen Rates der Kirchen, »Auf dem Weg zu einem Bekenntnis des gemeinsamen Glaubens,« *Ökumenische Rundschau* 29, no. 3 (1980): 367–376; Kommission für Glauben und Kirchenverfassung, »Apostolischer Glaube heute,« in *Schritte zur sichtbaren Einheit: Lima 1982. Sitzung der Kommission für Glauben und Kirchenverfassung. Berichte, Reden, Dokumente*, ed. Hans-Georg Link, Beiheft zur Ökumenischen Rundschau 45 (Frankfurt a.M.: Lembeck, 1983), 55–154; Kommission für Glauben und Kirchenverfassung: *Gemeinsam den einen Glauben bekennen. Eine ökumenische Auslegung des Glaubens, wie er im Glaubensbekenntnis von Nizäa-Konstantinopel (381) bekannt wird*, Faith and Order Paper 153 (Frankfurt a.M.: Lembeck, 1991); Link, *Bekennen und Bekenntnis*. See also Deutsche Bischofskonferenz/Rat der Evangelischen Kirche in Deutschland: »Erklärung zur 1600-Jahr-Feier des Glaubensbekenntnisses von Nizäa-Konstantinopel,« in *Der Lobpreis des Dreieinigen Gottes im Heiligen Geist. 1600 Jahre Bekenntnis von Nicäa-Konstantinopel*, ed. Evangelische Akademie Tutzing, Tutzinger Studien 2 (Tutzing: Evangelische Akademie Tutzing, 1981), 103–105.

[6] A critical assessment of the creeds of the Old Church and their ecumenical potential can be found especially among Protestanet theologians, e.g. Hans-Martin Barth, »›Alle eins‹ oder ›Streiten verbindet‹? Das Paradigma ökumenischer

However, this creed can develop its full ecumenical potential only in its original form, i.e. without the addition of the word »*filioque*«, which became common in the Western church from the sixth century onwards (proclaiming that the Holy Sprit derives from the Father »and the Son«). It would not be heterodox to omit this addition. Since Orthodox theology has strong objections against it – both for canonical and dogmatic reasons – and even regards it as a reason for the separation from the Western Church, this controversial term should, in my view, be omitted, for the sake of unity and peace.[7] The fifth World Conference on Faith and Order at Santiago de Compostela (1993) also voted in that sense.[8] The fact that the *filioque* can, in principle, be given up was also demonstrated, for example, by Pope Pauls VI, when he prayed the Great Creed, in its original Greek form, together with the Ecumenical Patriarch Athenagoras I during a solemn mass. Cancelling this *single* word, which has played such a fatal role in the schism between the East and West, would constitute a *unilateral confidence building act* and could help to bring about an improvement in the relations between the Orthodox Church on the one hand and the Catholic Church as well as the Anglican and Protestant Churches on the other hand. This proposal does not imply theological indifference or diplomatic calculation. Of course, the ecumenical difficulties created by issues such as the conflict in Ukraine, the ordination of women or divergent ethical viewpoints about homosexuality cannot be side-stepped simply by leaving behind the *filioque*. However, especially in view of such problems, it would be helpful to recall the common tradition of the faith we share. Moreover, renouncing the *filioque* does not necessarily express the dogmatic judgement that this term would be unorthodox. On the contrary, renouncing the *filioque* should be facilitated by *not* expecting such an explicit statement – a concession that would be helpful from the side of the Orthodox Church.

Theologie stimmt nicht mehr«, *Deutsches Pfarrerblatt* 83, no. 10 (1983): 474–477; Erich Geldbach, *Ökumene in Gegensätzen*, Bensheimer Hefte 66 (Göttingen: Vandenhoeck & Ruprecht, 1987), 46–51; Friedrich Loofs, »Die Geltung der drei ökumenischen Bekenntnisse«, *Die Eiche* 13, no. 3 (1925): 299–312; Jörg Zink, *Das christliche Bekenntnis: Ein Vorschlag* (Stuttgart: Kreuz, 1996).

7 Ecumenical dialogues have frequently come to this conclusion, for instance the »Klingenthal-Memorandum« about »Das Filioque aus ökumenischer Sicht,« in Link, *Gemeinsam glauben und bekennen*, 299–315. Cf. ibid., 284f. and 292.

8 Günther Gaßmann and Dagmar Heller (eds.), *Santiago de Compostela 1993: Fünfte Weltkonferenz für Glauben und Kirchenverfassung 3. bis 14. August 1993: Berichte, Referate, Dokumente*, Beiheft zur Ökumenischen Rundschau 67 (Frankfurt a.M.: Lembeck, 1994).

The Creed of Nicaea-Constantinople is not the only symbol of the Early Church that proclaims the catholicity of the church. The Apostles' Creed, too, which dates back as far as the second century AD, professes, in its third article, »the Holy Catholic Church«. Hence, here are only two *notae ecclesiae* mentioned, and the catholicity of the Church is one of them – a further hint to the fundamental importance of this concept. However, since the Creed of Nicaea-Constantinople is of eminent importance in the ecumenical context, the following considerations concentrate on this symbol and the term »Creed« hereinafter refers to that of Nicaea-Constantinople. This is not at all intended to deny the value of the different creeds in the various confessional traditions – rather, the aim is to highlight the unifying element of the multitude of confessions.[9]

2 The Credo as a Basis for the Catholicity of the Church

The fact that the creeds of the Early Church confess the catholicity of the church as one of the *notae ecclesiae* leads to the question: what is the relationship between the two dimensions of creed and *catholicity*? »Catholic« means all-encompassing or »universal«. As a statement about the church, this term has a territorial as well as a spiritual dimension. But *catholic* implies more: it is a kind of quality that the church claims for itself and, ultimately, it relates to faithfulness. The catholic faith is not only the »holistic« one (in terms of its content), but also the one which is generally shared – the one »that is believed at all times, in all places and by all people« as the famous *regula fidei* of Vincent of Lérins puts is.[10] The universal church is, at the same time, the faithful one – so there is a close relationship between the attributes »catholic« and »orthodox« – despite of the fact that later on, these terms became the names of different ecclesial traditions.

»Faithfulness« – this criterion again relates to the creed, for the Fathers of Nicaea and Constantinople intended to summarize the essence of the Christian faith in an authoritative manner. »The faith of the Holy Fathers, who had gathered in Nicaea in Bithynia, must not be abolished;

---

[9] For the rich variety of confessional traditions in the different Churches see for example Hans Steubing (ed.), *Bekenntnisse der Kirche: Bekenntnistexte aus zwanzig Jahrhunderten* (Wuppertal: Brockhaus, 1970).

[10] Vincent of Lerins: Commonitorum, II, 3.

it rather remains binding«[11] – this is what the participants in the Council of Constantinople added to the traditional text of the Creed. The Creed provides a conceptual qualification of the catholicity of the church.

If one turns this thought around, it leads to the conclusion: what is not specified in the Creed is not part of the elementary constitutions of the church's faith. Developing this idea further has far-reaching consequences for the ecumenical dialogue. This is because many questions which hamper the interconfessional dialogue today are not even mentioned in the Creed: neither the ministry (including that of bishops or the Pope, the apostolic succession or universal jurisdiction) nor other controversial teachings such as Mariology are included. Among the sacraments only baptism is mentioned, but not the eucharist, which is highly controversial among Christians.

Precisely this silence about many controversial theological issues is an important reason for the ecumenical quality of the Nicene-Constantinopolitan Creed. Nevertheless, the critical question may be asked:

> Is it true, that these creeds [of the Early Church] express all basic truths? These creeds make no mention of the concept of grace, which has occupied a central place in the theological traditions of both, East and West. They do not mention the true and complete humanity of Jesus or the relation of the two natures according to the formula of Ephesus and Chalcedon. Of the sacraments, only baptism is mentioned. They are silent on the Eucharist, which is generally regarded as the most important sacrament. No statements are made about the Pope, the bishops or any kind of *Ordo* or office within the Church.[12]

The most problematic gap within the text of this Creed is surely contained in the second article, which says about Jesus: »[...] and was made man; he was crucified for us under Pontius Pilate [...]«. Here, the birth of Jesus is mentioned and, immediately afterwards, his death. The entire *life* of Jesus of Nazareth, including his proclamation of the gospel of the kingdom of God is lacking. There can be no doubt: if an ecumenical

---

[11] Josef Wohlmuth (ed.), *Dekrete der ökumenischen Konzilien*, vol. 1: *Konzilien des ersten Jahrtausends. Vom Konzil von Nizäa (325) bis zum Vierten Konzil von Konstantinopel (869/70)*, 2nd ed. (Paderborn: Schöningh, 1998), 31.

[12] Avery Dulles, »Zur Überwindbarkeit von Lehrdifferenzen: Überlegungen aus Anlaß zweier neuerer Lösungsvorschläge,« *Theologische Quartalschrift* 166, no. 4 (1986): 278–289, here 280.

creed was to be written *today*, it would be a different one. However, the innumerable attempts to draft modern Christian creeds have clearly shown that such attempts, too, are not free from weaknesses regarding content and form and, in addition, are at least as much contextualized as are the creeds of the early churches[13] – a text of universal character, like that of the Nicene-Constantinopolitan Creed, could hardly be devised today.[14] The Creed of Nicaea-Constantinople does certainly not stipulate all elements of faith, but all those which were considered fundamental in the time of the Early Church. Since not *all* differences in faith, but only a dissent on *fundamental* beliefs, entail the break-up of the communion of churches, it is true for all Christian churches and communities affirming this creed: »What is common among us is stronger than what divides us.«[15]

3   The Creed as Space of Freedom

What would be the consequences for our ecumenical relations if we seriously acted according to this conviction? If we held to the principle that the faith as professed in the Symbol of Nicaea and Constantinople was not only a *necessary* but also *a sufficient* condition for full communion among churches? The consequences would be considerable. For there is a close and indispensable connection between these three dimensions: *communion in faith, communion of churches* and *communion in the eucharist*. According to traditional conviction, the communion in faith is the essential prerequisite for a communion of churches and the latter finds its strongest expression in the communion of the eucharist (»full communion«). This means that the problem of the (lacking) full communion, which many believers at the basis as well as ecumenical professionals consider the most pressing issue in interconfessional relations, could be solved (only) if a sufficient union in faith was ascertained. In the past,

---

[13]   Cf. Zink, *Das christliche Bekenntnis*.

[14]   Concerning the problems related to the formulation of new credal texts, see Konferenz Europäischer Kirchen in Europa/Rat der Europäischen Bischofskonferenzen »Unser Credo – Quelle der Hoffnung,« in *Gemeinsam glauben und bekennen*, 256–268, here 259.

[15]   Karl Lehmann and Wolfhart Pannenberg (eds.), *Lehrverurteilungen – kirchentrennend?*, vol. 1: *Rechtfertigung, Sakramente und Amt im Zeitalter der Reformation und heute*, Dialog der Kirchen. Veröffentlichungen des ökumenischen Arbeitskreises evangelischer und katholischer Theologen 4 (Freiburg: Herder, 1986), 196.

many churches have stated maximal demands for this. Especially the Roman Catholic Church (which does not grant union in the eucharist to the Anglican Church and all other Protestant churches) and even more so the Orthodox Church (which does not accept union in the eucharist with the Roman Catholic Church) state a lack of common faith as a reason for this. First and foremost, a lack of agreement on various aspects concerning the ministry are considered as an obstacle.

Over the past decades, academic ecumenical theology and numerous avenues of bilateral and multilateral dialogues between churches have sought to achieve a convergence regarding the question of ministry. The problems related thereto have turned out to constitute the »hard core« of the interconfessional dialogue. Although a clear definition of the respective positions and their theological premises has been achieved, the differences seem to remain insurmountable. One reason for this may be that the problems concerning ministry – more so than other dogmatic issues – correspond to a concrete reality, which leaves little room for vague formulae of compromise or competing truth claims. The ministers of the church themselves dispute the questions concerning their ministry and fail to find an agreement. Continuing the dispute with the means employed in the past seems to make little sense. However, it might help to adopt a different perspective with respect to the questions at stake – and even to change the paradigms. A return to the Creed of Nicaea-Constantinople could serve just that purpose: if the ministry of the church (like many other controversial theological issues) is not mentioned where the fundamentals of the faith are summarized, then it is probably not a fundamental of the faith.

Now, the decisive question is whether the »communion in faith«, which is the prerequisite for communion of the church and communion in the eucharist, only relates to these »fundamentals of the faith« (as they are stated in the creed) or to the »totality of the faith«. In the encyclical *Mortalium animos* of 1928, the Roman Catholic Church answered that question in the latter sense when Pope PIUS XI. stated: »Besides this, in connection with things which must be believed, it is nowise licit to use that distinction which some have seen fit to introduce between those articles of faith which are *fundamental* and those which are *not fundamental*, as they say, as if the former are to be accepted by all, while the latter may be left to the free assent of the faithful.«[16] This probably alludes to the »branch theory« that had been developed in the Anglican

---

[16] »Mortalium animos,« in: Denzinger, *Kompendium*, 998.

Church. However, the Second Vatican Council seems to converge on this idea in some way in its Decree on Ecumenism, which states: »When comparing doctrines with one another, one should remember that in the Catholic doctrine there exists a »hierarchy« of truths, since they vary in their relation to the fundamental Christian faith.«[17]

As we know, in the tradition of the Protestant churches, only a limited number of fundamentals of the faith and conditions for the unity of the church are stated – as, for example, in the famous *satis est* in Article VII of the *Confessio Augustana*.[18] Therefore, it is primarily the Roman Catholic Church and the Orthodox Church who consider the communion in faith – and thus the prerequisites for communion of the church and communion in the eucharist – to be lacking. These scruples could be overcome if one accepts that the Nicene-Constantinopolitan Creed summarizes all fundamental doctrines of Christian faith. At least this seems to have been the intention of the »318 Fathers« of the First Ecumenical Council, who drafted this text in order to distinguish the Catholic Church from the heretics. Had they only intended to reject the heresy of Arianism, they could have confined their propositions to the subject of Christology. Instead, they formulated a creed with three articles and they included many statements which had not been controversial. The threefold structure of the Creed refers to the trinity in God – another hint to the fact that this is to be understood as an all-encompassing summary of the essentials of the Christian faith. It begins with the *arche*, the creation of heaven and earth, and it ends with the *telos*, the life in the world to come.

Since the reference to the tradition of the early church is particularly important for the Orthodox and Roman Catholic Churches, the focus on the Creed as a basis for Christian unity could help them to take a new perspective on the ecumenical controversies. The »ambiguous relationship between diversity and unity«, which the Consultation of *Societas Oecumenica* is to reflect, would thus be seen from a new angle. For the Creed may serve the church for *two* purposes: it forms a basis for *unity* – and, at the same time, by virtue of its »open space« allows for *diversity*. Due to its limitation to the essentials, it opens a space of freedom that enables the catholicity and universality of the church.

---

[17] Unitatis redintegratio, No. 11, in *Kleines Konzilskompendium: Sämtliche Texte des Zweiten Vatikanums*, eds. Karl Rahner and Herbert Vorgrimler, 27th ed. (Freiburg: Herder, 1998), 240.

[18] Pöhlmann, *Unser Glaube*, 64.

Kirchliche Identitäten
und ökumenische Katholizität
Michael Plathow

Die Katholizität der Kirche wird im Nicaeno-Constantinopolitanum von fast allen Kirchen bekannt von der universalen Kirche Jesu Christi. Sie ist Gabe in Jesus Christus, real und aktualisiert durch den heiligen Geist je neu in den empirisch erfahrbaren partikularen Kirchen mit ihren ekklesialen Identitäten, für die die gegebene und bekannte Katholizität immer auch Aufgabe ist. Dem soll in methodischen Schritten nachgegangen werden.

Der Zugang für diese Überlegungen sind – eine Denkbewegung eröffnend – die sozialwissenschaftlichen und kultursoziologischen Regulative: Identität und Differenz, Differenz und Verständigung, Verständigung und Gemeinschaft in einer von der Spannung von Vielheit und Einheit geprägten pluralistischen Gesellschaft. Die Regulative könnten wohl einen geschichtlichen Prozess beschreiben, der dann allerdings das implizite Axiom eines Fortschrittsmodells in sich zu tragen droht. Diese Regulative stehen vielmehr in einer Wechselbeziehung, wie historische Beispielanalysen zeigen. Auch die ökumenischen Wechselbeziehungen der Kirchen sind entsprechend von ihnen beeinflusst.

Das Thema »Kirchliche Identitäten und ökumenische Katholizität« soll entfaltet werden in den Schritten 1. »Identität und Differenz«, 2. »Differenz und Verständigung«, 3. »Verständigung und Gemeinschaft«.

1 Konfessionelle Differenzen kirchlicher Identitäten heute

Der eine und die andere von uns mag noch die Fernsehwerbung einer bekannten Autofirma vor Augen haben: nicht nur das schwarze oder das weiße Schaf, sondern die verschiedenen einzigfarbigen Schafe werben durch Abgrenzung für das eigene Besonders- und Anderssein. Anderssein durch Abgrenzung schafft Aufmerksamkeit für das unterscheidende Selbstsein und für die eigene Identität – in der Autowerbung für den durch Identitätsmarker ausgezeichneten Klassewagen.

Irgendwie spiegelt sich hier die geistige und gesellschaftliche Situation unserer Zeit wider: in den ununterscheidbaren Zusammenhängen der Globalisierung durch Differenzierung mit eigenen Alleinstellungsmerkmalen identitätsstiftend und identifikatorisch zu sein, im Gleichmachenden und Gleichgültigen aufzufallen, aufmerken zu lassen und Einzigkeit auszustrahlen.

Diesen differenztheoretischen Trend spiegelt in seiner Weise die gegenwärtige Situation und Diskussion der ökumenischen Bewegung wider. Einige kurz genannte Beispiele mögen das veranschaulichen:

Die römisch-katholische Kirche und Theologie bewegt gegenwärtig die Auseinandersetzung über die Auslegung des Zweiten Vatikanischen Konzils und seiner Erklärungen durch einerseits die »Hermeneutik der Diskontinuität« und andererseits die »Hermeneutik der Kontinuität«[1] mit kirchlicher Tradition und Lehramt; das geschieht im Kontext gesamtkirchlicher und kurialer Zentralisierung.[2] Signifikant ist der Streit um das Verständnis des »subsistit in« in der dogmatischen Konstitution über die Kirche »Lumen gentium«, Kap 8 nach der abgrenzenden lehramtlichen Erklärung »Dominus Iesus«, Anm. 56 (6.8.2000) und den »Antworten auf Fragen zu einigen Aspekten bezüglich der Lehre über die Kirche« (29.6.2007). Und auch bei römisch-katholischen Theologen der Ökumene hat die Frage von »struktureller Kontinuität«[3] und »struktureller Identität«[4] eine methodische Funktion.

Im orthodoxen Bereich betont die Erklärung der Moskauer Bischofssynode »Grundlegende Prinzipien der Beziehung der Russischen-

---

[1] Ansprache PAPST BENEDIKT XVI. an das Kardinalskollegium und die Mitglieder der Römischen Kurie beim Weihnachtsempfang 2004, in: Verlautbarungen des Apostolischen Stuhls (VapS) 172, 11.

[2] Kongregation für die Glaubenslehre: Schreiben an die Bischöfe der katholischen Kirche über einige Aspekte der Kirche als Communio, in: VApS 107, 9.

[3] M. KEHL, Die Kirche. Eine katholische Ekklesiologie, Würzburg 1992, 277–319.

[4] W. BEINERT in: WOLFGANG BEINERT/ULRICH KÜHN, Ökumenische Dogmatik, Leipzig 2013, 535ff.

Orthodoxen Kirche zu den Nicht-Orthodoxen« (2000) die sich von westlichen Kirchen abgrenzend ausschließende Identifizierung mit der sichtbaren Kirche Jesu Christi; dem korrespondiert die Zunahme der kulturelle Identifizierung des neuen russischen Staates mit der Orthodoxie.

In der Anglikanischen Kirche, immer durch ökumenisches Engagement gekennzeichnet, wirft u. a. Paul Avis die Frage nach der »Anglikanischen Identität« auf. Entsprechend lässt sich ein differenztheoretisches Interesse in den sog. Freikirchen feststellen, um historisch aus der selbsteigenen Kirchengeschichte und ihren Urständen identifikatorische Merkmale wahrzugeben; es sei nur auf Hans-Jürgen Goertz Arbeiten zur »mennonitischen Identität« verwiesen.[5]

Seit 1977 ist das Thema »Lutherische Identität« in die Arbeit des Lutherischen Weltbundes involviert. Und im Zusammenhang der Reformationsdekade werden die konfessionsunterscheidenden Ansätze und theologischen Aspekte der verschiedenen Reformatoren etwa von J. Hus, M. Luther, Ph. Melanchthon, J. Zwingli, J. Calvin, von M. Luthers Katechismen und vom Heidelberger Katechismus historisch profiliert. Zudem gibt es Differenzen in der Zielgebung des Jubiläums 2017. Und auch innerhalb der Evangelischen Kirche in Deutschland entzündet sich die Auseinandersetzung über die Kirchengemeinschaft bekenntnisgleicher und bekenntnisverschiedener Gliedkirchen – trotz verstärktem Miteinander – immer wieder an grundlegenden und konkreten Fragen wie beim Thema »Ökumene der Profile«.

Das konfessionelle Gedächtnis verdichtet sich in der selbst vertretenen oder von außen zugesprochenen Identität und Differenz. Versuchen wir uns darum dem zu nähern, was mit Identität gemeint ist.

Von Identität sowie von Profil ist gegenwärtig viel die Rede. Nicht selten wird »Identität« und »Profil« bedeutungsgleich wechselseitig gebraucht. Jedoch entstammen sie verschiedenen Begriffstraditionen: zum einen der Individualpsychologie und gesellschaftlichen Sozialpsychologie, zum andern der mathematischen Geometrie.

»Profil« bedeutet der etymologischen Herkunft von »profilare« nach: einen Strich ziehen in einer Ebene; Umreißen mit einer Linie, die im Unterscheiden von Innen und Außen charakteristische Eigenbilder markiert, ein unverwechselbares Bild festhalten und nach außen erscheinen lassen. Es handelt sich um eine statische, festgelegte

---

[5] H.-J. GOERTZ, Art. Identität (mennonitisch), in: H.-J. GOERTZ, F. ENNS u. a. (Hrsg.), Mennonitisches Lexikon (MennLex), Bd. V.2, Hamburg 2010, 143ff.

Kennzeichnung mit ausstrahlender Wirkung. So bestimmen politische Parteien und soziale Hilfsorganisationen, Firmen und Kaufhausreihen, Universitäten und Schulen, Kirchengemeinden und kirchliche Werke ihr Profil.

Wolfgang Huber hat anlässlich der Begegnung mit Papst Benedikt XVI. beim Weltjugendtag in Köln das Modell der »Ökumene der Profile« für eine profilierte Ökumene ins Gespräch gebracht. Ein Modell bildet einerseits Beziehungsgefüge primärer Sachverhalte, gesellschaftlicher und naturwissenschaftlicher, ab. Andererseits wird es als »erklärungskräftige Anschauung«[6] verstanden, der in geschichtlicher Offenheit eine heuristische und didaktische Funktion eigen ist für Erkenntnis- und Erklärungsprozesse mit pragmatischer Absicht. Beim Symposium »Ökumene der Profile« mit Kardinal Karl Lehmann am 29.5.2006 erklärte Wolfgang Huber in Abgrenzung sowohl von einer Kontrovers- als auch von einer Rückkehrökumene:

> Es gibt nach meiner Wahrnehmung keine Kirche, keine Konfession, kein kirchliches Werk und keine Gemeinde, die nicht auf Grund der schwieriger gewordenen kirchlichen Situation in unserer Gesellschaft mit einer Profilierung des je Eigenen antwortet. ... Denn der Verlust an selbstverständlicher gesellschaftlicher Relevanz, die finanziellen Einbrüche und die neuen Herausforderungen führen unvermeidlich und Gott sei Dank dazu, dass wir das je Spezifische, das je eigene Profil, das sog. Alleinstellungsmerkmal betonen. ... Aber die unvermeidliche Rückseite dieser Herausforderung lautet: Je stärker das je eigene Profil betont wird, desto deutlicher treten auch die Unterschiede hervor. Damit verbindet sich die Gefahr einer Profilierungsfalle: Jede Kirche oder Konfession muss sich profilieren, aber gerade damit geraten die Sensoren und Andockstationen für ökumenische Gemeinsamkeiten in den Schatten.[7]

In diesem Sinn betont W. Huber am 13.9.2006 bei der 6. Vollversammlung der »Gemeinschaft Evangelischer Kirchen in Europa (GEKE)« in Budapest für das Modell der »Ökumene der Profile« »keine Einschränkung der ökumenischen Verpflichtung; sie beschreibt vielmehr ein unaufgebbares und unausweichliches Moment des ökumenischen Weges. Die Rede von einer Ökumene der Profile soll den ökumenischen

---

[6] D. RITSCHL, Modell und Methode – Implizite Axiome der Theoriewahl in der Psychosomatischen Medizin, in: P. HAHN u. a. (Hrsg.), Modell und Methode in der Psychosomatik, Weinheim 1994, 13.

[7] epd-Dok 24/06, 7f.

Einsatz unserer Kirche auf neue Weise unterstreichen. Wir wollen das Gemeinsame stärken. Den einen Glauben haben wir zu bekennen, weil wir an den einen Herrn gebunden sind. Die eine Taufe feiern wir, weil uns der eine Geist bestimmt. ... Auch darüber müssen wir Auskunft geben, was uns – einstweilen – an voller und sichtbarer Kirchengemeinschaft hindert«.[8]

Auf der Basis der Gemeinsamkeit wehrt somit das Modell der »Ökumene der Profile« zum einen eine Selbstdefinierung bloß vom Andern her ab, etwa des Protestantischen bloß vom typisch Römisch-Katholischen; zum andern setzt sie gegen exklusive Selbstverabsolutierung ökumenischen Einsatz frei: gemeinsames Zeugnis des Evangeliums in der Welt und arbeitsteilige Kooperation in einer Ökumene der Charismen. Denn nur wer die Frage »Wer bin ich? bzw. Wer sind wir?« zu beantworten vermag, wer um die eigene Gottes- und Lebensgewissheit weiß und um das Selbstverständnis seiner Kirche, ist in der Ökumene gesprächs- und dialogfähig und vermag profilierte Ökumene als Ökumene der Charismen zu leben.

Eine Fortführung des statischen Modells der »Ökumene der Profile« will das Bedenken der sozialpsychologischen und kulturwissenschaftlichen Beziehung von Identität und Differenz sein. Identität[9] – hier in der Unterscheidung, aber nicht Trennung von individuell-persönlicher und kollektiv-sozialer Identität verstanden – meint keine substantialistische Bestimmung, keine statische Festlegung; sie impliziert vielmehr die Relation von Innen- und Außenbild, von Selbstbeschreibung und Fremdbeschreibung, die Wechselbeziehung von Innen- und Außenperspektive. Identität erweist sich als Beziehung zum Andern und zu einer anderen Assoziation in Verbundenheit und Abgrenzung. Identität beschreibt die Selbigkeit, die Einzigkeit vor sich und vor Anderen, die Verschiedenheit mit sich und mit Anderen umfasst, Unverwechselbarkeit und Zugehörigkeit, Zugehörigkeit des einzelnen zu einer Gemeinschaft, einem Kollektiv, einer Gesellschaft, einem Staat, einer Kirche usw. In dieser Wechselbeziehung von Selbigkeit und Alterität zeigt sich Identität sowohl als fragmentarisch und als zukunftsoffen als auch – im verändernden Erneuern – als Grenze für den Andern. Zwischen Selbstdiffusion einerseits und Selbstgenügsamkeit andererseits erschließt sich Identität als unterscheidendes Selbstsein und Selbstwerden im Aneignen des Anderen bei Durchhalten der Differenz. Denn indem man

---

[8] epd-Dok 42/06, 52.
[9] Vgl. auch: K. GLOY, Art. Identität I. Philosophisch, in: TRE 16, 25–28; W. KERN, Art. Identität, in: Sacr. mundi 2, 788–795.

sich an die Stelle des Anderen als Anderer versetzt, ergänzen und bereichern sich Identitäten gegenseitig im Werden. So wächst Identität, wo Pluralität möglich ist und Wirklichkeit sich differenziert.

Christliche Identität konstituiert die exzentrische Beziehung des Menschen durch das gnädige Erbarmen des dreieinen Gottes in seiner Selbsterschließung in Jesus Christus durch den heiligen Geist, wie sie Glaubenden in der Taufe zugeeignet wird und in der ökumenischen Kirchengemeinschaft bekannt wird. Man kann mit Jan Assmann[10] sagen, dass christliche Identität »kanonische Qualität« im Differenzverhältnis zu anderen Religionen hat. Konfessionelle und kirchliche Identitäten stellen »Stil«-Differenzen dar; so ist der Makrostil der Orthodoxen, des römischen-Katholizismus, des pluralen Protestantismus und der emergenten Pfingstler zu unterscheiden.

Protestantische Identität etwa[11] – wie Kirchenhistoriker, Dogmatiker und Ökumeniker nachweisen – ist in ihrer Konfessions-, Kirchen- und Lebensgeschichte originär vom biblisch-reformatorischen Gedächtnis geprägt, d. h. von der Rechtfertigung allein aus Gnade um Christi willen durch den Glauben in der Anrede vom Wort des dreieinen Gottes und im Studieren der biblischen Schriften, d. h. von den vier reformatorischen Freiheiten: sola scriptura, solus Christus, sola gratia, sola fide im Bekenntnis des dreieinen Gottes. Bei aller Pluriformität ist den protestantischen Kirchen mit den Reformatoren die Verwurzelung in der Alten Kirche mit den altkirchlichen Bekenntnissen und den Kirchenvätern gemeinsam. Evangelisches Christ- und Kirchesein und -werden wird gelebt mit Bibel und Gesangbuch in Freiheit und Verantwortung als Priestertum der Getauften im Bekenntnis des Gottesdienstes am Sonntag und im Alltag. So erschließt protestantische Identität im Rechtfertigungsglauben von der »Freiheit eines Christenmenschen« ein neues Menschen- und Wirklichkeitsverständnis: die externe Beziehung vor Gott und vor der Welt als gelebten Glauben in der Selbigkeit und Differenz von »zugleich Gerechter und Sünder« und »zugleich sündige und gerechtfertigte Kirche« im Vorletzten getroster Heilsgewissheit

---

[10] ALEIDA UND JAN ASSMANN, Kanon und Zensur, in: dies. (Hrsg.), Kanon und Zensur. Archäologie der literarischen Kommunikation 2, München 1987, 7–27; vgl. auch: TH. SUNDERMEIER, Christliche Identität angesichts der Vielfalt der Konfessionen und Religionen, in: MD-EZW 7/2002, 199–205.

[11] Vgl. auch: M. PLATHOW, Heute evangelisch sein: Evangelische Identität und Ökumene, in: K.-R. TRAUNER/B. ZIMMERMANN (Hrsg.), 100 Jahre Evangelischer Bund in Österreich. BH 100, Göttingen 2003, 146–164; DERS., Gabe und Aufgabe auf dem ökumenischen Weg. Evangelische Identität und Kirchengemeinschaft, in: evangelische Aspekte 13, 2003, 15–18.

und freier Gewissensentscheidung der Liebe – eine fragmentarische Identität des gerechtfertigten Sünders, die Anfechtungen und Diskrepanzerfahrungen kennt und zugleich zukunftsoffen durch die Gnade in Jesus Christus die Ganzheit im Letzten bei Gott erhofft.

Damit ist evangelische Identität zugleich geprägt durch Differenzurteile in der historischen Beziehung zum römisch Katholizismus: etwa zum römischen Messopfer, zum Ablasswesen, zur Mitwirkung des Menschen am ewigen Heil, zum Priesterzölibat, zur geistlichen Höherwertigkeit der Mönche, zur hierarchischen Struktur der Kirche nach göttlichem Recht mit dem unfehlbaren und jurisdiktionellen Papstprimat. Damit bedeutet zusammen mit den spätscholastischen, mystischen und humanistischen Strömungen die Reformation die Geburtsstunde der Pluralität, der kirchlichen und gesellschaftlichen, auf dem Kontinent, der mit diesem Profil Europa heißt. Identität wächst, wo Pluralität und Freiheit möglich ist und Wirklichkeit sich differenziert, d. h. in einer freiheitlich pluralistischen Gesellschaft.

Kirchengeschichtliche und dogmatisch-theologische Forschungen sind es, die die Wechselbeziehungen von konfessionellen Differenzen und kirchlichen Identitäten in Geschichte und Gegenwart aufzeigen.

2 Ökumenische Verständigung in der Mannigfaltigkeit konfessioneller und kirchlicher Differenzen

Die dynamische Wechselbeziehung von Differenz und Verständigung schließt die Spannung von Einheit und Vielheit, »unum et multum« ein.[12] Seit den griechischen Naturphilosophen Parmenides und Heraklit bestimmt sie – bei der sich durchsetzenden Dominanz des Unum im Begründungszusammenhang platonischen und neuplatonischen Denkens – nicht nur das philosophische Denken, sondern auch kirchliche und gesellschaftliche Strukturen und Lebensformen. Die Vielheit erfährt demgegenüber im hebräischen Denken und in den biblischen, besonders auch den neutestamentlichen Schriften, ihre eigene Bedeutung. Grundlegend sind, wie die historische Forschung der Exegeten zeigt, die unterschiedlichen Genera kanonischer Schriften, die situativ geprägten Zeugnisse, die jeweiligen Aussagestrukturen, die von der Sache her paradoxal formulierte Glaubensrede etwa von Jesus von Nazareth, Gottes eingeborenem Sohn unserm Herrn und Bruder, die

---

[12] W. BEINERT, Wieviel Einheit braucht die Kirche Christi?, in: Cath 58, 2001, 1–18.

Polyphonie zur Heilsbedeutung des Todes Jesu, die Mannigfaltigkeit der Auferstehungsberichte und Hoheitstitel Jesu, die differierenden Gemeindeformen.

Der Ökumeniker E. Schlink stellt Unterschiede in den dogmatischen, d. h. auch in den konfessionellen und kirchlichen, Aussagen fest,

> wenn Augustin über den menschlichen Willen gegenüber einem selbstsicheren Voluntarismus und ethizistischen Aktivismus spricht und wenn gleichzeitig östliche Theologen die Willensfreiheit gegenüber einer naturhaften und deterministischen Verkennung des Menschen durch die Gnosis behaupten, – wenn Thomas von Aquin über Gottes Sein und Wesen vor allem in aristotelischer, Gregor Palamas aber vor allem in neuplatonischer Begrifflichkeit lehrt, – wenn das Chalcedonense in der Struktur der Doxologie oder in einer theoretischen Verhältnisbestimmung der göttlichen und menschlichen Natur entfaltet wird, wenn die Reformatoren die Rechtfertigungslehre in der Struktur personaler Begegnung des göttlichen Wortes mit dem Hörer oder wenn das Tridentinum seine Aussagen zum selben Thema in der Struktur der Beschreibung des Rechtfertigungsvorgangs macht.[13]

Aber nicht auf die phänomenologische Analyse von Differenzen ist die ökumenische Methodologie ausgerichtet; vielmehr zielt sie auf Verständigung und nimmt den Ausgang beim Gemeinsamen. Signifikant ist dafür die gerade den Kirchenhistorikern eigene konfessionskundliche Forschung: von der komparativen Symbolik der Kontroverstheologie wandte sie sich über den Vergleich der Konfessionen hin zur ökumenischen Konfesssionskunde. Römisch-katholischerseits steht dafür die Veränderung von den Werken J. A. Möhlers[14] hin zur »Konfessionskunde« Konrad Algermissens (1930).[15] Evangelischerseits steht dafür die Entwicklung von Karl v. Hases[16] »Polemik« über Ferdinand

---

[13] E. SCHLINK, Die Aufgabe einer ökumenischen Dogmatik, in: ders. mit A. PETERS (Hrsg.), Zur Auferbauung des Leibes Christi, FS Peter Brunner zum 65. Geburtstag, Kassel 1965, 90f; ders., Die Methode des ökumenischen Dialogs, in: KuD 12, 1966, 207f.

[14] J. A. MÖHLER, Symbolik der Darstellung der dogmatischen Gegensätze der Katholiken und Protestanten nach den öffentlichen Bekenntnisschriften, Mainz 1832.

[15] in 8. Auflage 1970 herausgegeben von H. FRIES, E. ISERLOH, L. KLEIN, W. DE VRIES.

[16] K. V. HASE, Handbuch der protestantischen Polemik gegen die römisch-katholische Kirche, Leipzig 1862 ([6]1894).

Kattenbuschs[17] »Vergleichende Confessionskunde« hin zu den ökumenisch ausgerichteten Konfessionskunden von Ernst Benz,[18] Peter Meinhold,[19] Friedrich Heyer[20] und Reinhard Frieling.[21]

Die Abkehr von der Kontroverstheologie hin zur Methode, vom Gemeinsamen her die konfessionellen und kirchlichen Differenzen zu analysieren, wurde auf der Konferenz für »Glauben und Kirchenverfassung« in Lund 1952 festgeschrieben. E. Schlink beschrieb sie in seiner »Ökumenischen Dogmatik« als »kopernikanische Wende«:[22]

> Wir haben die anderen christlichen Gemeinschaften nicht mehr so anzusehen, als ob sie sich um unsere Kirche als Mitte bewegen, so wie vor Kopernikus die Planeten als sich um die Erde drehend verstanden worden waren, sondern wir müssen erkennen, dass wir mit den anderen Gemeinschaften zusammen gleichsam wie Planeten um Christus als die Sonne kreisen und von ihm das Licht empfangen ... (wir) werden nur so, von Christus her, die eigene und die fremde Wirklichkeit erkennen. Wir müssen lernen, uns gewissermaßen von außen zu sehen.

Die Abkehr von Kontroverstheologie und kirchlichen Anathematisierung und die Kehre hin zur ökumenischen Verständigung und Theologie wurde in eminenter Weise verstärkt durch das Zweite Vatikanische Konzil (11.10.1962–8.12.1965). Das II. Vaticanum erweist sich als Wende gegenüber der Enzyklika »Mortalium animos« (6.1.1928) durch das Sich-Einbringen der römisch-katholischen Kirche in die ökumenische Bewegung und in das partnerschaftliche Mitwirken in der Abteilung für »Glauben und Kirchenverfassung« des ÖRK seit Löwen 1971. Sein »aggiornamento« mit den Entscheidungen der Konzilsväter in den Konstitutionen, Dekreten und Erklärungen stellt ein Paradigmenwechsel dar. Besonders hervorgehoben seien die biblisch-theologische Grundlegung der Verlautbarungen, die Unterscheidung zwischen Inhalt des Glaubens und seiner Aussageform, ferner die Liturgiereform; zu verweisen ist auf die – wie Wolfgang Thönissen mit Lothar Ulrich

---

17 F. Kattenbusch, Lehrbuch der vergleichenden Confessionskunde, Freiburg i.Br. 1890.
18 E. Benz, Die Ostkirche im Licht der protestantischen Geschichtsschreibung, Freiburg/München 1952.
19 P. Meinhold, Ökumenische Kirchenkunde, Stuttgart 1962.
20 F. Heyer, Kirchenkunde, Berlin 1977.
21 R. Frieling/E. Geldbach/R. Thöle, Konfessionskunde. Orientierung im Zeichen der Ökumene, Bensheim 1999.
22 E. Schlink, Ökumenische Dogmatik, Göttingen ²1985, 696.

feststellt – »Öffnungsklausel« des »subsistit in, verwirklicht in«, der dogmatischen Konstitution über die Kirche, Kap. 8 im Modell gestufter Kirchengemeinschaft entgegen dem »est« in der die sichtbare römisch-katholische Kirche mit dem Leib Christi identifzierenden Enzyklika »Mystici corporis« (1943), sowie auf die Bezeichnung der aus der Reformation hervorgegangenen Christen und christlichen Gemeinschaften als »Brüder« im »Ökumenismusdekret« (21.11.1964) gegenüber der Abwertung als Schismatiker oder Ketzer; hervorzuheben ist weiter die Veränderung durch die Erklärung der Religionsfreiheit in »Dignitatis humanae« (7. 12. 1965) gegenüber den lehramtlichen Verlautbarungen Papst Gregors XVI. (1831–1846) und überhaupt des 19. Jahrhunderts, die heilende Wertung anderer Religionen in »Nostra actate« (28.10.1965) gegenüber früherer Verurteilungen als »falsae religiones« und natürlich das Ökumenismusdekret »Unitatis redintegratio« (21.11.1964); Dialog und Verständigung werden nicht nur ermöglicht, sondern postuliert, initiiert und realisiert. Mit der Wende zur Ökumene und der methodologischen Kehre wurde das Gemeinsame, das Koinon, als größer erkannt als das Trennende und der ökumenische Weg, der auf Konvergenz und Koinonia ausgerichtet ist, als unumkehrbar anerkannt.

Der Verständigung über ökumenische Gemeinsamkeiten diente E. Schlinks strukturanalytische Methode, die in den verschiedenen konfessionellen Antworten auf das eine Evangelium die Möglichkeit einer theologischen Konvergenz oder eines Konsenses erkennt; vertieft wird dieser Ansatz durch die historischen Analysen zeitbedingter Gegenpositionen und situationsbedingter Polemiken oder Missverständnisse und sachbezogener Paradoxien.

Dieser methodische Ansatz fand im evangelischen Raum als Sternstunde das differenzierte Dialogergebnis in der »Leuenberger Konkordie« (1973) und in der Kirchengemeinschaft der »Gemeinschaft Evangelischer Kirchen in Europa«. Im weiten ökumenischen Raum führte er zur Konvergenzerklärung von Lima zu »Taufe, Eucharistie, Amt« (1981) und mit der methodischen Weiterentwicklung durch den »differenzierten Konsens« in Grundwahrheiten der evangelisch-lutherischen und römisch-katholischen Rechtfertigungslehre zur offiziellen »Gemeinsamen Erklärung der Rechtfertigungslehre« (31.10.1999). Auch die Selbstverpflichtungen der »Charta oecumenica« (2001) und die gegenseitige Anerkennung der Taufe in Magdeburg am 29.4.2007 sind in diesem methodischen Zusammenhand zu verstehen.

Diese Verständigung als theologische »Konvergenz« oder als »differenzierter Konsens« ist – bei bestehenden Differenzen – in der Ökumene des Dialogs und des Lebens durch die »Hermeneutik des Anderen«

und des »Vertrauens« geleitet: der Andere wird in seiner Andersheit anerkannt und zugleich, indem das eigene Selbst sich vom Anderen her wahrnimmt, die Andersheit als Vertiefung und Bereicherung der eigenen Identität verstanden, weil eine gemeinsame Vertrauensbeziehung vorausgesetzt ist: der Glaube an Jesus Christus, in dem sich der dreieine Gott gegenwärtig im Heiligen Geist offenbart zum Heil der Menschen durch Wort und Sakrament, wie die Christen im Geschenk der Taufe bekennen.

Auch hinter dem neuen ökumenischen Projekt »Grund und Gegenstand des Glaubens nach römisch-katholischer und evangelisch-lutherischer Lehre«[23] steht dieser methodische Ansatz: Indem evangelische und römisch-katholische Theologen die Themen »Offenbarung und Glaube« sowie »Sakrament und Wort« gerade in Theologie und Kirche der »Schwesterkirche« analysieren und die dabei festgestellte Mannigfaltigkeit der Bezeugung der Sache des christlichen Glaubens in seiner Perspektivität wahrnehmen, erkennen sie die »res« des Glaubens in seiner geschichtlichen und dynamischen Identität zwischen Erkennen, Neu-Entdecken und Neu-Artikulieren.[24] D. Ritschl umschrieb diese »res« des Glaubens – über dogmatisch festgestellte Konsense[25] hinaus – im »Christus praesens«, der sich nach den neutestamentlichen Zeugnissen in folgender Weise zu erkennen gibt: (1) die Anbetung des dreieinen und barmherzigen Gottes, (2) das Weitererzählen der Geschichte von Abraham bis zu Jesu Kreuz, Auferstehung und Kommen in Herrlichkeit, (3) das persönliche Eintreten für diese Geschichte, (4) das Eintreten für andere, auch für Nichtglaubende, (5) die Freiheit, sich im ethischen Verhalten immer als Glied einer Glaubensgemeinschaft zu verstehe,[26] die – wie ich ergänze – im Glauben an Jesus Christus und in der Taufe im und auf den Namen des dreieinen Gottes gründet.

Ökumenische Verständigung in der Mannigfaltigkeit konfessioneller und kirchlicher Differenzen setzt somit voraus die christliche Identität

---

[23] E. HERMS/L. ZAK (Hrsg.), Grund und Gegenstand des Glaubens nach römisch-katholischer und evangelisch-lutherischer Lehre. Theologische Studien, Tübingen 2008. Vgl. dazu: F. NÜSSEL, Glaubensgegenstand und Glaubenslehre. Zur Dynamik der Lehrentwicklung und Lehrverständigung in der Geschichte des Christentums, in: MdKI 59, 2008, 89–93.

[24] Vgl. auch: J. WERBICK, Grundfragen der Ekklesiologie, Freiburg/Basel/Wien 2009, 56.

[25] E. SCHLINK, Ökumenische Dogmatik, 673–685.

[26] D. RITSCHL, Konsens ist nicht das höchste Ziel. Gründe für eine Hermeneutik des Vertrauens in den Christus praesens, in: K. RAISER/D. SATTLER (Hrsg.), Ökumene vor neuen Zeiten, Freiburg/Basel/Wien 2000, 531–547, hier 545.

als Grund des christlichen Glaubens in den differierenden konfessionellen Identitäten, wobei die konfessionellen Identitäten bezogen sind auf den Grund des christlichen Glaubens und in »konfessionellen Selbstverständigungsprozessen«[27] mit anderen konfessionellen und kirchlichen Identitäten die eigene Identität sich vom Grund des Glaubens her neu versteht. Kirchengeschichtliche Analyse und dogmatische Reflexion sind in diesen ökumenischen Verständigungsprozessen unabdingbar und kooperieren in Verantwortung vor dem, was sie verbindet: die Sache des christlichen Glaubens.

3 Verständigung und Gemeinschaft als Katholizität der Einheit in Mannigfaltigkeit kirchlicher Identitäten

Auf theologische Konvergenzen und Konsense sowie auf die Koinonia der Kirchen und Menschen ist die differenztheoretische Ökumenehermeneutik des Anderen und des Vertrauens ausgerichtet: auf das Sichtbar-, Erfahrbar- und Lebbarwerden der geglaubten Einheit und Katholizität der Kirchen.

Im Nizäno-Konstantinopolitanum wird die eine, katholische Kirche bekannt. Als geglaubte ist sie die verborgene, real in Jesus Christus als Gabe und Aufgabe des universalen Volkes Gottes, aktualisiert in fragmentarisch sichtbaren Gestaltwerdungen auf die eschatologische »Fülle« und Vollendung hin. Die geglaubte eine, katholische Kirche des dreieinen Gottes versichtbart sich durch den heiligen Geist im gepredigten Wort Gottes, in den Gaben der Sakramente und in den daraus erwachsenden Taten der Liebe in Freiheit und Gerechtigkeit als Gemeinde und Kirche. Es ist der Christus praesens in der Koinonia mannigfaltiger Gemeinden und Kirchen, eine Gemeinschaft in und durch Vielheit.

Denn das Gemeinsame – bei Differenzen – in Inhalt und Aussageform, in Gehalt und Gestalt des christlichen Glaubens ist größer als das Trennende. Dazu gehört das Bekenntnis zum dreieinen Gott, der sich in Jesus Christus, wahrer Gott und wahrer Mensch, als der Liebende zum Heil der Welt offenbart hat, das Vaterunser-Gebet, die biblische Megastory, das gemeinsame Geschenk der Taufe und das Liebesgebot, die

---

[27] Vgl. hierzu: S. DANGEL, Konfessionelle Identität und ökumenische Prozesse. Analysen zum interkonfessionellen Diskurs des Christentums, Berlin/Boston 2014.

Kirchenväter, die Entsprechungen in Liturgie, Hodegetik, Aszetik, Apologetik, Ethik und Ästhetik.

So werden in der Koinonia in und durch Vielheit ökumenische Wortgottesdienste, Andachten und Bibel- und Gebetswochen gefeiert; es werden ökumenische Versammlungen und Kirchentage gemeinsam vorbereitet und gestaltet. Es gibt ökumenische Sozialstationen, diakonisch-karitative Kooperationen der kirchlichen Wohlfahrtsverbände, gemeinsame Erklärungen, Stellungnahmen und Denkschriften zu gesellschaftspolitischen Herausforderungen. Manche Formen des »geistlichen Ökumenismus«, der »kooperativen« und »missionarischen« Ökumene sind heutzutage selbstverständlich geworden; bisweilen tendieren sie zur Selbstgenügsamkeit, so dass die »Charta oecumenica«[28] (22.4.2001) an die Selbstverpflichtung erinnert, »auf allen Ebenen des kirchlichen Lebens gemeinsam zu handeln, wo die Voraussetzungen dafür gegeben sind und nicht Gründe des Glaubens oder größerer Zweckmäßigkeit dem entgegenstehen«.

Trotz mancher Unkenrufe über eine ökumenische Flaute oder eine ökumenische Eiszeit geht der ökumenische Weg weiter. Das gilt besonders für den »geistlichen Ökumenismus« des Lebens in Gebet, Dienst und Sendung, aber auch für die Beziehung von Verständigung und Gemeinschaft in der Dialogökumene, die sich zugleich vor weitere Aufgaben für Kirchenhistoriker, Dogmatiker und Ökumeniker gestellt weiß. Mit E. Schlinks Aspekten der »Darstellung der einen Kirche in der Einigung der getrennten Kirchen«[29] werden in der »Gemeinsamen Erklärung zur Rechtfertigungslehre«, Nr. 43 die weiterhin historisch und theologisch zu behandelnden Themen genannt: »Wort Gottes und kirchliche Lehre, von der Autorität in ihr, von ihrer Einheit, vom Amt und den Sakramenten, schließlich die Beziehung zwischen Rechtfertigung und Sozialethik«. Einige Aspekte sind in der theologischen Studie »Grund und Gegenstand des Glaubens nach römisch-katholischer und evangelisch-lutherischer Lehre« von 2008[30] aufgenommen worden. Unterscheidungsthemen werden das ökumenisch Gespräch weiter bestimmen wie weiterhin »Sakramentsverwaltung und Amt (Priester/PfarrerIn – BischöfIn – Papst – Konzil)« im Kontext der »Ortskirchen«, weiter »Glaube und Vernunft« nach den Enzykliken »Veritatis splendor«[31] und »Fides et ratio«[32] und »Schrift –Tradition – Lehramt«

---

[28] Nr. II,4.
[29] E. Schlink, Ökumenische Dogmatik, 684.
[30] Vgl. E. Herms/L. Zak, Grund und Gegenstand des Glaubens.
[31] VApS 110 (1993).

nach der dogmatischen Konstitution »Dei verbum« (21.11.1964) im Zusammenhang der von Melchior Cano aufgestellten Bezeugungsinstanzen Wort Gottes, Tradition, Lehramt, Theologie und Glaubenssinn. Gerade die zuletzt genannte Bezeugungsinstanz des in »Lumen gentium« Kap. 12 anerkannten und betonten sensus fidelium, der jedoch im CIC (1989) keine Erwähnung findet, sollte nicht nur für den »geistlichen Ökumenismus«, sondern auch für die ökumenischen Lehrdialoge eine zukünftige Forschungsaufgabe von Kirchenrechtshistorikern und ökumenischen Theologen sein; damit ist verbunden das spannungsvolle Verhältnis zwischen geistlicher Rezeption ökumenischer Dialogergebnisse und dem formal rechtlichen Rezeptionsverfahren.[33]

Ökumenische Verständigung und Gemeinschaft zielt auf die konziliare Gemeinschaft versöhnter Verschiedenheit sich gegenseitig als Kirche Jesu Christi anerkennender Kirchen mit wechselseitiger eucharistischer Gastfreundschaft, »damit die Welt glaube« (Joh 17,21), also auf die Katholizität der Einheit in Mannigfaltigkeit konfessioneller Identitäten, die gegründet im und bezogen auf den Grund des christlichen Glaubens sind: den sich im Christus praesens durch den Heiligen Geist zum Heil der Menschen offenbarenden dreieinen Gott, wie die Christen mit und in der Taufe bekennen.

Die wechselseitige Beziehung der sozialwissenschaftlichen und kultursoziologischen Regulative Identität und Differenz, Differenz und Verständigung, Verständigung und Gemeinschaft in Spannung zwischen Vielheit und Einheit impliziert so einen Weg ökumenischer Katholizität des eines Volkes Gottes in Mannigfaltigkeit kirchlicher Identitäten.

---

[32] VApS 135 (1998).
[33] Vgl. M. PLATHOW, Rezeption und Verbindlichkeit. Zur Rezeption ökumenischer Lehrgespräche, in: ZevKR 51, 2006, 49ff; W. BEINERT/U. KÜHN, Ökumenische Dogmatik, Leipzig/Regensburg 2013, 582f, 588.

From Divisive Diversity to Catholic Fullness?
Canon and Ecclesial Unity Reconsidered

Peter-Ben Smit

1 Introduction

At least since Ernst Käsemann forcefully voiced his view that the New Testament canon, with the diversity of views that is inherent to it, provided not so much a basis for ecclesial unity, but rather a justification for denominational diversity,[1] an intense discussion has been taking place on the interrelationship between the (ecumenical ideal of) ecclesial unity and the study of the New Testament, specifically: of New Testament ecclesiology,[2] often arguing against Käsemann,[3] (and the diversity of early Christian texts as such). The question concerning the role of the New Testament canon in all of this, is time and again of importance in this debate: does the canon play a role at all in the study of the New Testament (and early Christian writings in general), and: what should one make of the undeniable diversity in this second part of the canon of the Christian Bible? This contribution purports to give a

[1] Published as: Ernst Käsemann, »Begründet der neutestamentliche Kanon die Einheit der Kirche?,« in *Exegetische Versuche und Besinnungen*, Ernst Käsemann (Göttingen: Vandenhoeck & Ruprecht, 1960), 214–223. – See for a typical critique, e.g. Kurt Koch, »Eenheid van de Kerk in oecumenisch perspectief,« *Communio* 39 (2014): 373–387.

[2] See e.g. influential studies such as J.D.G. Dunn, *Unity and Diversity in the New Testament: An Inquiry into the Character of Earliest Christianity* (London: SCM Press, 1990), and Jürgen Roloff, *Die Kirche im Neuen Testament* (Göttingen: Vandenhoeck & Ruprecht, 1993).

[3] See e.g. the typical critique of Koch, »Eenheid.«

partial answer to such questions, with as its point of departure some recent research on the characteristics of canonical texts, from the fields of biblical studies, cultural studies, and intercultural theology.[4] In doing so, it will become clear that, with a particular, dynamic and dialogical understanding of unity and of canon, it is well possible to argue that the diverse canonical texts (with their diverse historical interrelationships), as they have been brought and bound together in one corpus, the New Testament canon, can be understood as having been placed into a permanent dialogue with each other and the reader in a conversation that is both aimed at discovering the fullness of the meaning of texts and at interpretation in communion through a process of mutual interpretation in each other's context and from each other's perspectives.[5] Unity and the meaning of a (canonical) text appear, when understood from this perspective, both as processes, rather than as somewhat static facts from the past or the present. On this basis, then, it can be argued that reading canonically is always a reading in dialogue, a reading for the fullness of the meaning of texts, and a reading for unity, or at least a reading in communion. In this way, this contribution also aims at creating a bridge between the disciplines of ecumenical studies and New Testament studies.

2 Perspectives on Unity and Canon

When considering the overall trends in New Testament studies concerning the canon and ecclesial unity, two large developments are significant. First, a development concerning the canon can be mentioned. As a topic of serious exegetical concern, the canon has made a comeback from virtual extinction, especially due to new historical scholarship into the phenomenon of canons as such, notably from the field of cultural studies,[6] and because of the influence of various

---

[4] This research is indebted to insights gained while working on a larger project, the monograph *From Canonical Criticism to Ecumenical Hermeneutics* (Leiden: Brill, 2015).

[5] To be sure, this does not infringe upon the need for research into early Christian texts as »non-canonical« as well, both approaches are needed, see for this: Francis Watson, *Gospel Writing: A Canonical Perspective* (Grand Rapids: Eerdmans, 2013).

[6] Especially as influenced by the work of Jan and Aleida Assmann, see, e.g. Jan Assmann, *Das kulturelle Gedächtnis: Schrift, Erinnerung und politische Identität*

branches of *canonical criticism* within the field of biblical studies that seek to take into account the canonical character of biblical texts when interpreting them.[7] Second, concerning the unity of the church in the New Testament, significant developments can also be noted, even if these are less pronounced than those concerning the role of the canon in exegesis. A major impulse for considering early Christian (dis)unity or diversity has been, both prior to and after Käsemann's contribution,[8] Walter Bauer's *Rechtgläubigkeit und Ketzerei im ältesten Christentum*, to which paradigmatic significance has been attributed.[9] Bauer's work reverses an important historiographical paradigm which dominated (at least the most prominent) accounts of the history of early Christianity, as it can be found in texts as early as the Acts of the Apostles, or as influential as the work of Eusebius of Caesarea, and which considers the starting point of the history of the Christian churches an original and orthodox unity, which, due to heresy and sin, developed into a plethora of mutually incompatible churches and denominations. Instead, Bauer argued that at the beginning of early Christianity there was diversity, pluriformity, and even divisiveness, rather than unity, while striving for one church can be seen as a later development, influenced by imperial interests in unity in the realm, now containing a substantial number of Christians, all too prone to infighting and disagreement. In contemporary New Testament studies, Bauer's argument has become hugely influential and continues to be popularized, for example through the influential work of Bart Ehrman, notably in his popular introduction to the early Christian writings.[10] At the same time, just as the notion of the canon is being reconsidered, also the notion of early Christian unity is being revised and reconsidered and,

---

in frühen Hochkulturen (München: Beck, 1992); Aleida Assmann and Jan Assmann (eds.), *Kanon und Zensur* (München: Fink, 1987).

[7] See on this, especially the on the founding fathers of this movement, Brevard S. Childs and James A. Sanders, e.g. Robert W. Wall, »Reading the New Testament in Canonical Context,« in *Hearing the New Testament: Strategies for Interpretation*, ed. Joel B. Green, 2nd ed. (Grand Rapids: Eerdmans, 2010), 372–396. – See also my forthcoming *Canonical Criticism*. The volume Thomas Hieke (ed.), *Formen des Kanons: Studien zu Ausprägungen des biblischen Kanons von der Antike bis zum 19. Jahrhundert*, SBS 228 (Stuttgart: KBW, 2013) gives a good overview of the various perspectives and approaches that play a role in this new field, which has been growing since 1970.

[8] This chronological oddity is due to the later reception of Bauer's work in the Anglophone work, i.e. only following its translation in 1970.

[9] Tübingen: Mohr, 1934.

[10] Bart D. Ehrman, *The New Testament: A Historical Introduction to the Early Christian Writings*, 5th ed. (Oxford: Oxford University, 2011).

while it is widely acknowledged that diversity has been part and parcel of the Christian movement (virtually) since its inception, so have been attempts to look for unity, communion, and the mutual reception of Christians of each other and each other's communities.

With this as (very) broad background, it is now possible to present an argument concerning canon and ecclesial unity in a new light and to show how two nearly extinct topics in the field of New Testament studies, can offer a surprising potential for ecumenical theology. For this purpose, two (representative) biblical scholars concerned with the canon will be studied first and, second, attention will be given to intercultural perspectives on the dynamics of the canon.

3   The Return of the Canon: The Example of James A. Sanders

The work of the Presbyterian academic James A. Sanders (*1927; Union Theological Seminary/Claremont School of Theology; not to be confused with Ed P. Sanders) can be taken as a representative inroad into the rediscovery of the canon, given that his work prefigures in many ways insights from cultural studies and even intercultural theology.[11] Sanders is originally a textual critic, and like the other »founding father« of the canonical approach to Scripture, Brevard S. Childs, an Old Testament scholar. Sanders, however, has developed his own distinct approach to and understanding of canonical criticism,[12] while he has

---

[11]   Somewhat surprisingly, Watson does not interface with the work of Sanders, even though there seems to be much proximity between their approaches. – The material that follows here will also feature in my *Criticism*.

[12]   See for outlines of his position e.g. James A. Sanders, *Torah & Canon* (Philadelphia: Fortress, 1972), 117–121, idem, *Canon and Community: A Guide to Canonical Criticism* (Philadelphia: Fortress, 1984), as well as the essays collected in idem, *From Sacred Story to Sacred Text: Canon as Paradigm* (Philadelphia: Fortress, 1987), especially »Biblical Criticism and the Bible as Canon,« »Canonical Context and Canonical Criticism,« and »From Sacred Story to Sacred Text« (75–86, 153–174, 175–191). See also the bibliography in Shemaryahu Talmon and Craig A. Evans (ed.), *The Quest for Context and Meaning* (Leiden: Brill, 1997), xxv–xxxvix. – Scholars that have taken up Sanders' approach include Mary Callaway, *Sing, O Barren One* (Atlanta: Scholars, 1986), Peter Pettit, »Shene'emar: The Place of Scripture Citation in the Mishna,« Ph.D. diss., Claremont Graduate School, 1993, and James E. Brenneman, *Canons in Conflict: Negotiating Texts in True and False Prophecy* (Oxford: Oxford University, 1997), who expands Sanders' approach by taking into account community dynamics and power structures.

made a contribution to the (canonical) exegesis of the New Testament.¹³ For this reason, and because Sanders' approach has been formative for the development of canonical criticism at large, his contribution will be considered here. As he notes himself, his own contribution to this debate has its roots in the publication (by himself) of the Psalms Scroll found at Qumran,¹⁴ which, together with other finds, challenged the then current (albeit already debated) consensus surrounding the formation of the canon of the Old Testament/Hebrew Bible. This study of the formation of the canon also led to the study of the question of the nature of canonicity itself, given that scant attention was being paid to the subject at the time, while the question what the dynamics of the use of a text that was obviously intended for use in one context in another context, part and parcel as it is of the functioning of canonical literature, was being left without due attention.¹⁵

---

13   See e.g. James A. Sanders, »Dissenting Deities and Philippians 2:1–11,« JBL 88 (1969): 279–290, »The Ethic of Election in Luke's Great Banquet Parable,« in *Essays in Old Testament Ethics*, eds. J.L. Crenshaw and J.T. Willis (New York: Ktav, 1974), 245–271, »From Isaiah 61 to Luke 4,« in *Christianity, Judaism, and other Greco-Roman Cults*, vol. 1, ed. J. Neusner (Leiden: Brill, 1975), 75–106, »Torah and Paul,« in *God's Christ and His People*, ed. W.A. Meeks (Oslo: Universitetsforlaget, 1977), »The Conversion of Paul,« in *A Living Witness of Oikodome* (Claremont: Disciples Seminary Foundation, 1982), 71–93, »A New Testament Hermeneutic Fabric: Psalm 118 in the Entrance Narrative,« in *Early Jewish and Christian Exegesis*, eds. C.A. Evans and W.F. Stinespring (Atlanta: Scholars, 1987), 177–190, with Craig A. Evans, *Luke and Scripture: The Function of Sacred Tradition in Luke-Acts* (Minneapolis: Fortress, 1993), »Paul and Theological History,« in *Paul and the Scripture of Israel*, ed. J.A. Sanders and C.A. Evans (Sheffield: JSOT Press, 1993), 98–117, and »Ναζωραῖος in Matthew 2.23,« in *The Gospels and the Scriptures of Israel*, eds. Craig A. Evans and W. Richard Stegner (Sheffield: Sheffield Academic Press, 1994), 116–128, as well as the example discussed below in 2.2.2.

14   See Sanders' retrospective remarks in: James A. Sanders, »What's up Now? Renewal of an Important Investigation,« in *Jewish and Christian Scriptures: The Function of »Canonical« and »Non-Canonical« Religious Texts*, eds. Lee M. McDonald and James H. Charlesworth (London: T&T Clark, 2010), 1–7, here 1. Sanders provides a similar review of his own scholarly career in relation to canonical criticism in »Scripture as Canon for Post-Modern Times,« *Biblical Theology Bulletin* 26 (1995): 56–63. – See also his earlier contribution, »Cave 11 Surprises and the Question of Canon,« in *New Directions in Biblical Archeology*, eds. D.N. Freedman and J.C. Greenfield (New York: Doubleday, 1969), 101–116. For the Psalms scroll, see: James A. Sanders, *The Dead Sea Psalms Scroll* (Ithaca: Cornell University, 1967) and idem, *Discoveries in the Judean Desert* 4 (Oxford: Clarendon, 1965).

15   Sanders, »What's up Now?,« 2: »Still, it was important to deal with the issue of canon because no biblical discipline so far had done so. The focus shifted in our

In Sanders' work, engaging these questions gave rise both to the field of »comparative midrash« and to theoretical reflecting on the recycling of texts, searching for meaning in them in new contexts, which influenced both the reception of older texts and the production of new ones. In interaction with insights from literary study, such as Kristeva's notion of *relecture*, a hermeneutical triangle was developed, which Sanders describes as follows:

> One angle of the triangle (#1) represents the older Scripture being cited or echoed, the second angle (#2) represents the historical/social situation the newer addressed; and the third (#3) represents the differing hermeneutics perceived in the later literature being compared.[16]

Thus, for Sanders, canonicity is an important aspect of biblical literature, both with regard to its authoring and its functioning; indeed, canonicity is, for him, part of the texts themselves.

4   The Canonical Approach of James A. Sanders

Like Childs, Sanders wants to relate the Bible again to the community of faith that reads and interprets it, and to take into account the canonical nature of the texts involved, i.e. the canon is not seen as something that was imposed upon the texts at a later stage, but canonicity is part and parcel of the texts themselves. In this way, Sanders seeks to correct a trend in biblical research dating back, according to Sanders, to Spinoza.[17] At the same time, there are also significant differences between the two scholars, as has often been noted.[18]

---

work to the problems arising out of how a piece of literature clearly intended by its authors to address one set of issues of a particular community went on to speak to other communities in other circumstances with quite different issues – the very nature of canonical literature.« – See on the broader context and on the current situation e.g. Eileen Schuller, »The Dead Sea Scrolls and Canon and Canonization,« in *Kanon in Konstruktion und Dekonstruktion. Kanonisierungsprozesse religiöser Texte von der Antike bis zur Gegenwart*, Eve-ed. Marie Becker and Stefan Scholz (Berlin: de Gruyter, 2012), 293–314.

[16] Sanders, »What's up Now?,« 3.
[17] See Sanders, »Scripture,« 56–58.
[18] See also, e.g. the following observations by Jan Gorak, *The Making of the Modern Canon. Genesis and Crisis of a Literary Idea* (London: Athlone, 1991), 40–41: »Childs reattaches to the idea of canon the narrative dimension described by Irenaeus and Augustine, the orderly canon of texts and religious practices

Sanders refers to his work on the canon as »canonical criticism« and considers it as one among the many sub-disciplines of biblical studies. It is concerned with the dynamics of canonicity, i.e. the process of reception, application, re-reception, collection of texts and traditions that are considered as authoritative, specifically in relation to the Bible as the book of the churches. Thus, rather than a history of the canon or a discussion of the authority of Scripture per se, canonical criticism aims at understanding the process that leads to a text becoming canonical and functioning as such.[19] As a result of his work on canonical criticism, he is able to state that »[t]he primary character of canon or authoritative tradition, whatever its quantity or extent, is its adaptability;

> which has aesthetic qualities we normally find in art. Similarly, for James A. Sanders, the Old Testament canon endures not as a collection of prohibitions ›but because of its essential diversity, its own inherent refusal to absolutize any single stance as the only place where one might live under the sovereignty of God.‹ When he emphasizes the experience of exile at the heart of the Jewish canon, Sanders conforms to the pattern of modern experience reported by a Kafka or a Raymond Williams. When he aligns canon with ›the community's historic memory,‹ he suggests its consonance with the deep hope for continuity in the midst of change that secular authorities from Mathew Arnold to Frank Kermode have associated with culture. When Sanders interprets canon as transmitting the eschatological fears and hopes of a particular community, he speaks of Scripture in terms that Northrop Frye and Walter Benjamin use to discuss the apocalyptic potential of art and mythology. Sanders' emphasis on its diversity not only validates the biblical canon for a plural society but renders it a potentially useful instrument for literary and cultural critics as well. Some of these critics may be surprised to hear the Bible described as ›veritable textbook in contemporization of tradition.‹ ... As a practitioner of what he calls ›canonical criticism,‹ Sanders discovers in the Bible the kinds of patterns earlier commentators found in church customs and laws. Sanders' canon conforms to the assumptions of a plural society, while the canons of Irenaeus, Gregory, and Augustin conform to their assumptions of a hierarchical universe. In both cases, however, the power of the canon lies in its ability to suggest the ultimate shape and destiny of Christian existence. All these writers agree that the Christian canon impresses on believers a set of values which scriptural narrative perpetually confirms,« with which Sanders agrees in »Scripture,« 61–62.

[19] Sanders, *Story*, 82: »Canonical criticism should be viewed as another sub-discipline of biblical criticism and complementary to the earlier developments. It takes seriously the authoritative function of the traditions that compose the Bible in the believing communities that shaped its various literary units, compiled and arranged its several parts in the conditions received, and continues to adapt its traditions in their ongoing lives. The Bible is the churches' book (in Christian terms) in every sense of the expression. The early believing communities created and shaped it and passed it down to their successors today – hence the term »canonical criticism« and not history of canon.«

its secondary character is its stability.«[20] Sanders also moves beyond a primarily descriptive approach to the processes involved in a text's becoming canonical and functioning as canonical. For him, canonical criticism also leads to a particular hermeneutical position, that is to say: having understood and reconstructed the dynamics involved in ancient canonicity, these very same dynamics should be used as a hermeneutical tool for the interpretation of the canonical texts, thereby doing justice both to their letter and to the spirit of the canonical process.[21]

This understanding of canonical criticism leads to a highly dynamic and creative approach to both biblical traditions and contemporary conventions, as Sanders puts it:

> Canonical criticism can liberate biblical study from the pervasive tendency to moralize upon reading all biblical texts thus absolutizing ancient Bronze Age or Iron Age or Hellenistic customs and mores. It stresses the ontology of the Bible as a paradigm of God's work from creation through re-creation out of which we may construct paradigms for our own works, rather than as a jewel box of ancient wisdom to be perpetuated. It seeks the biblical hermeneutics whereby we may adapt the new wisdoms of our age just as they back then adapted the wisdom of the ancient Near East from many peoples.[22]

Thus, building up on his work on »comparative midrash« (»midrash« understood in the broad sense of re-reading old Scriptures for new

---

[20] Sanders, *Canon*, 83. – See also idem, »Adaptable for Life: The Nature and Function of the Canon,« in *Magnalia Dei: The Mighty Acts of God*, eds. G.E. Wright, F.M. Cross, W.E. Lemke, and P.D. Miller (New York: Doubleday, 1976), 531–560, as well as idem, »Stability and Fluidity in Text and Canon,« in *Tradition of the Text: Studies Offered to Dominique Barthélemy in Celebration of His 70th Birthday*, eds. C.J. Norton and S. Pisane (Göttingen: Vandenhoeck & Ruprecht, 1991), 203–217.

[21] Sanders, *Canon*, 83: »Hermeneutics is the midterm between canon's [sic] stability and its adaptability. Discerning the hermeneutics used by the ancient biblical thinkers and authors in adapting the early authoritative tradition to their contexts, for their people, is the essence of canonical criticism. And those hermeneutics cannot be discerned without as much knowledge as possible of the ancient historical (cultural, economic, political, etc.) contexts addressed. Hence, responsible use of all the tools available from biblical criticism is necessary.«

[22] Sanders, *Canon*, 84.

situations), for Sanders, as different from Childs,[23] the development of the canon and the appertaining text, i.e. the »canonical process,« as he terms it, is of central importance, both theologically and hermeneutically.

In developing his theory with regard to this, building up on his work in comparative midrash and the functioning of sacred texts, he takes his point of departure in the historical observation that »a canon begins to *take shape* first and foremost, because a question of identity or authority has arisen, and a canon begins to *become unchangeable* or invariable somewhat later, after the question of identity has for the most part been settled.«[24] From this, Sanders deduces that »canonical criticism starts by defining the hermeneutics of that generation which gave the canon its basic shape.«[25] Sanders' aim in doing »canonical criticism« is, on the one hand, to uncover the process that led to the canonization of particular texts and on the other hand, find a way of using this process in the present, in other words »to apply the Bible's own ›unrecorded hermeneutics,‹ which lie between the lines of most of its literature.«[26] Thus, Sanders seeks to uncover a particular hermeneutical process that continues in the present.[27]

In developing his model of canonical criticism, Sanders emphasizes both the historical fact of a process of the traditioning of authoritative texts and traditions and the continuation of such processes today, with

---

[23] As indeed noted by Sanders, see *Canon*, 101: see for Sanders' view of Childs' *Introduction to the Old Testament as Scripture:* Sanders, »Context.«
[24] Sanders, *Guide*, 21.
[25] Ibid., 21.
[26] Sanders, *Canon*, 46.
[27] See: James M. Robinson, »Foreword,« in *A Gift of God in Due Season* (Festschrift James A. Sanders), eds. Richard D. Weiss and David M. Carr (Sheffield: Sheffield Academic Press, 1996), 14–15, 14: »At the core of canonical criticism as developed by Sanders is the perception that to call a tradition, text, or collection of texts canonical or authoritative is to recognize that it is enmeshed in a symbiotic relationship with communities of believers to whom the tradition, text, or collection, ›gives life,‹ and who at the same time ›give life‹ to it. Canonical or authoritative materials give such communities life by providing a source for a communal identity that enables the establishment of maintenance of communal integrity in a particular historical context. The believing communities give life to such traditional materials as each new generation grants them authority to name the community's life, thus selecting, transmitting and elaborating them for succeeding generations.« See in this volume also various studies interacting with the approach of Sanders.

all the pluralism that this implies.[28] This means both a full validation of the historical critical method *and* a recognition of the formative role of communities in the interpretation of texts. For this reason, Sanders is also able to integrate textual scholarship and canonical criticism. In fact, his work on the canon is a direct result of his work as a textual scholar.[29]

Having reviewed Sanders' work, and noting how his line of argument, which is shared by others, indicates that »canonicity« is inherent to writings with a claim to authority and not somehow alien to it, now the work of another biblical scholar much concerned with the canon can be considered, that of Francis Watson, specifically his latest work *Gospel Writing*.

5 Francis Watson and the Canon

Francis Watson in his major publication of 2013: *Gospel Writing. A Canonical Perspective*,[30] proposes nothing less than a new paradigm for the study of the (canonical) New Testament. This paradigm he understands as »an exercise in historically informed theological hermeneutics«,[31] with a historical component, comprising of an account of »the genesis of the canonical gospel within the context of early Christian gospel production as a whole,«[32] a hermeneutical component, consisting of a reflection on the »implications of the fourfold canonical form for interpretative practice,«[33] and a theological component, which is concerned with underlining the »mediated character of all knowledge of Jesus – over against the claim that we can have access to an uninterpreted ›historical‹ figure by abstracting him from his own reception.« For Watson, a (canonical) gospel text that is interpreted properly is

---

[28] See e.g. Sanders, »Scripture,« 61–62; the ultimate meaning of the text is eschatological for Sanders.

[29] See: James A. Sanders, »Text and Canon: Concepts and Method,« in idem, *Story*, 125–151 (published earlier in *JBL* 98 [1979]: 5–29 as Sanders' 1978 SBL presidential address).

[30] In what follows text has been incorporated from a review of Watson's work which has appeared as Peter-Ben Smit, Review of Francis Watson, *Gospel Writing: A Canonical Perspective*, *Review of Biblical Literature*, http://www.bookreviews.org, 2015.

[31] Watson, *Gospel*, 9.

[32] Ibid., 7.

[33] Ibid., 8.

both read as part of the process of formation of the (now) canonical gospels as well as part of the (new) canonical text that is a literary artefact of its own right and needs to be taken into account in order to be able to interpret a canonical text *as canonical text*. The result of this all is a new perspective on what it means to study Jesus in relation to the Gospel text, with much emphasis on the necessarily mediated character of any knowledge of Jesus. This is summed up by Watson in his concluding »Seven Theses on Jesus and the Canonical Gospel.«[34]

In order to arrive there, Watson travels through the entire history of the canon, or, to be more precise: the process of the formation of the canonical fourfold gospel, both in terms of the prehistory of the gospel texts and in terms of the way in which this fourfold canon has come to be treated in exegetical (always historical, always theological) scholarship throughout the last 20 centuries. Watson's starting point is the wrestling of Augustine with the fourfold canonical narrative, in particular with its inconsistencies and internal contradictions and his various ways of resolving them, both with recourse to an account of Gospel origins and various ways of harmonizing (apparently) contradictory accounts.[35] The major point that Watson makes in relation to his account of Augustine's view of the canon has everything to do with the chapter to which the chapter on Augustine is paired: »Dismantling the Canon: Lessing/Reimarus,« a scholarly and historical development of which Watson gives a highly readable account.[36] The reason why both are included into his book and paired with each other appears at the end of Watson's treatment of Augustine:

> Augustine held (1) that real contradictions between canonical gospels on matters of empirical fact would seriously undermine their authority, but (2) that no such contradictions can be established. The modern scholarly consensus that (2) is false is fully justified – as is all too evident from the harmonizers' inability to make coherent sense of the events of Easter morning. Given that (2) is false, however, the crucial question is whether one rejects or accepts (1).[37]

What appears at the end of the chapter covering Lessing/Reimarus (c.s.!) is that these modern scholars share with Augustine (and others)

---

[34] Ibid., 604–619.
[35] Ibid., 13–61.
[36] Ibid., 62–113.
[37] Ibid., 61.

a preoccupation with and predilection for a single, authentic, and authoritative narrative, be it a (more synchronously understood) gospel harmony or a historical (and harmonizing) account of Jesus' life or the reconstruction of the single narrative of the original gospel, be it in the shape of an *Urevangelium* or Q. Authority, originality, and singularity remain closely bound together in any of these proposals. This is, for Watson, an important vantage point for the next part of his book, which, in great depth and at great length, explores the process of the formation of gospels in relation to each other. This section of Watson's book is entitled »Reframing Gospel Origins.«[38] This large section of the book provides the reader with a discussion of the process of gospel formation that moves with great ease (and elegance) between detailed tradition- and source-historical discussions, the broader history of early Christianity, and the implications for the interpretation of the resulting gospels. The latter depend on the entire account of Watson's reconstruction of early Christian gospel production and not on, for example, his argument against Q (for which *Gospel Writing* will no doubt also become known). The first of Watson's (hermeneutical) conclusions is, accordingly, that »canonical and noncanonical gospels are intimately related and that they can and should be read in the light of each other. In other words, they can and should initially be read as though the distinction between canonical and noncanonical did not exist.«[39] At the same time, it can also be observed that processes of normativization are part of the production process of early Christian gospels, of which the four gospel canon is the most enduring one.[40] The creation of the latter Watson considers »fundamentally a creative move as well as a restrictive one. It brings into being a new composite textual object which enshrines the principles of plurality and relativity and excludes any monopolistic claim to embody the ›gospel of Jesus Christ‹ rather than a self-limiting ›gospel according to....‹«[41] As a result, a double perspective on any extant gospel emerges: »it can be viewed as a further contribution to the single ongoing project of writing the gospel. Or it can be viewed in relation to a canonical boundary that

---

[38] This part of Watson's book contains the following chapters »The Coincidences of Q« (117–155), »Luke the Interpreter« (156–216), »Thomas versus Q« (217–285), »Interpreting a Johannine Source (Jn, *GEger*)« (286–340), »Reinterpreting in Parallel (Jn, *GTh*, *GPet*)« (341–407).
[39] Watson, *Gospel*, 406.
[40] Ibid., 406.
[41] Ibid., 407.

defines it as something which, in itself, it is not.«[42] It will be Watson's insistence that *both* perspectives are needed in order to do justice to an early Christian gospel, canonical or not. In fact, as one could argue, Watson's argument also implies that the canonical depends for its (precise) meaning on the non-canonical books as well as on the canonical construct itself. With this, one has arrived at the third and last part of Watson's *opus*, which is entitled »The Canonical Construct« and contains the chapters »The East: Limiting Plurality,«[43] »The West: Towards Consensus,«[44] »Origen: Canonical Hermeneutics,«[45] and finally »Image, Symbol, Liturgy.«[46] As the titles of these chapters indicate, here the history of the canon *sensu stricto* is discussed, both from a historical perspective and from the perspective of (theological) hermeneutics, as the treatment of Origen and the extensive chapter on »Image, Symbol, Liturgy« show. What emerges is the construction of the canon as a centripetal development within different strands of early Christianity, a development that one could term, anachronistically, »ecumenical« in nature. At the same time, as in particular the discussion of Origen (which builds on the discussion of other authors, such as Irenaeus) shows, one can arrive at the following conclusion concerning the hermeneutical functioning of the four gospel canon, due to its fundamental enshrinement of the plural into the one canon:

> No interpretation of the fourfold gospel is mandatory because integral to its object from the outset. The form of the gospel is theologically underdetermined and could be put to a variety of uses ... [T]he fourfold gospel requires interpretation like any other canonical text. Arguably, an interpretation is only truly canonical when its attention to one of the four is such as to evoke echoes in the other three, and where the differences that come into view are seen as promising rather than threatening.[47]

Thus, diversity appears as a something that is (theologically and hermeneutically) productive rather than something that ought to be suppressed, either in a synchronic or diachronic gospel harmony (see, e.g., Watson's discussion of Augustine and modern biblical scholarship in

---

[42] Ibid., 407.
[43] Ibid., 411–452.
[44] Ibid., 453–509.
[45] Ibid., 510–552.
[46] Ibid., 553–603.
[47] Ibid., 552.

the first part of his book). In the final chapter that is part of this section of *Gospel Writing*, Watson extends the dynamic of the canon by placing it into the (liturgical) life of the church: here also echoes are evoked and, for example in Christological discussions the potential of the four gospel canon unfolds – both in word, artefact, and ritual.[48]

Finally, by way of conclusion, Watson offers seven theses on »Jesus and the Canonical Gospels.«[49] It becomes clear (thesis 1) that the early Church's notion(s) of Jesus are all part of a dynamic process of reception and interpretation; also, Jesus is only to be known through the »mediation of his own reception« (thesis 2), while this mediation and the reception thereof is characterized by an interplay of the oral and the textual (thesis 3 – one could add: of the practical and theoretical); also, there is no differentiation possible between canonical and non-canonical gospels based on »identifiable criteria inherent to the texts« (thesis 4), also, the notion of »canonical« implies an ongoing production and usage of gospel literature (thesis 5); furthermore, the reception of the gospel literature is determined by the canonical divide, accounts of this reception should therefore differentiate between pre- and post-canonical stages (thesis 6), finally, »A ›canonical perspective‹ models a convergence of historical, theological, and hermeneutical discourses, rejecting the assumption that these are necessarily opposed to one another« (thesis 7).

When looking back on reading and rereading Watson's *Gospel Writing*, it seems that especially his hermeneutical proposal (see thesis 7, but also 1 and 2) pose the biggest challenge to contemporary scholarship in New Testament studies and are simultaneously the most fruitful for the ecumenical question that is at the centre of this essay: The (re)discovery of plurality-in-unity as both a centripetal aspect of the canon and the vantage point for the dynamic and productive process of reception is a gain – and a challenge to any and all more monolithic accounts of biblical meaning or historical narrative or truth. At the same time, now that both Sanders and Watson have shown that canonicity is inherent to the (now formally) canonical texts and not alien to them and while they have also indicated that the canonical process (i.e., the process of canon formation) can be understood as a dialogical search for meaning and truth in the setting of a reading community,

---

[48] Ibid., 553–603.
[49] Ibid., 604–619.

which discovers both what being in communion entails and,[50] at the same time, discovers the texts through this process of reading, by means of which the canonical process continues in the process of canonical interpretation, the question remains whether and how this can be related to ecumenical theology. This will be done in the following and last section of this paper, which highlights a number of insights from intercultural theology.

6 Canon and Unity: Intercultural Insights

The writings of Sanders and Watson, as they were just discussed as (representative) examples of certain developments in the study of (Christian) canonical texts, offer a vantage point for further reflection on the canon. In particular, the question, underlined (and answered affirmatively) by both, whether the way in which a writing, or a corpus of writings has come into existence should not be taken into account in its interpretation, can be considered further. This can, and has been, demonstrated in various ways, both for the canonical gospels and for other writings.[51] In the case of the Gospels, as well, to be sure, in the case of the work of Paul and its reception (in pseudepigraphical Pauline letters, as well as in those of James and Peter), part of the documents pertaining to the prehistory of the canonical writings has been canonized as well. Because Mark and Luke, Matthew, and John have become part of the canon, documents belonging to at least two stages of the process (Mark on the one hand, the rest on the other) of the formation of the authoritative memory of Jesus has been enshrined in its authoritative Scriptures. If Matthew, Luke, or even John had been intended to replace Mark, the canon partially reverses this development: now all four are canonical.[52] All of this applies also to the work of Paul and its diverse reception, already in the writings that are now canonical. The ongoing search for identity »in Christ« with the appertaining production of ever new authoritative or at least supplementary texts is docu-

---

50 See also: Angela Berlis and Stephan van Erp, »Het Woord is lichaam geworden: Geschiedenis en traditie in de theologie van Rowan Williams,« *Tijdschrift voor Theologie* 54 (2014): 115–126.
51 See, e.g. Theo K. Heckel, *Vom Evangelium zum viergestaltigen Evangelium* (Tübingen: Mohr Siebeck, 1999), as well as the essays in Richard Bauckham (ed.), *The Gospels for All Christians: Rethinking the Gospel Audiences* (Grand Rapids: Eerdmans, 1998).
52 See on this the general argument of Watson, *Gospel*.

mented in the canonical writings themselves, which, therefore, are only authoritative in concert with each other, no longer on their own.[53] All of this constitutes, in fact, a prolonged reflection on the hermeneutical consequences of a principle of historical-critical, more specifically tradition-historical research, that is to say: the principle that the genesis of a text is of importance for understanding it. If this is the case, then it becomes particularly inviting to further reflect on the question what it would mean for the interpretation of the canonical writings whether the fact that historical emergence of the canon had many centripetal aspects does not need to be taken into account when reading its contents. Doing so invites considering the following insights of the New Testament scholar Michael Wolter:

> Die intensive Suche nach einer sprachlich wie existentiell ausdifferenzierbaren und einheitsstiftenden Mitte der christlichen Identität und die Unmöglichkeit, sie eindeutig...zu bestimmen, [war] bereits von Anfang an integraler Bestandteil der geschichtlichen Existenz der christlichen Gemeinden ... Die Spannung zwischen Einheit und Vielfalt wäre demnach nicht ein erst mit dem Kanon gegebenes Problem, sondern eine fundamentale und damit unaufhebbare Gegebenheit der geschichtlichen Existenz des Christentums überhaupt.[54]

When following Wolter's line of thought the conceptualization of the notion of the »unity of the church« (as well, to be sure, as that of the »meaning of the canon«) shifts from a historical or current situation to that of a process. The image that emerges is one, in which the canonical writings do not so much constitute a stable and clear form (or source) of Christian identity and unity and communicate this (when read cor-

---

[53] See Michael Wolter, »Die Vielfalt der Schrift und die Einheit des Kanons,« in *Die Einheit der Schrift und die Vielfalt des Kanons*, eds. John Barton and Michael Wolter (Berlin: De Gruyter, 2003), 45–68, here 65, and Judith Gruber, *Theologie nach dem Cultural Turn: Interkulturalität als theologische Ressource* (Stuttgart: Kohlhammer, 2013), 20, 25–26; see further also: Judith M. Lieu, *Neither Jew nor Greek? Constructing Early Christianity* (London: T. & T. Clark, 2002), 2–3: »Texts do not simply reflect a ›history‹ going on independently of them, they are themselves part of the process by which...Christianity came into being. For it was through literature that ... a self-understanding was shaped and articulated, and then mediated to and appropriated by others, and through literature that people and ideas were included or excluded. What the texts were doing is sometimes as, if not more, important than what they were saying.«

[54] Wolter, » Vielfalt,« 52–53.

rectly) in an unequivocal way, but are rather the witnesses of (and catalysts for) an ongoing dialogical and even conflictuous search for such unity and identity. This search is evidenced precisely also by the various differences and disagreements between the canonical writings, given that these have been enshrined into one single canon and thus made to be in conversation with each other.[55] While this might sound like a relativization of what one might want to see as »Biblical« view of Christian identity, according to Wolter's line of thought, this is not at all the case; the question is rather how one understands notions such as »unity« and »identity« from the perspective of the emergence of the early Christian writings, including the canon itself, which is also a literary construct. Following this line of thought, one might agree with Wolter again:

> Die Ausdifferenzierung des einen Bekenntnisses in unterschiedliche und miteinander konkurrierende Heilskonzepte einschließlich ihrer lebensweltlichen Implikationen [darf] nicht als Verlust einer ursprünglichen Einheit verstanden werden, sondern [ist] ein integraler Bestandteil der Plausibilität des Bekenntnisses selbst gewesen, ohne die die Rezeption der christlichen Heilsbotschaft nicht möglich gewesen wäre. Was das Zeugnis vom Christusereignis konkret bedeutet (d.h. mit welchen Zeichen diesem Zeugnis welche Bedeutung zugeschrieben wird) steht nicht von vornherein fest, sondern wird in kontextabhängigen Bedeutungsprozessen ausverhandelt; das wird im Kanon dokumentiert.[56]

Identity, accordingly, is a continuous process of conversation and even of »negotiation.« Precisely the differences between the canonical texts provide the necessary conditions for this – without difference, no conversation is possible – and create the space for this.[57] This conversation takes place among different communities and their »cultures« (e.g., those of Matthew and Mark) and between different political and/or cultural settings (e.g., those of Luke and John, the Seer), in order to discover and narrate again and again what faith is. This conversation

---

[55] The diversity that exists concerning the text of the canonical Scriptures of Christianity can be understood along the same lines.
[56] Wolter, »Vielfalt,« 55.
[57] See also the notion of the »epiphanic space« opened up by the (different) »other«, as underlined by Hans de Wit, »My God«, She Said. »Ships Make Me so Crazy,« Reflections on Empirical Hermeneutics, Interculturality and Holy Scripture (Amsterdam: VU University, 2008), 65, 87.

can be termed »intercultural«, as it has been formulated in the work of the Austrian theologian Judith Gruber as follows:

> Die Differenzen, die ein genealogischer Blick im Kanon offenlegt, lassen ihn als eine Kompilation von partikularen Theologien erscheinen von Theologien, die vom Christusereignis im Rückgriff auf die Bedeutungsstrukturen ihres kulturellen Kontextes Zeugnis ablegen. Die Differenzen werden nicht ausgeblendet, sondern innerhalb des Kanons zusammengestellt. In den Differenzen konstituiert sich – so wurde oben aufgezeigt – ein Raum der Interkulturalität. Indem der Kanon Differenzen sichtbar macht, schafft er einen Raum der Interkulturalität, in dem christliche Identität verhandelt wird; Als normativ gesetztes Dokument normiert er sie damit als disparates Produkt interkultureller Übersetzungs- und Transformationsvorgänge zwischen partikularen Theologien.[58]

The kind of identity and unity that becomes visible in this way in the writings of the New Testament (or even Biblical) canon is one that is less conceptual in character but rather has the shape of an ongoing search for identity and unity, which is fed by the diverse perspectives and witnesses of the canon in conversation with each other and the location of the person and/or community that participates in this search. Conflict and diversity are no longer a threat to unity, but rather necessary for the (ongoing, even eschatologically oriented) search for it.[59]

Based on these considerations, it is now possible to proceed towards a number of conclusions concerning a new perspective on the question of ecclesial unity, interpretative fullness, and the canon of the New Testament.

---

[58] Gruber, *Theologie nach dem Cultural Turn*, 19.
[59] See Gruber, *Theologie nach dem Cultural Turn*, 20: »Christliche Identität geschieht hier performativ im Konflikt – gerade weil über unterschiedliche Interpretationen verhandelt wird, zerfällt christliche Identität nicht. Die im Kanon normative gesetzte konfliktive Interkulturalität weist so einen Weg zwischen einem Verständnis von christlicher Identität, das Differenzen ausblendet, und ihrer Zersplitterung entlang der im Kanon dokumentierten Bruchlinien.«

7 Conclusions

Recent history on the canon, both of a historical and of a more hermeneutical kind, help to understand the phenomenon of »canon« in its centripetal function and to gain more knowledge of the function of canonical texts in processes of identity formation in (reading) communities.

Reflection on research on the New Testament canon has led to an appreciation of both the centripetal character of this collection of writings as well as to an understanding of unity in terms of an ongoing process that is characterized by dialogue, which, in turn, is fuelled by the differences that are part of the canonical writings.

The previous point also means that reading New Testament texts without relating them to other New Testament texts, does little justice to their character as canonical texts, while, more specifically, reading these texts without the centripetal function of the canon in mind equally fails to do justice to the »grammar« of their interpretation provided by the genesis of the canon. Reading canonically always means reading centripetally, dialogically, and with an eye to the fullness of the meaning of texts as it enfolds through reading in communion.

A canonical perspective on the New Testament, therefore, brings out the fullness of the meaning of the biblical texts, both historically and, for lack of a better word, theologically, i.e., as interpreted in the communities reading the canonical texts, which is a centripetal process. Reading canonically is reading for communion in its fullness, it is reading for unity, or, if you like, reading canonically is reading for catholicity.

Die Autoren/Index of Authors

James **Amanze**, Ph.D., is Professor in the Department of Theology and Religious Studies at the University of Botswana,

Augoustinos **Bairactaris**, Ph.D., is Assistant Professor of Ecumenical Theology, History of the Ecumenical Movement and inter-Christian Dialogue at the Patriarchal Ecclesiastical Academy of Heraklion (Crete). He is also an associated member of the Volos Academy for Theological Studies.

Henk **Bakker**, Dr., is Professor of Baptist Studies at VU University Amsterdam (Netherlands), and Fellow Researcher at the Centre for Evangelical and Reformation Theology in Amsterdam.

Viorel **Coman**, is a Ph.D. student and research assistant at the Faculty of Theology and Religious Studies at the Catholic University in Leuven (Belgium). He is a member of the Research Unit Systematic Theology and the Study of Religions.

Jelle **Creemers**, Ph.D., is Assistant Professor at the Evangelische Theologische Faculteit in Leuven (Belgium). His research traces developments in theology and praxis of evangelical free churches in ecumenical and societal contexts.

Peter **De Mey**, Dr., is professor of ecclesiology and ecumenism at the Catholic University of Leuven (Belgium). He was secretary and president of Societas Oecumenica from 2004 to 2010 and is currently member of the Reformed-Roman Catholic international dialogue commission.

Sara **Gehlin** is a doctoral student at the Centre for Theology and Religious Studies at the University of Lund (Sweden).

Margriet **Gosker**, Ph.D., is a retired pastor of the Protestant Churches in the Netherlands and an Ecumenical Theologian. She is the Project Manager of 500 Years of Protestantism for the Protestant Church in the Netherlands and a member of the Faith and Order Board of the Council of Churches in the Netherlands.

Dagmar **Heller**, Dr. theol., is professor of Ecumenical Theology and Academic Dean at the Ecumenical Institute Bossey (Switzerland) and Executive Secretary for Faith and Order at the World Council of Churches, Geneva. Since 2012 she serves as President of Societas Oecumenica.

Mihai **Iordache**, Ph.D., is an ecumenical researcher currently holding the UNESCO Chair for Inter-Cultural and Inter-Religious Exchanges at the University of Bucharest (Romania). He also leads both the Olari Church (www.bisericaolari.ro) and the Cultural and Social Centre ADORNO in Bucharest.

Kirsteen **Kim**, Ph.D., is Professor of Theology and World Christianity at Leeds Trinity University, UK. She served as vice-moderator of the Commission on World Mission and Evangelism of the World Council of Churches in 2007-2013.

Jutta **Koslowski**, Ph.D., is junior pastor of the Protestant Church of Hesse and Nassau (EKHN) in Germany and lecturer for ecumenism and interreligious dialogue at the Pädagogische Hochschule Ludwigsburg.

Mihály **Kránitz**, Dr., is a diocesan priest and since 1996 Professor for Fundamental Theology at the Faculty of Theology of the Catholic University in Budapest (Hungary).

Christine **Lienemann-Perrin**, Dr. theol. habil., is Professor em. for Ecumenical Studies and Missiology at the Theological Faculty of the University of Basel (Switzerland).

Wolfgang **Lienemann**, Dr. theol. habil., Prof. em. für Ethik an der Theologischen Fakultät der Universität Bern (Schweiz).

Friederike **Nüssel**, Dr. theol. habil., since 2006 Professor of Systematic Theology and Director of the Ecumenical Institute of University of Heidelberg (Germany).

Dorin **Oancea**, Dr. theol., Professor of Theology at the Orthodox Theological Faculty „Andrei Şaguna" of the Lucian Blaga University of Sibiu (Romania).

Michael **Plathow**, Dr. theol. habil, pastor of the Protestant Church of Baden (Germany), em. Director of the Konfessionskundliches Institut in Bensheim, teaches Systematic Theology at the University of Heidelberg.

Risto **Saarinen**, Dr. theol., Dr. phil., is Professor of Ecumenics at the Faculty of Theology at the University of Helsinki (Finland)

Dorothea **Sattler**, Dr. theol. habil., ist Professorin für Ökumenische Theologie und Dogmatik an der Katholisch-theologischen Fakultät der Westfälischen Wilhelms - Universität Münster (Deutschland).

Peter-Ben **Smit**, Th.D., Dr. theol., holds the extraordinary chair of Ancient Catholic Church Structures and the history and theology of Old Catholicism at Utrecht University (Netherlands) and serves as assistant professor of New Testament at VU University Amsterdam. He is also an assistant priest in the Old Catholic parish in Amsterdam.

Ferenc **Szűcs**, Dr. theol., is Professor emeritus at the Theological Faculty of Károli Gáspár University of the Reformed Church in Hungary (Budapest), where he had the Chair of Systematic Theology and Ecumenical Studies.

Péter **Szentpétery**, Ph.D., senior lecturer at the Lutheran Theological University (School of Theology) in Budapest (Hungary) for ecumenical and religious studies. From 2000 to 2015 he served as Secretary of the Ecumenical Study Centre, Budapest, and from 2012 to 2014 as Secretary of Societas Oecumenica.

Georgios **Vlantis**, M.Th. (Philosophy of Religion); theologian, assistant of the Chair of Orthodox Systematic Theology, Faculty of Orthodox Theology, Ludwig-Maximilians-Universität, Munich (Germany); member of the academic team of the Volos Academy for Theological Studies (Greece).

Henk **Witte**, Ph.D., is associate professor at the Tilburg School of Theology, Department of Systematic Theology and Philosophy (Netherlands) and extraordinary professor on the Xaverius chair.